Cowboy Poets & Cowboy Poetry

Cowboy Poets & Cowboy Poetry

Edited by

David Stanley and Elaine Thatcher

University of Illinois Press
Urbana and Chicago

Manufactured in the United States of America

This book is printed on acid-free paper.

Library of Congress Cataloging-in-Publication Data
Cowboy poets and cowboy poetry / edited by David Stanley and
Elaine Thatcher.
p. cm.
Includes bibliographical references (p.) and index.
ISBN 0-252-02520-2 (alk. paper)
ISBN 0-252-06836-X (pbk. : alk. paper)
1. Cowboys' writings, American—History and criticism.
2. American poetry—West (U.S.)—History and criticism.
3. Ranch life in literature. 4. West (U.S.)—In literature.
5. Cowboys in literature.
I. Stanley, David, 1942–
II. Thatcher, Elaine.
PS153.C67C69 2000
811.009'92636—dc21 99-6289
CIP

1 2 3 4 5 C P 5 4 3 2 1

For our parents,
David and Helen Stanley
and
Ted and Zella Thatcher,
who introduced us to a West of
beauty, space, and diversity

Contents

Part 5: Connections

Part 6: Developments

Preface

A collection of essays on cowboy poetry was first discussed by Suzi Jones and David Stanley after the second Cowboy Poetry Gathering in Elko, Nevada, in 1986, and although Suzi found it necessary to withdraw from the project when she took a new job on the East Coast, her input was of great importance in the early stages. Soon after, Elaine Thatcher volunteered to coedit the manuscript, with each editor responsible for roughly half of the essays. With the exception of the contributions of John I. White and Teresa Jordan, all of the essays were written especially for this collection and have not been previously published.

By design, the editors strove to elicit writing from the greatest possible variety of contributors: public-sector folklorists, college and university teachers, and cowboy poets. We hoped to provide a wide range of perspectives—historical, literary, and internationally comparative—with the collection framed by the creative work of Kim Stafford and William Kittredge. Recognizing that the volume would probably be read not only by cowboy poets and other deeply knowledgable readers but also by people broadly interested in the West and its cultural heritage yet unfamiliar with the tradition of cowboy poetry, we tried to group the essays to reflect both the variety and the interrelated nature of the subjects. The first essay in the collection, an overview of cowboy poetry's history and current prospects, is intended to provide necessary background for general readers.

In the last few years, three men who were actively involved in cowboy poetry have died, and we wish to acknowledge their contributions here. John I. White, once a singing cowboy on New York–area radio stations and later an important collector of cowboy song and poetry, died in 1992 at the age of ninety. Buck Ramsey, whose poems, songs, and stories became a vital part of cowboy poetry gatherings throughout the West in the 1990s, died unexpectedly in January 1998 at the age of fifty-nine. Blanton Owen, Nevada's first state folklorist and an independent fieldworker/photographer who contributed to festivals, concerts, publications, and exhibits of ranch culture, cowboy crafts, and cowboy poetry, was killed in an aircraft accident early in the summer of 1998. Taken together, these three men spanned the entire era of the cowboy revival to which they contributed so much as scholars, performers, and artists.

In the process of assembling the collection, we have received wonderful advice and help from dozens of people, especially the twenty-six contributors, all of whom provided leads, suggestions, and advice. Hal Cannon, Carol Edison, Jim Griffith, Guy Logsdon, and Charlie Seemann as a group have completed well over a hundred years of research in the oral expression of cowboys, and they have constituted an informal board of advisors and editors whom we consulted frequently. Their writings on cowboy poetry and song anticipate many of the ideas in these essays.

In addition, we've had a lot of help from the staff of the Western Folklife Center in Elko, particularly Meg Glaser, Debbie Fant, Sue Wallis, and Tara McCarty, and from a corps of folklorists and scholars throughout the country, especially David Brose, Tom Carter, Alan Davison, Liz Dear, Georgi Donavin, Andrea Graham, Joe Graham, Annie Hatch, Mike Korn, Jack Lamb, Bob McCarl, Steve Ohrn, Ray Ownbey, Bea Roeder, Jan Roush, George Schoemaker, Greg Scott, Steve Siporin, Gary Stanton, Paul Stone, Jessie Sundstrom, Steve Tatum, Barre Toelken, Nicholas Vrooman, Don D. Walker, Bert Wilson, and Joy Woolf. The readers of the manuscript, Sandy Ives and Jim Hoy, provided sound criticism and advice that greatly improved the book.

Cowboy poets who have been characteristically generous with their time and ideas include J. B. Allen, Virginia Bennett, Baxter Black, Buster and Cheryl McLaury, Rod McQueary, Wallace McRae, Joel Nelson, Vess Quinlan, Georgie Sicking, and Paul Zarzyski. The staff of the Fife Folklore Archives at Utah State University, notably Barbara Walker, Randy Williams, Amy Rogers, and Erin Peterson, have patiently looked up obscure poems and poets for us. David Hales, Hildy Benham, Oresta Esquibel, and the other librarians at Westminster College sought out important reference materials to help us complete the work. Joe Hickerson at the American Folklife Center in the Library of Congress found materials that we never would have located otherwise. Our editors at the University of Illinois Press, Judy McCulloh and Mary Giles, were wonderfully patient and painstaking.

Our greatest debt is to the student assistants who did so much of the legwork: Mike Santarosa, Stephanie Sherman, Matthew Irwin, and Sarah Rudd. Sarah and Matt in particular edited essays, looked up sources, checked references, and handled all of the copyright permissions so necessary to a work like this. Their organizational and computer skills and their endless patience were absolutely invaluable.

Generous financial support for publication was provided by the Utah Humanities Council; by the Charles Redd Center for Western Studies at Brigham Young University in Provo, Utah; by the Arizona Humanities Council; the Arizona Cowboy Poets Gathering; and by Sharlot Hall Museum, Prescott, Arizona. Finally, a Weyher summer research grant to David Stanley from Westminster College in the summer of 1993 provided the time and support that really got this project moving.

1

Cowboy Poetry Then and Now: An Overview

David Stanley

When Charles Badger Clark, an Iowan–South Dakotan living temporarily in southern Arizona, invented "The Legend of Boastful Bill" in 1907, he managed to synthesize half a dozen traditional themes that had long animated the home-grown poetry of those who spent their working lives with cattle and horses in the American West. The great American heritage of braggadocio, so beloved of Mark Twain and the humorists of the Old Southwest in the nineteenth century, was combined here with cowboy socializing, tall-tale telling, the ghost story, and the stubborn refusal of nature and animals to be mastered by humans:

At a roundup on the Gily, [Gila River]
    One sweet mornin' long ago,
Ten of us was throwed right freely
    By a hawse from Idaho.
And we thought he'd go-a-beggin'
    For a man to break his pride
Till, a-hitchin' up one leggin,
    Boastful Bill cut loose and cried—

"I'm a on'ry proposition for to hurt; [ornery]
I fulfill my earthly mission with a quirt;
    I kin ride the highest liver
    'Tween the Gulf and Powder River,
And I'll break this thing as easy as I'd flirt."

But the horse bucks so hard that Bill's cinches snap, and he is propelled skyward, so high that he never comes down.

Like his near-contemporaries Theodore Roosevelt, who had glamorized cowboy life in the North Dakota Badlands in the 1880s, and Owen Wister, a friend of Roosevelt's at Harvard who "went West" and wrote the novel *The Virginian* in 1902, Clark both romanticized the cowboy way of life and gloomily predicted its end:

Stardust on his chaps and saddle,
    Scornful still of jar and jolt,
He'll come back some day, astraddle
    Of a bald-faced thunderbolt.
And the thin-skinned generation
    Of that dim and distant day
Sure will stare with admiration
    When they hear old Boastful say—

"I was first, as old rawhiders all confessed.
Now I'm last of all rough riders, and the best.
    Huh, you soft and dainty floaters,
    With your a'roplanes and motors—
Huh! are you the great grandchildren of the West!" [1]

That theme of a disappearing way of life under assault from industrialized society is as much a part of cowboy poetry as its parallel celebration of organic wholeness, camaraderie, and individualism. Since cowboy poetry's first appearance after the Civil War, its practitioners have been ever-alert for signs of its passing, expressed through a combination of romantic nostalgia, an unblinking description of the harsh realities of range life, and a tongue-in-cheek set of exaggerations. Back in the nineteenth century, the cowboy way of life was threatened by the Homestead Act, barbed wire, the end of the trail drive, and the closing of the open range, as Clark recalled in "The Old Cow Man":

Oh, it's squeak! squeak! squeak!
    Close and closer cramps the wire.
There's hardly play to back away
    And call a man a liar.
Their house has locks on every door;
    Their land is in a crate.
These ain't the plains of God no more,
    They're only real estate. [2]

By the 1920s the gravest threat to the cowboy life—at least from the poets' point of view—was tourism and the ubiquitous dude ranch. Thereafter, much of the poetry alludes to the exaggerations and misrepresentations that Hollywood had foisted upon the cowboy and the resultant public misunderstandings of the economies of the West. During the 1990s, emphasis in the poetry shifted to the political, portraying environmentalists, vegetarians, animal-rights activists, large corporations, and the developers of second homes and destination resorts as the destroyers of the range-herding way of life. In truth, cowboys—and their poetry—have always struggled to stay afloat in the turbulence of western waters, and both have consequently become, in Clark's phrase, "on'ry propositions."

The roots of cowboy poetry can be found in the post–Civil War period, when the open grasslands of the American West, increasingly emptied of their Native populations by disease, assault, and forced movement to reservations, became available for exploitation by grazers and herders using cattle from Mexico and Texas and herding techniques learned in large part from the vaqueros of Old Mexico. Trail drives moved herds from Texas northward to railroad stockyards, summer grazing range, and Indian reservations. Along the way, a variety of poem and song traditions were recalled, modified, reinvented, and regionalized, particularly the verbal art of sailors and soldiers, largely English and Irish in origin, which combined with the songs and hollers of black cowboys and the *corrido* tradition of the vaqueros.[3] In fact, the invention of poems and songs describing the hazards and triumphs of their occupation is remarkably common among herding people throughout the world and dates back hundreds of years in those cultures.[4]

Cowboy poetry and song are frequently interchangeable because poems were frequently set to music, often to traditional tunes or popular music of the day. Songs were sometimes recited, perhaps for greater dramatic effect or as a last resort by a tone-deaf performer.[5] The distinction between poem and song, in other words, has never been of much moment to working cowboys, except that some seem to define themselves as singers, others as reciters, and still others as composers of poetry. So cowboy singers, poets, and reciters adopted and adapted an enormous variety of materials as the basis for their occupational art: British and Irish sung ballads, a tradition of rhymed poetry created to memorialize an occasion or an individual, exaggerated tales for humorous effect, and considerable ribaldry. These materials they combined with the widespread Victorian affection for parlor and public—often schoolhouse—recitations, a mass of popular poetry from Shakespeare to Stephen Vincent Benét (particularly the outdoor, work-related, exotically set poetry of Rudyard Kipling and Robert W. Service), and the ample opportunities for entertainment and performance afforded by chuck wagons and campfires, bunkhouses and line camps, and barrooms and hotel rooms.

From this complex matrix of verbal art, derived from Ireland, Scotland, England, and Wales with a strong admixture of Mexican- and African-derived performance traditions and popular culture, individual singers, reciters, and wordsmiths shape a lasting heritage of occupational verse. But singers and reciters from the nineteenth century to the present day have never adopted wholesale the traditions of the past, nor did cowboy poetry shift from an anonymous oral tradition in the nineteenth century to one that relied heavily on individual composition and publication in the twentieth.[6] Instead, cowboy poetry and song have consistently combined time-honored poetic forms, job-specific language, and traditional metaphor with innovations by singers, reciters, and composers in expression, form, rhyme, meter, and subject matter. And although cowboy poetry was—as recently as 1985—defined as regularly rhymed and metered ballads composed and recited by men who have spent their lives in the cattle industry, rapid evolution since then has resulted in the use of unrhymed and irregularly metered open forms; in the expansion of subject matter to domestic, environmental, political, and personal topics; and in the increasing participation by women, Native Americans, Hispanic Americans, Canadians, Hawaiians, and even children. At the same time, cowboy poets have become more aware of the traditional herding poetry of Australia, Argentina, and the British Isles.

Cowboy poetry has been primarily the province of literate people since the first publication of poems in western newspapers in the 1870s. That is true both of poets, who compose original verse, and of reciters, who memorize and perform poems composed by others (although certainly some reciters in the past were barely or not at all literate and relied on prodigious feats of memory to absorb the poems). Some people both invent and recite; others specialize. And although many contemporary poets compose their poetry in their heads, on horseback or while driving a pickup, and refuse to write anything down until the poem is complete to their satisfaction, writing has always been a vital part of an only partially oral tradition. The written poem is an aid to memory and a device by which poems are passed on to others, and publishing has aided the spread of specific poems and of poetry in general.[7] Yet most reciters still value—and insist upon—memorization of any poem that they recite in public, in sharp contrast to the academic "poetry reading" in which poets seemingly read their poems, even if they are, in fact, memorized.[8]

Nor are cowboy poets primitive versifiers who create poetry instinctively from their working lives and experiences. Many cowboys of both the nineteenth and twentieth centuries have been well read, sometimes astonishingly so. One of the best-known nineteenth-century poems, "The Cowboy's Soliloquy," was composed by Allen McCandless, a working cowboy on the Crooked L Ranch in the Texas Panhandle, sometime before 1885. The third stanza reads:

My ceiling the sky, my carpet the grass,
My music the lowing of herds as they pass;
My books are the brooks, my sermons the stones,
My parson's a wolf on a pulpit of bones.

The imagery is taken directly from Shakespeare's *As You Like It,* in which Duke Senior, living in banishment in the Forest of Arden, exclaims:

And this our life, exempt from public haunt,
Finds tongues in trees, books in the running brooks,
Sermons in stones, and good in everything:
I would not change it. (II, i, 15–18)

In his allusion-filled poem, McCandless cleverly converts the forest wilderness of England into the harsh realities of the American West, wolf, bones, and all. The poem begins:

All day o'er the prairie alone I ride,
Not even a dog to run by my side;
My fire I kindle with chips gathered round,
And boil my coffee without being ground.[9]

The range of literary influences at work on cowboy poets is illustrated by the influential Texas poet Carlos Ashley (1903–93), who wrote modestly:

> I have never considered myself to be a real (certified) poet. Just a rhymer; some call it doggerel. Most so-called poets fall into this category, even a few famous ones like Dorothy Parker, for instance. Some critics put Longfellow on that list.
>
> Now who is a "real" poet? There are many, but as an example, how about the Richmond mystic, Edgar Allan Poe?[10]

More recently, contemporary cowboy poets have begun reading and reciting poets whose roots are deep in Anglo-American literary history. Paul Zarzyski recites Dylan Thomas; Buck Ramsey borrowed stanza forms from Housman and Pushkin and liked to recite from memory Eliot's "The Love Song of J. Alfred Prufrock"; Andy Wilkinson and Teresa Jordan recite Frost; John Dofflemyer composes Shakespearean sonnets about cowboy life; and Wallace McRae confesses unabashedly to "plagiarism" of forms and rhyme schemes from half a dozen English and American poets.

Cowboy poets, in other words, don't conform to most readers' perceptions or expectations of who or what a folk poet might be. For example, T. M. Pearce's early (1953) formulation, "What Is a Folk Poet?" concluded that folk poets write often of community events and of the joyful or sorrowful experiences of individuals in their communities, using traditional poetic forms that are sometimes "irregular or modified in the direction of informal and freer communication." The poet's "identity as an author is not suppressed, but his individuality as a poet is submerged in the stream of group or community feeling."[11] That definition does fit some cowboy poets and some cowboy poetry, but it implies a lack of technical skill on the part of the poet and an effort to conform totally to group norms, neither being standards by which cowboy poets measure themselves.

Américo Paredes's 1964 review also describes the subject matter and form of folk poetry but goes beyond Pearce's discussion to identify the folk poet specifically as performer and the poem as an oral performance for a specific audience in which context is all-important. The performer, says Paredes, is

> an actor, a personality. In the comic song he may play the clown. In the folksong of high seriousness he will be serious; he will take a detached attitude toward himself as performer. But he is far from detached in respect to his subject. . . . no matter how he submerges himself in his part, the performer will be effective to the extent that he is a personality in his own right.
>
> Here of course is a fundamental difference between folk and sophisticated literature. Folk literature is always a vehicle for the performer, who supplies a feeling of immediacy—of passion and power—through his own performance.[12]

Roger deV. Renwick's study *English Folk Poetry* identifies three major types: orally disseminated, anonymous songs from the rural working class; local songs commemorating community individuals or occurrences; and local poetry closely tied to the poet's "bounded and knowable world."[13] Cowboy poetry probably has most in common with the third category, yet differences are readily apparent. Although some cowboy poetry is composed to mark community occasions—weddings, funerals, baptisms, celebrations of community history, commemorations, and natural disasters—other poetry is universal to the cowboy trade. Still other poems may be highly personal, even confessional. Beyond their geographic communities, cowboy poets increasingly consider themselves part of a large group spread throughout the West, a "family" who communicates constantly by letter, telephone, sometimes e-mail.

Cowboy poetry, then, is elusive of definition and in constant flux. Although some poems originate in local circumstances and are centered on identifiable individuals and events within a community, many of the most lasting ones lack that sense of specific locality or perhaps lose their local references over time and through repeated recitation. The genre is writing- and print-dependent yet remains intensely oral in performance. Nor did cowboy poetry originate in some preliterate, primitive culture, but instead has borrowed since its beginnings from the forms, metrics, and images of folk song, the Bible, classic literature, and contemporary verse. Cowboy poetry has over the years expanded rapidly in its use of available poetic forms, subject matter, and technique, moving outward from its balladic center to other fixed forms and, increasingly, to free verse. And although the most-admired poets of the pre–World War II era, Bruce Kiskaddon and Curley Fletcher, were experienced riders and stock handlers, ranching people have also embraced verse by non-cowboys—James Barton Adams, Lawrence Chittenden, Charles Badger Clark, E. A. Brininstool, and Henry Herbert Knibbs—whose acquaintance with livestock and cattle management was mostly secondhand.

Many of the earliest cowboy songs and poems were anonymous in origin, but signed poetry began appearing in western newspapers during the 1870s. McCandless's "The Cowboy's Soliloquy" and Chittenden's "The Cowboys' Christmas Ball" were well known in the West before the turn of the twentieth century; Chittenden, in fact, published a volume of verse with a New York publisher in 1893. Yet by trade he was a dry-goods salesman, then a correspondent for a New York newspaper; he got into Texas ranching in partnership with an uncle but after seventeen years gave it up and returned East in 1904.[14]

About the same time, James Barton Adams (1843–1918), an Ohioan by birth, veteran of the Civil War and the construction of the transcontinental railroad, became a newspaperman, editor, and columnist in Denver, where he began publishing his own poetry of western life. In 1899 he published a collection called *Breezy Western Verse,* poems based on a bare two years of ranch employment in New Mexico when he was in his late forties. His poetry soon became known and recited by cowboys throughout the West.[15]

In 1889, N. Howard "Jack" Thorp set out on a year-long, 1,500-mile circuit of ranches in New Mexico and Texas, collecting songs and poems as he went. He was inspired enough to compose the well-known "Little Joe the Wrangler" in 1898, and in 1908 he published, at his own expense, *Songs of the Cowboys,* the first important anthology of cowboy songs and poems collected from working cowboys—although Thorp himself wrote six of the twenty-three songs.[16] Despite his work as a cowboy, Thorp had been raised in New York City, the son of a well-to-do lawyer who suffered financial reverses. Forced to forgo the college education that he had expected, Thorp trained polo ponies, worked as superintendent of an Arizona mine, got involved in a South American railroad scheme, and eventually became a successful rancher.[17]

It may seem that cowboy poetry was a decidedly marginal avocation at the beginning of the twentieth century, given its partly oral roots and the apparently ephemeral nature of the few poems that did get into print in newspapers, magazines, and a few individual, mostly self-published, collections. Yet in 1905 there appeared a mammoth (seven-pound) publication, *The Prose and Poetry of the Live Stock Industry of the United States.* Sponsored by the National Live Stock Historical Association, the volume was intended to be the first of three that would provide a "complete, reliable and interesting history" of the cattle industry in the western United States. This first volume contained no poetry at all, however, and the second and third volumes were never published because of financial problems. Yet the very title of the publication demonstrates that cowboy poetry was already an established and significant part of ranching life by the turn of the century, recognized by the livestock industry as a vital chronicle of an endangered occupation.[18]

Most of the cowboy poets active in the period before and after World War I—those whose poetry still lasts—were not native westerners, Thorp being something of an exception in his successful adaptation to ranching life. By 1906, for example, Charles Badger Clark—the "Badger" is a family name, not a nickname—was sending poems to the *Pacific Monthly* from the Arizona ranch near Tombstone where he was caretaker. But like Thorp, Clark (1883–1957) was not reared around ranching. His father was a minister in Iowa and South Dakota, and Clark was in Arizona primarily because his doctor thought he had tropical fever and that the dry climate might effect a cure. Thus, most of Clark's knowledge of the cowboy life was from observation rather than direct experience.[19] Yet his "A Cowboy's Prayer," "The Glory Trail" ("High-Chin Bob"), and "A Border Affair" ("Spanish Is the Lovin' Tongue") have become standards for recitation.[20]

E. A. Brininstool (1870–1957), a New York native, moved to Los Angeles at age twenty-five, where he became a prominent reporter and editor for a series of newspapers. He wrote a daily column, feature articles, and verse, finally becoming a full-time freelance writer in 1915. He was the author of dozens of books on popular western history, particularly the Indian wars, and also wrote in his lifetime some five thousand poems, most of them treating cowboy and range life.[21] His *Trail Dust of a Maverick* (1914) was published in New York by Dodd, Mead with poems on a variety of topics, one of which, "The Old Trail Songs," demonstrates Brininstool's familiarity with cowboy singing, possibly via Thorp's collection.

In 1910 John Lomax—one of the most important American folklorists—published his first collection, *Cowboy Songs and Other Frontier Ballads* (New York: Macmillan). Lomax had grown up near a branch of the Chisholm Trail in north Texas and had begun collecting cowboy songs as a young man. But it wasn't until he began studying for an M.A. at Harvard when he was in his late thirties that he received encouragement to spend the next three summers roaming the Southwest, collecting ballads, songs, and poems. The publication of *Cowboy Songs*—only a few had music accompanying the lyrics, and many were probably composed first as poems before being set to music—resonated with an American public preoccupied with urbanization, industrialization, and immigration and still imbued with a sense of inferiority with respect to Europe. Here, it seemed, was a native American voice of epic quality to challenge European culture.[22]

The popular success of *Cowboy Songs* encouraged John Lomax to collect farther afield, and in 1919 he published *Songs of the Cattle Trail and Cow Camp*, not—as the title suggests—another collection of songs but an anthology of cowboy poetry gleaned partly from published collections. Included were two poems by Brininstool, eight by James Barton Adams, ten by Badger Clark, and four by

Henry Herbert Knibbs, another easterner. A few of the poems were listed as "anonymous" or "from recitation," which suggests that Lomax's collecting endeavors included transcribing poetry as well as song and recognizing that recitation was a popular entertainment and recreation among cowboys.

Not until after the publication of Lomax's first collection did the two poets who had the most experience with livestock, Bruce Kiskaddon (1878–1949) and Curley Fletcher (1892–1953), begin writing. Like most of the other prominent cowboy poets of the first third of the twentieth century, Kiskaddon was an easterner, born in Pennsylvania, although his family later relocated to the mining town of Trinidad, Colorado. Until his forty-eighth year he was employed primarily as a range hand in Colorado and Arizona, with a short stint of work in Australia. Then, in 1926, Kiskaddon went to Hollywood to work in the nascent motion-picture industry, where he wrote most of his reminiscent poems about his days as a working cowboy.

Information about Kiskaddon's life remains fragmentary, but he did develop a cooperative partnership with the magazine *Western Livestock Journal* and its publisher, Nelson Crow. Each month Kiskaddon would send Crow a poem that was then sent to illustrator Katherine Field for an appropriate sketch before publication. *Western Livestock* was a magazine of great popularity, subscribed to by thousands of ranch families all over the West, so Kiskaddon's poetry was often clipped, carried in purses and wallets and pocket notebooks, pasted into scrapbooks, and memorized. His lyric and descriptive powers and his technical abilities make him the most influential cowboy poet of all, as in the beginning lines of "The Creak of the Leather":

It's likely that you can remember
A corral at the foot of a hill
Some mornin' along in December
When the air was so cold and so still.
When the frost lay as light as a feather
And the stars had jest blinked out and gone.
Remember the creak of the leather
As you saddled your hoss in the dawn.[23]

Carmen "Curley" Fletcher, the son of an English father and an Italian mother, grew up in farming country around Bishop, California, and became familiar with cowboy work through the Paiute cowboys in the area. He was a successful rodeo rider who scraped by on his winnings and wrote poems on the side, notably "The Strawberry Roan" and "The Flyin' Outlaw." A slim booklet, *Rhymes of the Round-Up,* was self-published by Fletcher and his brother in 1917; apparently Lomax had not encountered it when he assembled *Songs of the Cattle Trail and Cow Camp.*

Fletcher published a larger collection, *Songs of the Sage,* in 1931. He spent the remainder of his life promoting rodeos, developing mines, and advising publishers and filmmakers on western topics.[24]

Prominent poets of the World War II era included S. Omar Barker (1894–1985), a college-educated New Mexican from a ranching background who spent most of his career as a freelance writer, and Dartmouth graduate Gail Gardner (1892–1988), a rancher and postmaster in Prescott, Arizona, who wrote "The Sierry Petes" ("Tyin' Knots in the Devil's Tail").[25] Carlos Ashley was a "country lawyer," as he liked to describe himself, when he wasn't writing poetry, ranching, and developing real estate.

It must be apparent, then, that virtually none of the most respected cowboy poets of the last century have been itinerant working cowboys scribbling heartfelt verses in lonely line camps. Almost without exception, cowboy poets have been men and women of the world, aware of politics and economics, war and peace, environmental conflicts, shifting cultural values and mores. Despite massive misconceptions about the origins of cowboy poetry, it is clear that the great majority of poems are of known authorship; that they nevertheless exist in multiple versions; that they are widely transmitted by oral, written, and—now—electronic means; and that although the geographic origins and occupations of the poets are considered significant and relevant, it is a poem's fidelity to the cowboy experience and its ability to reflect accurately the ups and downs of the cowboy life that determine its lasting appeal.

In short, cowboy poetry seems to defy categorization. A hybrid of folk and popular kinds of poetry, it borrows deftly from popular and commercial images of the West, appropriating, parodying, and critiquing. Cowboy poets are intensely aware of their occupational traditions, poetic and otherwise, but they also read widely in the classics and popular literature. Like the rest of the cowboy's occupational heritage, cowboy poetry has borrowed heavily from a diversity of cultural backgrounds. Nineteenth-century cowboys got their cattle-herding techniques largely from the Spanish and Mexican practices of vaqueros. They learned horsemanship in many cases from Native Americans, and black cowboys, both slaves and freemen, were a vital part of the development of the cattle drive and roundup. By some estimates, African American and *Mexicano* cowboys may have made up as much as 37 percent of the working hands during the trail-drive era that ended in the 1890s. And the continuing influence of Native Americans as horsemen, cowboys, and independent ranchers is just beginning to be assessed by historians of the West.[26]

Similarly, the oral traditions of working cowboys represent an amalgam of cultural expressions and forms, not only the ballads and broadsides of Great Britain and the songs and poems of outdoor workers like sailors and loggers but also field hollers, spirituals, and work songs from African American cowboys; *corridos, versos,* and guitar-accompanied singing from *Mexicanos;* and poems and songs from Native American cowboys.[27] It is not just a matter of cultural traditions and occupational skills influencing each other but a complex of traditions coexisting and sometimes hybridizing, even as far away as Argentina and Australia.

The subject matter of the poetry, once relatively narrow, has expanded radically since the mid-1980s, yet familiar topics are still at the heart of the tradition. Work is, of course, the primary subject, but it can be treated in a variety of ways—with humor, as in poems about memorable "wrecks" (bucking accidents) or, more grimly, by capturing the sheer drudgery of long days on the range and the dangers that await unwary cowboys. Yet work-centered poetry frequently has an instructional function as well and carries with it embedded debates over work techniques, appropriate dress, and preferences in gear that continue to animate conversations among cowboys throughout the West.

Thousands of poems, unsurprisingly, have been written about animals—favorite horses and dogs, notable bucking horses, and wild cows and steers with more-than-human intelligence and craft. Frequently the poetry celebrates the wildness still inherent in supposedly domesticated stock, a theme that recurs in a different form in the numerous poems about cowboys who try to rope truly wild animals: Badger Clark's "The Glory Trail" (sometimes called "High Chin Bob," the name of the proud cowboy who ropes a mountain lion and is doomed to have it follow him for the rest of his days); S. Omar Barker's "Bear Ropin' Buckaroo"; and Curley Fletcher's "Yavapai Pete" (the cowboy who rides a grizzly bear for ranch work).[28]

Much poetry has been composed in memory of fallen comrades as well, often when the death is the result of stampede, drowning, or other accident. Another favorite topic is the system of values prevalent among cowboys (usually referred to as "the code of the West"), which celebrates the virtues of bravery, loyalty, steadfastness, honesty, honor, and courtesy, especially to women and the elderly. Value-laden statements—which may again provide instruction in norms and values to youngsters and outsiders—are often embedded in a set of traditional metaphors: "he'll do to ride the river with," "he never sold his saddle," "he'll make a hand," and "he rides for the brand."[29] More memorably, "Let me be easy on the man that's down / Let me be square and generous with all."[30]

Nature is, of course, central to the cowboy life, and it's a rare poem that doesn't include references to the rugged yet beautiful landscape and the fickleness of the western climate. The confinement of the city in contrast to the freedom of the outdoor life, the beauties of the changing seasons, the contrast between mountain and prairie or desert and river, the sun, rain, and open sky—these are major topics that portray the cowboy's harmonious interplay with nature.

Although rarely published until recently, bawdy poetry and song have been a vital part of cowboy expressive culture since the trail-driving days of the nineteenth century. One of the oldest poem/songs, "The Old Chisholm Trail," had hundreds of verses, many of them dealing with sex, masturbation, sodomy, and excretions, both human and animal. Vulgar parodies of well-established cowboy poems and songs were also common, notably "The Castration of the Strawberry Roan," a parody of Curley Fletcher's "The Strawberry Roan" and written by Fletcher himself.[31] Bawdy poetry and song probably occurred in proportions similar to those in the repertoires of soldiers, sailors, loggers, college fraternity members, and other relatively isolated all-male groups.

Bawdy poetry is still a common bill of fare among working cowboys, although the emphasis on "family entertainment" at poetry gatherings has mostly driven the performance of such materials back to line camps, bunkhouses, and saloons. The 1986 and 1987 Cowboy Poetry Gatherings in Elko, Nevada, each set aside a late-night session specifically for men—and women—who wanted to hear and recite off-color poems and songs, but protests by many attending the gathering ended the practice thereafter. Yet small groups of poets and reciters maintain the bawdy tradition by getting together in motel rooms and bars and by continuing to compose and recite such works.

Cowboy poetry has a social and domestic side as well. The cowboy's pridefully raucous social life is celebrated in dozens of poems about dances and other social gatherings, and love, courting, and family also play a surprisingly important role in the poetry. Although women poets were extremely rare during the "golden age" of cowboy poetry between 1905 and 1935, an increasing number of women have been writing and reciting and developing their own perspectives and styles. Women write of family and children, the unpredictability of ranch life (and husbands), and the frustrations and beauties of rural living. But they also write of their work as ranchers, riders, and working cowboys; their struggles to maintain their independence; and the limiting nature of traditional gender relations in the West. Women are now at the forefront of developments in cowboy poetry, adopting newer and more open forms and forging into hitherto untouched subject areas: domestic relations, family problems, and women's roles.

The ethnically diverse makeup of the West has been a topic, too, and despite the major influence of Mexico (and before that, Spain) on the gear, lingo, and working techniques of American cowboys, vaqueros (and other ethnic minorities) were generally harshly treated in the early poetry, both stigmatized and stereotyped. In keeping with widespread racist attitudes in the first half of the twentieth century, *Mexicanos* were treated with disdain but were also portrayed as exotic and sensual, as in Frank Desprez's well-known "Lasca" and Badger Clark's "A Border Affair" ("Spanish Is the Lovin' Tongue"). Yet there were apparent exceptions. "The Texas Cowboy and the Mexican Greaser," for example, which is anonymous, describes a cowboy's defense of a Mexican hand about to be murdered by a mob.[32]

Clark's "A Border Affair" has often been bowdlerized to remove what many singers and reciters consider an offensive line in the last stanza:

> Never seen her since that night,
> I kain't cross the Line, you know, [the Arizona-Mexico border]
> She was Mex and I was white;
> Like as not it's better so.
> Yet I've always sort of missed her
> Since that last wild night I kissed her,
> Left her heart and lost my own—
> *"Adios, mi corazon!"*[33]

The resignation of "like as not it's better so," however, suggests that it was social pressures—the embedded racism of American society—that militated against the pair, and the speaker's use of Spanish at the end of each stanza suggests that the "Mex" of the third line is not the cowboy's term but what he hears—or expects to hear—from others; thus the poem becomes an indictment of the racism that refuses to allow relationships of this kind. Yet as Jim Griffith has pointed out, the entire poem describes an American cowboy's crossing the border, meeting and possibly seducing a Mexican woman, getting in a "foolish gamblin' fight," and fleeing back across the border, never to return: a powerful emblem of American imperialism that creates an unresolved political tension within the poem.[34]

The belief that cowboy poetry is a vital means of expression of western ways of life, that it has political as well as aesthetic power, has meant that hundreds of poems throughout the tradition address the issues of a vanishing West—of the economic pressures on independent ranchers and cowboys and political tensions throughout the region. This awareness of poetry as speaking for an entire regional occupational group has led to a large group of poems that are highly self-conscious and that speak of the nature of memory, of the process of writing poetry, and of the mystery of making poems that can have effect as well as affect in a difficult world.

Poems have been written about the debate between those favoring strictly metered and rhymed ballad forms and those who experiment with open forms. Other poems deal with the stark contrasts between the romantic Hollywood image of the cowboy life and its harsh realities, or between the easy humor of cowboy poetry and the struggle of many ranch families to hang onto their land and to make a living. Poems have taken sides on environmental questions, have castigated vegetarians, have commented on politics and international trade agreements, and have asserted the right of women to work and be respected as cowboys. As Sue Wallis has said, "cowboy" is a verb, not a gender-exclusive noun.

And poems have described cowboy poetry gatherings and the remarkable network of cowboy poets that has developed throughout the West.[35]

The success of cowboy poetry gatherings all over the West has not only brought the poetry to a far greater audience than it enjoyed previously but also changed the poetry permanently. The first of the gatherings was organized in 1985 by Hal Cannon, at the time working out of the Sun Valley (Idaho) Center for the Arts and Humanities, although the idea for a regional celebration of cowboy poetry was originally proposed by Jim Griffith, director of the Southwest Folklore Center in Tucson, at a caucus of public-sector folklorists from the West in Washington, D.C. The project, a truly regional one, called on the talents and energies of folklorists throughout the region, and a majority of the fieldwork to locate active poets and reciters was done by Gary Stanton with a grant from the National Endowment for the Arts.

The folklorists decided to host the gathering in Elko, Nevada, then a relatively small town heavily dependent on ranching but boasting a convention center with a thousand-seat auditorium and ample motel rooms because of its lively casinos. It was also home to a number of outstanding cowboy poets and had been the site of a Pioneer Arts and Crafts Festival a few years earlier at which cowboy poetry was featured. The gathering—so called because of its allusion to the "gathering" of cattle during roundup and to emphasize that the event was not a contest or competition and that no prizes would be awarded—was scheduled in the dead of winter, the end of January, the quiet time when ranchers and working cowboys could most easily leave their stock for a weekend, assuming that neighbors, friends, or family could pitch in to feed and water.

The first gathering in Elko drew a few hundred people, primarily ranchers and buckaroos from Nevada and surrounding states, many of whom had been reciting and writing poetry for years without knowing that others were doing the same thing. In the ensuing years, attendance at the Elko gathering has grown dramatically to about eight thousand, a figure limited only by the number of available rooms in the city's motels. The audience has changed as well. As costs and ticket prices have increased, the gathering has drawn an increasing number of middle- and upper-middle-class people, many of them from retirement communities in California, Nevada, and Arizona. And although the majority of the audience still seems to have a background in ranching, stock raising, or farming, a substantial number of contemporary fans of cowboy poetry has little personal knowledge of ranching life. At the same time, the number of independent working cowboys, traditionally single and highly itinerant, has declined sharply as ranching becomes ever more mechanized and dependent on family labor.[36]

In response to this shift in audience, the Western Folklife Center, the nonprofit organization in Elko founded by Cannon to run the gathering, has begun sponsoring free concerts and other events the weekend before the gathering for ranch families and the citizens of Elko. Another result of the changing makeup of audiences is the Western Folklife Center's marketing of books, tapes, and CDs of poetry and music along with scarves, T-shirts, jewelry, and artwork. At the same time, cowboy poetry has been buoyed by the faddish appeal of western and southwestern motifs and crafts, which in turn has enabled hundreds of traditional craftspeople throughout the West to make a living, even though much of their rawhide, horsehair, and silver artwork may never be used for working with horses or cattle and may be sold primarily to non-ranching collectors.

The Elko gathering has spawned dozens of smaller events throughout the West as well. At least 150 regional, state, and local gatherings are held every year, often in schools, churches, or community halls. These are sometimes the enterprise of a single individual; others are held in association with a state or county fair or other event. Some of the larger state gatherings, like those in Montana and Arizona, attract thousands. The major draw seems to be more than nostalgia for an Old West that is disappearing (if it ever existed) and more than the compelling mix of understated humor, outlandish exaggeration, and frankly acknowledged emotion that sometimes crosses the line into sentimentality. The appeal may have something to do with the sense of encountering an authentic community of like-minded people in touch with the land and their heritage. Besides, cowboys have a reputation in the public mind for reticence, for being "strong but silent," and their willingness to acknowledge deep feelings, express personal difficulties, and perform an intensely private poetry before audiences far different from their network of family and friends seems to be another reason for cowboy poetry's mass appeal.

The gatherings have, inevitably, wrought major changes on cowboy poetry. Exposure to the most skilled and innovative cowboy poets has meant that other poets have tested themselves and found their techniques wanting. As poets exchange their latest works, as they hear critiques and questions from their colleagues, they refine their rhythms and rhymes (avoiding, one hopes, rhyming "horse" with "of course") and seek out images and metaphors that are less clichéd and formulaic than "grass-grown prairie" or "brown-eyed steed." Other poets have brought to the gatherings their readings of non-cowboy poetry, beginning first with Rudyard Kipling and Robert W. Service, the great balladeers, but increasingly embracing a variety of writers, from Homer, Shakespeare, and Browning to Stephen Vincent Benét, Walt Whitman, and the Beat poets of the 1950s. These influences assure that cowboy poetry will continue to change, perhaps as drastically as it did in the 1990s, as poets experiment with form, gain an increasing sophistication in meter and rhyme, and try out subjects beyond ranch work.

The future of cowboy poetry is as unpredictable as cattle futures and the beef market. It is possible that the mass enthusiasm that landed cowboy poets on

Johnny Carson's "Tonight Show" for several years in the late 1980s will wane and audiences will contract to a hard core of ranching people who will continue to seek out vivid forms of expression for their working lives. But it is equally possible that the poetry's greatest strengths—its honesty, its wry self-deprecation, and its quest for beauty, meaning, and continuity in the day-to-day ordinariness of human existence—will make it prosper as a form of art that is at once subtle, complex, and accessible.

Notes

1. Charles Badger Clark, "The Legend of Boastful Bill," in Clark, *Sun and Saddle Leather, Including "Grass Grown Trails" and New Poems,* 5th ed. (Boston: Richard G. Badger, 1920), 52–56. The poem was composed in 1907 during Clark's residency near Tombstone, Arizona; it was first published in *Pacific Monthly* magazine in February 1908. *Sun and Saddle Leather* is still available, along with other works by and about Clark, from the Badger Clark Memorial Society, P.O. Box 351, Custer, SD 57730–0351.

2. Charles Badger Clark, "The Old Cow Man," in Clark, *Sun and Saddle Leather,* 5th ed., 88. This poem was first published by Clark in the 1915 edition, but it was probably written in Arizona between 1906 and 1910 (personal communication from Greg Scott, 25 June 1997).

3. Alan Lomax, "Introduction," in John A. Lomax and Alan Lomax, *Cowboy Songs and Other Frontier Ballads* (1910), (New York: Macmillan, 1986), xviii–xxix.

4. Lomax, "Introduction," xxix–xxx.

5. W. K. O'Neil, "Introduction," in *The Oral Tradition of the American West: Adventure, Courtship, Family, and Place in Traditional Recitation,* ed. Keith Cunningham (Little Rock: August House, 1990), 14 and note 19.

6. This is the argument of Blake Allmendinger, *The Cowboy: Representations of Labor in an American Work Culture* (New York: Oxford University Press, 1992).

7. Compare Dianne M. Dugaw, "Anglo-American Folksong Reconsidered: The Interface of Oral and Written Forms," *Western Folklore* 43, no. 2 (1984): 83–103.

8. For additional perspectives on recitation and monologues, especially in Great Britain, see "Monologues and Folk Recitation," ed. Kenneth S. Goldstein and Robert D. Bethke, special issue of *Southern Folklore Quarterly* 40, nos. 1–2 (1976); and Bethke, "Recitation," in *Folklore: An Encyclopedia of Beliefs, Customs, Tales, Music, and Art,* ed. Thomas A. Green (Santa Barbara: ABC–CLIO, 1997), 2:695–97.

9. In *Cowboy Poetry: A Gathering,* ed. Hal Cannon (Salt Lake City: Gibbs Smith, 1985), 1. See also Harry E. Chrisman, *Lost Trails of the Cimarron,* 2d ed. (Denver: Sage, 1964), 284–87; and Jim Bob Tinsley, *He Was Singin' This Song: A Collection of Forty-Eight Traditional Songs of the American Cowboy, with Words, Music, Pictures, and Stories* (Orlando: University Presses of Florida, 1981), 1–7.

10. Personal communication, 21 March 1988.

11. T. M. Pearce, "What Is a Folk Poet?" *Western Folklore* 12, no. 4 (1953): 248. Com-

pare Duncan Emrich's narrow, erroneous description: "The folk poet is not conscious of form. He knows nothing of and is totally unconcerned about sonnets, madrigals, epics, quatrains, hexameters, free or blank verse, couplets, or whatever." See *American Folk Poetry: An Anthology* (Boston: Little Brown, 1974), xxvi.

12. Américo Paredes, "Some Aspects of Folk Poetry," *Texas Studies in Literature and Language* 6, no. 2 (1964): 225. For more on the performative nature of cowboy poetry, see Carol A. Edison, *Cowboy Poetry from Utah: An Anthology* (Salt Lake City: Utah Folklife Center, 1985), 8–14.

13. Roger deV. Renwick, *English Folk Poetry: Structure and Meaning,* Publications of the American Folklore Society: New Series, vol. 2 (Philadelphia: University of Pensylvania Press, 1980), 5.

14. Allen McCandless, "The Cowboy's Soliloquy" and Lawrence Chittenden, "The Cowboys' Christmas Ball," in Tinsley, *He Was Singin' This Song,* 144–47.

15. James Barton Adams, *Some Letters and Writings of James Barton Adams,* Publications in History (Socorro, N.M.: Socorro County Historical Society, 1968), 4:5–6.

16. Although Thorp is usually credited with publishing the first collection, a patent-medicine salesman named Clark Stanley anticipated Thorp by producing in 1897 a pamphlet that combined cowboy songs with advertisements for "snake-oil liniment." See Glenn Ohrlin, *The Hell-Bound Train: A Cowboy Songbook* (Urbana: University of Illinois Press, 1973), xvii. Even before that, in 1886, a cowboy named Lysius Gough printed a collection of his own poems; see Guy Logsdon's essay in this volume. See also Thorp's autobiographical sketch, "Banjo in the Cow Camps," *The Atlantic* 167 (Aug. 1940): 195–203, in N. Howard ("Jack") Thorp and Austin E. Fife and Alta S. Fife, *Songs of the Cowboys* (1908), (New York: Clarkson N. Potter, 1966), 11–27.

17. John I. White, *Git Along, Little Dogies: Songs and Songmakers of the American West* (Urbana: University of Illinois Press, 1975), 198.

18. Don D. Walker, "Prose and Poetry of the Cattle Industry: Fact and Image as the Centuries Changed," in *Clio's Cowboys: Studies in the Historiography of the Cattle Trade* (Lincoln: University of Nebraska Press, 1981), 46–60.

19. "Preface," in Clark, *Sun and Saddle Leather,* 6th ed. (1922), vii–xix. See also Greg Scott, ed., *Poems of the West by Charles Badger Clark, Jr.: Previously Unpublished and Out of Print Poetry* ([Nogales, Ariz.]: Moco Seco Press, 1997).

20. Charles Badger Clark, "A Cowboy's Prayer," "The Glory Trail" ("High-Chin Bob"), and "A Border Affair" ("Spanish Is the Lovin' Tongue"), in White, *Git Along, Little Dogies,* 126–36.

21. *Who Was Who in America* (Chicago: A. N. Marquis, 1960), 3:104.

22. Lomax, "Introduction," xi–xxxvi.

23. Bruce Kiskaddon, "The Creak of the Leather," in *Rhymes of the Ranges: A New Collection of the Poems of Bruce Kiskaddon,* ed. Hal Cannon (Salt Lake City: Gibbs Smith, 1987), 41. Kiskaddon's biography appears in the introduction to *Rhymes of the Ranges.*

24. Hal Cannon, "Preface" to Curley Fletcher, *Songs of the Sage: The Poetry of Curley Fletcher,* ed. Cannon (Salt Lake City: Gibbs Smith, 1986), v–xiii.

25. See, for example, S. Omar Barker, *Rawhide Rhymes: Singing Poems of the Old West*

(Garden City: Doubleday, 1968); and Gail I. Gardner, *Orejana Bull for Cowboys Only* (1935), 7th ed. (Prescott: The Sharlot Hall Museum Press, 1987).

26. Richard W. Slatta, "Cowboys and Indians: Frontier Race Relations," *Cowboys of the Americas* (New Haven: Yale University Press, 1990), 159–73. See also Peter Iverson, *When Indians Became Cowboys: Native Peoples and Cattle Ranching in the American West* (Norman: University of Oklahoma Press, 1994); and Morgan Baillargeon and Leslie Tepper, *Legends of Our Times: Native Cowboy Life* (Vancouver: University of British Columbia Press, 1998).

27. See the program books from the Elko, Nevada, Cowboy Poetry Gathering, particularly those from the 1992 and 1993 gatherings that featured vaquero traditions and those from 1995 and 1996, which highlighted Native American contributions. See also Joe S. Graham, *El Rancho in South Texas: Continuity and Change from 1750* and *Ranching in South Texas: A Symposium,* ed. Graham (both, Kingsville, Tex.: John E. Conner Museum, 1994). Also see Jerald Underwood, "The Vaquero: Forerunner and Foundation of the American Cowboy," in *The Catch-Pen,* ed. Len Ainsworth and Kenneth Davis (Lubbock: Texas Tech University, 1991), 171–75; and María Herrera-Sobek, *Northward Bound: The Mexican Immigrant Experience in Ballad and Song* (Bloomington: Indiana University Press, 1993), especially ch. 1.

28. Charles Badger Clark, "The Glory Trail" and "High Chin Bob" (two versions), in John A. Lomax, *Songs of the Cattle Trail and Cow Camp* (1919), (New York: Macmillan,1927), 30–35; S. Omar Barker, "Bear Ropin' Buckaroo," in *Cowboy Poetry,* ed. Cannon, 14–15; Curley Fletcher, "Yavapai Pete," in Fletcher, *Songs of the Sage,* 15–17.

29. See in particular the poetry of Red Steagall in *Ride for the Brand* (Fort Worth: Texas Christian University Press, 1993); Eugene Manlove Rhodes, "The Hired Man on Horseback," in *Best Loved Poems of the American West,* ed. John J. Gregg and Barbara T. Gregg (Garden City: Doubleday, 1980), 189–93; Georgie Sicking, "To Be a Top Hand," in *Just Thinkin'* (Fallon, Nev.: Loganberry Press, 1985), 8; Thorp and Fife, *Songs of the Cowboys,* 61–65; and Jack Lamb, "American Cowboy Poetry: History and Orality," unpublished essay.

30. Charles Badger Clark, "A Cowboy's Prayer," in Clark, *Sun and Saddle Leather,* 5th ed., 36.

31. Guy Logsdon, *"The Whorehouse Bells Were Ringing" and Other Songs Cowboys Sing* (Urbana: University of Illinois Press, 1989), 60–69, 86–96. See also Clifford P. Westermeier, "The Cowboy and Sex," in *The Cowboy: Six-Shooters, Songs, and Sex,* ed. Charles W. Harris and Buck Rainey (Norman: University of Oklahoma Press, 1976), 85–105.

32. "The Texas Cowboy and the Mexican Greaser," in Lomax, *Songs of the Cattle Trail and Cow Camp,* 11–13.

33. Charles Badger Clark, "A Border Affair" ("Spanish Is the Lovin' Tongue"), in Clark, *Sun and Saddle Leather,* 5th ed., 44; see also White, *Git Along, Little Dogies,* 126–36.

34. Personal communication, 14 July 1996.

35. Sue Wallis, "Gatherings" in chapter 17 of this volume; Charles A. Kortes, "Poets Gathering, 1985," in *Cowboy Poetry,* ed. Cannon, 110–11.

36. See Teresa Jordan, "Preface to the Bison Book Edition," *Cowgirls: Women of the American West* (Lincoln: University of Nebraska Press, 1992), xiii–xx.

Part 1
Backgrounds

The origins of cowboy poetry are obscured by the smoke and dust of the mid-nineteenth century, but it seems likely that Texas settlers of northern European ancestry in the period between Texas independence and the Civil War first combined their own oral traditions of balladry with the hard facts of cattle and horse work under the tutelage of Spanish-speaking vaqueros to produce poems and songs redolent of the cowboy life. Once the war was over, Jesse Chisholm, Joseph G. McCoy, and others established the utility of driving cattle from the vast Texas rangelands north to the railroad terminuses of Kansas. Eventually, new trails were established to take cattle as far north as Montana and Canada, and it was along these trails as well as on the home ranches of the West that cowboy poetry became established as a distinctive genre of folk art identified with a small but culturally significant occupational group.

As Kim Stafford—essayist, fiction writer, and director of the Northwest Writing Institute at Lewis and Clark College in Portland, Oregon—demonstrates, cowboy poetry has much in common with other forms of folk expression of the rural American West. Its emphasis on exacting craftsmanship, its thoughtful combination of individual innovation and expressive tradition, and its deeply spiritual qualities in its reflection of the natural world make it resonate with the cultural heritage of Native Americans and other groups dating back to the singers and poets of the Middle Ages.

At the same time, cowboy poetry has a deeply functional role within the ranching community, providing sociability, emotional release, and the opportunity for commentary on the political and social issues most directly affecting ranchers and working cowboys throughout the West. This is the thesis of James Griffith, formerly the director of the Southwest Folklore Center at the University of Arizona and the first public-sector folklorist in the western United States. Jim's deep knowledge of the folk traditions of southern Arizona led him to early friendships with the late Van Holyoak, Slim Kite, Gail Gardner, and other old-time poets, reciters, and musicians. In fact, it was Jim who first suggested the idea of a get-together of cowboy poets from throughout the West—an idea that led to the first Cowboy Poetry Gathering in Elko, Nevada, and to the hundreds of local, state, and regional gatherings it has spawned.

Scott Preston, an independent poet, critic, and editor, suggests that cowboy poetry has deep affinities with other American literary forms, even including the nonacademic poetic tradition established by Walt Whitman and William Carlos Williams. At the same time, the performance of cowboy poetry bears strong resemblance to worldwide forms of ethnopoetry, the traditional kinds of folk expression often performed in ritualistic, ceremonial, or festival atmospheres throughout the world.

Cowboy poetry's oral qualities are balanced by its long-time reliance on printed texts, as Guy Logsdon shows. Logsdon, the Tulsa, Oklahoma-based dean of American historians of cowboy music and song, has collected dozens of examples of cowboy poetry from nineteenth-century newspapers and magazines, demonstrating that the genre is virtually coterminous with the first periodicals in the western part of the United States.

The beginnings of printed cowboy poetry roughly parallel the rise of the cowboy as an American cultural hero, and the impact of the dime novel, the Hollywood film, and the singing cowboy of recordings, radio, and television have deeply affected cowboy poetry, especially in its themes. What Hal Cannon calls a "poetry of exile" was the result as poets increasingly reacted against the mass marketing of the cowboy at the same time that economic prospects for independent ranching began to flag in the face of drought and corporate buyouts of family ranches. That these processes occurred at precisely the same time that the finest and best-loved cowboy poetry was being composed (the golden age of cowboy poetry—1905 to 1935) is another irony in the development of American popular culture as well as an insistent reminder of mass culture's power to adapt, adopt, and exploit the hand-wrought craftsmanship of working people. Cannon, founding director of the Western Folklife Center in Elko and producer of the first Cowboy Poetry Gatherings, has edited five anthologies of cowboy poetry, including the popular collections *Cowboy Poetry: A Gathering* and *New Cowboy Poetry: A Contemporary Gathering.* Examined together, they demonstrate the dynamic tension between tradition and innovation that has been the hallmark of cowboy poetry for 150 years.

2

Making Something Fine

Kim Stafford

We were coming across the Salt Flats west out of Salt Lake, and I started to think about the way things get done well. I thought how the desert does silence really well. And the moon does a nice soft light on the sage. In the morning, if it's not too cold, the thing the birds do well is to sing and make a smooth pattern through the wind when they fly. Then I got to us. I thought, "What do we do well, we humans?" One of the things we do best is language, braiding it for meaning and delight. For me, cowboy poetry is one of our best artifacts, one of the best tools in our kit, one of the sweetest locations of delight in the use of language.

I think back to a fellow I visited up in Hermiston, Oregon, by the name of Loren Wood. He had a shop there with some tack and harness, and I was admiring some of the special pieces in his glass case.

"How about that white rawhide bridle there?" I said. "Who made that?"

"A kid up in Idaho made that," he said. "If he keeps at it, someday he'll be really good."

"What does it go for?" I said.

"Twenty-five dollars."

"Well," I said, "how about that finer piece next to it?"

"Old fellow in town made that," Mr. Wood said. "That's seventy-five. He's one of the best around."

It was a nice headstall, all right, but I was working up to the best piece, the black and white counted strands of the round braid bosal. "And that horsehair work there beside it," I said. "What about that?"

"Oh that?" he said. "I made that. I think I'm going to have to just give it away."

And he drifted down the aisle to help a customer while I gazed on work too fine to tease money. It had to be a gift.

Mr. Wood taught me something there about how the best things get made and used. In the realm of language, too, we live by giving away the best we make. We try to be responsible to those depending on us, but we really live by giving things away. Cowboy poems talk about the human spirit by talking about horses and leather and rope, but I also think of cowboy poetry in terms of gifts and friends and Indians.

I was up in Idaho one time and at the end of a program we had, a fellow came up with a little package, and he started telling me a story. He said, "When I was a kid, I lived up around Lapwai in that Lawyer Canyon. I was always the one in the family who had to go sit with Grandma in the evenings, because she got lonely and she lived up in this little side canyon where she couldn't get TV or even radio reception. She got lonely in the evenings, so I'd go sit with her. I got kind of mad about it at the time, because my brothers and sisters always got to watch TV and all, but she told me stories, and over the years I was glad it worked out that way.

"Then when I come to graduate from high school she gave me this beaded belt buckle, made by an old lady named Viola Morris up there, a Nez Perce woman. Grandma said, 'Now Dan, I'm going to give you this buckle on one condition. In your life when you meet someone who deserves this beautiful thing, you will give it away without hesitation.'"

At this point Dan handed me the little bundle. I opened it, and it was that buckle. He said, "I've met the person who should have this now, and on the same condition. When *you* meet someone who deserves this beautiful thing, you'll give it away without hesitation."

"Dan," I said, "how am I going to recognize that person?"

"Well," he said, "I did."

And that was that. I think Dan taught me how we make it through the world—by carrying these gifts we have for a time and then passing them on without a second thought, because we know more will come to us.

There was an old-timer on the dry side of the mountains who told me about going away to college in the city when he was young. He knew he would get homesick, so he got himself a little matchbox and filled it with sage. When he was sitting in the lecture hall with a couple of hundred other agricultural students taking notes on a lecture and he got a little dizzy and disoriented—the way the city will do that to you—he would quietly take out this little box and smell the sagebrush, and feel a lot better, and put it away. Every time he got home, he'd freshen that little bit of sage, and every time he got lost in the city he'd pull it out.

That little bit of sanity that's portable over time and distance, that's what we need. And that's what a cowboy poem, done right, can give.

The way they do it up in Lapwai, some of the Nez Perce people carry a little bag inside their shirts. It has powerful things in it that are connected to experiences they have had, places they have been, maybe certain people they have known. I was up there visiting an old woman, and I came away with this little bag. I said to her, "Well, what am I supposed to put inside this little bag?" She will never look you in the eye. That would be impolite. She looked down and spoke softly.

"That's for your life to tell you what you put in there," she said. "You will know."

So I carry my matchbox filled with sage, and I carry my little bag, and sometimes when I'm at the Root Feast, I put a chokecherry seed in the bag to remember. Or if I'm at a place in the desert that teaches me something, I put a tip of pine needle in the bag. If I'm in a cafe and I have a good, deep conversation, I might put in a little crumb from my whole wheat toast.

I'm circling around cowboy poetry, but I hope those of us who live with metaphors and seasons and lost relatives and other distant yet immediate things will understand. Cowboy poetry works like that little bag, like that matchbox, like a story that brings good people along, over your shoulder or in your heart as you walk through life. The way a horse carries a rider through the wilderness, a poem carries wisdom through time, from a distant place to where you live now.

When your boots are full of water and your hat brim's all a-drip,
And the rain makes little rivers dribblin' down your horse's hip,
When every step your pony takes, it purt near bogs him down,
It's then you git to thinkin' of them boys that work in town.
They're maybe sellin' ribbon, or they're maybe slingin' hash,
But they've got a roof above 'em when the thunder starts to crash.
They do their little doin's, be their wages low or high,
But let it rain till hell's a pond, they're always warm and dry.[1]

A poem like S. Omar Barker's "Rain on the Range" brings a fragrant and delicious piece of experience from out on the range into the room where you sit listening or reading. It carries that other place to you like a horse carrying a rider.

Now Mr. Boomer Johnson was a gettin' old in spots,
But you don't expect a bad man to go wrastlin' pans and pots;
But he'd done his share of killin' and his draw was gettin' slow,
So he quits a-punchin' cattle and he takes to punchin' dough.[2]

Henry Herbert Knibbs's poem works its magic by hauling someone from the grave to stand before us. With a poem you can rope a person or a place and bring it in close.

I thank You, Lord, that I am placed so well,
    That You have made my freedom so complete;
That I'm no slave of whistle, clock or bell,
    Nor weak-eyed prisoner of wall and street.
Just let me live my life as I've begun
    And give me work that's open to the sky;
Make me a pardner of the wind and sun,
    And I won't ask a life that's soft or high.[3]

Badger Clark's poem brings a moment of understanding close, the kind of moment that is rare in a lot of our lives. I know it's rare in mine. When you get one of those understanding moments, you want to hold onto it, to bring it along. And that's just what the poem is made to do.

We grow up with people telling us that doors are opening in front of us all the time. Every day, a new opportunity awaits. We grow and we learn. But I have found, getting partway through life, that you look over your shoulder and there are some doors closing behind you, too, and you want to have your baggage with you, in your heart and mind—your little bag, your box, your poem.

As a writer, when I think of making something fine I remember a remark by Carol Bly, author of *The Passionate, Accurate Story,* I heard up in Wyoming a few years ago. Partway through her talk, she started into a sentence I realized I wanted to own for the rest of my life. It's similar to what the cowboy poets say when they hear a good poem: "I want that poem." They don't mean they want a photocopy; they want to memorize it, to have it inside. And when Carol Bly started into this sentence, I had to focus deep and memorize. She said, "How can I take the neat dimple on the lid of a canning jar well-sealed, or the plain look of surprise on the face of a cow when it meets you on the highway and will not turn aside, or the way snow when it first falls in the mountains is so fragile you're afraid to touch it at all, and turn those things through my writing into something so clear and so passionate that teenage boys in America will not be so bored they have to go do a war somewhere to feel alive?"

I heard that sentence and I thought, yes, how *do* I take those simple passionate things close to me and turn them into language that lasts and changes people? How do I take Ray Lashley gnawing on his pipe as he gets ready to launch into a poem, or Sunny Hancock sighting past the forebrim of his hat as he gets into a recitation, or Gwen Petersen with a mean twinkle in her eye just before she slides into a limerick?

As a writer, I ask myself this all the time—how do I take the prickle on my nose at seven below, or the ache in an old love gone, and turn those things into something so passionate and clear they will help me survive and then survive me? How can I turn those things into a poem, a story, a love letter to us all that will make us value our lives daily, locally, always?

That's the question for those who make something fine in cowboy poetry, it seems to me, and in all poetry. I don't have an answer, but every time I write I feel the friction of trying.

I once heard Georgie Sicking being interviewed live on the radio, and I admired many things she said but especially one. She told the interviewer, "Well, a woman has a certain understanding with animals, and maybe a certain patience training a horse that a man might not have." I thought then that making a good cowboy poem may be the closest a man comes to the kind of patience a woman has naturally. I don't know. I'll never get to find out. But when I try to do language well, maybe I come close.

One of the special things about cowboy poetry, one thing that makes it fine, is that we speak it to each other aloud. We recite, we play the music of its language out loud. Others know a lot more about this than I, but this custom of sharing poetry aloud seems to go back to the tradition of families gathering in the evening to entertain themselves trading poems. Parlor recitation was a common habit in the last century. Radio and then TV killed it off for most Americans. Maybe the cowboys were just out there, too far away from anything to get good reception, so their stories and poems kept right on happening. However it came about, this poetry spoken aloud is our good luck.

But the tradition of poetry memorized and recited is a lot older than a century. Before the printing press, before writing, all poetry was composed orally and revised with each telling. There was a rule in a monastery of the fourteenth century that "monks shall not read while others are trying to sleep." This meant that reading often meant reading aloud, loud enough to keep others awake. Chaucer tells us about the Canterbury pilgrims telling stories and reciting poems to each other as they rode along together. He exaggerates but not much. Many people in those days, educated or not, did take turns reciting poems, tales, and songs to each other on a long ride or by a winter fire.

Many centuries earlier in *The Phaedrus,* Socrates had said, "When we learn to read we will forget how to remember." Books killed much of spoken literature long before the radio.

This is why I think the cowboy poetry of today has a special importance and a special connection with the oral literature of the Middle Ages. Many of these old poems are anonymous. We don't know who wrote them, but we do know they were part of a tradition of poetry recited aloud. This was true in Chaucer's time, and it was true of the troubadours in southern France beginning in the twelfth century. The word *troubadour* means "inventor" or "the one who finds." A poet back then might have been attached to a particular court for a time, inventing pleasing songs, creating and reciting poems in exchange for hospitality, then moving on. Others stayed at one court for years.

There is a poem called "The Wanderer" from very early in the English tradition that reminds me in some ways of cowboy poetry—and like many cowboy poems, it's quite stylized, with allusions to other poems, including written ones. A traveler, someone hard-bitten by years on the road, looks back at his life and wonders:

Where is the horse? Where is the man?
Where is the one who gave good things?
Where is the place we feasted, our joys together?
Alas the bright cup! Alas the rider armed!
Alas the glory we shared! How that time went,
Slid away into the night, as if it had never been.[4]

That sounds to me like one of those dark cowboy poems from a thousand years ago, especially if you can hear the actual words of the poem in the Old English of its making: "Hwaer cwom mearg, hwaer cwom mago, hwaer cwom maþþumgyfa?"

From several centuries later, here is a passage describing the gear on a horse, in this case Gringolet, the particular horse ridden by Sir Gawain of King Arthur's court. Gawain is riding out to his doom, but he is sitting tall in the saddle and his horse is wonderfully dressed:

Then Gringolet was ready, and fit with a saddle
That gleamed with joy by many gold fringes
All riveted new, neat-stamped for that work,
The bridle braided with strands of gold,
The breast harness fancy, the proud side flap,
The crupper and cloth matched to the saddle-bow,
And all set in red with rich gold nails
That glittered and glinted as the sun gleams.[5]

The poem that comes from, *Sir Gawain and the Green Knight,* was written in the fourteenth century by some anonymous poet out in the west of England. It only exists in one manuscript book, and there was a period of four hundred years when no one read it. That book sat in a library while poetic fashions changed, while the language itself changed so much the original is difficult to read: "Bi that watz Gryngolet grayth, and gurde with a sadel / That glemed ful gayly with mony golde frenges." The poetic traditions of the West Country in England in the fourteenth century—out in Derbyshire and Staffordshire along the Welsh border—have certain similarities to the custom of cowboy poetry today. The poetry of the West Country was looked down upon by the urbane readers of the East, meaning London, and the European continent. The West Country poets used an old-fashioned style with lots of alliteration. Their work was looked upon as provincial and archaic by Chaucer and the other London poets. This reminds me of the attitudes about cowboy poetry sometimes expressed by the culture guardians of our own East Coast. A writer in the *New York Times Book Review* a few years back branded cowboy poetry plain doggerel. Like most insults, that's an easy word to lay on a complex tradition.

The fact remains that out in the west of England, where poets recited traditional verse at the small but artistically active courts of the lesser barons, some of the best English poetry got written and saved. Chaucer's Parson could scoff that he does not "rum, ram, ruf by lettre" (that he does not follow the provincial alliterative style), just as readers outside the tradition of cowboy poetry often don't take it seriously, either. The fact remains that when a poetry tradition lives a long time and people keep doing what they like, some of the best poetry in the language can happen. It won't make the authors rich, but it's something fine getting made.

In my own work I sometimes get in the middle of writing a poem or story and find I'm not sure just where it's going. Maybe I thought I knew for a while, but then, like my life, the poem seems to take on a mind of its own. In making a poem I think I learn how to make a life—by taking the best things close at hand and going on.

I was talking with an old woman one time by the name of Belle. She was discouraged about things.

"You know," she said, "there isn't any future for a person my age. You can't half see, you can't hear, you can't share. Friends come to visit, and—well, the folks got me a hearing aid, and while the sound is loud enough, it isn't distinctive, you know. So I don't use it. I'm just practically what they call a vegetable."

"Belle," I said, "it's okay."

"What do you know, son?" she said. "What do you know?"

"Well, I guess I don't know much. Tell me a story so I will."

"Tell you a story?"

"Tell me a story about when you did get out. Did you ever go tramping around in the hills here?"

"Did I go hiking? Why, I had to look after my sheep, you know. They went clear over in that Cataract country and over the hill and down the gulch and all that land was timbered. It started in to snow. I turned to go home, I didn't know where I was. You know how the trees will bend down, and nothing was familiar.

"I had a little shepherd dog that always went with me. I said, 'Rex, go home!' He started off. I said to myself, 'You're not going right, but I'll follow you anyway. Maybe we'll come to a little stream or something and can follow that down.' But he *was* going right. He took me right home."[6]

When I heard that story from Belle, I thought, yes, I've had that feeling in the making of a poem or the living of a life. Sometimes I want to say, "You're not going right, but I'll follow anyway." You just keep doing what you know how to do, what you think you're put here to do, and hope to make it fine.

My last story for cowboy poetry is about Indians again, and growing up, and the little bag. I was up on the Duck Valley Reservation a few years ago, acting like a folklorist along with the real pros, Blanton Owen and Andrea Graham and Steve Siporin. We were looking at some cradleboards the Shoshone people and the Paiute people had made. One of the dangers of acting like a folklorist for me is I'm always right on the verge of making a terrible mistake. I just live in ignorance.

It turned out the woman we were visiting had just finished a cradleboard. It had taken her quite a while to make, and she had it sitting on the couch. I was just about to sit down when I turned around and saw it there. I had almost crushed it. I stood and gazed.

It had a tiny beaded bag hanging from the dream shade. They would prop their child in the cradleboard up against a juniper tree, and the dream shade would keep the sun out of the kid's eyes, and that little beaded bag would sparkle there.

"What's that?" I said, pointing to the little bag. I was impertinent, but I couldn't help it.

"That's where we put the umbilical cord after it falls off," she said. "It sort of stays connected to the cradleboard as the child grows. Then when the child grows a little more, you take that beaded bag and you go bury it somewhere. That's so the kid can never go too far from home. It sort of keeps them around."

So that's what I've been learning lately. I've been learning that cowboy poetry tethers me to the best things other people have known and said. I'll never stray too far as long as I can go back every so often and listen to one of these poems, or—if I'm desperate—go read it in a book.

Some of the old Indian people, when they finished with their stories and their dancing, would take off their masks and say to their audience, "You do not see us dancing today, you see your ancestors dancing today. And now you will wear their stories. You will wear their stories that never grow old."[7]

Notes

This essay is adapted from the keynote address at the 1989 Cowboy Poetry Gathering in Elko, Nevada.

1. From S. Omar Barker, "Rain on the Range," in *Cowboy Poetry: A Gathering,* ed. Hal Cannon (Salt Lake City: Gibbs Smith, 1985), 12.

2. From Henry Herbert Knibbs, "Boomer Johnson," in *Cowboy Poetry,* ed. Cannon, 47.

3. From Badger Clark, "A Cowboy's Prayer," in *Sun and Saddle Leather: A Collection of Poems by Badger Clark* (Tucson: Westerners International, 1983), 41.

4. My translation. The original of this passage can be found in *The Wanderer,* ed. T. P. Dunning and A. J. Bliss (London: Methuen, 1969), 121–22.

5. My translation. The original of these lines can be found in *Pearl and Sir Gawain and the Green Knight,* ed. A. C. Cawley (London: Dent, 1962), 73.

6. A fuller version of this story can be found in Kim Stafford, *Entering the Grove* (Salt Lake City: Gibbs Smith, 1990), 87–88.

7. See Kim Stafford, *Having Everything Right: Essays of Place* (1986), (Seattle: Sasquatch Books, 1997).

3

Why Cowboy Poetry? Some Thoughts toward an Answer

James S. Griffith

Cowboy poetry has been an important literary and performance genre within western cattle culture since the 1870s. More recently, partly as a result of intensive fieldwork on the part of a number of public-sector folklorists in the western states and the resulting Cowboy Poetry Gatherings in Elko, Nevada, the genre has come to the attention of the mainstream American media. The outside world is beginning to have available a pretty clear idea of what cowboy poetry is. We know its stylistic characteristics and main themes as well as who writes and recites it and under what circumstances. An intriguing question remains: Why does cowboy poetry exist in the first place? Why do hard-working ranch people, not necessarily overburdened with vast quantities of leisure time, bother to create, memorize, and recite verse about their lives and experiences?

In reaching for answers to these questions, I will be using a very old tool employed by cultural anthropologists and others interested in the workings of culture. This is the notion, suggested by Ralph Linton in *The Study of Man* (1935), that every item of human culture has four aspects: form, use, function, and meaning.[1] The form is what one can see and record (a specific poem, for instance). The use of the poem is what folks do with it: They write it, learn it from others, recite it, perhaps publish it. The poem's function is what it does in the context of its culture, while meaning includes the sum total of all the conscious and subconscious associations the poem carries with it.

The primary use of cowboy poetry seems to be as a pastime. People in the cattle industry memorize, recite, and compose poetry to please and entertain themselves and their peers. Poetry writing, at least in recent years, seems to be a solitary affair; I am not aware of any truly communally composed poems (in which several or many people contribute lines and verses) after the manner of "The Old Chisholm Trail."[2] Many of the poets I have interviewed have described making poetry as something they did while riding alone on horseback or in a pickup, keeping alert to their environment but needing to occupy their minds as well. Much cowboy work involves long travel to the job site, and the state of relaxed watchfulness needed for the "getting there" seems conducive to such exercises as poetry composition. Sometimes the poems thus composed will be jotted down later at home; it may then occasionally be the task of a spouse or some other relative to set them down in readable form. Talking with some cowboy poets, I get the impression that the process of putting poems together is often as important to them as the poems that result from this process. Both Van Holyoak and Vess Quinlan have told me that they composed poetry as a solitary pastime long before they succumbed to the urging of family members to put their work on paper.

Some poems are composed for specific occasions like weddings and funerals and are written down or typed up as memorials or mementos. Van Holyoak composed a poem for each of his children when they came of age; he also wrote and recited one for his father's funeral.[3] Ross Knox made a poem for a friend as a wedding present.[4] The late Gail Gardner, composer of at least four poems that entered oral recitation tradition back in the 1930s, used to produce a new poem annually for a friend's rodeo. In fact, he claimed in the introduction to his collection *Orejana Bull for Cowboys Only* that he published the book in self-defense because he was tired of writing his poems down for fellow cowboys.[5]

Performance, like composition, can be a solitary occupation. Van Holyoak used to sing and recite while he was riding or driving alone; others have described similar situations. As Slim Kite of Chino Valley, Arizona, told me, "It beats talking to yourself." Recitation can be a social activity as well, taking place while driving a vehicle, after dinner in a line camp or bunkhouse, or in a bar or motel room. In all these instances the object is to pass the time for oneself and one's fellows. For some reciters, solitary recitations may be a kind of rehearsal for later group sessions, but more often they are full-blown performances in their own right, done for the pleasure of the performer.

If the major use of cowboy poetry is to pass the time and amuse oneself and one's fellows (I am reminded of Gail Gardner's often-repeated claim that his poems were created for the sole purpose of amusing cowboys), what are its functions? In the first place, the employment of shared experiences, values, and language serves as a bond among members of this occupational subculture. This seems to be just as true in the case of solitary composition or recitation as it is for recitation in groups. Each time a cowboy sings or recites "Windy Bill," with the lines "and take your dallywelters to the California law / And your Sam Stack tree and new magee won't go driftin' down the draw," he automatically assumes a circle of listeners for whom this rather esoteric bit of advice is meaningful. The poem describes a cowboy who fails to catch a wild steer because his insistence on tying his rope "hard and fast" to the saddle horn—the Texas-Arizona technique—results in the snapping of his cinches and the loss of his saddle and rope. Instead, the poem advises using the California method of wrapping the rope several times around the saddle horn and letting it "run" against friction ("dallywelters," like dozens of other cowboy terms, is from the Spanish—in this case, *dale vuelta,* "give a turn").[6] A "Sam Stack tree" is a particular kind of carved wooden framework for a saddle; a "magee" is a rope made from the maguey, or century plant.

Here and in many other poems, the reciter identifies the common language and experience that separate this occupational group from everyone else. It doesn't matter if the reciter is alone or with other cowboys; this in-group/out-group division is implied anyway. (With these particular lines, he also revives the long-running dispute between the Texas "tie fast" men and the "dally-ropers" as to the proper way to rope an animal—a dispute grounded in differences in geography and ethnicity that can still provide an hour's diversion for all concerned.) Such words as "sull," "sunfishing," "gut line," "seago," and many others attest to the richness of the cowboy's occupational vocabulary as well as to its opacity for the uninitiated.

It is not only shared language that is celebrated through cowboy poetry. Cowboying is hard, dangerous work, and men and women can still get seriously injured or killed while pursuing it. Death is taken seriously, and when it occurs in poems it is treated seriously or sentimentally. "When the Work's All Done This Fall" and "Little Joe, the Wrangler" are two well-known examples.[7] Both of these are best known as cowboy songs, but it is my experience that a single text is often available as both poem and song, the choice depending on the tastes and abilities of the performer.

Anything short of death, however, is considered a subject for humor, and many popular cowboy poems both old and new demonstrate this. Potentially serious and life-threatening situations—being thrown off a horse or getting chased by a bear—are treated as humorous situations in well-known cowboy poems.[8] Why is this so? Probably because no matter how badly you are hurt in the process of doing your work, the only course open to you is to shrug or laugh it off, pick yourself up, and keep doing your job. This is a deeply held value within the cowboy subculture that is constantly reinforced by the poetry. In fact, in one poem, D. J. O'Malley's "D-2 Horse Wrangler," this value is made explicit when the tenderfoot narrator, after what must have been a spectacular wreck (bucking accident), asks for special treatment:

They picked me up and carried me in,
And rubbed me down with a rolling pin,
"Now that's the way they all begin,
You are doing well" says Brown.
"And tomorrow morning if you don't die,
I'll give you another horse to try."
"Oh won't you let me walk?" says I.
"Yes," says he, "Into town."[9]

Other values are celebrated in the poetry as well. Bravery and tenacity, for instance, are qualities in man and beast that are still needed for cow work; they are lauded in poem after poem.[10] Although comparatively few cowboy poems take landscape and scenery as their overt subject matter, nature in all its guises—friendly and otherwise—is always present as a setting, providing the conditions under which the work must be done. A passionate attachment to the land and the animals as well as to the work lies just below the surface of much cowboy poetry. Only occasionally, in poems like Baxter Black's "The High Lonesome" or Owen Barton's "Early Morning Roundup" does one get lyrical, even passionate descriptions of natural beauty for its own sake.[11] This is a cultural tradition that values understatement, especially in matters of great importance, and a lot gets implied rather than expressed forthrightly.

The traditional dime-novel stereotype of the laconic cowboy has, in my experience, a certain amount of truth, even though many cattle folk I know can be positively garrulous and take great joy in playing with words. Words, after all, are one resource always on hand in an environment that otherwise demands thriftiness by necessity. When I inquired once after Van Holyoak's health, he replied, "I've never felt better—and, by God, it's about time I did." Everett Brisendine, in response to a similar question, said, "Well, Jim, I've got the forked end down, and I can't ask for much more." This is not the talk of word-shy men by any means. The economy with words comes into play when serious or emotional subjects are raised, and that is where poetry becomes a useful tool for many. As Vess Quinlan told me, "It lets you say things that are too important to say right out."

Thus one function of cowboy poetry is to forge and strengthen the bonds of common language, experience, and values among individuals who share an occupational tradition. The poems as they are recited or sung remind performer and listener of their shared cultural identity while reaffirming the values that keep many ranch people going despite hard times and harder work. Cowboy poetry, in short, provides some of the "glue" that keeps this particular subcultural system stuck together.

On a different level, it may well be that cowboy poetry's traditionally rhymed, metered verse echoes other important cultural themes. Open-range stock raising is and always has been a gamble at best. The cowboy or rancher is at the mercy of the climate, disease, market conditions, and many other factors. To survive in the business takes consummate skill and craftsmanship. One has to be able to "read sign" in a dozen natural communication systems and must be willing and able to take on and accomplish any kind of work on the spur of the moment. Halfway measures and sloppy work are almost invariably rewarded with disaster. The job, whatever it is, must be well and carefully done if one is to survive in the cattle industry.

This preoccupation with craftsmanship, with mastery of techniques and with tight control over material, carries over into traditional cowboy leisure-time activities like rodeo and team roping and to traditional cowboy crafts like rope twisting, rawhide braiding, and leatherworking. Cowboys think it appropriate that utilitarian objects be given richly textured surfaces and that this surface texturing itself be a visible sign of the artistry and control of the maker. This repeated emphasis on the importance of controlled craftsmanship does not explain why rhymed, metered verse, an extremely popular narrative and expressive medium in the late nineteenth century, was adopted by members of cow culture in the first place. But it might explain why this highly crafted, richly textured art form has remained so popular within that culture long after it has been set aside by mainstream American society. The strong survival value of cowboy poetry may be the result of its ability to satisfy a central aesthetic need.

There is an attitude in ranch culture that often finds expression in phrases like "he'll make a hand" or "I'll try to make a hand." To make a hand, as I understand it, is first to be willing to work hard and, more important, to develop the ability to rise to any challenge or solve any problem with a workable solution of one's own. It involves the sort of self-sufficiency so necessary to survival in a sparsely occupied region where the choice was often limited to "do it yourself or do without." This emphasis on competence, basic to ranch culture, may explain why so many cattle people have tried writing poetry. I know two people with long experience in cowboy culture who wanted to include poems in books they had just written. Neither one had much experience as a poet, yet each rose to the occasion and composed appropriate verses. In other words, each author responded to the need in a manner that reflected the traditional values of ranch culture. Each "made a hand."

With comments and speculations such as these we are entering the realm of "meaning," or the sum total of all the associations—some of them subjective or even unconscious—connected with the composition, recitation, and enjoyment of cowboy poetry. The power of these associations is immediately evident to anyone who has witnessed a performance of cowboy poetry among ranch people. The strongest verbalized response is usually to the content of the poem, with the listeners often being reminded of similar incidents or situations they have experienced or heard of. In fact, cowboy poetry often acts as a trigger that provokes conversation, reminiscence, and sharing of experience.

Montanan Wallace McRae remarked after attending the first Cowboy Poetry Gathering in Elko that he had discovered that a whole bunch of people all over the West had written the same poem he had about a favorite horse. He was not talking about plagiarism or copyright infringement but rather about a set of values and associations he shared with other members of his occupational tradition and that they expressed in traditional ways. In other words, cowboy poetry creates meaning within the values and experience of an allied group.

One more point should be made. Despite its deep tradition of recitation, performance, and composition, contemporary developments in cowboy poetry and fundamental changes in ranch life and work now are taking place, and cowboy poetry itself is in the process of changing. That is nothing new, of course. Careful analysis of cowboy poems from different periods of cattle-industry history demonstrate changes in theme, in language, and in verse form. For instance, the spate of "tall-tale" poems like those composed in the 1920s by Gail Gardner may very well coincide with the rise in popularity of dude ranching and the need for "authentic cowboy entertainment" for paying guests. And now change may well be accelerating.

A few cowboy poets are becoming full- or part-time professional reciters. Poets like Baxter Black and Waddie Mitchell have become performers, not only within the region and culture of the cattle industry but also in relation to the outside world as well. This has long happened, of course, in dude ranch and rodeo contexts, but at least there the cattle world was more or less in control of the environment in which the recitation took place. Earlier in this century, when cowboy verbal skills were presented in the mass media—on radio or records or in Hollywood films—they were often interpreted by professional actors and singers who had little connection with the cowboy world. The major exception is the 1920s recordings of cowboy songs by Carl T. Sprague and Jules Verne Allen, who knew range life firsthand. But their records had a much narrower audience than those, for instance, of Gene Autry, Roy Rogers, and the Sons of the Pioneers. The interactions in which traditional cowboy singers, poets, and reciters present their own cultural traditions to outsiders on alien turf, however, are bound to have effects on the artists who participate, just as dude ranches, Wild West shows, national parks, and other sites affected cowboy poetry and song in the 1920s.

At the first Cowboy Poetry Gathering, an often-heard comment was, "I didn't know anyone else was writing this stuff." That comment is heard less and less with each passing year. In addition to changes having to do with poets' and reciters' perceptions of their roles within their culture and within the dominant society, a series of drastic changes is taking place in ranch and range life. Various powerful interests are converging on western lands that have been traditionally used for cattle grazing. Some conservationists wish to end much or all grazing on federal lands. Popular authors such as Edward Abbey have attacked the cattle industry in harsh terms. Urban and suburban people in increasing numbers are encroaching on rangeland for recreational purposes and for second-home development. All of these are affecting the way members of cattle culture perceive themselves and their relationship to the rest of society, and those changes are, in turn, affecting cowboy poetry.

Cowboy life and poetry today are vastly different from what they were in the days before the turn of the century when D. J. O'Malley, Jack Thorp, and others were composing, reciting, singing, and swapping what have since become classics in the genre. Only the passing of time will reveal what effect current changes will have on the culture and on the literary art form to which it gave birth and which it has supported for more than a century.

Notes

An earlier version of this essay was presented at the annual meeting of the American Folklore Society in Baltimore, Maryland, in October 1986. I am grateful to many colleagues, especially Suzi Jones and Dave Stanley, for their helpful comments and suggestions.

1. Ralph Linton, *The Study of Man: An Introduction* (1935), (New York: Appleton-Century-Crofts, 1964).

2. The communal authorship of "The Old Chisholm Trail" is described by John A. Lomax and Alan Lomax in *Folk Song U.S.A.: The 111 Best American Ballads* (New York: Duell, Sloan and Pearce, 1947), 193–94.

3. Van Holyoak, *The Cowboy and Horses* (privately mimeographed booklet, 1976). The poem for his father's funeral, "Prayer for a Cowboy," was also printed on the program card for Van's own funeral.

4. Ross Knox, "Gettin' Put in Double Harness," in *Easy Chairs and Saddle Sores: Cowboy Poetry and Songs by Waddie Mitchell, Ross Knox, and Earl Rogers* (Prescott: Sharlot Hall Museum, 1986), side B, band 10.

5. Gail I. Gardner, *Orejana Bull for Cowboys Only* (1935), 7th ed. (Prescott: Sharlot Hall Museum Press, 1987), xiii.

6. "Windy Bill," in Glenn Ohrlin, *The Hell-Bound Train: A Cowboy Songbook* (Urbana: University of Illinois Press, 1973), 12–14.

7. "When the Work's All Done This Fall," in D. J. O'Malley and John I. White, *D. J.*

O'Malley, Cowboy Poet (Helena: Montana Folklife Project, 1986), 8; "Little Joe, the Wrangler," in N. Howard ("Jack") Thorp and Austin E. Fife and Alta S. Fife, *Songs of the Cowboys* (1908), (New York: Clarkson N. Potter, 1966), 28.

8. The following poems, published in *Cowboy Poetry: A Gathering,* ed. Hal Cannon (Salt Lake City: Gibbs Smith, 1985), illustrate this theme: "The Gol-Darn Wheel" (10), "Bear-Ropin' Buckaroo" by S. Omar Barker (14), and "Silver Jack" (21). See also "Jake and Roany" in Ohrlin, *Hell-Bound Train,* 113.

9. "D-2 Horse Wrangler," in O'Malley and White, *D. J. O'Malley, Cowboy Poet,* 11.

10. A good modern example of this is Bob Schild's "Two of a Kind," in *Cowboy Poetry,* ed. Cannon, 101. Note also the admiration expressed for the horse in "The Strawberry Roan" in Curley Fletcher, *Songs of the Sage: The Poetry of Curley Fletcher,* ed. Hal Cannon (Salt Lake City: Gibbs Smith, 1986), 11, and for the rider in "The Zebra Dun" in *Cowboy Poetry,* ed. Cannon, 8.

11. Baxter Black, "The High Lonesome" and Owen Barton, "Early Morning Roundup," both in *Cowboy Poetry,* ed. Cannon, 109, 176.

4

"The Rain Is the Sweat of the Sky": Cowboy Poetry as American Ethnopoetics

Scott Preston

Poetry must sing or speak from authentic experience.
—Gary Snyder, "Poetry and the Primitive: Notes on Poetry as an Ecological Survival Technique"

The American poet and anthropologist Jerome Rothenberg first proposed the term *ethnopoetics* in the late 1960s as a catch-all phrase for a wide variety of world poetry traditions then being investigated by poets (primarily in America, although there were important European contacts in the movement) in search of inspired alternatives to traditional, academically based Eurocentric poetry. Rothenberg's contributions to ethnopoetics have been most effective when demonstrating the actual energy potential of divergent traditions (as in his still remarkable anthologies) or in such aphoristic dares as "study the *Popol Vuh* where you now study Homer and study Homer where you now study the *Popol Vuh,*" essentially a jibe aimed at reversing the perceptual assumptions of writers who rely wholly on imported traditions in the New World.[1]

As a would-be academic discipline, however, far too much time has been expended in trying to satisfactorily define ethnopoetry. Rather than do so here, I will consider cowboy poetry as a form of exotic anthropology in an attempt to open it up for a wider consideration of its values and practices in common with other world traditions.

Since I first began composing this essay, about 1987, the Cowboy Poetry Gathering at Elko has operated, at least in part, as a virtual host of comparative ethnopoetics of pastoral people. Native Hawaiian, Australian, British, Welsh, Scottish, Irish, Peruvian, Mexican, and Native American ranch people have offered their oral literatures on the Elko stage, and plans continue to eventually include Asian cowboys as well. Ethnopoetry refers to poetry characteristic of any group, particularly poetry lying outside the academic realm that has usually defined poetry for Europeans and North Americans. Fiji Islanders, Mississippi Delta bluesmen, Inuit, you name it—all have poetry of some sort, and ethnopoetists study that poetry for its beauty and for the possibility that it may help revitalize their poetic traditions.

In other words, ethnopoetry centers most frequently on folk traditions with which the entire working knowledge of a culture—historical, ethical, practical, spiritual, or comic—can be taught to the community through poems, songs, and chants that have a strong, probably undifferentiated link to dance, ritual, and ceremony. It might be called the "theater of the people" in the value it places on the transmission of cultural knowledge and heritage through entertainment. After all, the ritual of storytelling by firelight has as its first purpose entertainment, but the drawing together of the community created by such entertainment also brings with it the chance to educate the young and pass on the inner light of the culture in a perpetual drama of voice-activated memory and recognition.

Despite the frequent confusions and conflicting definitions of ethnopoetics, which generally seem the contradictory result of attempting to write about cultures that are themselves free of writing, three primary components of ethnopoetic inquiry will serve as a framework for the comparisons to follow:

1. *Poetry as an oral tradition.* This refers to the transmission of cultural traditions by oral, personal means as opposed to the use of books as primary teaching tools. Most of the so-called primitive societies that ethnopoetists have studied have relied on the oral tradition exclusively for centuries, having no written language. In this tradition, poetry serves as instruction for the young, as community ritual, as work accompaniment, and as private entertainment.

2. *Poetry as public performance.* Although most poets in America, even in academia, make a large part of any money they earn from public readings, they bitterly deny that public readings are a form of theater. The majority of poets in the world of intercultural literature do not share this hang-up. An inevitable side effect of the oral tradition, poetry as theater—an event freed from the page, the book, the publisher, and all rigid standards of decorum and niceness—is a nearly universal phenomenon in preliterate societies.

3. *Poetry as ideogrammic symbol.* Hieroglyphs, pictographs, and petroglyphs all possess elements of poetry in attempting to realize a representational beauty outside the conventions of phonetic language.

A technical note concerning "doggerel," that vicious term implying sing-song rhythms and unimaginative rhymes: Yes, much cowboy poetry—traditional and contemporary—is predictable in stanza form, meter, and rhyme. In that way it has parallels with world poetics as a kind of private music. Quite often a poem, as defined by ethnopoetic standards, may consist of only one central line or idea that is then bent, altered, revocalized, or reemphasized for as long as the poet wishes. Doggerel works in much the same fashion. To an inexperienced ear, repetitive language and its accompanying sound may seem a lulling, sleep-inducing ordeal (if singing cattle to sleep on the great trail drives could be allowed as an early practical application of cowboy poetry principles, one could consider the somnaic rhythms of today as an archaic carryover from a more deliberate age). And yet the sounds and rhythms of doggerel have an astonishing ability to blend as a whole, as a unified sound-object. To those within the culture used to such poetry, who enjoy a shared emotional expectancy for the poem, a sophisticated entertainment is created in which the reciter's subtle variations and commentaries, presented within a traditional framework, are the center of interest.

The Cowboy Poem as Song

It's in the field of song that the contemporary cowboy poet's literary practice most directly connects as ethnopoetry, both in terms of actual performance and in its implied critique of academic definitions in mainstream culture that separate "song" and "poem" as two distinct categories. Many of the most popular classic cowboy songs began as poems, but the impulse to re-create them as music was seemingly irresistible. In fact, cowboy poetry, song, and music have rarely been distinct categories; they are often combined and transformed. Poems can become songs and then poems again.

In a conversation in 1987, Alan Lomax pointed out to me that song performance on the great cattle drives probably did not feature continuous musical accompaniment and that the a cappella verses of the song were punctuated by fiddle or banjo breaks (these being far more portable instruments than guitars). The practice sounds intensely similar to that of West African village *griots* who bridge their epic narratives with interludes of music played on the *kora* (thumb piano), itself a precursor of the banjo. The technique encourages audience attention and reflection during long recitations. Lomax went on to say that the introduction of the guitar, with a heavier, flatter resonance in its chording, resulted in a diminished vocal nuance in the cowboy song. He felt that the link between poetic recitation and popular song was simple, plain, unaccompanied singing as it had been practiced on the trail drives and as it had originated back at the beginnings of nomadic herdsmanship in the Middle East and North Africa.[2]

Even modern cowboy performers disposed toward a more traditional presentation of their work have used musical accompaniment as a natural collaborator in moving it along. Ross Knox has been the most distinguished of classic reciters in this regard. His recitation of Bruce Kiskaddon's "The Old Night Hawk" may have been the first guitar-backed recitation of the cowboy-poetry revival, and it marks something of a before-and-after phase in recorded tapes of cowboy poetry.[3] Knox's later contributions to this genre have been more understated, a co-writing credit with Ian Tyson for "I Outgrew the Wagon" notwithstanding. In contrast, Wallace McRae's poem "Put That Back . . . Hoedown" is almost a sound-generated text rising out of square-dance rhythms and performed accordingly.[4] Meanwhile, Waddie Mitchell, perhaps the best known of traditional reciters, has toured and recorded with a band of musicians.

The Cowboy Poem as Theater

The archaic roots of poetry lie in theater, the physical ritualization of language in public performance. Just as modern specialization in the arts insists on a separation between song and poem, so has there developed an unimaginable distance between "poetry" and "theater." But certainly the basic practice of reciting poetry from memory has been a revelation in terms of opening the possibilities for performance of literature on the stage. Despite occasional attempts by avant-garde writers, performers, and musicians since the mid-1950s, poetry reading has become ever more stifled and predictable, increasingly aimed at a tiny audience of intellectuals and cognoscenti.

The desire to incorporate the body into performance, to go beyond merely standing up and reading aloud, has given rise to a number of expansive attempts at extending the range of performance. Wallace McRae's accompanying soft-shoe on "Put That Back . . . Hoedown," Jon Bowerman's kneeling demonstration—using a folding chair—of a calf-pulling fiasco, and even the controlled and precise gestures of Baxter Black are examples. So is the use of props like Leon Flick's well-known bull slippers, Drummond Hadley's blanks-loaded revolver, or the scores of hats, boots, and ropes used as visual focal points for poetry. All break down barriers between reciter and audience.

The outstanding example of physicality in cowboy poetry is, of course, the legendary performances of the often-bruised Nyle Henderson, whose hair-raising jaunts across the stage on a bucking chair seemed nearly as life-threatening as the bull and bronc rides he described. Compare his performance to that of the Kirgiz-Tatar poet described by J. Castagné as running around the tent, springing, roaring, and leaping: "[He] barks like a dog, sniffs at the audience, lows like an ox, bellows, cries, bleats like a lamb, grunts like a pig, whinnies, coos, imitating with remarkable accuracy the cries of animals, the songs of birds, the sound of their flight, and so on, all of which greatly impresses his audience."[5] Henderson didn't imitate an entire menagerie, of course, but his ability was such that it created a profound recognition in his audience of certain events, certain relationships with animals, that all present could feel in their bones—and not without a wince.

The Cowboy Poem as Cultural Transmitter

Beyond the obvious entertainment values inherent in cowboy poetry, an essential underlying function is that of a transmission vehicle for cultural values and instruction. As in preliterate societies, the role of the poet is doubled into that of religious leader, teacher, and historian.

That is especially true as the spiritual function of the cowboy poet continues to manifest itself. Repertoires of virtually all poets in the modern cowboy tradition contain at least one poem praising the Creator. It is often self-composed but also includes recognized classics like "A Cowboy's Prayer" by Charles Badger Clark and "The Cowboy's Prayer" by Curley Fletcher. Indeed, on some levels differentiating between secular and religious poetry may be beside the point because the secular and the spiritual aspects of the culture are often acknowledged in the poems to be inseparable. Clark's poem begins:

Oh Lord, I've never lived where churches grow.
  I love creation better as it stood
That day You finished it so long ago
  And looked upon Your work and called it good.[6]

It is as a transmitter of practical knowledge that cowboy poetry most clearly serves its audience as an educational tool. The errors and foibles of the protagonists in even the most humorous poems are firmly based on an instructional ethic. From the disgrace of "Windy Bill," who loses his rope and saddle in attempting to capture an especially wild steer, to Rod McQueary's "Chicken Outfit," a hilarious self-parody of a rancher who can't quit treating chickens like cattle, poetry provides both practical guidance and a commentary on self-knowledge for an audience constantly faced with a rapidly changing and perilous occupation.[7]

Another function of cowboy poetry might also be noted: It allows for humor to be directed at areas of frequent dissatisfaction, resulting in a sort of pressure-release valve that simultaneously identifies and diffuses tensions. Rod Nelson's poems describing the tribulations he has gone through in having his wife help jump-start the combine or replace the bulb in the yard light can be seen as both a primer in what not to do in such circumstances and an opportunity to reveal the difficulties of adapting traditional gender-based roles to new ranching circumstances. Gwen Petersen sees many of the same issues from a woman's very different perspective.

Linguistic Parallels between Cowboy Poetry and Ethnopoetries

Although narrative as a binding coherence in all cultures is probably the central factor relating cowboy poetry and other ethnopoetries, there are a number of linguistic parallels as well. In the introduction to his anthology of ethnopoetry, *Technicians of the Sacred,* Jerome Rothenberg describes the problem of isolating language in primitive poetry, in which meaning may be centered in one line alone yet the line be repeated with phonetic or emphatic alteration or with other syllables or sounds inserted. A poem that translates merely as "a splinter of stone which is white" (in one example) may achieve a profound metamorphosis of meaning through extended repetition in company with other lines similarly modified and enhanced.[8]

Cowboy poetry does not do that directly. And yet, beyond the superficial similarities of chant fragments like "Whoopee Ti Yi Yo" being incorporated into formal verse structures, and the less obvious similarity of words phonetically altered from Spanish sources (which in their loving preservation reflect the historical and cultural transmission described previously), several areas bear closer inspection for linguistic interrelatedness.

The most striking, especially on the written page, is the distortion of formal English—and again, I mean that favorably—in order to achieve specific sonic ends. The diversity of vernacular respellings and reworkings of even common words to reflect more accurately their truest sound is one of the finest gifts cowboy poetry has made to American literature by reordering contemporary language and providing variation within the structures of the form. These respellings frequently take on the flavor not just of regional, rural, western dialect but present, in the most deliberative way, a continuously re-realized interaction with language on an individual basis, unrestricted by academic formalizations of vernacular speech patterns.

While the rhyming of "barn" and "iron" manages to make a subtle joke at the expense of grammarians and create an end-line sound that sonically propels the poem forward, other sound spaces exist without hard meaning—another linguistic parallel to ethnopoetry. As some poets have observed, the lean, hard lines of classic cowboy poems owe as much to their constant usage as to any compositional economy at their birth. Like a steer run hard on a cattle drive, the fat, superfluous lines of any poem are likely to disappear in continual retelling. Yet the use of "filler" verses and time-worn rhyme schemes can be seen as fulfilling a perhaps subconscious need for a fuller rhythmic, even musical, accompaniment not fully served by word choices favoring meaning. Take, for instance, the use of the phrases "and such" and "that much" to fill out the action of verses in poems and songs throughout the tradition. The best-known example is Wallace McRae's "Reincarnation," where that final rhyme is the punch-line of the best-known contemporary cowboy poem:

I thinks of reincarnation,
Of life, and death, and such.
I come away concludin': "Slim,
You ain't changed, all that much."[9]

McRae is renowned for his skill and care in creating poems (he is also, not coincidentally, an outstanding creator of original vernacular forms). I've come to realize that his use of that rhyme was less an accident than a subtle comment on the use of such clichés—or, rather, sound-devices—throughout the tradition, a comment underlined by the subtlety of the near-rhyme of "reincarnation" and "Slim" as well as by variations in rhythm and diction.

As another example, written cowboy poetry uses many, although not all, of the symbol devices of the modern keyboard but individualizes itself primarily through punctuation symbols. These are used with vast effect. McRae, for example, had a difficult fight with an editor over the proper way to punctuate the letter *n* when used as a colloquial *and.* The editor insisted it needed two apostrophes: *'n'.* McRae, however, wanted no hash marks at all cluttering up his work, n they finally compromised on *'n,* which is worse than either. One of the most curious phenommena in cowboy poetry has been a reduction of punctuation since the mid-1980s, perhaps because of confidence that the intrinsic beauty of rural speech does not need to be qualified by signs that the writer really knows formal English and is just kidding around in these here funny little poems. Alternatively, poets may be reacting to the increased amount of publishing by further emphasizing the oral nature of their work.

Numerous other combinations come to mind, most immediately what Paul Zarzyski has called the "Mr. Ed syndrome" in which "horse" always rhymes with "of course." It's open to debate just how unconscious this language selection process is. The surface repetitions of even the most banally composed cowboy poems serve a rhythmic function that may extend beyond meaning to create a music of spoken or intoned words where the sound of the performance is possibly more crucial than the actual meaning it evokes. Consider the massive bridging of cultures represented by the work of Henry Real Bird, whose Native American song rhythms create a fascinating and difficult tension within the English words and standard rhymes he uses as seed syllables.

Another important impact on written cowboy poetry comes from the iconography of brands and other symbolically rendered devices, which cut a deep influence through the entire culture. Although brands have an accepted "reading" or pronunciation, the sign—the picture—of the actual brand is a kind of pictograph that would read like a version of a Chinese ideogram.[10] One example is Henry Ellard's use of brand imagery throughout *Tales of the Rockies,* privately printed in Cañon City, Colorado, in 1899. Ellard used the phonetic rendition of various ranch brands within his verse text but added, in every instance, the pictographic brand in the right-hand margin. Considering how often brands are incorporated into signatures, autographs, and stationery, it seems as if a form of ideogrammic nonverbal communication has long been taking place in the private exchanges within cowboy culture. Perhaps the idiosyncrasies of punctuation reflect a similar private exchange between poet and reader, an exchange that recognizes the vast differences between oral and written transmission.

In summary, then, my preference for "raw balladry" is based on this: Although cowboy poetry quite rightly can be traced to the ballads of Britain and other European oral sources, it has resonances and flavors that probe the deepest roots of human life no matter the sheen of contemporary political or social or economic details that inform the whole. A willingness to incorporate the emergent issues of the day into a culture's literature is a phenomenon that has often been practiced more readily around the world than in the self-consciously limited United States, where the inner life of the individual has long been promoted as the only correct focus for the literary author, a stance that often eliminates laughter, the music that accompanies a plain, honest, physical engagement with the world.

Cowboy Poetry as American Literature

These differences between academic and ethnopoetic traditions point to a primary conflict in American literature, an intrinsic uneasiness pulsing in the heart that frequently renders U.S. literary tradition a contradiction in terms, a hybrid of such impossibly self-cancelling attributes that it could only exist in the mythic bestiary of a critic. The conflict might be broadly located as inhabiting the gulf between a literature based wholly on experiences and perceptions formed by life on the North American continent and that which seeks to extend the biases of tradition, generally that of Europe, specifically Great Britain.

The conflict has apparently accompanied English-language poetry from the very beginning. Geoffrey Chaucer was responsible for a dual innovation in his poetics. He wrote primarily about the common people (as opposed to chivalric or legendary heroes), and he did so in English even though French had been the preferred language of the British aristocracy since the Norman invasion and was thereby enshrined as the language of high art. Chaucer opened the gates of an English-language renaissance that has never been eclipsed. The pull of Romance language–based courtly pretense, however, remained a most powerful current.

A few hundred years later, John Milton strenuously applied the rules of Latin grammar to his verse, a technique that virtually destroyed English poetic syntax and persisted as a habit in the fledgling poetry of anyone, child or grandparent, who attempted to elevate conceits by reversing noun and adjective to score a rhyme and a "poetic" sound.

Nearly half a millennium separates Walt Whitman from Chaucer, but even the pioneering free verse of America's first great poet frequently resorts to self-consciously poetic flourishes, syntactical mutations, and cheap dramatic heightenings that impede the raw outpouring of pure American energy he sought to capture and create. Whitman is a genuine watershed, his celebration of the working people no less a revolution in content than the form he developed.

The radical breakthrough in the creation of an American English for an American poetry came early in the twentieth century with William Carlos Williams. After a long, frustrating apprenticeship when he imitated John Keats, Williams embarked on a wrenching reappraisal of line, image, and subject matter that often seems simplistic yet is fresh and uncontrived. It's a peculiar combination that has made him the most widely imitated American poet of the twentieth century yet also the most extraordinarily misread and misunderstood.

The desire to imitate European standards as a means of acquiring legitimacy as a writer in the New World (and the subsequent conflict with environmental and cultural reality) has created a curious state of tension that hasn't gone unnoticed. Philip Rahv's famous distinction between "paleface" and "redskin" tendencies in American writing was echoed by Robert Lowell in his even more famous categories of "cooked" versus "raw" poetry.[11] Lowell preferred the parboiled variety to the extent that he was at least as claimed by England as by his native country. That conflict still continues, a stunning blur between the poles of raw authenticity and refined contrivance, between outspoken spontaneity and carefully rewritten craft. It's a conflict that exists even in the world of cowboy poetry. It is so central to the concerns of the genre that it provides most of the critical fascination and debate the movement has to offer.

As a popular literary genre, cowboy poetry has always been subjected to outsiders' definitions of authenticity. The pure oral narrative balladry admired by folklorists may have briefly existed at an early stage in western Euro-American culture, carried over from older, European traditions, but it was affected from the outset by the impact of formal education, widespread literacy, and other influences. In any case, the most rigid definitions of cowboy poetry contain a paradox at their roots. Supposedly a naturally occurring, natively pure expression emanating from a specific occupational group whose primary education is that of the job itself, it nevertheless insists on a highly formal compositional structure. It attempts to produce a totally authentic voice yet is presented via a totally artificial linguistic construct. It is the ultimate meeting ground of raw and cooked impulses in American poetics.

One critical perception debated around the fringes of cowboy poetry gatherings concerns whether the best poets were necessarily the best cowboys. Charles Badger Clark, Henry Herbert Knibbs, and Carlos Ashley were essentially outsiders to the culture that nevertheless adopted them as artistic spokesmen. Elements of literary self-consciousness and genteel attitudes frequently inform their work, from unmistakable flourishes of "heightened" language to the underpinnings of entire poems like Clark's "The Legend of Boastful Bill," a remarkably successful attempt at fusing the grit of a day's work with the emergence of a mythological hero.[12]

With a writer like Bruce Kiskaddon, the idea is much more problematic, even though most of his writing was produced after he stopped range work. His authenticity can be measured both by content (Kiskaddon wrote some of the most defiantly demystifying, unromantic poems of the cowboy experience) and by form. Kiskaddon's voice is paced to the rhythms of everyday workers' speech as closely as any rhymed poetry in the English language. His syntax rarely gets displaced to accommodate a rhyme scheme, and the deep, grass-roots survival of his poems is testimony to his success in avoiding artifice. Few contemporary poets have managed to match him. Compare, for instance, Kiskaddon's "The Cowboys' Christmas Dance" with S. Omar Barker's "Bunkhouse Christmas."[13] The terrain is almost exactly the same, yet where Barker uses his space to toss off a few platitudes about the true meaning of the holiday before cutting to a joke about cowboy diet, Kiskaddon offers a deep reflection on the way such occasions maintain social civility on the range. The polarity between Kiskaddon and a slightly later writer like Barker is significant. Whereas Kiskaddon's nostalgia is melancholy in the extreme and rarely glorifies previous hardships, Barker turns the West into a romantic joke marketable to a far vaster audience than Kiskaddon ever reached.

The issue of proper form in cowboy poetry—particularly concerning whether unrhymed poetry of irregular meter can even qualify—has long been a subject of intensive debate. Viewed as an ongoing, albeit unrecognized, product of basic compositional conflicts in American poetry as a whole, the argument over the appropriateness of "free verse" in cowboy poetry seems completely predictable even if it is nearly a century behind similar arguments in mainstream American poetry between Longfellow and Whitman or Benét and Williams. The dispute first developed over whether free verse could actually ever be free, given the syllabic basis of the iambic foot. It's an amusing sidelight to note that even this debate in English poetics often echoed the French *vers libre* rebellion of the late nineteenth century.

More important, the intuitive adopting of free verse in the American vernacular—that is, a poetry attempting to re-create the rhythms of native speech patterns—has been used by cowboy poets from the beginning. Their incorporation of storytelling and other anecdotal devices to frame the presentation of their poems may be as important to the poetic event as the poem itself. Many stories told orally by cowboy poets, if committed to the page with line breaks determined by natural pauses and points of particular emphasis, would make superb American free-verse poetry.

Vess Quinlan has emerged as one of the leading exponents of open-form poetics in cowboy poetry, using a short, tightly constructed line to present his stories. Nevertheless, his sense of underspoken, almost elliptical, styled narrative is in a direct line that runs back to Williams and the other writers of the objectivist movement. Especially distinctive is Quinlan's use of simple objects to unadornedly create imagery and his reliance on everyday speech patterns and vernacular language to mask the close crafting of the finished poems.

Quinlan's influence and example have led a number of other writers associated with cowboy poetry to attempt their own versions of free-verse poems. The most striking result has been the emergence of new subjects and forms such as poems about the Vietnam War written by veterans like Bill Jones and Rod McQueary who are also cowboys. These writers have since made some contact with nationally recognized figures in the Namvet poetry movement.

It is ironic that open forms often engender hostility and resentment within the cowboy poetry establishment. Often raw, unadorned, and very different from the unrhymed poetry usually written in American universities, it still finds itself lumped in and condemned with the "other" poetry written outside the folk-ballad tradition. The debate has centered not only on the importance of maintaining traditional forms but also on the necessity for keeping what is most distinctive about cowboy poetry.

John Dofflemyer's response to the ballad-form purists places the debate squarely in the American tradition. In an essay published in *Boots* magazine, he expresses fear that the stipulation to play to nostalgia would reduce cowboy poets and storytellers to popular clowns, to be paraded onstage for wages while changing economic conditions destroyed the work and the life that made the poetry possible in the first place. To Dofflemyer, cowboy poetry potentially offers a means of comprehending the changing West, a potential that far outweighs its attraction as an embodiment of history or a symbolic rendition of American values. It may, in fact, become a significant tool in the American cowboy's struggle to survive. To do so, says Dofflemyer, the poetry must adapt formally and linguistically; it must find new forms of expression to accommodate its intellectual growth and visibility.[14]

But cowboy poetry can do more than just serve itself and its practitioners.

Rodeo poet Paul Zarzyski has defended cowboy poetry as the intuitive embodiment of several virtues central to the redevelopment of an audience for poetry in the United States. Zarzyski praises the cowboy poetry movement for its knowledge and promotion of writers from its past, for its willingness to experiment with other art forms (music and dance) in its live presentations, and for the phenomenal sense of community it fosters.[15] To that I would add that cowboy poetry demands a reexamination of assumptions about the development of American literature and its role in the life of the country. Like it or not, from any side or angle of the debate it is an example that will continue to express and define itself, probably well into the twenty-first century.

Notes

1. Jerome Rothenberg, "An Academic Proposal," in *Pre-Faces and Other Writings* (New York: New Directions, 1981), 175.

2. See also Alan Lomax's introduction to the Collier Books edition of John A. Lomax and Alan Lomax, *Cowboy Songs and Other Frontier Ballads* (1910), (New York: Macmillan, 1986), xi–xxxv.

3. A music-plus-recitation version of Badger Clark's "A Bad Half Hour" and the folk song "Annie Laurie" by Ross and Patty Knox is included on the anthology *The Cowboy Poetry Gathering* (Rhino Word Beat CD R2 71573, cassette R4 71616, 1994).

4. Wallace McRae, "Put That Back . . . Hoedown," in McRae, *Cowboy Curmudgeon* (Salt Lake City: Gibbs Smith, 1992), 86–88.

5. Quoted in Mircea Eliade, *Shamanism: Archaic Techniques of Ecstasy* (1951), trans. Willard R. Trask, Bollingen Series 76 (New York: Pantheon, 1964), 97.

6. Badger Clark, "A Cowboy's Prayer," and Curley Fletcher, "The Cowboy's Prayer," both in *Cowboy Poetry: A Gathering,* ed. Hal Cannon (Salt Lake City: Gibbs Smith, 1985), 65–70.

7. The anonymous "Windy Bill" is in *Cowboy Poetry,* ed. Cannon, 26–27; Rod McQueary, "Chicken Outfit," in *Dry Crik Review* 4 (Winter-Spring 1994): 40–43.

8. Jerome Rothenberg, comp., *Technicians of the Sacred: A Range of Poetics from Africa, America, Asia, and Oceania* (Garden City: Doubleday, 1968), xxi.

9. Wallace McRae, "Reincarnation," in *Cowboy Curmudgeon* (Salt Lake City: Gibbs Smith, 1992), 49.

10. Compare Ezra Pound's use of the Chinese ideogram in his *Cantos* and his frequent reference to Ernest Fenollosa's *The Chinese Written Character as a Medium for Poetry* (New York: Arrow, 1936).

11. Philip Rahv, "Paleface and Redskin," *Kenyon Review* 1 (Summer 1939): 251–56. Lowell made his distinction in an acceptance address for the National Book Award, 23 March 1960; quoted in Ian Hamilton, *Robert Lowell* (New York: Random House, 1982), 277.

12. Charles Badger Clark, "The Legend of Boastful Bill," in *Sun and Saddle Leather,* (1915), 3d ed. (Boston: Richard G. Badger, 1919), 43–47.

13. Bruce Kiskaddon, "The Cowboys' Christmas Dance," in *Rhymes of the Ranges: A New Collection of the Poems of Bruce Kiskaddon,* ed. Hal Cannon (Salt Lake City: Gibbs Smith, 1987), 34–35; S. Omar Barker, "Bunkhouse Christmas," in *Rawhide Rhymes: Singing Poems of the Old West* (Garden City: Doubleday, 1968), 146–47.

14. John Dofflemyer, "Now or Never," *Boots* 2 (Fall 1991): 20.

15. Paul Zarzyski, "The Lariati Versus/Verses the Literati: Loping toward Dana Gioia's Dream Come Real," *Writer's N.W.* 6 (Fall 1991): 1–2, 10, 12.

5

The Tradition of Cowboy Poetry

Guy Logsdon

Beef cattle had been raised in the states east of the Mississippi long before Texans started driving their beef northward to market in the years before the Civil War. But the men who tended and herded those cows and who built the foundation for the development of cattle ranching in the West have received little recognition in the romantic imagination of the nation. Instead, it was the working man of the range cattle industry that developed first in post–Civil War Texas who captured the fancy of the country—and, eventually, the world—and became "the American cowboy," the nation's mythical national hero. Cowboy poetry as it is now defined was born among those working men more than a century ago.

Strangely enough, the origins of cowboy poetry remain obscure even though ballads, work songs, music-hall and parlor songs, and hymns among first- and second-generation cowboys have been well documented, as have the adaptations of folk and popular poetry and songs into cowboy settings. An example is "The Dying Cowboy," an imitation of Edwin Hubbell Chapin's "The Ocean-Buried," which was first published in 1839. But the identity of the poet who rewrote the poem (or song—it isn't clear whether the revision first saw light as verse or music) into the cowboy genre will probably remain unknown.

The same loss of identity applies to the poets who composed "Sam Bass" and "Billie Vanero." The outlaw Sam Bass was killed by Texas Rangers on 21 July 1878, and it is probable that the poem (or song) was written shortly after his death. Cowboy poet and collector N. Howard "Jack" Thorp believed that John Denton of Gainesville, Texas, wrote it in 1879, but there is no hard evidence to support Thorp's statement. Nor is there much information about the source of the tune, although Charles A. Siringo claimed it was that of "Jim Fisk, who carried his heart in his hand," and Austin and Alta Fife tracked its similarities to a pre–Civil War song, "The Range of the Buffalo."

The song "Billie Vanero" describes Billie's death from wounds inflicted by Apaches while he rides to warn the ranch where his sweetheart lives. The setting is Arizona, and the last major Indian uprising in that state occurred in July 1882. The poem/song is a localization and adaptation of Wisconsin poet Eben E. Rexford's poem "The Ride of Paul Venarez," published 29 December 1881; the death of Billie Vanero would have been seven months later. Again, the identity of the individual who rewrote the poem and the date of adaptation remain unknown, along with the identity of the person who first set it to music.[1] All three of these early popular cowboy poems/songs, then, were probably written—or rewritten—in the late 1870s or early 1880s, and, with additional evidence from printed sources, they suggest that cowboy poetry as a genre first developed in the mid-to-late 1870s.

When death, disaster, or other memorable events happen, poems and songs soon follow. Does this mean that no dramatic deaths or other memorable events happened on the cattle ranges of the West between 1867 and the death of Sam Bass in 1878? Certainly other narrative poems with a cowboy theme (such as "Utah Carroll") may have been written earlier, but again there is no solid evidence to support an earlier date. Also, it is possible that whatever ballads were composed in those early years of the range cattle industry were unworthy of entering oral tradition, perhaps because they lacked mnemonic devices or because early-day cowboy poets wrote in styles that discouraged or hampered memorization and diffusion. Another possibility is the slow growth of occupational idiom, an essential ingredient in cowboy poetry and song. The terminology of the cowboy, as with all occupations, required time to develop, and it is probable that it took until the mid-1870s for a distinctive idiom to spread widely enough to distinguish cowboy language, poetry, and song from those of ordinary citizens.

Other poems and songs with cowboy themes have uncertain dates that rely on the memories of informants, primarily those associated with the collecting activities of Thorp and John A. Lomax along with memoirs written by first- and second-generation cowboys. These memoirs indicate that hymns and popular sentimental songs were familiar to many cowboys, so it seems likely that poetry recitation would have used popular poems of the day along with well-known bawdy materials. But only a few texts of cowboy poems and songs exist in memoirs printed before 1900. A better source is the newspapers published in settlements along the cattle trails and in communities that were cattle-shipping centers.

The Cheyenne *Transporter* was published in Darlington, Cheyenne and Arapaho Reservation, Indian Territory (now Oklahoma) from 5 December 1879 to 12 August 1886. Darlington was near the Chisholm Trail, and the newspaper published information primarily about the cattle drives, cowboys, cattlemen's associations, and ranches in Indian Territory. The *Western Central Kansas Cowboy* was published in Sidney, Kansas, for approximately ten months in 1883–84 and continued in Dodge City as the *Kansas Cowboy* for an additional eighteen months. Dodge City had a variety of newspapers such as the *Ford County Globe* (later the *Globe Live Stock Journal*) and the Dodge City *Journal*. The *Stock Growers' Journal*, established in Miles City, Montana, in 1884, lasted much longer than most other early livestock publications. Each of the cattle states had similar publications that generally began—and usually ceased—publication in the 1880s. And all of them printed cowboy poems and songs.

"The Cowboy," an anonymous, six-verse poem, is a good example of newspaper transmission. It depicts its subject as a wanderer who loves his work. He is also a gunman, a jovial consumer of strong drink, and a big-hearted prankster. "The Cowboy" is one of the earliest representations of the mythical cowboy and, given the vocabulary, it likely was not written or rewritten by a working cowboy:

What is it has no fixed abode.
Who seeks adventures by the load—
An errant knight without a code?
    The cowboy.

Who finds it pleasure, cows to punch,
When he would a whole herd "bunch"—
Who ready for a fine grass lunch?
    The cowboy.

Who is it when the drive is done,
Will on a howling bender run,
And bring to town his little gun?
    The cowboy.

Who is it paints the town so red,
And in the morning has a head
Upon him like a feather bed?
    The cowboy.

Who is it with unbounded skill
Will shoot big bullets with a will
That generally has the effect to kill?
    The cowboy.

Who is it, after all, who make
Town trade good, and uniformly take

For big treats what is called "the cake?"
The cowboy.

The poem appeared in the Cheyenne *Transporter* on 5 November 1884, in the *Kansas Cowboy* on 8 November 1884, and in the *New Mexico Daily Optic* on 12 November 1884.[2] It probably was published in many other western newspapers at about the same time. Such widespread distribution implies that copies of the poem were mailed or telegraphed to many newspapers. The poem also appears to be a romanticized version of "The Cow Boy," which had been published in the *Colorado Weekly News* on 28 September 1882—two years earlier:

Who rides his broncho through the street,
And shouts at each friend as they meet:
"Hello! Come in and I will treat"?
The Cow Boy.

Who "packs" a pair of Colt's Frontiers,
And sets the town upon its ears,
And man nor devil neither fears?
The Cow Boy.

Who plays "high ball" and "stud poker,"
And drinks whisky like an old soaker,
And gambles like a stock broker?
The Cow Boy.

Who trips the light fantastic toe
To violin or old banjo,
And yells, more gin, *poco tiempo?*
The Cow Boy.

Who "runs" the town at dead of night,
And puts the people in a fright,
Because he is a little tight?
The Cow Boy.

Who, when all is said and done,
Has only had a little fun,
And from the bake shop takes a bun?
The Cow Boy.[3]

It is possible that a cowboy actually wrote this version, which contains language closer to that a cowboy would use and depicts him as more of a rough hell-raiser than the romanticized versions of 1884. It is the earliest printed text of a poem on a cowboy theme that I have seen.

The earliest printed collection of cowboy poetry is *Western Travels and Other Rhymes* by L. (Lysius) Gough, who cowboyed in Texas from 1882 to 1884 and wrote poems about "actual life on the trail and ranch." Gough put his poems together in book form in 1886 and had a thousand copies printed in Dallas, Texas. It was a small paperbound volume that easily fell apart and was then discarded, which explains why I have located a copy only at the Barker Library of the University of Texas at Austin, although a copy is also reported to be in the Library of Congress. Many of Gough's poems in this collection are about his life after leaving the cowboy world. In 1935 he published *Spur Jingles and Saddle Songs* (Amarillo, Texas: Russell Stationery Company), which included many of his ranch poems, along with the dates they were written and information about the events that inspired them. It is a valuable collection of reminiscences and experiences, but there is no evidence that any of his poems were popular with cowboys or that any of his poems entered oral tradition. Gough's poem "Damn Fool"—written on 5 February 1883—is in the "Come All Ye" tradition and similar in theme to the folk song "Bad Companions." It contains thirteen verses, of which the first, fifth, and last follow:

Come all you young boys who long the west to see,
Come listen to my story and warning take from me;
And never while in youth do you attempt to roam;
For you can never find a place like your father's home.

. . . .

I longed to be a cowboy, to work upon the trail,
And face the cold stormy rains, also the snow and hail.
For the life of a cow boy I surely thought it best,
And onward I traveled to the country of the west.

. . . .

So come all you young boys, be you rich or poor,
Never start to rambling, 'twill teach you a lesson sure,
Though you can ramble for twenty years or more
You will never find a place like your father's door.

The first major collection of cowboy poetry was William Lawrence "Larry" Chittenden's *Ranch Verses,* published by G. P. Putnam's Sons in 1893. Chittenden referred to himself as the "Poet-Ranchman" and on the dedication page wrote: "The verses in this little volume are offsprings of solitude—born in idle hours of a Texas ranch [near Anson]." His poetry is varied in themes, and not all the poems address cowboy or western subjects. Only a few use cowboy idiom, metaphors, or imagery.

Chittenden's "The Cowboys' Christmas Ball" became a favorite among cowboys, and even though the book was also popular and went through numerous printings, most reciters probably learned the poem from newspaper printings before the book's publication.[4] Through the folk process, cowboys shortened and adapted the poem to fit their tastes. Chittenden's poetry did receive excellent reviews in eastern newspapers and in London, but, except for the one poem, working cowboys were not so enthusiastic.

The first important collector of cowboy poetry and song was N. Howard "Jack" Thorp, a New Mexico cowboy, poet, and singer, although Mary J. Jaques, Grace B. Ward, and Sharlot M. Hall published some cowboy song lyrics before Thorp.[5] In 1889 Thorp started a song-collecting trek in New Mexico that led him into Texas and Indian Territory (Oklahoma). A few of those songs, along with his own well-known "Little Joe, the Wrangler" and other poems, were published as *Songs of the Cowboys* in Estancia, New Mexico, in 1908. Thorp paid a local printer to print two thousand copies of his collection of twenty-three items, and many continue to be standards in the cowboy repertoire.

Thorp, born 10 June 1867, was, like Chittenden, an educated easterner who in his late teens became a cowboy. He remained a cowboy until his death in 1940 and wrote poetry about cowboy culture all of his adult life. He had no desire to return to the East or to change occupations as most men with his background did. He was the first cowboy poet who dedicated his entire life to cowboying and poetry. Consequently, Thorp's poetry appealed to working cowboys because it included their distinctive metaphors and imagery.

Working cowboys like Thorp wrote primarily for other cowboys rather than for literary acclaim, so to them writing poetry in the "language of the gods" instead of their own was wrong. Romanticized poems about cowboys, in contrast, seldom contain working cowboy language, and cowboys smile disdainfully when they hear them. It is the language combined with the sense of cowboy experience that has made the poetry of Curley Fletcher and Bruce Kiskaddon popular among cowboys for more than fifty years, for the language guarantees that the poet knows his subject. Distinctive cowboy jargon also often makes it difficult or impossible for non-cowboys to understand the subtlety, humor, and beauty of much cowboy poetry.

Not all cowboy poetry qualifies as folk poetry, a term often understood to refer to ancient epics or to the efforts of illiterate, anonymous poets. It suggests that the poet has inherited no literary traditions, a blatantly erroneous assumption when applied to cowboys. Many cowboys were and are well educated; many others with less education were and are well read. Reading—especially in the isolation of line camps, bunkhouses, and roundup camps—was and is a pastime widely enjoyed and practiced, and books (including many classics) and magazines were and are readily available in most ranch houses.

I knew an old-time cowboy who was well schooled in the classics and wrote poems primarily because he loved poetry. His name was Herb McSpadden, and he was Will Rogers's nephew and father of Clem McSpadden, the legendary rodeo announcer. To the stranger who casually met and visited with him at his ranch near Bushyhead, Oklahoma, he looked and sounded like a wise old weather-beaten cowpuncher who had little book learning; he never saw the need to impress people with his knowledge. He spoke and wrote the language of cowboys, but he could quote Shakespeare when he wanted to. His poems were not crafted to look and sound like any well-known poet's works, for, like most cowboys, he was too independent to imitate others—unless he was writing a parody.[6]

The tremendously influential collectors and writers John A. Lomax and J. Frank Dobie both had strong backgrounds in classical literature and so judged cowboy poetry as doggerel. Lomax did not hesitate to revise, edit, expurgate, and bowdlerize many of the songs he collected to make them fit for what he judged to be the genteel tastes of the public. After publishing *Cowboy Songs and Other Frontier Ballads* (1910) on the heels of Thorp's collection, he compiled a collection of cowboy poetry, *Songs of the Cattle Trail and Cow Camp* (Macmillan, 1919), which incorporated texts from printed as well as oral sources. In his introduction, he disparagingly qualified the poems as "attempts, more or less poetic, in translating scenes connected with the life of a cowboy."[7] A few selections were anonymous, but most poets were identified: James Barton Adams, William Lawrence "Larry" Chittenden, Arthur Chapman, Charles Badger Clark, Jr., Henry Herbert Knibbs, and others. Lomax had received most of the poems from cowboys and individuals interested in cowboy culture, who had clipped them from newspapers and magazines. At least Lomax appreciated the fact that poetry was popular among working cowboys.

Dobie was far less kind. In *Guide to Life and Literature of the Southwest* (1952), he devoted a chapter to "Poetry and Drama," stating:

> No poor poetry is worth reading. Taste for the best makes the other kind insipid.
>
> Compared with America's best poetry, most poetry of the Southwest is as mediocre as American poetry in the mass is as compared with the great body of English poetry between Chaucer and Masefield.[8]

Dobie listed a few poets he considered meritorious, mostly from the Santa Fe–Taos literary colony, and gave qualified praise to Eugene Manlove Rhodes's "The Hired Man on Horseback": "[It is] a long poem of passionate fidelity to his own decent kind of men, with power to ennoble the reader, and with the form necessary to all beautiful composition. This is the sole and solitary piece of poetry to be found in all the myriads of rhymes classed as 'cowboy poetry.'"[9]

Rhodes may have spoken to Dobie's sense of power and form, but he didn't speak to the working cowboy. He did not use cowboy idioms, the language of cowboys; instead, he wrote in the style of G. K. Chesterton, so it is not surprising that few, if any, cowboys learn "The Hired Man on Horseback" for bunkhouse recitation:

> Harp and flute and violin, throbbing through the night,
> Merry eyes and tender eyes, dark head and bright
> Moon shadow on the sundial to mark the moments fleet,
> The magic and enchanted hours where moonlight lovers meet;
> And the harp notes come all brokenly by night winds stirred—
>   But the hired man on horseback is singing to the herd![10]

The cattle industry's major bibliographer, Ramon Adams, seemingly shared Dobie's opinion, for he did not include poetry in his monumental bibliography *The Rampaging Herd.* Very few writers have consumed cowboy culture as did Adams, but he dismissed cowboy poetry and song with a short statement: "I have purposely omitted books on cowboy songs, cowboy poetry. These, I feel, do not belong to the range cattle industry and would only add to the printing costs."[11]

Among the bookmen, bibliographers, and writers of cowboy culture, Louis P. Merrill stands out as the individual most aware of what cattle people read and enjoyed. He made no literary value judgments in *Aristocrats of the Cow Country,* an annotated bibliography of one hundred of the best and rarest of cow-country books. He also provided a fine description of the place of reading and books in the ranch house:

> The reading habit among livestock producers, particularly the men and women of the cattle country, is much more pronounced than in any other segment of America's rural society. As a matter of fact, it probably equals or exceeds that of any group outside of the professions. It is possible to account for this in a measure by isolation, or seasonal leisure, or the highly complex nature of the range livestock production and management which requires an unusual stock of basic information in addition to current trends of economics and weather.
>
> Not only is it significant that cowfolks read much, they like most to read about their own country. This is probably because the occupation they were born in represents an epoch in America unlike anything before or since. An occupation further from common experience than any other with customs having the force of law, its own standards of conduct, its own philosophy and lore. Ranch headquarters are noted for sizable libraries of good books, well used but well cared for.[12]

Among his hundred "aristocrats," Merrill included seven books of poetry along with additional books that contain a few poems. The poets were James Barton Adams, William Lawrence "Larry" Chittenden, Wallace D. Coburn, Nathan Kirk Griggs, F. W. Lafrentz, N. Howard "Jack" Thorp, and C. C. Walsh. Not all were cowboys but at least they each had a solid knowledge of the occupation.

Much cowboy poetry, then, demonstrates clearly that cowboys did and do read. Many had and have a knowledge of literature, and as soon as their occupational language became solidified they began to express themselves with rhymed, metered, structured verse, using their own language and style and influenced by a variety of both traditional and literary models. Even though many newspaper and journal poems were anonymous, it is remarkable how many of the best and most lasting are ascribed to known poets. Larry Chittenden wrote "The Cowboys' Christmas Ball"; Jack Thorp scratched out "Little Joe, the Wrangler" on a piece of brown paper in 1898; D. J. "Kid" O'Malley wrote "A Cowboy's Death" ("Charlie Rutledge"), "After the Roundup" ("When the Work's All Done This Fall"), and "D-2 Horse Wrangler"; Charles Badger Clark, Jr., provided "The Glory Trail" ("High Chin Bob"), "A Border Affair," and "A Cowboy's Prayer"; Curley Fletcher wrote "The Strawberry Roan" and "The Flyin' Outlaw"; Bruce Kiskaddon wrote dozens of poems that became cowboy favorites; and Gail I. Gardner added "The Sierry Petes" to traditional cowboy lore. All of these poems were written after 1885, after cowboy language had begun to reflect occupational ways, and they were written for cowboys. These poets and their anonymous compadres created a cowboy literary tradition from which contemporary cowboys still draw inspiration.

Notes

Some ideas in this essay also appear in Guy Logsdon, "Cowboy Poets," in *Hoein' the Short Rows,* ed. Francis Edward Abernethy (Dallas: Southern Methodist University Press, 1988), 181–99; for additional information about printed sources and the transmission of cowboy poems and songs see the bibliographical essay "A Singing Cowboy Roundup" in Logsdon, *"The Whorehouse Bells Were Ringing" and Other Songs Cowboys Sing* (Urbana: University of Illinois Press, 1989), 281–345.

1. For information about "Sam Bass" see N. Howard ("Jack") Thorp, *Songs of the Cowboys* (Boston: Houghton Mifflin, 1921), 135–38, and Jim Bob Tinsley, *He Was Singin' This Song: A Collection of Forty-Eight Traditional Songs of the American Cowboy, with Words, Music, Pictures and Stories* (Orlando: University Presses of Florida, 1981), 174–79. For information about "Billie Vanero" see Logsdon, *"The Whorehouse Bells Were Ringing,"* 42–47.

2. A photocopy of the Cheyenne *Transporter* is in my collection; the *Kansas Cowboy* copy is found in *Ballads of the Great West,* ed. Austin E. Fife and Alta S. Fife (Palo Alto:

American West Publishing, 1970), 71; for the Las Vegas *Daily Optic,* see Clifford P. Westermeier, *Trailing the Cowboy: His Life and Lore as Told by Frontier Journalists* (Caldwell, Idaho: Caxton Publishers, 1955), 259–60.

3. "The Cow Boy," in Westermeier, *Trailing the Cowboy,* 259.

4. For additional information see Tinsley, *He Was Singin' This Song,* 144–47.

5. Logsdon, *"The Whorehouse Bells Were Ringing,"* 290–92.

6. See Guy Logsdon, "Herbert Thomas 'Herb' McSpadden: Oklahoma Rancher on the Verdigris," in *Cowboys Who Rode Proudly: Carrying Cattle . . . and the Methods of Handling Them,* ed. J. Evetts Haley, Jr. (Midland, Tex.: Nita Stewart Haley Memorial Library, 1992), 97–101.

7. John A. Lomax, *Songs of the Cattle Trail and Cow Camp* (1919), (New York: Duell, Sloan and Pearce, 1950), 6.

8. J. Frank Dobie, *Guide to Life and Literature of the Southwest: Revised and Enlarged in Both Knowledge and Wisdom* (Dallas: Southern Methodist University Press, 1952), 184.

9. Dobie, *Guide,* 185.

10. Eugene Manlove Rhodes, "The Hired Man on Horseback," in May Davison Rhodes, *The Hired Man on Horseback: My Story of Eugene Manlove Rhodes* (Boston: Houghton Mifflin, 1938), ix.

11. Ramon Adams, *The Rampaging Herd: A Bibliography of Books and Pamphlets on Men and Events in the Cattle Industry* (Norman: University of Oklahoma Press, 1959), 18.

12. Louis P. Merrill, *Aristocrats of the Cow Country* (Eagle Pass, Tex.: Pack-Saddle Press, 1973), 4.

6

Cowboy Poetry: A Poetry of Exile

Hal Cannon

The cowboy accompanied us as we sent our young men and women into two world wars. The cowboy struggled with us through a depression. He helped us find social justice as personal and civil rights were reformed in the 1950s and 1960s. His image gave Americans strength and hope. He entertained us. He gave us identity. In him we found, for the first time, a national symbol. This was the heyday of the cowboy in popular culture, between 1900 and 1965.

The popular cowboy image has been important both artistically and historically, but its history tells us more about the American people than it does about the lives of cowboys. From the moment Buffalo Bill Cody staged his first Wild West show in 1883, we can follow the vision Americans have sought in the cowboy as popular symbol. The earliest representations are heroic accounts of frontier life and settlement with a healthy dose of Victorian sentiment. The first Hollywood cowboys and dime-novel heroes scripted pure Arthurian story with undercurrents of regret for values lost in the dramatic move from nineteenth-century rural America to the fast-paced city. Later themes turned toward social justice and an examination of courtship and gender roles. These themes played themselves out in the 1960s when the cowboy was replaced with more progressive heroes suited to a technological age. But of late there has been a revival of the cowboy image. It is based on the American struggle to cope with a world that is seemingly changing in uncontrollable ways. The myth of the independent, freewheeling cowboy living in the unfettered West still appeals to many Americans, most of whom value the Old West for what they nostalgically feel society has lost and who use the mythic cowboy, once again, to find new paradigms.

I suspect that most representations of true cowboy tradition are fated to be swept up in this way by popular culture and to become stereotyped, hackneyed, and frivolous. Because cowboy poetry did not fit the archetype of singing cowboys on horseback, because it often dealt with serious and in-group coded subjects disdainful of the popular cowboy image, and because all poetry was increasingly defined in highbrow terms, it was slow to follow cowboy painting, sculpture, and music on the path to B-movies, pulp fiction, and spangled four-part harmony.

Cowboy poetry reached its height between 1905 and 1935. At first glance, stories of cowboy experience put to rhyme and meter might be seen as just another way that Americans reveled in the cowboy image. Examining the poetic script, however, reveals a very different purpose than simply entertaining Americans or confirming their basic values. Rather, the cowboy poetry of the twentieth century shows the claw marks of traditional agrarian life being dragged into the modern age.

It is a poetry laced with tragedy and immortality. Although sometimes humorous, it is often born of loss, remembrance, and grief. The Greek root of "nostalgia" means, after all, "return home," and cowboy poetry so chronicles the slow march of country people to the city. Because there was no home to return to, even early cowboy poetry from the 1800s is a song of exile from the American promise of the West:

They filled up the grave, and each herder
Said good-by, till the Judgement Day.
But the fiddler stayed, and he sang and played,
As the herders walked away

A requiem in a lonesome land,
In a mournful minor key:
"No matter how long the river,
The river will reach the sea!"[1]

Every artistic tradition has a murky past, a past marked by high creativity, low self-consciousness, and marginal popularity to outsiders. For cowboy lore in general, the focus is the trail-drive days of the 1870s and 1880s, when the American West was still a frontier and the expressive life of the cowboy became legendary.

There are no narratives from the trail drives following the Civil War that fully explain the chemistry of a diverse lot of men relying on each other and their animals on long and trying odysseys. From this experience came an amazing amalgam that forever would represent the American character. It was a jazz of Irish storytelling and lore, Scottish seafaring and cattle tending, Moorish and

Spanish horsemanship, European cavalry practices, African improvisation, and a reluctant observation of the means of Native American survival. All can be heard and seen in this way of life, even today.

Starting in the 1890s, books of cowboy poems started to trickle out, cowboy novels spread like prairie fire, and by 1908 cowboy song collections appeared. The image of the cowboy was set on course, a course that eventually followed through music, film-making, and literature and, as the years passed, strayed increasingly from the reality of ranch life. Because the poetry and oral storytelling of working cowboys were not included in the popular cowboy stereotype, these forms of expression, for the most part, remained as insiders' forms.

Before the century's turn, cowboy poetry and song absorbed the sentimentality of the Victorian era, describing loneliness on the trail for loved ones back in civilization and sometimes pleading for respect, as in this traditional verse from the nineteenth century:

The cowboy's name is butchered by the papers in the East
And when we're in the city we're treated like the beast
But in our native country our name is ever dear,
And you bet we're always welcome by the western pioneer.[2]

Yet simultaneously there was a new sense of engagement in the stories, the dialect, and the credo of the cowboy. William Lawrence "Larry" Chittenden, probably the first man to publish a book of cowboy poems for the popular market, made a hit with "The Cowboys' Christmas Ball." Written in cowboy dialect, it is one of the few poems in his 1893 collection not rife with Victorian stuffiness and sentimentality:

The dust riz fast an' furious, we all just galloped round,
Till the scenery got so giddy, that Z Bar Dick was downed.
We buckled to our partners, an' told 'em to hold on,
Then shook our hoofs like lightning until the early dawn.
Don't tell me 'bout cotillions, or germans. No sir-'ee!
That whirl at Anson City just takes the cake with me.
I'm sick of lazy shufflin's, of them I've had my fill,
Give me a frontier breakdown, backed up by Windy Bill.[3]

This was a caricature of a cowboy Christmas dance that ranch folks embraced, and in the early part of the century John Lomax recognized that the poem had been improved by folk editing as it strayed from the published text: "One night in New Mexico a cowboy sang to me, in typical cowboy music, Larry Chittenden's entire 'Cowboys' Christmas Ball'; since that time the poem has often come to me in manuscript form as an original cowboy song. The changes—usually, it must be confessed, resulting in bettering the verse—which have occurred in oral transmission, are most interesting."[4] The piece is still sung and performed, and Anson, Texas, is known for its annual Christmas Ball, a dance boosters would have discontinued years ago but for the resonance of this one poem.

Chittenden, the self-proclaimed "poet-ranchman," was not only a resident of Anson but also had seaside homes in Florida and Bermuda; he also founded the National Autograph Library at Christmas Cove, Maine. Yes, he was a rancher, but he was an opportunist as well, one of the first exploiters of the cowboy image. And like most cowboy interpreters since, he treaded the dilettante's path between the real cowboy's world and polite society.

When John Lomax published his second collection, *Songs of the Cattle Trail and Cow Camp,* in 1919, he had actually collected original poems that he claimed had been "set to music by the cowboys, who, in their isolation and loneliness, have found solace in narrative or descriptive verse devoted to cattle scenes."[5] Unlike his groundbreaking *Cowboy Songs and Other Frontier Ballads,* there is no musical notation; to my knowledge, most of the poems never had music. Yet Lomax claimed that they were songs. Had Lomax invested in the idea that cowboys were singers rather than poets and reciters? Was he attempting to uphold the then-current emphasis by folklorists on old ballads? Or was he playing up to a new and potentially popular commodity, the singing cowboy? Perhaps the definition of poems and songs has changed since the turn of the twentieth century, when the most prevalent singing style was the unaccompanied. The old ballads were sung with little regard for strict rhythm because the drama of the story dictated the rhythm rather than a strict regularity. In other words, singing may have been closer to storytelling; the line between song and recitation may have been less distinct than it is now. I recall Alan Lomax, attending a Cowboy Poetry Gathering as the keynote speaker, listening patiently to several cowboy music sessions but later angrily decrying modern cowboy music, its incessant guitar and strict dance rhythms. In his opinion, these confining elements had ruined the power of the song and story.

Regardless, the golden age of cowboy poetry before and after World War I marked the intersection of two parallel and interacting poetic traditions, one oral with traditional recitation performance at its heart, one literary with reading at its core. Cowboys learned poetry for recitation both through oral means and by gaining access to printed texts, even though their access to published material was scant.

The poetry that first reached them came out of periodicals, small-town newspapers, stock growers' newsletters, and ephemeral advertising material. An early example is Frank Desprez's "Lasca," first published in an 1882 issue of the Montana *Stock Growers' Journal.* The poem was widely recited by cowboys but eventually attracted a far larger audience, becoming a popular performance piece in Chautauqua presentations all over the county. Frank Deprez, a London theater critic, had only brief experience in the Wild West yet was able to combine western landscape and nostalgia for the past:

And the buzzard sails on,
And comes and is gone,
Stately and still, like a ship at sea.
And I wonder why I do not care
For the things that are, like the things that were.
Does half my heart lie buried there
    In Texas, down by the Rio Grande?[6]

Self-published and small-press books and pamphlets have always been prevalent in cowboy poetry. Most notable is Curley Fletcher's 1917 pamphlet, which included "The Strawberry Roan." Fletcher and his brother produced the booklet and peddled it at the original Prescott (Arizona) Rodeo. Another poet from Prescott, Gail Gardner, produced only one book (*Orejana Bull for Cowboys Only*) and kept it in print throughout his long life. Bruce Kiskaddon, too, self-published three of his four books, the other being published by his principal benefactor, the magazine *Western Livestock Journal,* which used his poems on Union Stockyard Auction notices as well as in the monthly.

A small group of poets during this time had an impact on the cowboy poetry tradition through books published and distributed widely through mainstream publishers in New York and elsewhere. Notable among these were Charles Badger Clark, Henry Herbert Knibbs, James Barton Adams, E. A. Brininstool, Arthur Chapman, Larry Chittenden, Elliott Lincoln, S. Omar Barker, and Robert Carr. All wrote a good deal of poetry for the popular market, and it shows in their subjects and style. Few of their stories of gunfighters, prostitutes, and gold prospectors made any impact on cowboys and ranchers. Some are written in a stilted cowboy dialect tinged with sentimentality. This was stuff more suited to the pop market, where it blended with a mass of like product from Hollywood and elsewhere.

Of these widely published poets, S. Omar Barker and Henry Herbert Knibbs display in many of their poems an honesty and straightforwardness, a knowledge of horses and cowboy life, which rang true to cowboys. I interviewed Barker shortly before his death in 1985. He corrected me when I asked about his life as a cowboy poet. "I'm a western poet, not a cowboy poet," he said. He explained that some of what he wrote was about cowboy experience, something he had experienced firsthand, but he wanted to differentiate his writing, the writing of a professional, from that of the folk versifiers.

Probably the most widely published of the early poets—and the most influential—was Badger Clark. The son of a Methodist minister, he was born on New Year's Day in 1883. The family moved from Iowa to South Dakota, where the young Badger experienced the taming of Deadwood. As a young man he spent a couple of summers working for a rancher uncle in Wyoming. Later he traveled to Cuba, where he got into a scrape with the law. In a dingy cell he lost himself in the *Rubaiyat* of Omar Khayyam. A long legal battle ensued, and by the time he was acquitted he was physically and mentally exhausted. He was diagnosed with tropical fever and doctors told him he must move to a dry, healthy climate. He found a place in Arizona as caretaker on a small ranch. There he wrote his finest poems, poems written for the neighboring cowboys who came to his cabin for entertainment. As an afterthought he sent one of them to his mother, who in turn sent it to a magazine. When he returned to South Dakota four years later, "The Glory Trail" or "High-Chin Bob" had already entered folk tradition:

'Way high up the Mogollons,
Among the mountain tops,
A lion cleaned a yearlin's bones
And licked his thankful chops,
When on the picture who should ride,
A-trippin' down the slope,
But High-Chin Bob, with sinful pride
And mav'rick-hungry rope.[7]

In 1915 Clark self-published his classic collection *Sun and Saddle Leather.* After several successful editions, the Boston publisher Richard Badger took it over for a time, after which Chapman and Grimes obtained the rights. By 1942 it had sold more than thirty thousand copies, and the book has stayed in print almost continuously since. Clark eventually was named South Dakota's poet laureate and lived out his life as a lecturer and minor celebrity.

Bruce Kiskaddon represents the poetry of loss more than any other cowboy poet of the early part of the century, and his work permeates ranching country more than that of any other. He was a tragic figure who traded his boots and spurs for a bellhop's monkey suit and a bottle of whiskey after he came to Hollywood in 1926 to take an extra's role in the original film *Ben Hur.* Although he lived in the heart of the Hollywood cowboy scene, he never found much work there, and his poetry was always written for ranch people of the old school. He had no use for the romantic cowboys in the movies, for, after all, he was the little man who piloted the stars up and down in the hotel elevator for the last quarter of his life. In a book he published shortly before his death, he said with typical cowboy understatement: "I never really completed grammar school and my powers of imagination are not what some writers are gifted with. So you will find these rhymes are all written from actual happenings or from the old legends of the cow country. Hoping it brings back memories to the old boys and that the younger ones enjoy them."[8]

Poetry is singular in its demands. It is an artistic expression that chronicles history. It is a form that asks that language be as succinct as possible. It demands not only the facts but also the emotion behind the facts.

Rural and agrarian life go hand in hand. As life on the land, life with animals, life producing food becomes rarer and rarer in America, the poetry of ranch people will continue to be disquieting in its sense of exile from land, from history, and from tradition:

The Wrangler Kid is out with his rope,
He seldom misses a throw.
Will he make a cow hand? Well I hope,
If they give him half a show.
They are throwin' the rope corral around,
The hosses crowd in like sheep.
I reckon I'll swaller my breakfast down
And try to furgit and sleep.

Yes, I've lived my life and I've took a chance,
Regardless of law or vow.
I've played the game and I've had my dance,
And I'm payin' the fiddler now.[9]

Notes

1. Eugene Ware, "The Blizzard" (1860s), in *Cowboy Poetry: A Gathering,* ed. Hal Cannon (Salt Lake City: Gibbs Smith, 1985), 25.

2. "The Western Pioneer" is also known as "Texas Jack," one of the earliest cowboy songs to be published. This version was collected by Ellen J. Stekert from Ezra Barhight. See Austin E. Fife and Alta S. Fife, *Cowboy and Western Songs* (New York: Clarkson S. Potter, 1969), 125–26.

3. William Lawrence "Larry" Chittenden, "The Cowboys' Christmas Ball," in John A. Lomax, *Songs of the Cattle Trail and Cow Camp* (1919), (New York: Duell, Sloan and Pearce, 1950), 116.

4. Lomax, *Songs of the Cattle Trail and Cow Camp,* ix–x.

5. Ibid., xi.

6. Frank Desprez, "Lasca," in Lomax, *Songs of the Cattle Trail and Cow Camp,* 26.

7. Charles Badger Clark, "The Glory Trail" ("High-Chin Bob") in Lomax, *Songs of the Cattle Trail and Cow Camp,* 30.

8. Bruce Kiskadden, introduction to *Rhymes of the Ranges and Other Poems* (Los Angeles: Heitman Printing, 1947), iv.

9. Bruce Kiskaddon, "The Old Night Hawk," in *Rhymes of the Ranges: A New Collection of the Poems of Bruce Kiskaddon,* ed. Hal Cannon (Salt Lake City: Gibbs Smith, 1987), 88.

Part 2
Process

A commonplace in folklore scholarship is that folklore—whether folk song, folk poem, folk tale, or other material—exists in variation. That is, in the course of being passed from one individual to another, or in the course of the material's being performed many times over a long period to a variety of audiences, the poem or song or tale inevitably undergoes change, so that one teller or singer may perform the same piece quite differently from another performer. For that reason, cowboy poems and songs often exist in many different versions, each fitted or responsive to the particular requirements of performer, audience, time, and place. The transmission of this material from person to person—often called "the folk process"—is especially likely to create variation because of the lack of a stable written text.

This is the process closely examined by folklorist Warren Miller, education director at Sharlot Hall Museum in Prescott, Arizona, and a specialist in the traditional poetry and song of Arizona. Miller was able to collect different versions of several well-known cowboy poems from reciters who had learned the poems from other cowboys rather than from written texts. The differences among the texts provide instructive examples of the influence of local conditions and personal preferences on traditional performances.

At the same time, cowboy poetry has been powerfully influenced by text-based materials, particularly classical literature. Buck Ramsey, a former bronc rider who turned to composing and performing cowboy poems and songs before his untimely death in 1998, recalls the fascination that cowboys had for inexpensive pocket literature and for vivid wordplay. Buck's essay is a fine counter to the myth of the cowboy as "strong and silent."

David Stanley, who teaches folklore and American literature, also looks at the literary backgrounds of cowboy poetry, showing that the best cowboy poems—like many of the best poems of the literary canon—maintain a tension between the orderly predictability of rhythm and rhyme and a richness of variation that creates emphasis, contrast, and humor. The interplay between sound, rhythm, and content, in other words, creates meaning in cowboy poetry.

Two essays, one by former rodeo hand, rancher, and cowboy singer Glenn Ohrlin and one by Charlie Seemann, executive director of the Western Folklife Center in Elko, Nevada, examine the close relationship between cowboy music and cowboy poetry. Because some well-known songs began as poems that were later set to music and because some original songs have been frequently recited as poems, many texts have had two different forms of existence and have gained or lost lyrics in the process. Ohrlin's description of his adventures as a poem- and song-collecting itinerant rodeo rider demonstrates how widespread cowboy expressive culture was in the 1940s and 1950s and what different forms it took. Seemann examines the different cultural environments in which poetry and song flourished and the changes that occur when a poem becomes a song.

Rancher Bill Lowman, who works out of the badlands of western North Dakota, provides a personal glimpse of the composing process. Inventing poetry, Lowman observes, is often part and parcel of the working day, with the best poems coming from direct experience on the ranch. Lowman says he composes many poems entirely in his head before he even begins to set them down on paper—a revealing statement that reemphasizes the essentially oral nature of cowboy poetry.

7

Change and Oral Tradition in Cowboy Poetry

Warren Miller

The poems of the cowboy, like other forms of oral literature, exist in a state of constant flux. These poems are heard as recitations, and they often are passed orally from one reciter to another. Firm, unchangeable, written texts are never established; even published versions of poems seldom intersect with versions circulating orally. Folklorists have tended to view change in oral tradition as being largely anonymous, the organic result of circulation within a community, requiring many generations of retelling. Cowboy poems also change in retelling, but the changes are not necessarily either anonymous or unintentional. Cowboy poetry is the unique province of that occupational group working livestock in the American West, and changes in the poems must be viewed as legitimate parts of the folk process, whether the changes are made by known individual folk artists or appear without attribution. Changes to folk poetry within the cowboy tradition result from several different mechanisms.

Cowboy oral lore, for example, although firmly rooted in older traditions, is still relatively young. The earliest reports of specifically cowboy song and verse come from the mid-1870s, during the formative period of the great cattle drives. There are living reciters whose personal histories span fully half the history of cowboy recitation. Because of the relative youth of this folk tradition, it is possible to observe and comment anecdotally on the nature of change in cowboy oral traditions. The observations that follow are drawn from interviews, field recordings, and public presentations of cowboy folk artists (reciters, storytellers, and singers) that I did in northern Arizona between 1984 and 1996.

Reciters often state that it is their intention to reproduce a poem exactly as they first heard it. That is a difficult goal and one that is seldom completely achieved.

There may be references, terms, and words in the original that a listener does not understand but must approximate to the best of his or her ability if he or she is to attempt a recitation. Sometimes whole lines have to be reconstructed around concepts that are part of the reciter's experience. The style of the language may be awkward for the reciter, and he or she may change the incidental language to better suit his or her own conversational style. Work-related concepts and terms, common in cowboy verse, differ from region to region and may be altered by the working cowboy reciter to fit his or her expertise. Work-specific terms present a more difficult problem for the reciter who has not done the kind of work in question but who may nevertheless learn and recite a poem well enough to pass it on—leaving out or misquoting technical terms. And, of course, the reciter's memory may alter the poem over time.

Such changes can be characterized as passive because they act upon the text of a poem without any conscious decision on the part of the reciter. There are also conscious, or active, factors that effect change. These include the reciter's exercise of artistic license to modify the poem to suit personal notions of propriety and authenticity, to fit local geographic and work settings, and/or to satisfy his or her aesthetic judgment.

Particular periods over the last century have seen intense activity in the publishing of cowboy verse. The first of these periods was approximately 1905 to 1915. The 1930s also saw a wealth of cowboy verse published, and the period since the first Cowboy Poetry Gathering at Elko, Nevada, in 1985 has been the most active. Through early publications, the original composed versions of poems that have circulated in oral tradition are sometimes available. These poems may be changed or altered in many ways as they pass from one reciter to the next. Many of these changes are inadvertent and unconscious, but some are deliberate acts of creativity. The original published versions provide a baseline against which later oral recitations may be contrasted.

"The Sierry Petes" (also known as "Tyin' Knots in the Devil's Tail") is one of the most widely known cowboy poems. It has been subjected to a variety of changes over the years since it was written in 1917 by Gail I. Gardner of Prescott, Arizona. The poem relates the story of two rough-country cowhands who triumph over evil, personified as the devil himself. Its universal theme, clever and colorful construction, and descriptions of wild-cow work around the turn of the century made it immediately appealing to all who heard it, and it passed quickly into the body of oral cowboy lore.

Gardner, who died in 1988 at the age of ninety-five, was for more than seventy years regularly treated and subjected to different versions of his poem, usually containing changes and misquotes. In 1935 he published a booklet entitled *Orejana Bull* in an effort to put the original wordings of his poems into circulation.[1]

Gardner's subtitle, *For Cowboys Only,* reasserted his belief that only cowboys who understood the work and the language of the range could properly appreciate (and correctly quote) his poems; they were written, he reiterated in the introduction, "solely for the amusement of cowboys." His usual reaction to hearing "bunged-up" versions of "Sierry Petes" and others of his poems was to get hopping mad and rail against "drugstore cowboy singers" who couldn't bother to get the words right.

Gardner's "Sierry Petes" was, at root, autobiographical. It was inspired by a conversation he once had with his partner, "Sandy Bob" Heckle (son of "Texas Bob" Heckle and uncle of Marty Robbins). Returning to camp after a trip to town during which Gardner and Heckle had attempted the popular local challenge—to down a drink in every one of Prescott's twenty Whiskey Row saloons—Heckle had ventured the opinion that "the devil gets cowboys for doing what we done." Gardner himself was the "Buster Jig" of the poem; he had acquired that nickname as the offspring of J. I. Gardner, who was addressed by his friends and general store customers as "Jig," after his initials. Reciters who didn't know this bit of the author's personal history usually changed "Jig" to "Jiggs," a more common nickname. The change was frequent and inadvertent and did not alter the meaning of the poem at all: It is an example of passive change.

Another example of passive change can be drawn from "Sierry Petes." In Gardner's original version, "Sandy Bob" says, "I'm sick of this cow-pyrography, and I 'lows I'm a-goin' to town." Pyrography was a popular parlor craft at the turn of the century. An iron stylus heated red-hot in the fireplace was used to burn designs on leather throw-pillows and other decorative objects. The parallel to branding was obvious, and Gardner applied it with humorous result. By the 1920s, however, pyrography had gone out of fashion, and few people remembered it. Reciters heard a variety of things in the line and repeated it as best they could. "Cow-pyrography" became "cow biography," "cowboy-ography," "cow biology," "cow geography," just plain "cow-ography," and even "cowpie-ography."

By 1935 Gardner had heard his clever line misquoted so many times that when he published *Orejana Bull* he changed the line himself. His new version read, "I'm sick of the smell of burnin' hair, and I 'lows I'm a-goin' to town." This less-colorful line was not open to so much misinterpretation, but the poem was no longer Gardner's to shape: It had been happily appropriated by thousands of cowboy reciters who would continue to repeat it and pass it on in their own individual versions.

I once had an illuminating experience with variations of "Sierry Petes" in front of a public audience at a gathering of cowboy reciters in the Verde Valley of Arizona. In a session devoted to the poems of Gail Gardner, a twelve-year-old boy had given a fine and quite accurate-to-the-original recitation of "Sierry Petes," which he had recently committed to memory from a printed text. I asked a Canadian reciter who was present if he would give his version of the same poem. I knew that he had learned it in Alberta in the 1930s and that it had different names for the two characters and other regional variations. I thought it would be interesting for the audience to hear the two contrasting versions.

The Canadian came to the microphone and announced that as far as he could tell his poem was exactly the same as the one the young man had recited. He then proceeded to recite his own (and, to my ear, very different) version of "Sierry Peaks," reiterating afterward that it was just the same poem. When he had finished, Bud Brown, a local old-timer with a broad traditional repertoire, stood up from the audience and verbally raked the Canadian over the coals for botching so many important parts of his friend Gail's poem. He was particularly critical of the Canadian's line "where the yellow-jack pines was tall" and pointed out that yellow pines are ponderosa pines, which are tall. Jack pines, however, are small trees, and there is no such thing as a yellow-jack pine. Jack pines are unknown in Canada, so the anomaly did not trouble the Canadian.

The lesson I learned was this: To the traditional reciter, the critical elements of a poem are the story line and the rhyming words. Everything else can and does change, but the changes may be inadvertent, unnoticed, or considered to be of little importance. What follows is the Canadian reciter's version of "Sierry Peaks." The full text of Gail I. Gardner's original poem may be found in *Orejana Bull for Cowboys Only.*

Way out West in the Sierry Peaks,
Where the yeller jack pines grow tall,
Six-foot Sam and Buster Jiggs
Had a roundup way last fall.

Any old cow that flopped long ears
And didn't show up by day,[2]
Got his long horns chiseled and his old hide sizzled
In a most artistic way.

Said Six-foot Sam to Buster Jiggs
As he threw his long legs down,
"I'm gettin' tired of this old cow ranch,
And I reckon I'll jog to town."

They both set out at a campsite lope
Just a-packin' up a damn good ride,
Those were the days when a good cowpoke
Could ride out his inside.[3]

They stopped at the old Kentucky Bar
At the end of the whiskey row,
And they wound up tight in the middle of the night[4]
Some forty drinks below.

The room went around, and it set them off,
And they started on a different way,
And, honest to goodness, to tell you the truth,
Those boys got stewed that day.

They both set out for the Sierry Peaks,
A-packin' up a damn good load,
When who should they meet, but the devil himself,
Come a-prancin' down the road.

"Confound yer ornery cowboy skunks,
You better had a-hunt yer hole,
Fer I am the devil from the Hell rim rock
Come to gather up your soul."

"The devil be damned," said Buster Jiggs,
"Us boys, we know, are tight,
But before you corral any cowboy soul,
You'll surely see a beautiful fight."

He threw his rope, and he threw it straight,
And it spun down good and true.
And he roped the devil by his splendid horns
And he tooken his dollies[5] too.

Now Six-foot Sam was a lariat man,
With a gut-line coiled up neat,
He threw his rope, and he threw it straight,
And he roped the devil's hind feet.

They threw him down and they stretched him out,
While the sizzlin' irons grew hot,
And they trimmed his horns with a de-horn saw,
And they branded him a lot.

They tied ten knots in the old boy's tail,
And they left him there for a joke,
And the bellers and the cries of the cowboy
Made up fer the blackjack oak.[6]

If you ever go ridin' down that Sierry trail
And you hear an awful wail,
Remember it's the devil with the owls and the fowls
And the knots tied in his tail.

Some discussion of the changes wrought in "Sierry Petes" as it wandered from the high desert country of northern Arizona to the frozen north will further illustrate passive change. The Canadian reciter's "Six-foot Sam" may be an alliterative cousin of "Sagebrush Sam," one of the characters in a northern U.S. version of the poem usually attributed to Powder River Jack Lee and published as "Tying Knots in the Devil's Tail" in *The Stampede*.[7] Powder River Jack published and recorded the song as his original composition and was considered by Gail Gardner to be his principal artistic nemesis.

The Canadian reciter told me how he had learned his version of the poem: "A guy came to our place on the farm, and he got stormed in for a few days, and he was singing it. I say it as a poem, but he was singing it. I don't remember his name. That was in Alberta, over fifty years ago. He come in to the farm and got stormed in there, him and his wife, for a couple of days, and he had his guitar and he was singing away. I learned it from him. He wrote it down for me. He used to be in the States, but he had been in Alberta for a few years. It must have been sixty years ago since he learned it." This version of "Sierry Peaks" bears such a close resemblance to Powder River Jack's version that I wonder if Charlie's "guy with a guitar" who was stormed in for a few days might have been Powder River Jack himself, who traveled and performed extensively during the 1930s accompanied by his wife, "Pretty Kitty" Lee.

In stanza three, Gardner's original has Sandy Bob announce "as he throwed his seago down" that he intends to go to town. In the Canadian version, the term *seago,* meaning a tightly woven rope of vegetable fiber manufactured for use on ocean-going vessels and also called a "yacht line" by some cowboys, has been lost. The hole left has been filled in with "threw his long legs down."

Stanza eleven contains another anomaly that the reciter's version shares with Powder River Jack's. In Gardner's original, Buster Jig was a "riata man with his gut-line coiled up neat." A riata is a catch-rope made of braided or twisted rawhide, also sometimes called a gut-line, as in the following line. Every working cowboy is a "lariat man" because "lariat" indicates a catch-rope but does not specify what kind, material, or manufacturer.

In stanza twelve, the order of work has been inverted from Gardner's original. Roped head and heels, a cow was stretched out between the two cow ponies as a way of getting her onto her side on the ground so the branding could proceed. A stretched-out cow that managed to keep on its feet would be "tailed down."

One cowboy would dismount, leaving his well-trained horse to keep the rope taut. He would then grab the cow by the tail and give a swift sideways yank, throwing the animal off balance and onto the ground.

The line in the concluding stanza, "Remember it's the devil with the owls and the fowls and the knots tied in his tail," is a radical departure from Gail Gardner's original ("you'll know it's the devil a-bellerin' about, with the knots tied in his tail") but bears a closer resemblance to Powder River Jack Lee's concluding lines: "You'll know it's the Devil as he yowls and prowls, with the knots tied in his tail."

To illustrate the nature of active, intentional change, we can turn to Bud Brown, the same reciter who objected to the Canadian's version of "Sierry Petes." Brown came to Arizona to work as a cowhand in 1926. He spent many years working on ranches throughout Arizona and then established Friendly Pines Summer Camp near Prescott, where he taught generations of youngsters to ride and to drive teams of miniature mules. Bud Brown was, perhaps, an atypical cowboy. He had graduated from Dartmouth and taken graduate courses at Columbia University before coming west in 1926. He was fascinated with cowboy poems and songs from his first exposure and sought to learn them whenever he could. During the years that he operated the Friendly Pines camp, he would often entertain the campers with his recitations and songs. In 1986 and 1987 I conducted several interviews with Bud, who spoke candidly about the changes he had made in a number of poems he had adopted.

In the case of "Little Joe the Wrangler's Sister Nell," Bud first told me that he had heard that this sequel was written by the same man who wrote "Little Joe, the Wrangler" but didn't believe it. When Little Joe first came to work at the cow ranch, he "didn't know straight up about a cow." In contrast, Sister Nell, Bud pointed out, had volunteered "I'll wrangle in the morning" on her arrival several months later. "How," Bud asked, "did Little Joe's twin sister get to be a skilled hand so quickly?" He applied the same critical thinking to the poem and decided that he could not sing it the way he had learned it. It violated one of the tenets of Bud's personal Code of the West: A man must own up to his responsibilities, no matter how difficult. "The ending to the song just chills me," Bud said. "Can you imagine a group of grown men just waiting for her to read the brand on the horses? And letting her judge from the looks on their faces that she never again would see her brother Joe? When I find a song that irks me as bad as that one, I just make my own version of it and hope that the author will at least be able to sense my reason for the change and not be offended."

This is one traditional ending for "Little Joe the Wrangler's Sister Nell":

Soon we heard the horses comin', a-headin' into camp;
'Twern't daylight but we plainly heared the bell,

And then someone a-cryin' a-comin' on behind,
It was Little Joe the Wrangler's sister Nell.

We couldn't quite console her, she'd seen the horses' brand
As she drove 'em from the river bank below.
From the look upon our faces she seemed to realize
That she ne'er again would see her brother Joe.[8]

Bud not only corrected what he saw as a serious breach of responsibility by the cowhands but also added a happy ending:

Soon we heard the cavvy, a-comin' into camp,
'Twern't yet daylight, but we plainly heard the bell.
And behind them, she was sobbin', like her heart was gonna break,
Little Joe the Wrangler's sister Nell.

We hardly could console her, she'd seen the horses' brand,
As she drove them from the river bed below,
But the boss, he kindly told her what she already knew,
That she never again would see her brother Joe.

Now this story has a happy end, as every story should,
For the boss's wife adopted little Nell.
Gave her all the tender care and love her life had never known,
And at age nineteen she married very well.

She still comes to the wagon for roundup spring and fall,
She's a real top hand and always on the go.
And the little kid that trails her on that faithful pony, Chaw,
Is her oldest boy we all call Wrangler Joe.

Another poem that didn't feel right to Bud was Henry Herbert Knibbs's "The Bosky Steer" (often called "Jake and Roany").[9] "The way I learned it," Bud says, "Roany answered 'in a voice that was weak and queer.' Well, I don't think a cowboy's going to answer to a guy up in a tree in a voice that's weak and queer. Besides which, it spoils the punch line if you sing it. If you have to do it weak and queer, it doesn't even get across." Bud's concluding stanza is:

Jake hollered, "You old fool, keep back out of sight,
Ya act like yer hankerin' to make him fight."
But Roany hollered for the world to hear,
"Stay back, Hell, there's a bear in here!"

Changes such as these, wrought with purpose and design by individual reciters, are likely to be carried on in oral tradition if they ring true, discarded if they do not. I have since recorded another reciter who has never met Bud Brown and who uses verbatim the same line Bud claims as his original work: "Roany hollered for the world to hear."

I gained more insight into the mechanisms of change in recitation through an unusual fieldwork experience. I made recordings of two excellent traditional reciters, Slim Kite and Mike Landon, and discovered that they had both learned the same several poems from the same source, one Ray Ailee, at the same time and place more than fifty years before. Slim Kite had lived all his life around livestock and had worked on many ranches in New Mexico and Arizona, including a ranch west of Flagstaff where he worked with Ray Ailee and Mike Landon on a roundup crew about 1934. Slim also worked at the Grand Canyon as a mule wrangler and tourist saddle-guide in the mid-1930s, where he entertained tourists with his traditional recitations and fiddle-playing. Mike Landon had been a working cowboy all his life and was unusual in that he had been employed at the same ranches (those operated by the Babbitt brothers in the Flagstaff area) for fifty years. His daily and life-long connection with cattle work comes out strongly in his recitations.

One of the poems Slim and Mike both learned from Ray Ailee was Curley Fletcher's "The Flyin' Outlaw," which both reciters knew as "The Mustang with Wings." I knew that both reciters had heard the same version of the poem from Ray Ailee, so any differences between their recitations had to be due to changes one or both had made. Yet both Slim and Mike stated that they recited the poem exactly as they had learned it; neither was aware of having made any changes. Each had recited the poem numerous times over the fifty years but never in the presence of the other. A comparison between these two versions of the poem shows the nature and extent of changes possible in just one generation of oral transmission.

I transcribed the two versions and made a careful comparison between them. I also compared them with Curley Fletcher's original poem, which had first been published in 1931, just a couple of years before the two men learned it from Ray Ailee. I did not have access to the interim oral version Slim and Mike heard from Ray but have assumed it to be closer to the original than either Slim's or Mike's recitations. Some changes from Fletcher's original that are the same in both Slim's and Mike's versions, such as the omission of stanzas eighteen through twenty-one, were probably the same in Ray's version.

There are numerous differences between Slim's and Mike's recitations, and these are instructive because they must have been made by one or the other reciter. Changes between Curley Fletcher's original and the derivative versions reflect changes wrought in a very few generations of oral transmission—perhaps only two.

Fletcher's original "Flyin' Outlaw" is a poem of twenty-eight stanzas of four lines each. Each line has three stressed syllables and varying numbers of unstressed ones, with the second and fourth lines rhyming. The story relates the Pegasus legend of Greek mythology, retold in cowboy vernacular. What follows is Mike Landon's recititation; Curley Fletcher's original version appears in *Songs of the Sage*.[10]

Mustang with Wings

Come gather around me, you waddies,
Listen to me real close.
'N I'll tell you a yarn about a mustang
That must have been a ghost.

Now, you-all must have heard of this cayuse
In the days when folks called them steeds.
He ranged in the sky with the angels,
And he only come down for his feed.

He was owned by a big outfit,
Sisters, the Methuses, they say.
They always kept him in hobbles,
Till he broke 'em and got away.

For years they tried hard to catch him,
But he kept right on runnin' free.
Riders wore way too much clothing;
Cowboys were knights then, you see.

Well, he went by the name of Pegasus
And he had him some wings for to fly.
He watered and grazed in the badlands
And he ranged around in the sky.

He sure has a bad reputation,
I don't savvy just how it begins,
Part eagle, part horse and part devil,
They claim that he's meaner than sin.

Well, I was ridin' that old rimrock country,
One day above Wild Horse Springs,
When I fell nearly out of my saddle
As this cayuse sails in on his wings.

It seemed like I must be plumb crazy,
As I gaze up over the bank,

I'm a-watchin' this albino mustang,
He's a-plumin' his wings while he drank.

Soon, he filled up on water.
Wings folded, he starts in to graze.
I notice he's headin' up my way,
So I straighten myself in a daze.

Then I come to all excited,
My hands are both tremblin' with hope,
I reaches down on my saddle,
And fumbles as I loosen my rope.

Ready, I rode right out at him,
I'm a-spurrin' and a-buildin' a loop,
An' before he could turn or get goin',
I throwed, and it fit like a hoop.

Well, I jerked in my slack and I dallied,
I turned, and my bronc throwed him neat.
He let out a blood-curdlin' beller
While I'm at him, a-hogtyin' his feet.

I put my hackamore on him,
Made a blindfold for his eyes,
Then hobbled his wings close together
So he can't go back to the skies.

Then I set my saddle down on him,
My cinches cut deep in his hide,
And take out the slack in my spur straps
'Cause it looked like a pretty tough ride.

Well, I stepped on him, just like he was gentle,
I'm a little bit nervous, you bet,
But I felt pretty sure I could ride him,
'Cause I still got his wings hobbled yet.

Well, I raised the blinds and he snorted,
He stepped like he's walkin' on eggs,
Then he grunts and explodes like a pistol
And I see he's at home on his legs.

Well, I have a deep seat in my saddle,
My spurs are both bogged in the cinch,

I ain't gonna take any chances;
He ain't gonna budge me an inch.

Wolves, panthers an' grizzlies,
Catamounds, tarantlers and such,
Rattlesnakes, wild women and bad whiskey,
All stacked up beside him wasn't much.

Well, he keeps gettin' rougher and rougher,
I'm weary, and I kinda wish that he's through,
I have me both hands full of leather,
'Cause he's spinnin' and sunfishin', too.

Then he hit the ground with a twister
That broke those wing hobbles right there.
And before I could turn loose or quit him,
We're a-sailin' way out in the air.

Well, he smoothed out and he kept right on climbin',
Till away down, miles below,
I could see the tops of the mountains
And their peaks are all covered with snow.

While up through the clouds I'm a-freezin',
I'm sick and I'm dizzy, to boot,
I was wishin' that I had one of them things
That they call a parachute.

Then I must have gone plumb loco,
Or maybe I dropped off to sleep,
'Cause when I come to, I'm a-lyin'
Right down on the ground in a heap.

Now, he might have had wings like an angel,
He might have been light on his feet,
But he'd oughta had horns like the devil
And a mouth fit for eatin' raw meat.

I've lost me a saddle and a blanket,
Hackamore, rope and some things,
But I'm right proud to be here to tell you,
To stay away from these horses with wings.[11]

In both Slim's and Mike's versions, several changes seem due to imperfect understanding. The first concerns Curley's classical allusion to the Muses. Slim calls them "some sisters, the mooses."[12] Mike, however, has named them "the Methuses." In Slim's version, the name "Pegasus" is replaced by the cryptic "Euchias" (Yew-ky-us); Mike says "Pegasus" but pronounces it "Pe-GAY-sus." Neither reciter has this avian Pegasus "preenin' his wings" as in Fletcher's original. Slim's mustang is "pruning his wings as he drank" (an arresting image), and Mike's is "a-plumin' his wings."

Both reciters modified the language substantially to suit their own conversational styles, and, perhaps surprisingly, both also corrected Curley Fletcher's vernacular. The conversational changes were made to the incidental language of the poem, the verbal mortar that holds the substance of the story together. Thus, where Fletcher's original has "yuh mighta heard of a cayuse," Slim says, "You've probably heard of a cayuse," and Mike's version is "now, you-all must have heard of this cayuse." And where Curley's original is "I grabs me both hands full of leather," Slim's recitation has "I got both hands full of leather," and Mike says, "I have me both hands full of leather." In general, Slim's recitation emphasizes the regular meter of the poem; Mike's, however, is more casual in tone and sometimes departs from regular meter in favor of a more off-hand conversational style.

Curley Fletcher made liberal use of vernacular devices in "The Flyin' Outlaw" and in all his cowboy poetry, including nonstandard verb forms that dropped final *gs* and appended an *a-*:

And then I comes to, all excited,
My hands is a-tremblin' in hope,
As I reaches down on my saddle
And fumbles a noose in my rope.

Both Slim's and Mike's recitations modify grammatical irregularities present in the original poem. Often these changes correct errors contained in the original; sometimes they modify Fletcher's vernacular in favor of the reciter's own. Instead of Curley's "I lets him up when he's saddled," Slim says, "I put my saddle on him"; Mike comments, "Then I set my saddle down on him." Where the original has "I raises the blinds and he's snortin'," Slim's version has "I pulled up the blinds, and he's snorting," and Mike says, "Well, I raised the blinds and he snorted."

Several changes in Mike's recitation are particularly intriguing because they illustrate the close fit between Mike's narrative and his methods of working stock. I suspect that Mike could not tell a story that did not make sense in the way it described cowboy work. In his tenth stanza he relates, "I reaches down on my saddle, and fumbles as I loosen my rope." This is a departure from Fletcher's original ("I reaches down on my saddle and fumbles a noose in my rope"), which is closely paralleled by Slim's version. The difference is important to a working cowboy. Mike's narrator has not yet made his loop, so he has to proceed to this critical step in the next stanza: "Ready, I ride right out at him / I'm a-spurrin' and a-buildin' a loop." In both the original and Slim's recitation, however, the line is "spurrin' and swingin' my loop."

The second work-related change in Mike's recitation has to do with blinders. "I put my hackamore on him, / and a pair of blinds on his eyes," state Curley and Slim. Mike, however, must have thought that the average range-riding cowboy didn't carry a pair of blinds and says, "I put my hackamore on him, made a blindfold for his eyes." Also, both Slim's and Mike's narratives have "cinches," plural, sunk in the mustang's hide (stanzas thirteen and fourteen), compared with the original's singular cinch. Slim and Mike were accustomed to riding double-rigged saddles that had two cinches, whereas Curley Fletcher probably used the single-rigged saddle more popular in the buckaroo country of northern California and Nevada where he did much of his cowboy work.

Perhaps the most remarkable finding from this comparison is how little the substance of the poem has changed. Very few changes affect the overall course of the narrative, and substantive changes are relatively minor, such as Mike's substitution of "wild women" for Curley's "scorpions" in the catalog of comparative dangers that pale beside the marauding mustang. The narrative survived intact in all important features. The other element that survived completely unaltered in both reciters' versions—through fifty years of memory—was the integrity of the rhyming pairs. Neither reciter had lost or replaced a single rhyming word out of the twenty-four rhyming pairs in the stanzas they recited.

Anecdotal evidence from fieldwork with cowboy reciters yields insights into the processes through which folk poetry changes. These changes are not always anonymous but may be traceable to individual reciters. They are often the result of imperfect understanding, faulty memory, or regional differences in work and terminology. They are also sometimes the result of the exercise of deliberate and purposeful artistic intent.

Notes

1. *Orejana Bull for Cowboys Only* was self-published by Gail I. Gardner in six editions, the first issued in 1935. A seventh edition was published in 1987 by the Sharlot Hall Museum Press, 415 W. Gurley St., Prescott, AZ 86301, and remains in print.

2. This line, a puzzler, indicates a lack of understanding of the work involved, either on the reciter's part or one of his sources. Its meaning is opposite from Gardner's original "didn't bush-up by day." A cow that bushed-up successfully hid from the cowboys—or made it so difficult to capture her by getting into the thickest brush available that they would leave her for another day. A cow that "didn't show up by day" was not likely to be handled at all.

3. This is another puzzler, perhaps created by the necessity of finding something to make a line ending in "his inside." Gardner's original line is "could ile up his inside." The rhyming pair survived intact, but the meaning of the line was lost somewhere along the way.

4. This clever line with its internal rhyme occurs in many variants of "Sierry Petes," including Powder River Jack Lee's.

5. The reciter clearly said "dollies" instead of Gardner's original "dallies" (turns of rope taken around the saddle horn to secure the catch rope).

6. This line is hard to interpret and probably is another instance of loss of meaning due to imperfect understanding of the work involved. In the rough, mountainous country of northern Arizona, a wild cow full of fight and difficult to lead would be "necked to a black-jack oak," or tied by the neck with a short line to a stout scrub-oak tree and left overnight to work its fight out against the tree. The rhyming pair survives intact, requiring the reciter to fill in a line that more or less makes sense and ends with the words "black-jack oak."

7. Powder River Jack Lee, "Tying Knots in the Devil's Tail," in *The Stampede, and Other Tales of the Far West* (Greensburg, Pa.: Standardized Press, [1938?]).

8. This text is excerpted from Katie Lee, *Ten Thousand Goddam Cattle: A History of the American Cowboy in Song, Story, and Verse* (Flagstaff, Ariz.: Northland Press, 1976), 122–23. "Little Joe, the Wrangler" is in N. Howard ("Jack") Thorp and Austin Fife and Alta Fife, *Songs of the Cowboys* (1908), (New York: Clarkson N. Potter, 1966), 28–37.

9. The original text of "The Bosky Steer" can be found in Henry Herbert Knibbs, *Songs of the Lost Frontier* (Boston: Houghton Mifflin, 1930), 73–74.

10. Curley Fletcher, *Songs of the Sage* (1931), reprinted as *Songs of the Sage: The Poetry of Curley Fletcher,* ed. Hal Cannon (Salt Lake City: Gibbs Smith, 1986). "The Flyin' Outlaw" appears on pages 60–64 in the latter edition.

11. Mike Landon, "Mustang with Wings," fieldwork audio tape no. FLK 077, Sharlot Hall Museum folklore collection.

12. Slim Kite, "Mustang with Wings," fieldwork audio tape no. FLK 038, Sharlot Hall Museum folklore collection.

8

Cowboy Libraries and Lingo

Buck Ramsey

Although I have never seen one, I would give two red blankets plus all I can make braiding bridles for all 303 of the Bull Durham Classics. I had begun to fear that a few lines spoken by a Eugene Manlove Rhodes character and my cowboy gullibility were the only evidence that this set of books ever existed, because I contacted Bull Durham headquarters and folks there had never heard of them.

I was dead certain that once, years ago, I was reading along in a book by Rhodes, and one of his characters, taking a mental census of cowpunchers, attributed to bunkhouse libraries stocked with this set of books a large portion of the general intellectual overload peculiar to cowboys. The claim was made, as I recall, that those cowboys out of the old rock—many of whom read like monks in the great old literature shunted aside by all but a few readers—could mail in a dime with a tag from a Bull Durham tobacco pouch and get in return one of those 303 literary classics ranging from the old Greeks to books by early American authors whose copyrights had run out.

It turns out my ideas were part gullibility and part fact. I unreasonably imagined a tag and a dime would get you a complete volume of the classic requested, but it turns out they were abridged to warbag or chap-pocket size. At the 1993 Cowboy Poetry Gathering in Prescott, Arizona, I ran into an old-timer, Mike Dawson, who holds forth in conversation or before a crowd like he read every one of them. He was carrying around a small stack of the old booklets. Not hefty enough to be a burden to the light traveler or reader, they were past adequate for teasing the fancy and for whipping and spurring the imagination.

With the exception of those who still live in about the same way as in the old days, modern cowboys don't seem to be as deep and avid readers as the old-timers, although they still probably read more for pleasure and a private kind of enlightenment than the average citizen. But those old birds never flashed their feathers. For every hundred, surely twenty-five were real readers, and an outsider would not have guessed it of more than one of them. For those old cowboys partial to books, reading jags were the regular winding down of the day's circle.

Most of the bunkhouse bookers I have known were very eclectic in their reading. Cowboys seldom claimed expertise at anything; they just showed it. With regard to intellectual matters, they would not have given sign of any knowledge unnecessary to their tasks. But there were specialists among them. I recall one scholar who read the Bible to fortify his faith and a debunker who read it to delve for evidence that it just didn't add up.

Speaking of the Bible, there is no doubt that in the cowboy poems and songs out of the old leather, the Bible among the old books was the most prominent source of reference. It says something about the cowpuncher's religious attitudes that the Bible was used more for relating to fellow herdsmen than as a source of inspiration. For instance, Badger Clark—a preacher's son—often referred to Old Testament characters in his poems: "Bachin'" is about Adam, and the "Old Cow Man" about Job. Here is the last stanza of "From Town" as the puncher, riding up the rocky trail from town, reflects on days of yore:

Since the days that Lot and Abram split the Jordan range in halves,
    Just to fix it so their punchers wouldn't fight,
Since old Jacob skinned his dad-in-law for six years' crop of calves
    And then hit the trail for Canaan in the night,
There has been a taste for battle 'mong the men that follow cattle
    And a love of doin' things that's wild and strange,
And the warmth of Laban's words when he missed his speckled herds
    Still is useful in the language of the range.[1]

With regard to church-house religion, Harry E. Chrisman, clearly a very religious man himself, summed up the attitude of nearly all the cowboys he knew: "He was quick to deny any particular awareness of religion in its orthodox sense or admit to any attachment for the 'sky pilots' who traveled the missionary routes around the ranches, attempting to foist their brand of religion upon men who had been living a deep and full brand of work-a-day Christianity every day, month in and month out, for years."[2]

There is a touching and typical moment of cowboy religious testimony in the song "Cowboy in Church," when the cowboy finds himself in town, and, as he tells it, "I heard the churchbell ringing, I didn't know 'twas Sunday, / For on the plains we scarcely knew a Sunday from a Monday." He wasn't rigged out in Sunday-go-to-meeting garb, and the congregation seemed to regard him as someone out of place: "Although the goodly parson in his vestry garb arrayed / Was dressed the same as I was in the trappings of his trade." And although it appeared a cowboy might not fit too well in a church house, he concludes (and here the great Glenn Ohrlin in his version cribs a little from Robert Service):

But at that last great roundup when before the throne we stand,
When it is decided what will be our final brand,
I have a hunch that we'll be judged by what we are inside,
And He alone shall judge His own, so I His judgment bide.[3]

Most of the trail drivers were southern boys, and the old gospel hymns as much as any literature probably influenced their use of the written language when dealing with fate and the serious side of life. "Little Joe, the Wrangler" and "My Little Old Sod Shanty on the Plain" are two of many cowboy songs that have the same tune as a hymn; both are sung to the tune of "Lily of the Valley."[4]

I have never met a cowboy puffed up enough with tribal hubris to make the claim, but I am sure that when the range was grass side up and cows wore horns some of those old graduates of the camp and trail felt close enough to the gods to think that when the cowboy race was created, sometime around the middle of the nineteenth century, the lingo was handed down to them complete, springing whole from the brow of some Olympian range boss.

That, of course, was not the case. But a healthy portion of the language did spring directly or indirectly from Olympus. When you stay up late, flipping station to station on your TV, and hear a big-hatted dude say he saw some hombre "bite the dust," he is using a bit of the language the old-timers lifted from a translation of Homer's *Iliad* by Samuel Butler that was popular in the nineteenth century. I first opened the *Iliad* because I was assured it was one salty tale of horsemen. I was not disappointed. The description Homer rationed to the best men of the book was "breaker of horses," and because I was one I took care to count the phrase in one translation (Richard Lattimore's) fifty-three times, including the moving final line of the tale: "Such was their burial of Hektor, breaker of horses."[5]

Most if not all cowpunchers consider themselves to some extent "breakers of horses." But they have a special place in their hearts for the real rough-stock riders, the bronc stompers and peelers who handle the rough string. A song called "Pitch, You Wild Outlaw, Pitch," which I learned from a Montana cowboy-song encyclopedia named Duane Dickinson, captures the spirit of this class of cowpuncher:

You been roped and saddled and bridled and straddled,
  I've spurred you and quirted you, too.

You squealed and cavorted and sunfished and snorted
As 'round the corral we both flew.
Your temper is sassy, your actions are classy,
For buckin' you sure got an itch.
Course, I'll never trust you till after I bust you,
So pitch, you wild outlaw, pitch.
Your eyes are a-burnin' and you are a-yearnin'
To git me down there in the dirt.
So hop to it feller, there's no streak of yeller
Beneath my old blue denim shirt. . . .

This puncher clearly loves what he is doing and loves as well the adversary that gives him the chance to do it:

You are a jimdandy, you're tough and you're sandy,
The way that you do it is rich.
So keep on a-humpin' your back up and jumpin',
And pitch, you wild outlaw, pitch.

But he is one happy adversary who knows how this contest will end:

In spite of your kickin', you'll still find me stickin',
So let me just hand you this hunch.
You got me disgusted, you're gonna git busted,
Jist rode to a frazzle and sich.
If you only knew it, you'd give and come to it,
But pitch, you wild outlaw, pitch.[6]

I will always regret I didn't start taking notes when I was a boy among the cowboys along the Canadian River and while working around them later. So much colorful, wonderful language, although relished in the moment, was set on air and floated away forever. I recall being puzzled by something a cowboy (this same cowpuncher, I would later discover, liked to compare English translations of Homer) said about a puncher who had taken up farming. It was something like, "There's no way in hell anybody could ever get me yoked to a Sisyphus rock like that." I went scampering after the source of what he said and into Greek mythology. And to this day it is as near to a perfect metaphor as any I have heard or read for people who till the soil for a living.

There was something about the Greeks that greatly appealed to the old cowpunchers, probably because they thought of the Greeks as the first in that long and noble lineage of men on horseback that ended with, as best they could tell, their noble selves. Pegasus got a lot of play, of course—in Curley Fletcher's "The

Flyin' Outlaw" and where Badger Clark writes: "When my Pegasus is lopin', / Ory-eyed and on the bust."[7]

There is a curious little publication called *A Bronco Pegasus* (1928), a mixed bag of poetry by Charles F. Lummis. He was a Harvard man, a friend and confidant of Teddy Roosevelt, and he was assisted in putting his book together by Henry Herbert Knibbs, one of the more talented and prominent writers of cowboy fiction and poetry early in the twentieth century. Lummis, like Badger Clark, came west for its healing powers and soon fell to writing verse about the people and places around him. As a study in cowboy attitude or lingo it wouldn't rank high as recommended reading, but it has its moments. One is a poem from 1889 called "Sartor Resartus"—the title of a famous book by the English writer Thomas Carlyle—subtitled "While the Train Stops at Albuquerque." A professor and a pretty widow are in conversation, and, spotting a cowboy, she exclaims, "Ah, what a *man!* / I mean yon cowboy—what embodied force!" The professor tries to distract her attention from the heathen: "But hear his speech, how cultureless and slack—/ 'Hello, old maverick! How they comin', Pard?'"

The Pretty Widow:
"Well, I don't *care!* He's lovely! And I hate—"
The Professor, savagely:
"Those who do not so ignorantly speak as your Eureka?"
The Cowboy:
"Sir, the aspirate!
You'll find the word's Heureka in the Greek!"
The Professor, quite losing himself:
"Were you at Squantum University
I'd beat some information into you!"
The Cowboy, blandly:
"Thanks awfully! I collared one degree,
Summa cum laude, Harvard, '82!"[8]

The labors of Hercules and such were no doubt parodied by those old punchers until they became the big-brag, wild-wolf-of-the-world stories turned into poems by cowboy poets. The literature is rife with larger-than-life tales of cowboys roping mountain lions and bears. At least one folklorist—or was it Carl Sandburg?—claimed Clark's "The Glory Trail" ("High Chin Bob") was the best folk song to come out of the cowboy West, and then there's "Bear Ropin' Buckaroo" by S. Omar Barker.[9] But for imaginative cowboy lingo and outlandish braggadocio, Badger Clark's "The Legend of Boastful Bill" is hard to beat:

"I'm the one to take such rakin's as a joke.
Some one hand me up the makin's of a smoke!

If you think my fame needs bright'nin'
W'y I'll rope a streak of lightnin'
And I'll cinch 'im up and spur 'im till he's broke."

Bill goes off on one hell of a ride, but as a challenge this raging bronc is for Boastful Bill about like hairpinning Aunt Maude's milk cow. "I'm too good for earthly ridin'" he says as he disappears into the heavens. His pals figure he is spending his time yanking at "some celestial outlaw's bit." But they are sure "when the lightnin' flares and flickers" that they can hear him shouting, in some of the best lingoistic superlatives in the literature, messages to the thin-skinned generations to come, messages to the effect that he and his kind were the best and there will never be any more like them.[10] (In fact, how many of us became Icarus in our longing to ride too close to the sun?)

One of the most remarkable offerings in the literature of the West is the 1959 Folkways album of a cappella cowboy songs by Harry Jackson, who learned the songs working with cowboys and who has since become preeminent among western artists and sculptors. He sings the songs the way we first heard them on the range, and there is no better way to get the full effect of cowboy talk than listening to this album. And while we're on the subject of brag talk, sample this passage by Jackson:

> I was full-growed with nine rows of jaw teeth and holes bored for more. There was spurs on my feet and a rawhide quirt in my hand, and when they opens the chute I come out a-riding a panther and a-roping the long-horned whales. I've rode everything with hair on it, and I've rode a few things that was too rough to grow any hair. I've rode bull moose on the prod, the grizzlies and long bolts of lightning. Mountain lions are my playmates and when I feels cold and lonesome, I sleeps in a den of rattlesnakes 'cause they always makes me nice and warm. To keep alive I eat stick dynamite and cactus.[11]

Before you know it, he turns into a cowboy who would make Paul Bunyan want to go to work on his reputation.

Mining those old epics, the cowboys and their singers and poets and tellers of tales fashioned their own epic with its own powerful language, and it became the one mythology the United States would give to the world. There was no better commercial fodder for hack writers and, later, movie-makers. But the western fabulists and oaters missed what the cowpuncher was all about. (Basically, he was hired to go out and tend to cattle, to be in the right place on horseback at the right time. His was perhaps the highest skill for the lowest pay in the country. And intertwined with all this was a calling, a way, an idea of self and tribe that will be understood by but a few until the end of time.) But those who created the oaters also had sense enough to go back to the old sources for their plots and advice. Zane Grey wrote or confessed in an interview somewhere that in plotting his novels he stuck strictly to Aristotle's plot prescriptions in *The Poetics,* and surely there could be no better plot of a hero coming to the rescue and riding off into the sunset with cries of gratitude trailing behind him than Hercules in Euripides' *Alcestis.*

Could a cowpuncher read *Don Quixote* without imagining himself and some pardner in the roles of the knight-errant and his sidekick Sancho Panza? In fact, how many others (Roy and Gabby, Gene and Smiley) followed the formula but allowed the hero to be true-blue and tall in the saddle on a Rocinante sleek and strong and tireless, letting the sidekick play the foil and carry the burden of absurdity?

How many of those lingo-laden poems and tales grew out of that Quixotic quest? The solid old literature is full of well-meaning tenderfeet wanting to share in the glory they saw in the cowboy manner and idea of himself. D. J. O'Malley's "D-2 Horse Wrangler" takes a twist on the theme wherein the town-dude gets the job and greatly regrets it, concluding about cowpunching:

Before you try it, go kiss your wife,
Get a heavy insurance on your life,
Then shoot yourself with a butcher knife,
It's far the easiest way.[12]

On the other hand, E. A. Brininstool's dude in "The Disappointed Tenderfoot" is disenchanted in a far different manner. He comes west seeking all the glories he has been told about, and the poem concludes:

And no one knew of a branding bee or a steer roundup that he longed to see.
But the oldest settler named Six-Gun Sim rolled a cigarette and remarked to him:
"The West hez gone to the East, my son, and it's only in tents sich things is done."[13]

The pranksters and their foils inevitably created a flip side of the coin. Out of these situations grew poems and songs like the great classic "The Zebra Dun," in which a fellow who looks and acts and talks every inch the tenderfoot takes the bait, in this case the worst horse in the remuda, and rides the living thunder out of it to the utter amazement of the pranksters gathered for the show.[14]

Cowboys would read of the Knights of the Round Table and of feats by men and horses with the involvement and wonder of children watching Saturday-morning television and would enter into the plots like cloistered homemakers reading grocery-store novels or watching soap operas. Virtually all the cowboy code concerning how best to go about your labors, treat friends and strangers, and hang or be hanged was drawn from times when the best men were horseback, from Bellerophontes on Pegasus to Robert E. Lee on Traveler.

S. Omar Barker was good at defining the cowboy code in poems like "The Unpardonable Sin," "Cow Country Saying," and "Cowboy Saying" ("don't whittle towards you, and don't spit against the wind"). Curley Fletcher said it well in "The Cowboy's Prayer":

I've always been good to my horses,
Till today I ain't never ate sheep.
I never did shirk on no round-up,
And I've always been worth my keep.[15]

One of my favorite cowboy sentiments is one I heard in a bunkhouse or around some wagon: "I don't care if he's purple and has orange breath as long as his head is screwed on straight and his heart is cradled right in his breast."

That body of literature contained in the 303 Bull Durham Classics has influenced all of Western civilization, but it's an influence that has seeped in over the centuries. The portion of those classics having to do with men horseback seems to have been a revelation for cowboy readers and bards, and maybe that is one reason the cowboy tribe, in the minds of many, was made into, or contrived to become, or became by providential anointment a race apart with its own mythology and code and lingo.

Other groups since—honky-tonk musicians, truck drivers, Hell's Angels, government spooks, politicians, Wobblies (who came close but were infected with doctrine, which always eats away at integrity)—have tried to become something special and apart, or publicists and hack writers have tried to do it for them, but all have fallen short. Just about all such groups have resorted to fashioning themselves "the last cowboys," but at best they lack understanding of what the cowboy was all about and at worst they drag him into a philosophical or aesthetic gutter.

Waylon Jennings and Willie Nelson are damn good old boys and bring enough joy to cowboys to be forgiven for fashioning themselves as the nostalgic vestige of the breed, but for all its hats and boots the honky-tonk crowd is no closer to the cowboy in character and attitude and lingo than actors in movie and television westerns. Henry Kissinger, who might get my vote for America's representative to the International Pantheon of Culprits, said somewhere, "I've always acted alone. Americans admire that enormously. Americans admire the cowboy leading the caravan alone, the cowboy entering the village alone on his horse . . . a Wild West Tale, if you like." Offering himself up as America's cowboy, he dragged the tribe down to a level no one bottomed until Ronald Reagan was inducted into the Cowboy Hall of Fame. When political leaders such as these cause murder and mayhem to people who won't act the way American corporate bosses think they should, pundits call them "cowboys," intending disdain. They greatly insult the thing compared to and lend honor undeserved to that compared.

One politician, Teddy Roosevelt, stood himself in pretty good stead with cowboys. Even though they recognized his patronizing way with them, they blamed it on inbred infirmities typical of his class, recognized his good intentions, and forgave him. He seemed to have admired the cowboy way, its skill and manner, and saw in the cowpuncher the kind of man he wanted around him in battle. A wordsmith himself, Roosevelt recognized their lingo "of strong effect," as Mark Twain described it, and jotted down a good bit of it for his own use. His pithy, straightforward manner with the language was, more than anything, what set him apart from other presidents. He is credited with sayings like "clean as a hound's tooth" and "pussyfootin'"; once he called the president of Venezuela a "pithecanthropoid." Teddy was an honest man, and he probably somewhere admitted picking up most of this kind of colorful talk from the cowboys he was around during his Dakota days. You can bet that's where it came from.

In *Ranch Life and the Hunting-Trail* Roosevelt tells of a miserable night when he and some of the cowboys who worked on his outfit were getting ready to bed down. They could see in the distance, where the cattle were beginning to drift out of control with the storm: "Just as we were preparing to turn into bed, with the certainty of a night of more or less chilly misery ahead of us, one of my men, an iron-faced personage, whom no one would ever have dreamed had a weakness for poetry, looked towards the plain where the cattle were, and remarked, 'I guess there's "racing and chasing on Cannobie Lea" now, sure.'"[16] The cowboy had done his reading. He was quoting a line from "Lochinvar," a song sung by a character in *Marmion* by Sir Walter Scott, who, like Bobby Burns, was very popular among the cowboy tribe, thickly populated by Scots and heavily influenced by the Celtic spirit.

Although dime novelists and oater-writers figured into the creation of a cow-country literature, others wrote with a higher level of authenticity and came across with enough genuine lingo and attitude for the cowboys who read them to confer levels of merit according to how close each was to the mark. Andy Adams was great. Teddy Blue and Ike Blasingame were wonderful, but one read them wishing they had stuck to their own language, their own way of speaking, and written without interference. Some fine cowboy improvisations on normal thought and language are to be found in the writings of Owen Wister, Emerson Hough, B. M. Bowers (Mrs. Bertha Muzzy Sinclair), Alfred Henry Lewis, Hamlin Garland, Clarence E. Mulford, Henry Wallace Phillips, James Barton Adams, and Larry Chittenden. O. Henry had such an uncanny ear for language and accurate eye for manner and detail that he was able, for my taste, to write some of the best moments in cowboy literature in his stories about the West. Will Rogers, one of my heroes, left the cowboy life to make a living entertaining—or, rather, informing—the general public. But he never sold his saddle, and the code and tradition of the true-blue cowboy informed his every word and deed. J. Frank Dobie, though, might have been right when he advised anyone wanting to learn about cowboys to read the writings of Charlie Russell, Ross Santee, and Eugene Manlove Rhodes, all of whom earned wages horseback in cow country and wrote about what they knew to be true.

As good a line as ever described a cowboy was Santee's: "The best you could say about a man was that he was good to his horse, and the worst was that he wasn't." Rhodes wrote well and truly from his experience horseback (it was said in his cowpunch days he could ride anything with hair), but I can't help thinking he fell a little short by trying too hard. He never really seemed to aim his writings at his cowboy pals, aspiring instead to interpret the West for a more universal audience. But better to try greatly and fall short than to try commonly and succeed. As for Russell, on any day when I have done my duty I will have taken a moment to thank the gods for what little writing he left us and wonder why they didn't allow more of it. Open one of the books of this greatest of cowboy painters at any page and you'll encounter cowboy prose lingo in its highest form. I am particularly fond of these three cowboy writers because the deep-down decency that makes the starter dough rise in those called to the cowboy way was full dose in them and because they had the genuine cowboy's bottom savvy that what a man can do is what counts, not what he can get.

There was a time in my life when I occasionally took notes while reading and listening, thinking I might someday compile a sort of cowboy-lingo glossary. Then someone gave me one of Ramon Adams's books and I realized again you are never the first to cross a river. He got down a lot of lingo but not as an insider. I suspect he rode as in bridlepaths and spent nights on the prairie in the Big House of the boss rather than at the wagon or in the bunkhouse. For all his keen attention to their lingo and manner, he so misunderstood what the cowboy was all about that he could think he was complimenting a certain cowboy by commenting that he seemed bright and competent enough to become a productive member of society if he ever chose to sell his saddle and get a real job in the business world. Still, he preserved a lot of the old lingo, so bless him.

If philosophy is, as someone wrote, the sublime ability to say the obvious, then many an old cowpuncher muttering observations on matters at hand deserved the label. There are apt sayings enough to fill books, but some come especially to mind: "If that son-of-a-bitch don't go to hell, there ain't no use in having one"; "some minds let more out than in"; and "he's like the stuffed fish—shoulda kept his mouth shut." And there was the cowboy who was asked by a proper sort of Englishman, "Tell me, my good man, where is your master?" He replied, "That son-of-a-bitch ain't been born yet."

He could be like the philosopher in other ways, wandering in his talk off the clear path to take the dimmest trail. It might have been because his mouth wasn't keeping time with his head, but he might have just been stringing it to a greener, as in Barker's "A Turkey Tale for Tenderfeet" or "The Ballad of Cowboy Lou."[17] John H. Dewing is credited with saying, "Ranch lingo is perfectly easy to understand. All you've got to do is know in advance what the other fellow means, and then pay no attention to what he says."

But cowboys liked most of all in their talk to frame an image and let it shine, playing the language down so subtly that an idea would almost pass by before it grabbed you or prickling it up to where an idea would slap you like a cactus. They would take in what was around them at a glance, mine its ore, and come up with a gem: "It was so dark the bats stayed home"; "she looked at me like I was a blizzard in a fairy tale"; "that horse was as ganted as a gutted snowbird; its legs looked like the running gears of a katydid"; "it was so dry the range wouldn't graze a horny toad"; and "Curly had about as much hair as a Mexican dog, and they're fixed for hair 'bout like a sausage."

Until a few years ago it appeared the literary bell mares of the Victorian era had succeeded in keeping cowboy cussing off the printed page, but Guy Logsdon has resurrected enough to provide an idea of its depraved eloquence in *"The Whorehouse Bells Were Ringing."*[18] Cussing contests were common around the wagon, and not a few cowboys kept their cussing skills honed contest-sharp. Some of them developed a strain of cussing to be used strictly in polite society. For example, a flustered cowboy wishing to cut some civilian in with the culls while socializing among the manicured set might call him a "rancid left-handed dadgummed parallelogram."

I suppose a caricaturist reading all this might draw a cowboy with a tasseled mortarboard on his head, his chin in his hand and an elbow on his knee. I will no doubt outrage a lot of the school crowd with these claims to cowboy literacy. Worse yet, I will probably anger some cowpunchers who think I'm suggesting that a bunch of effete waddies are riding out there among them. In truth, there have always been many cowboys who shunned the books. An old puncher in Agnes Morley Cleaveland's *No Life for a Lady* sums up the attitude of his kind when he says, "I never read atall 'cept when I don't want to think, which ain't often."[19] One would be foolish to underestimate the mental census of the watchers, listeners, and thinkers of the tribe because many of them who will not get near a book can sing a dozen songs or string poems end to end from memory. And books are by no means necessary to intellectual discussion and philosophical debate in the bunkhouse or cow camp. There are always canned, bottled, and packaged goods around with labels, and as lengthy and interesting confab as I was ever privy to was about how "ozs." should be pronounced.

There are enough poems, articles, and books entitled something like "The Last Cowboy" to fill a parlor of library shelves. The trend started in the 1890s when ranchers began fencing the range and shutting off the long trails. It seems every other poem or piece written these days is about the cowboy's disappearing way of life. Rewriting this piece, I lost count of the "old's" I edited out. In fact, writing about the cowboy tribe, I notice I stayed mostly in the past tense, as if the consummate nostalgia of what the old puncher said constantly shrouded my thought: "Like anything worth talking about, it happened a long time ago." Here is Badger Clark in "The Passing of the Trail":

The trail's a lane, the trail's a lane.
    Dead is the branding fire.
The prairies wild are tame and mild,
    All close-corralled with wire.

The sunburnt demigods who ranged
    And laughed and lived so free
Have topped the last divide, or changed
    To men like you and me.[20]

And that true-blue master of the old cowboy poets Bruce Kiskaddon wrote about "The Old Night Hawk":

I can see the East is gettin' gray,
I'll gather the hosses soon,
And faint from the valley far away
Comes the drone of the last guard's tune.
Yes, life is just like the night-herd's song
As the long years come and go.
You start with a swing that is free and strong,
And finish up tired and slow.[21]

It was pure contrivance that allowed Badger Clark to bow out with the line about how men of the cow country have "changed / To men like you and me," with grace and modesty admitting that as fine a representative as he was at its poetry roundups, he was not a part of the cowboy tribe. Clark was a well-educated man who sojourned west to Arizona for his health. A friendly rancher set him up in a camp where he was neither a paying boarder nor a paid hand. He was gifted with language, and he had an uncanny ear for cowboy lingo and an eye for style and mannerisms. But with regard to cowboy literature, the essential facts are that he wrote from observation with an acquired language. He wrote from the heart but through a mental process that created a small fissure between his poetry and authenticity.

Of the poets of earlier generations, Bruce Kiskaddon is the most popular among contemporary cowboy poets, particularly for those who have earned wages punching cows. Very few cowboys who prefer Kiskaddon over Clark even know that Kiskaddon was a hired man horseback and Clark was not. They are drawn to Kiskaddon instinctively, although Clark by any formal measure would be judged superior. The deepest analysis I have heard from a cowboy about why he prefers Kiskaddon over such great poets as Clark or Knibbs or Curley Fletcher was that "his stuff just has the right smell to it." For a puncher that explanation is adequate—in fact, it speaks volumes.

I need to throw in a word for Fletcher here. He is deservedly a great favorite among cowboys and probably the most widely read of the earlier cowboy poets by the larger public. He was more of an arena hand than a pasture cowboy, but he had a great feel for livestock and knew cowboy thinking and the lingo. You might say he fell somewhere between Kiskaddon and Clark—an average of two poets of excellence. And as any cowman will tell you, it's the vigor of the hybrid that pays off when the gavel falls at the sale.

By all accounts Kiskaddon was a forkéd cowboy before going to Hollywood in the early days of the movies to try to make bigger money as a stuntman. But he found a more stable job as a bellhop in one of the Hollywood hotels of the stars, and once a month he would trek down to the Western Union office to send off to a magazine another poem reminiscing about the old days. They were written straight from raw experience in the only language he knew, and they had about them a knowledge of horse moves and stock sounds, the feel of a saddle in all its moods, the jolt of the tightening rope with a raging brute on the end, and the unspoken communication across a campfire or horseback to horseback. He wrote in a natural shorthand from his heart to the heart of the cowboy, and there was nothing in between.

Many of Kiskaddon's poems are all of a piece at making a point, so it is unfair to quote them in part. But to give you a whiff of his stuff, I pull from the shelf a volume of his poetry and let it fall open at random to lift some lines:

(From "Alone")
The hills git awful quiet, when you have to camp alone.
It's mighty apt to set a feller thinkin'.
You always half way waken when a hoss shoe hits a stone,
Or you hear the sound of hobble chains a clinkin'.

It is then you know the idees that you really have in mind.
You think about the things you've done and said.
And you sometimes change the records that you nearly always find
In the back of almost every cow boy's head.

(For your own joy and edification, look up and read "Between the Lines" and "The Time to Decide," poems that cannot be taken apart.)[22]

After contrasting these two earlier cowboy poets, in the interest of symmetry I will conclude by contrasting two modern cowboy poets. First there's Baxter Black. He is a singular phenomenon in cowboy poetry who by no means would accept a Badger Clark as his model or inspiration, although as a trained veterinarian he was schooled in the Latin-based language of science. But then he went coyote crazy with a hilarious lingo of Anglo-Saxon sprinkled with Latinate parodies and created a body of comic poetry that has made him easily the most popular poet in the cow-country West.

Although I won't try to compare Baxter to Badger, I *will* compare him to Shakespeare for the exuberance with which he attacks the language—or, more likely, in his rambunctious response when the language attacks him. Beyond that, the poetry of each could be compared only in the far reaches of their imagery and in the fact that both are written to be acted out on the stage. But Baxter's poetry is contrived to be acted out only by himself. He may be the best stand-up comedian never to play the Catskills.

Because so many of his poems are plotted jokes, it is a shame to break them up, but here are some samplings. In "The Fall Run," the feedlot rider has hired on with a high-risk operator trying once again to beat the odds:

He bought big ol' soggy weaners . . . soaked up virus like a sponge!
He bought dime-off little leppies when the market made a lunge.
He bought Terramycin junkies that had been around the world
And hungry auction refugees that stuffed their cheeks like squirrels!

The fall run, of course, is a wreck and makes a wreck out of all hands. Everyone, though, eventually gets back to normal—except the boss:

He's been checked into a clinic where they put 'im every year
To recover and rejuvinate and let his conscience clear.
Sort of Jiffy Lube for managers who've lost their sense of place,
Where they git their eyes reglittered and their memory erased!

With Baxter there is a prize in nearly every line, and he is full of surprises. He will give you a bellyache with laughter, then grab your attention with some serious poetics:

There's a fingernail moon hangin' low in the sky,
The crickets make small talk as he passes by . . .

A bachelor cloud, thin as fog on a mirror,
Crossed over the moon and then disappeared.[23]

J. B. Allen writes poetry in the pure tradition of Kiskaddon and the few great cowboy poets who wrote from knowledge punching cows a-horseback. He is the best of the contemporary poets writing in the tradition. If you had walked up to J.B. a few years ago and suggested that he should try his hand at writing a poem, although he is a quiet and gentle man he would have considered backhanding you just hard enough to let you know he didn't appreciate the implication that he was a sissy. Since then more than seven hundred poems have flowed from his pen, and he still seems puzzled about where they are coming from. In fact, until you get to know him the words on the page do not jibe with the image or personality of the short-spoken, crusty man standing in front of you. They are one and all gems, and polished ones at that, although each is let go in its first draft.

In contrast to Baxter (except when Baxter chooses to be dead serious), J.B. seems to be curried by the language, soothed into a sometimes pensive, sometimes whimsical, nearly always nostalgic reflection; his lines are an easy saddletrot on a slow prowl through what cowboys think about. Most of them are, in effect, like that short look in greeting or parting, across the campfire or corral, that sends a message an hour's conversation could not get said. Again, some random samples, this one from "Treasures":

Do you mind some cold, clear mornin' settin' horseback on a bluff
When the air was still and ringin' in yore ears,
And you orta been a-foggin' down amongst the rocks and brush
To make it to that gunyun 'fore them steers? [canyon]

There was sumpthin' sorta held you in that frozen speck of time,
Paintin' pictures for the mem'ry times a-comin',
Till you leaned up on them swells and put that bronc down off the edge
And heard that weathered hat brim go to hummin'.

Things were boomin' back at home while you was pullin' second guard,
Accordin' to the letter that was brought,
But the sudden thought of leavin' was a thing just too blame hard
When a feller had what wizards dearly sought.

Lanky yearlin' colts a-dancin' as the mares slipped in to drink
While you used them stunted cedars for a blind,

Takin' notice of a grulla runnin' circles 'round the rest— [a mouse-colored horse]
And you aimed to keep that hombre on yore mind.

Or them new calves just a bouncin' on that early springtime grass
As the sun was turnin' hair to shinin' silk,
While them high-horned baby sitters kept a watchful, wary eye
On a country from the Pecos to the Milk.[24]

In "Purty Ain't Pardners," J.B. writes about a subject as profoundly ordinary as it is commonly overlooked and misunderstood:

With a smidge of bakin' powder on the tip end of her nose
Or dust from ringy cattle in her hair,
A feller's female pardner puts to shame a blushin' rose,
Fer there never was another'n quite so fair.

Calvin' heifers in the moonlight or feedin' hungry hands,
The pardnership they planted blooms in fact,
Runnin' deeper than just *wife* or *friend* to mesh the toughest strands,
Cullin' out them foolish thoughts of turnin' back.

Rare indeed is that small creature sent to share a puncher's life,
Blendin' spirit, mind, and purpose to the task,
Prized much higher than them pompered pets more prone to simply take,
Hidin' mercenary ways behind a mask.

Fair maidens flit like butterflies too fragile for the work,
Leadin' men to chase a rainbow's lurin' hues,
Tradin' pride and joy of livin' for the means to gild their wings
Till the winter once agin reveals their ruse

Sonnets penned to silken tresses fade as fevered flame subsides,
Hollow soundin' when the hoax has been revealed,
Longer lastin' is the love-light in her pardner's shinin' eyes,
Quietly signin' that the pardnership is sealed.[25]

Pardnership. Far above the "rugged individualism" of the money-changers seeking profits, cowboys work in a cooperation glued by a love and sense of protection for one another sure as that of good soldiers hard in battle. Badger Clark writes of it in "The Lost Pardner" and other poems.[26] The feel of that unspoken caring seems to come through in Bruce Kiskaddon's every other poem. As Baxter says in "Take Care of Your Friends":

Friend is a word that I don't throw around.
Though it's used and abused, I still like the sound.
I save it for people who've done right by me
And I know I can count on if ever need be.[27]

And here is J.B.'s "Compadres":

"Hey, Pard!" I heard 'im holler
As he strode across the floor;
I turned and saw him grinnin' ear to ear.
We stood like long-lost buddies
Though we'd met just once before
And lookin' back it'd been almost a year.

He didn't look much older
And his eye and grip still firm
As we started in to ketch up on the news,
'Cause it seemed we'd knowed each other
Fer a whole lot longer term
While we shared some common idys, thoughts, and views.

Miles and years still separate us,
Though we meet from time to time
Where some cowboys chance to gether, here and there,
And the friendship, quickly started,
With some agein' rates as "prime,"
Though our natures now are kin to grizzly bear.

I 'spect we'll mind our manners,
Fer not often do we find
A feller who will overlook our faults
And still be glad to see us
When it seems we've lost our minds
While sprinklin' foolish statements with some salt.[28]

And for the lingo at its prime and a summing up of the spirit that lurks in all those camp and bunkhouse libraries, there is J.B.'s "Square Pegs":

Some mav'ricks never cease to pine when freedom's gate is shut
While they wither from effects of constant strife,
Gazin' always t'wards the distant hills with longin' in their gut
Till frustration fin'lly snuffs the flame of life.

The wheels of time and circumstance have ruint a many man
And left 'im crushed like grain beneath the stone
Fer the ones that's heard the callin' through the length of hist'ry's span
Kept the point and always led the other'n's on.

Their ways could stand no bound'ries, stayin' always on the edge
While the milder folk accepted rules and fence
Till there weren't no worlds to conquer and the roads were lined with hedge
In a system that just never made no sense.

The cowboys of an older time were men that fit the mold,
And a few still render homage to that creed,
Though the world has changed so quickly snake-eyes seems forever rolled
As reality outweighs the spirit's need.[29]

Notes

1. Charles Badger Clark, "Bachin'," "Old Cow Man," and "From Town," in Clark, *Sun and Saddle Leather, Including "Grass Grown Trails" and New Poems* (1915), 6th ed. (Boston: Richard G. Badger, 1922), 74–76, 92–94, 49.

2. Harry E. Chrisman, *Lost Trails of the Cimarron* (Denver: Sage Books, 1961), 285.

3. Glenn Ohrlin, "Cowboy in Church," in Ohrlin, *The Hell-Bound Train: A Cowboy Songbook* (Urbana: University of Illinois Press, 1973), 18–19.

4. "Little Joe, the Wrangler" and "My Little Old Sod Shanty on the Plain," in N. Howard ("Jack") Thorp and Austin E. Fife and Alta S. Fife, *Songs of the Cowboys* (1908), (New York: Clarkson N. Potter, 1966), 28–37, 87–96.

5. Homer, *The Iliad,* trans. Richard Lattimore (Chicago: University of Chicago Press, 1951), 496.

6. "Pitch, You Old Piebally" is claimed by "Powder River Jack & Kearney Moore" in Powder River Jack Lee, *Cowboy Songs* (Butte: McKee Printing, 1928), 38–39, but the poem was really written by E. A. Brininstool, "A Corral Soliloquy," in *Trail Dust of a Maverick* (New York: Dodd, Mead, 1914), 87–88.

7. Curley Fletcher, "The Flyin' Outlaw," in *Cowboy Poetry: A Gathering,* ed. Hal Cannon (Salt Lake City: Gibbs Smith, 1985), 59–63. The Clark quotation is in the sixth edition of *Sun and Saddle Leather,* xxi.

8. Charles F. Lummis, "Sartor Resartus: While the Train Stops at Albuquerque," in *A Bronco Pegasus* (Boston: Houghton Mifflin, 1928), 53–54.

9. Two versions of Charles Badger Clark's "The Glory Trail" ("High Chin Bob") appear in John A. Lomax, *Songs of the Cattle Trail and Cow Camp* (1919), (New York: Duell, Sloan and Pearce, 1950), 30–35. S. Omar Barker's "Bear Ropin' Buckaroo" is in *Cowboy Poetry,* ed. Cannon, 14–15.

10. Charles Badger Clark, "The Legend of Boastful Bill," in Clark, *Sun and Saddle Leather,* 63–64.

11. Harry Jackson, *The Cowboy: His Songs, Ballads and Brag Talk* (12" LP recording, Folkways FH 5723, 1959).

12. D. J. O'Malley, "D-2 Horse Wrangler," in *Cowboy Poetry,* ed. Cannon, 29.

13. E. A. Brininstool, "The Disappointed Tenderfoot," in Brininstool, *Trail Dust of a Maverick* (Los Angeles: Gem Publishing, 1926), 43; also in Lomax, *Songs of the Cattle Trail and Cow Camp,* 183.

14. "The Zebra Dun," in *Cowboy Poetry,* ed. Cannon, 8–10.

15. S. Omar Barker, "The Unpardonable Sin," "Cow Country Saying," and "Cowboy Saying," in *Rawhide Rhymes: Singing Poems of the Old West* (Garden City: Doubleday, 1968), 112, 114, 119; Curley Fletcher, "The Cowboy's Prayer," in *Cowboy Poetry,* ed. Cannon, 67.

16. Theodore Roosevelt, *Ranch Life and the Hunting-Trail* (New York: Winchester Press, 1969), 68.

17. S. Omar Barker, "A Turkey Tale for Tenderfeet" and "The Ballad of Cowboy Lou," in Barker, *Buckaroo Ballads* (Santa Fe: Santa Fe New Mexican Publishing, 1928), 98–99, 66.

18. Guy Logsdon, *"The Whorehouse Bells Were Ringing" and Other Songs Cowboys Sing* (Urbana: University of Illinois Press, 1989).

19. Agnes Morley Cleaveland, *No Life for a Lady* (1941), (Lincoln: University of Nebraska Press, 1977), 272.

20. Charles Badger Clark, "The Passing of the Trail," in Clark, *Sun and Saddle Leather,* 171–73.

21. Bruce Kiskaddon, "The Old Night Hawk," in *Cowboy Poetry,* ed. Cannon, 45.

22. Bruce Kiskaddon, "Alone," "Between the Lines," and "The Time to Decide," in *Rhymes of the Ranges: A New Collection of the Poems of Bruce Kiskaddon,* ed. Hal Cannon (Salt Lake City: Gibbs Smith, 1987), 15, 17–19, 108–9.

23. Baxter Black, "The Fall Run," in *Croutons on a Cow Pie,* vol. 2 (Brighton, Colo.: Coyote Cowboy Co., 1992), 132; Black, "Hangin' On, Hopin', and Prayin' for Rain," in *Coyote Cowboy Poetry* (Brighton, Colo.: Coyote Cowboy Co., 1986), 120.

24. J. B. Allen, "Treasures," in Allen, *The Medicine Keepers* (Lubbock: Grey Horse Press, 1997), 22.

25. J. B. Allen, "Purty Ain't Pardners," in Allen, *The Medicine Keepers,* 56.

26. Charles Badger Clark, "The Lost Pardner," in Clark, *Sun and Saddle Leather,* 75–77.

27. Baxter Black, "Take Care of Your Friends," in Black, *Coyote Cowboy Poetry,* 122.

28. J. B. Allen, "Compadres," in Allen, *The Medicine Keepers,* 39.

29. J. B. Allen, "Square Pegs," in Allen, *The Medicine Keepers,* 16.

9

Orderly Disorder: Form and Tension in Cowboy Poetry

David Stanley

Despite its current popularity, cowboy poetry has often been criticized for its frequent sentimentality, its limited subject matter, its sometimes anti-government and anti-environmental values, and its predictability. Because folk arts are generally considered to be conservative, it seems odd that commentators who gladly accept predictable and repetitive patterns in quilting, ballad singing, or ritual would find cowboy poetry flawed simply because contemporary cowboy poets are trying to replicate what previous generations have done.

The favorite angle of attack against cowboy poetry has been that it is "doggerel," a Middle English term that originally meant loose and irregular (usually for humorous purposes) but gradually came to mean trivial and predictable, especially in form. Doggerel verse tends to be of regular rhythm and predictable rhyme, so—the critics imply—the poet sees his or her greatest responsibility as the creation of the most regular possible rhythm, the most exact rhymes. Presumably, then, these critics assume that the cowboy poetry aesthetic focuses first and foremost on regularity and that deviations from this principle of exactness will be thoroughly criticized by the poet's peers. Cowboy poetry, goes this argument, is an endless succession of four-line stanzas in ballad form, with iambic tetrameter alternating with iambic trimeter lines rhyming a-b-c-b.

But folk poetry in English is probably never what it seems to be at first glance, especially if heard in recitation rather than read on the printed page. Cowboy poetry is no exception. Both the "classic" cowboy poems from the nineteenth and early twentieth centuries and the work of contemporary poets demonstrate great variety in form as well as subject matter, a variety that creates a constant set of tensions revolving around appropriate metrics, topics, and language to create what

Henry Herbert Knibbs, referring to a band of running horses, called "orderly disorder."[1] Like academic poets forever grappling with the problems of what T. S. Eliot called "Tradition and the Individual Talent," folk poets must simultaneously grapple with the cowboy poetry tradition and with their spirit of innovation and creativity.[2] They must absorb the tradition from which they spring and adapt it to personal interests and subjects.

Although much of the subject matter of cowboy poetry has remained constant over the years—work, cattle, horses, friendship, love, values, and family being steady companions—the contemporary poet has available an enormous range of forms, settings, and subjects, including politics, war, economics, and the environment. Stress patterns, line lengths, stanza shapes, and rhyme schemes are all increasingly flexible and less bound by convention than in earlier years thanks to the influence of great ballad poets such as Rudyard Kipling and Robert W. Service and a host of modern free-verse poets from Whitman to Cummings.

The variations that the poet plays on these forms, and the reciter's ability to deliver the poem tellingly in an oral rather than written setting, constitute the poet's competence within the tradition. Poets valued highly by the poetic community are those who know the tradition and are capable of maintaining it yet are innovators and individualists in their own right, recognizing and exploring the potentials of a poetic tradition that constantly explores new dimensions of form, subject, and expression.

The knowledge of the tradition is derived not from academic coursework or from reading essays that dissect and analyze the poetry but from being in the midst of a lively poetic subculture that also values hard, practical knowledge of cattle and horses. Out of this background, the active poet or reciter has read and listened to hundreds of poems, has committed many to memory, has recited them privately and publicly, has composed imitations and parodies, and has absorbed the formal traditions by immersion if not by concentrated study. The conventional norms of this poetic tradition—how far the poet can depart from standard forms, what the generally accepted limits are, how rules can be altered, and what constitutes a good or successful poem—exist within cowboy poetry and within cattle culture and are learned subconsciously and over time.

This strongly oral tradition implicitly attacks our culture's tendency to elevate written poetry over spoken. As John Hollander suggests in *Rhyme's Reason,* "[A]ll poetry was originally oral. It was sung or chanted; poetic scheme and musical pattern coincided, or were sometimes identical. Poetic form as we know it is an abstraction from, or residue of, musical form, from which it came to be divorced when writing replaced memory as a way of preserving poetic utterance in narrative, prayer, spell, and the like. The ghost of oral poetry never vanishes, even though the conventions and patterns of writing reach out across time and silence all actual voices."[3]

Even if Hollander badly understates the continuing vitality of oral forms of poetry, he still points to the power inherent in the oral delivery of poetry through recitation. Unlike academic poetry, folk poetry's true strength lies in its quality of potential, suspended orality, as if the poem is constantly ready to spring off the silent page into the mouth of an expert reciter.

Cowboy poetry demands memorization and recitation—and not just because reciters who can commit long poems to memory and say them flawlessly are admired and respected as court poets, sages, and singers have been in other societies. In the West, cowboy poetry was traditionally recited around the campfire during trail drives or roundups, in bunkhouses and line camps, and in bars and cafes when the hands were in town. Now, the same settings continue to offer performance opportunities, along with motel rooms, pickup cabs, rodeo grounds, and—increasingly—cowboy poetry gatherings.

Reciting the poetry aloud seems to work in two ways. The more regular of the poems (the "doggerel" ones) ask for—and need—personal interpretation to save them from their own on-the-page tedium. Yet poems that depart from a regular pattern—poems that may look amateurish and ill-formed when seen on the page—often take on an astonishing rhythm and life when skillfully recited. As Américo Paredes said in the mid-1960s:

> [F]olk poetry is performed; it is chanted or sung. Because it is a performance, and one of a very particular type, the complete context of a folk poem is not taken into account without a consideration of three factors contributed by the performance itself. One is the influence of the chant or song on both rhythm and diction, an element separate from the pure musical dimension. Lines that look rough or unrhythmical on paper may not be so when they are chanted or sung, while the most singable lines are not necessarily the most readable ones.[4]

Paredes concludes that the other two vital factors in performance are the context of the recitation, including the audience's reaction, and the personality of the performer.

Much of the subject matter of cowboy poetry—riding horses, rounding up cattle, toughing out bad weather, breaking broncs, and drinking in saloons—occurs in situations and settings totally inhospitable to written texts, so the culture of memory, reminiscence, and shared experience that flourishes within occupations like cowboying encourages the recitation of poetry within a group setting as opposed to the individual experience of reading the poem on the printed page. These considerations help explain why some cowboy poetry is repetitive in rhythm and predictable in rhyme, both as a concession to memorization and a bow to the oral sources from which the poetry came. It's as if all these poems had been composed on horseback and later, grudgingly, committed to paper and ink.

Cowboy poetry, then, is historically, inherently, and potentially oral, yet its forms vary widely. The increasingly common open forms and free verse now used by many poets have as their sources not only the innovations of Walt Whitman, Emily Dickinson, Arthur Rimbaud, William Carlos Williams, Robert Frost, E. E. Cummings, Marianne Moore, and others but also the formal experimentation of classic cowboy poets such as Bruce Kiskaddon, Charles Badger Clark, and Curley Fletcher. Experimentation and innovation, in fact, have been notable elements in cowboy poetry since the days of the trail drives, but it is an experimentation always based in the oral potential of the poem and in its capacity for recitation.

Within the relatively regular forms, cowboy poetry uses primarily two rhythms. Iambic alternates unstressed and stressed syllables ("One day I thought I'd have some fun / And see how punchin' cows was done"). Anapestic places each stressed syllable after two unstressed ones ("When my trail stretches out to the edge of the sky / Through the desert so empty and bright").[5] Line lengths vary all the way from two to seven feet (a "foot" being a single group of one stressed and one or more unstressed syllables). Stanzas may have anywhere from two to two dozen lines. Rhymes are frequent and occur in many different patterns; internal rhymes (thanks to the influence, again, of Kipling and Service), near-rhymes, alliteration, the repetition of vowel sounds ("assonance"), and the matching of consonant sounds but not vowels ("consonance") are also quite common.

At the formal center of cowboy poetry is the ballad, usually written as a four-line stanza with alternating lines of four and three iambic feet. The ballad is originally a medieval form used in many of the oldest folk songs in English. Later it was used for hymns as well, where the form is called "common measure." As several critics have commented, the four-stress line is basic to much English-language poetry, frequently occurring with a pause ("caesura") in the middle to further emphasize its symmetry. The alternating three-stress line in the ballad, however, often requires a pause or moment of silence at the end, a "rest" or "hold" that has rhythmic value, especially because the end of the three-stress line is almost always marked by a comma or period.

The three-stress line of the ballad, in other words, really counts as four stresses, with the last one silent. So the ballad—which contrasts the symmetrical and the asymmetrical, the even and the odd, voice and silence—creates a nice kind of tension that drives the language, as in Badger Clark's "The Glory Trail":

'Way high up the Mogollons, ["muggy-yones"]
    Among the mountain tops,
A lion cleaned a yearlin's bones
    And licked his thankful chops,

When on the picture who should ride,
  A-trippin' down a slope,
But High-Chin Bob, with sinful pride
  And mav'rick-hungry rope.[6]

Clark's ballad form is perfectly regular except for the first line, where he chose the dialectal and emphatic "'way" over the more regular but weaker "away."

Bruce Kiskaddon, like many other cowboy poets, adopted the ballad form but made it decidedly irregular, as in "The Old Night Hawk":

I am up tonight in the pinnacles bold
Where the rim towers high,
Where the air is clear and the wind blows cold
And there's only the horses and I.
The valley swims like a silver sea
In the light of the big full moon,
And strong and clear there comes to me
The lilt of the first guard's tune.

The numerous extra, unstressed syllables—in some lines there are so many that the rhythm verges on the anapestic—add to the reminiscent quality of an old man's reflections as he stands night guard. In its conclusion, the poem becomes even slower and more anapestic, almost like a three-count waltz rhythm at the end of the all-night dance used by the speaker as his final reflective metaphor:

Yes, I've lived my life and I've took a chance,
Regardless of law or vow.
I've played the game and I've had my dance,
And I'm payin' the fiddler now.[7]

The ballad form has dozens of other variations, and cowboy poets—deliberately or instinctively—have invented and adapted and played with the form endlessly. Another example, Gail Gardner's justly famous "The Sierry Petes," describes what happens when two drunken cowboys riding back to camp are confronted by the devil:

Sez he, "You ornery cowboy skunks, ["on-ry"]
You'd better hunt yer holes,
Fer I've come up from Hell's Rim Rock
To gather in yer souls."

Sez Sandy Bob, "Old Devil be damned,
We boys is kinda tight,

But you ain't a-goin' to gather no cowboy souls
'Thout you has some kind a fight."[8]

The contrast between the devil's precise and regular rhythm and the warped irregularities of Sandy Bob's statement both emphasize the cowboys' drunken state and provide a strong contrast between the relative formality of the devil and the informal "devil be damned" attitude of the cowboys.

Perhaps the most important of the variations on the ballad is the longer, fourteen-syllable line of iambic rhythm referred to as the "fourteener," essentially two lines of the ballad compressed into one.[9] It is a form that Roger Renwick has identified as a more modern means of representation of the ballad.[10] Henry Herbert Knibbs borrowed the fourteener to describe the camp cook, Boomer Johnson:

Now Mr. Boomer Johnson was a gettin' old in spots,
But you don't expect a bad man to go wrastlin' pans and pots;
But he'd done his share of killin' and his draw was gettin' slow,
So he quits a-punchin' cattle and he takes to punchin' dough.[11]

Much of the humor of this stanza resides not only in the contrast between "punchin' cattle" and "punchin' dough" (eventually Boomer Johnson forces the men to eat doughnuts at the point of a gun) but also in the extra unstressed syllable ("anacrusis") that begins each of the last three lines and provides an understated anticipation of the regular rhythms in the remainder of the lines.[12]

S. Omar Barker was fond of the fourteener and used it in primarily light-hearted poems like "Bear Ropin' Buckaroo," "Jack Potter's Courtin'," and "Rain on the Range." Other poets sensed a kind of inherent dance rhythm in the fourteener; Larry Chittenden adopted it for "The Cowboys' Christmas Ball" and James Barton Adams used it in "The Cowboy's Dance Song."[13] Even more interesting is Badger Clark's use of the fourteener in "The Bunk-House Orchestra," a poem intended to be sung to the melody of "Turkey in the Straw":

Wrangle up your mouth-harps, drag your banjo out,
Tune your old guitarra till she twangs right stout,
For the snow is on the mountains and the wind is on the plain,
But we'll cut the chimney's moanin' with a livelier refrain.

Shinin' 'dobe fireplace, shadows on the wall—
(See old Shorty's friv'lous toes a-twitchin' at the call:)
It's the best grand high that there is within the law
When seven jolly punchers tackle "Turkey in the Straw."[14]

The remainder of the poem—three verses alternating with three italicized choruses, each chorus ending with the phrase "Turkey in the Straw"—is identical in form to these stanzas. But in replicating the rhythm and spirit of the old fiddle tune, Clark shies away from a monotonously repeated fourteen-syllable iambic line with regularly alternating unstressed and stressed syllables. He begins the first two lines of each verse with stressed syllables; in fact, the first two lines of each stanza have only eleven syllables each. The missing syllables occur at the beginning of the line ("catalexis") and in "rests" or "holds" in the center of the line where the rhythm slows to replace unstressed syllables with silence, as in "mouth-harps, drag" and "twangs right stout." Clark's use of three stressed syllables in a row carries the syncopated feeling of the original fiddle tune and of the original lyrics of "Turkey in the Straw," where lines like "once upon a time in Arkansas" have all three syllables of "Arkansas" stressed. The next two lines of Clark's poem, however, have fifteen syllables because of anacrusis. In the chorus, an eleven-syllable line is followed by one of thirteen, of twelve (with two rests), and, finally, of fourteen. The last line, in other words, equalizes the less regular lines that precede it.[15]

Dozens of other forms animate cowboy poetry, from the four-line stanzas and three-beat lines of Curley Fletcher's "The Flyin' Outlaw" to the 4–4–4–3 pattern of D. J. O'Malley's "D-2 Horse Wrangler" and the alternating 3–4–5 stresses (a variation of the alternating 7–5–7–5 pattern found in many other poems) of Bruce Kiskaddon's "When They've Finished Shipping Cattle in the Fall":

And the saddle hosses stringin'
At an easy walk a swingin'
In behind the old chuck wagon movin' slow.
They are weary gaunt and jaded
With the mud and brush they've waded,
And they settled down to business long ago.[16]

As in this poem, many cowboy poems use lines beginning with two unstressed syllables, so that iambic poems frequently seem to be flirting with an anapestic rhythm. This rhythm, often referred to as the rhythm of hoofbeats, has long standing in cowboy poetry, from Allen McCandless's "The Cowboy's Soliloquy" (1885), Bruce Kiskaddon's "That Little Blue Roan," and Curley Fletcher's "The Strawberry Roan" to contemporary poems like Baxter Black's "A Time to Stay, a Time to Go," which describes an elderly couple's sale of their ranch:

Lookin' back over my shoulder
At the mailbox, I guess that I know

There's a time to be stayin', a time to be goin',
And I reckon it's time that we go.[17]

Most of the stanzas in this poem begin with an iambic foot, a form of catalexis, because most of the poem is anapestic. But in the first line of this final stanza Black omits both unstressed syllables, which makes the first line seem almost dactylic (a stressed syllable followed by two unstressed ones). Then he adds an extra syllable as line one carries over or enjambs into line two: "shoulder / At the mailbox." This variation illuminates the speaker's tension and hesitation before his final decision to leave, a decision reinforced by the regularity of the anapests in the last two lines. It's not necessary to imagine the hoofbeats of a family riding away from their ranch for the last time to recognize the subtlety with which Black handles the rhythms here. The assonance of the drawn-out *o* sounds throughout the stanza ("over," "shoulder," "know," "goin'," "go") and the consonance of "lookin'," "stayin'," and "goin'" provide a further unity within the stanza, which is in total contrast to the irregular rhythms, the relative lack of rhyme, and the conversational tone in the first stanza of the same poem:

Ya know, I got this ranch from my daddy,
He come here in seventeen.
He carved this place outta muscle and blood;
His own and his ol' 'percheon team.[18] [Percheron]

The tension between anapestic and iambic in cowboy poetry (between the rhythm of hoofbeats and the traditional rhythm of the ballad) occurs in hundreds of poems, especially because a seven-foot iambic line totaling fourteen syllables is very close to a four-foot anapestic line totaling twelve. Take Kiskaddon's "The Cowboy's Dream," for example:

A cowboy and his trusty pal
Were camped one night by an old corral;
They were keeping a line on the boss's steers
And looking for calves with lengthy ears.[19]

The poem starts with two lines of nearly regular iambic meter, but the next two lines are mostly anapestic. That alternation is repeated throughout the poem, which is, in the end, a humorous one about the conflict between the beauties of heaven and the cowboy's earthly (and earthy) habits. The conflict of the rhythms, in other words, mirrors the poem's subject.

The iamb/anapest conflict is especially apparent in poems with longer lines, like T. J. McCoy's frequently recited "Alkali Pete Hits Town":

Clear the trail, you short-horn pilgrims, hunt your hole or climb a tree,
Else I'll ride yu down and stomp yu in the earth.
I'm a ring-tailed he-gorilla on a hell-bent jamboree,
And I've rid to town to celebrate my birth.[20]

Formally, this poem alternates seven- and five-syllable iambic lines, often with anacrusis at the beginning of each line, a form also popular with James Barton Adams, Curley Fletcher, Badger Clark, and S. Omar Barker. But beside (or perhaps below) the iambic rhythm is an understated anapestic rhythm with extra unstressed syllables that places primary stress on "trail," the first syllable of "pilgrims," "hole," and "tree" in the first line while deemphasizing "short," "hunt," and "climb." In the second line, the deemphasized syllables are "down" and "in," words that would ordinarily get little or no stress in conversation. This quasi-anapestic variation that flows beneath the iambic alternates four and three stresses per line and therefore calls to mind the ballad form. And this duple rhythm not only alludes to a variety of traditional poetic forms but also creates a tension in rhythm and stress that affords the reciter tremendous freedom in emphasis, speed, and the inclusion of silence in the poetry.

Badger Clark is especially expert at using this 7–5 form to create mood, as in "The Rains":

It's sun and sun without a change the lazy length o' May
    And all the little sun things own the land.
The horned toad basks and swells himse'f; the bright swifts dart and play;
    The rattler hunts or dozes in the sand.
The wind comes off the desert like it brushed a bed of coals;
    The sickly range grass withers down and fails;
The bony cattle bawl around the dryin' water holes,
    Then stagger off along the stony trails.[21]

The many forms of variation in cowboy poetry demonstrate the wide variety of literary influences that have been passed on to cowboy poets over the years and then, eventually, recorded on the printed page. In oral recitation, however, the performer of the poem is equally capable of creating that orderly disorder, both by smoothing over irregularities and by adding pauses and emphasis to vary what the reciter may sense is too much regularity. Each poem in performance reflects a dynamic tension between regularity, predictability, and surprise—factors that help explain why a group of cowboys will listen attentively to a poem that they've heard dozens of times before and perhaps have memorized themselves, some well-worn but beloved classic like the anonymous "Zebra Dun" or "Windy

Bill" or "The Gol-Darned Wheel."[22] Another anonymous poem, "Murph and McClop," begins:

It was a late afternoon in a cowtown saloon
At the end of a big rodeo,
And the boys from the chutes in their Levis and boots
Were wandering in to hash over the show.

At first glance this poem looks amateurish and badly formed on the page. In recitation, however, especially when the recitation is by someone as skilled as Harry Taylor or Ross Knox, the irregularities are dampened and the more obvious poetic devices (like the internal rhyming of "afternoon" and "saloon," "chutes" and "boots") are deemphasized. Taylor, for example, pauses very little at the end of lines one and three to avoid the too-obvious emphasis of the internal rhymes; then he speeds up markedly in the last line to accommodate the extra syllables—which, after all, emphasize the barroom scene by doing some wandering themselves.

In the same poem, the dramatic speech of the young woman who has just gotten a divorce from a rodeo rider who can't settle down is prefaced by a totally irregular stanza:

The room was like death
and each man held his breath
Then she finally spoke
through the cigarette smoke.[23]

These are actually the first and third lines of a normal stanza; leaving out lines two and four maintains the internal rhyme of the longer stanzas while emphasizing the shift in the poem from objective description to the personal statement of the woman. In performance, Taylor slows down his narration at this juncture, taking nearly as much time for these lines as he would for a full stanza and creating the same tension between regularity and irregularity as before. And the irregularity works, especially because a waiting anticipation is exactly what's being described at this point in the poem.

Variation from regularity—what we might think of as defying the doggerel—has a number of purposes for both the composer of the poem and its reciter. First, it provides a conversational informality that emphasizes that this poetry is not academic or schoolhouse in its origins. Second, it affords the reciter great freedom for emphasis, humor, and emotion. Third, it creates a constant tension between the predictable and the unpredictable, a key element in performance for an audience likely to be familiar with the poem. Cowboy poetry (and perhaps all poetry dependent on oral recitation) is thus not entirely a literary form but is, in a sense, preliterary. Its performative qualities and close relation to song mean that what is reproduced on the printed page is frequently only one version of the poem, because it exists in multiple variation in the minds of both reciters and listeners.

At the same time, these variations point back to the often anonymous origins of the cowboy poetry tradition and to the shared heritage of linguistic representation and dynamic performance that goes back to the nineteenth century. Lines are dropped, stanzas move, and words change. Poets may even change their own lines, as Gail Gardner did when he became disgusted that his original line, "I'm tired of cow pyrography," was being missaid (most interestingly as "I'm tired of cowboyography") and so went back to the more easily memorized but less imaginative "I'm sick of the smell of burnin' hair."[24]

This flexibility on the part of reciters, and the constant tension that they maintain between printed texts more or less known to the audience and their emergent performance, suggest that reciters of cowboy poetry have as an aesthetic principle not the maintenance of regular rhythm, syllable after syllable at the same speed, but the subtle acknowledgment of an underlying rhythm that lies beneath often-irregular words and lines. Reciters of cowboy poetry are assuredly not wedded to an absolute, sing-song, tick-tock regularity based on the poem's dictatorship; the metronomic is not an aesthetic principle. Instead, poets and reciters seem to subscribe instinctively to a rhythm like Walt Whitman's, one that maintains natural breath groups and echoes the rhythms of nature—whether the pounding of the sea's breakers, the beat of the human heart, or the sound of hoofbeats. Cowboy poetry is, in effect, a collaboration between writer and reciter, a mutually creative effort based on a shared understanding of the culture's aesthetic.

The reciter maintains the ability and the freedom, whether by conscious decision or by instinct, to make rhythms more or less regular, to emphasize or deemphasize rhyme, or to pause at the end of each line or carry on to the next, regardless of end punctuation. Recitations may also differ from the original printed text in language; some reciters deliberately change lyrics to better fit rhythm or mood, and, of course, dozens of changes and variants creep into poems that have been in oral tradition for many years. It is not uncommon for a poet to hear his or her own poem recited with discernible alterations by other poets.

Modern-day poets are equally capable of using metrical variation to fit their meanings, even when they are working in less predictable or more open forms. Georgie Sicking, one of the first woman cowhands to write poetry about her working life, plays with rhythm at the same time that she asserts her membership in the cowboy fraternity:

When I was a kid and doing my best to
Learn ways of our land,
I thought mistakes were never made by
A real top hand.

He never got into a storm with a horse
He always knew
How a horse would react in any case and
Just what to do.[25]

The basic form here is the ballad, although both iambic and anapestic feet occur in the first two lines. The third line is totally regular except for the additional syllable at the end, and the fourth uses three stressed syllables in a row to emphasize Sicking's meaning. As Seymour Chatman says, meter "clearly collaborates with meaning, either the specific content of the poem or its broader implication of tone and feeling. The meter is the sign of the poet's control; it signals propriety of formalization and genre specification. And its resources are available, in their own small way, to confirm semantic movements and to render part or the whole salient."[26]

Nor is metrical variation the only reinforcement for meaning; cowboy poets use diction, tone, and sound as well. Word choice is especially important, of course, and not just the use of occupational jargon to create in-group solidarity for the cowboy audience. The well-worn cliché that describes the cowboy as soft-spoken or totally uncommunicative has been thoroughly undercut by poems that take delight in extravagant language, as McCoy's classic about Alkali Pete demonstrates. A more subtle play with words is evident in Wallace McRae's "Reincarnation," surely the best-known and most popular contemporary cowboy poem. It begins:

"What does reincarnation mean?"
A cowpoke ast his friend.
His pal replied, "It happens when
Yer life has reached its end."

These lines are in traditional ballad form (although McRae uses a stanza of eight lines rather than four) and are totally regular in meter except for the first line, which begins—as McRae recites it—with two trochaic feet followed by two iambs. Because it is the first line of the poem, the reader or listener gets no clue as to the prevailing rhythm. Attention therefore falls on the multisyllabic term *reincarnation,* with all its potential for misunderstanding and its contrast to the dialectical "ast," "pal," and "yer." The second stanza begins:

"The box and you goes in a hole,
That's been dug into the ground.
Reincarnation starts in when
Yore planted 'neath a mound."[27]

As in the first stanza, "reincarnation" warps the meter—requiring a trochee rather than an iamb in the first foot—and thereby calls attention to itself and to its contrast with the faulty agreement in the first line and the informal "yore."

Much the same is true of the poem's last stanza, when the term again changes the meter and makes the listener aware that the poem is not only a traditional joke at the expense of the listener but also a subtle contrast of linguistic conventions: the informality of cowboy speech versus the pretentiousness of formal or traditionally "poetic" language, a point emphasized by McRae's working into the poem phrases like "life's travails," "transformation ride," "rendered mound," "moldered grave," "vegetative bower," "essential to the steed," and the deliberately and archaically poetic "'neath." McRae's manipulation of diction, then, turns the poem from a rhymed and metered joke about horse manure into a tongue-in-cheek commentary on folk versus elite poetry and on the use of one or another kind of language to create meaning for an audience because the poem implies that the audience knows and understands—and finally rejects—those multisyllabic Latinate phrases. The final line of the poem—"You ain't changed, all that much"—uses a comma to break up the iambic rhythm and suggest that each of those one-syllable words should be stressed in a final putdown of the ideas and attitudes that lie behind a term like reincarnation.

Sound is also important in cowboy poetry, in the deliberate alliteration of *s* sounds in Badger Clark's "The Rains" or in the vowel sounds of Vern Mortensen's "Range Cow in Winter," which concludes:

Have you listened still on a desert hill
    When the world was cold and drear,
When the tinkling bells of a herd of sheep
    Was the nearest sound you'd hear,
And the haunting notes of a lone coyote whose
    Evening's hunting howl
Rose wild and clear in the cold blue night,
    And was answered by the hoot of an owl?

But when the scanty grass lies covered deep
    By the snow that lies like a pall,
Then the plaintive bawl of a hungry cow
    Is the loneliest sound of all![28]

Here the increasing use of open vowels, especially the long *o* and *ow* of "cold," "sound," "notes," "lone," "coyote," "howl," "owl," "snow," "cow," and "loneliest" in combination with the internal rhyme of the longer stanza and the rhyme of "pall" and "bawl" in the last stanza, create a real feeling for winter that is perhaps emphasized by the contrast between the regular meter of the first seven lines and the less regular lines that follow.

Diction is also important in poems with a political thrust and that depict with great clarity the difficult life ranchers face. Nyle Henderson, for example, uses multisyllabic terms and irregular rhythms to typify the dilemmas of the family rancher:

> And there's imports and embargoes and all the like,
> Remember now, as a rancher that you can't go on strike.
> There's politicians, vegetarians and ecologists, too,
> And a hundred government agencies tellin' you what to do.[29]

Yula Sue Hunting's poem to the Internal Revenue Service, "Dear Sirs," also moves radically away from the short-line ballad form. At first glance the poem appears to be some kind of rhymed free verse arranged in couplets of various lengths, although in fact virtually every line has four distinct stresses as Hunting performs it. The major exception is the ironically conceived second line:

> Out of all the headaches, hard work, taxes and expense,
> We managed to find three thousand, four hundred, thirty-six dollars and
> sixteen cents
> To support my husband, myself, six kids and three dogs, too,
> Now you expect me to send Self-Employment to you.
> Not even enough left over for any underwear,
> If God taxed us, we wouldn't even have prayer.[30]

Contemporary poets are increasingly using open forms and free verse, but the best seem to keep a foot in the traditional meters and stanza forms of the past. Here is Vess Quinlan's "Sold Out":

> The worst will come tomorrow
> When we load the saddle horses.
> We are past turning back;
> The horses must be sold.
>
> The old man turns away, hurting,
> As the last cow is loaded.
> I hunt words to ease his pain
> But there is nothing to say.
>
> He walks away to lean
> On a top rail of the corral

And look across the calving pasture
Toward the willow-grown creek.

I follow,
Absently mimicking his walk,
And stand a post away.
We don't speak of causes or reasons.

Don't speak at all;
We just stand there
Leaning on the weathered poles,
While shadows consume the pasture.[31]

Quinlan's poem maintains a basic three-beat line and iambic rhythm in the first three stanzas, but the last two stanzas swerve away from that pattern, first with the attenuated "I follow," then with the contrast between short, heavily accented lines like "don't speak at all" and "we just stand there" and longer, more meditative lines with extra unstressed syllables. This contrast juxtaposes lines suggesting decisiveness with lines suggesting thought, so the rhythms and line lengths of the poem emphasize the lack of answers and the impossibility of the rancher's situation.

Another politically loaded poem that attacks the popular romantic image of the West as it is reflected in cowboy poetry and that contrasts it with the day-to-day grind of hard work and constant financial pressure is Rod McQueary's self-referential "A Joker's Pay":

If you can make a week-old prolapse seem
Romantic as a schoolgirl's dream,
Describe the sweet and lovely things
Held together with hog rings,
You'll deserve your gold "B.S." degree
In western cowboy poetry.

But writing poems, and jokes, and such
For this cattle crowd won't pay too much.
You see, they can't afford to pay to hear
The real value of a dying steer,
Or all about this market mess
That brings on all their money stress
And doubt
About tiny checks toward giant notes,
Worn out overshoes and coats,
Old gloves turned inside out.

Please, don't forget the numbers, friend,
Write those great big numbers down.
All that pretty equity (and fifty cents)
Will buy a cup of coffee
Nearly anywhere in town.

And who here hasn't visualized
That long-dreaded day,
When some sympathetic crowd, somber auctioneer,
Sells your world away?
Some bitter husband, weeping wife,
Decide what now to do with life
Or where to go,
How *not* to feel like failures
At the only thing they know.

So if you write the poems and jokes
To entertain these western folks
Who watch the cows, or herd the sheep,
For their sake, keep it light,
And take the laughter for your pay,
Because right now, tears are cheap.[32]

This is a beautifully complex poem that begins, appropriately, with a line of perfectly regular iambic pentameter (after all, this is a poem about poetry and its failure to depict the realities of western life). The iambic pattern continues, primarily four stresses to the line, through the first twelve lines, with each couplet exactly rhymed. But then the unexpected "and doubt" interrupts that pattern and begins a sustained subversion of the poem's rhyme scheme, its meter, and of conventional notions of line, stanza, and mood. The lines that follow are almost all irregular, with frequent spondees (double-stressed words or phrases like "old gloves") and long lines varied with short ones, all of which emphasize the discontinuity and confusion in the contrast between the regularity of poetry and the roughness of real life.

Far from being doggerel, cowboy poetry, both classic and contemporary, is more complex and subtle than it may seem on the surface. But the poets' and reciters' constant attention to issues of form and their consistent creation of tension, not only between lines, words, and rhythms but also between dialect and slang, cowboy jargon, and the multisyllabic elite expression of the East, suggest something more: a reiterated subtextual focus on language and its power to represent (or mask) the realities of cowboy life. In other words, devices of form and language, in all their possible variations, interrupt the easy transference of linguistic sounds to established, recognized meanings. They call into question many of our deepest assumptions about language as defining and representing human life, as providing meaning and stability to existence.

Especially considering its increasingly politicized subject matter and the broadened fields of opportunity within—and tension between—traditional and contemporary forms, cowboy poetry exemplifies this continued questioning of language and of the stability of the text. And that is especially true because of the intensively oral nature of the poetry and its many ways of insisting that it exists only in recitation-performance, that its representation on the printed page is no more than a reminder of what it can be when spoken. In this sense, the reciter is at once shaping, repeating, and changing a series of texts that have as one of their principal subjects the nature of language and its relationship to the realities of human life. The text, constantly in process, always dynamic, is read, heard again and again, memorized, recited, passed on, and spoken into a world of silence. And cowboy poetry contains this silence as well in its pauses and hesitations; its rests and its holds; and its references to the silence of the plains, to the noise of wind and animals, and to the absence of the human voice. Silently learned and silently memorized, then spoken aloud, cowboy poetry speaks to the fickleness of language in defining our lives at the same time that it reflects the tensions of modern life in the West.

Notes

I am indebted to Lee Haring for his critique and suggestions for this essay.

1. Knibbs's phrase is in his poem "Where the Ponies Come to Drink"; the entire poem is quoted in chapter 14 of this volume.

2. T. S. Eliot, "Tradition and the Individual Talent," in Eliot, *The Sacred Wood: Essays on Poetry and Criticism* (1920), (London: Methuen, 1950), 47–59.

3. John Hollander, *Rhyme's Reason: A Guide to English Verse* (New Haven: Yale University Press, 1981), 4.

4. Américo Paredes, "Some Aspects of Folk Poetry," *Texas Studies in Language and Literature* 6 (1964): 224.

5. The first quoted lines are from D. J. O'Malley, "D-2 Horse Wrangler," in *Cowboy Poetry: A Gathering,* ed. Hal Cannon (Salt Lake City: Gibbs Smith, 1985), 28; the second are from Charles Badger Clark, "The Song of the Leather," *Sun and Saddle Leather, Including "Grass Grown Trails" and New Poems,* 6th ed. (1915), (Boston: Richard G. Badger, 1922), 42.

6. Charles Badger Clark, "The Glory Trail" ("High-Chin Bob"), in Clark, *Sun and Saddle Leather,* 77.

7. Bruce Kiskaddon, "The Old Night Hawk," in *Cowboy Poetry,* ed. Cannon, 42–46.

8. Gail I. Gardner, "The Sierry Petes," in *Cowboy Poetry,* ed. Cannon, 4.

9. See Derek Attridge, *The Rhythms of English Poetry* (London: Longman, 1982), 87–89.

10. Roger deV. Renwick, *English Folk Poetry: Structure and Meaning* (Philadelphia: University of Pennsylvania Press, 1920), 97–98.

11. Henry Herbert Knibbs, "Boomer Johnson," in *Cowboy Poetry,* ed. Cannon, 47.

12. For this and other terms, see Babette Deutsch, *Poetry Handbook: A Dictionary of Terms* (New York: Funk and Wagnalls, 1962).

13. S. Omar Barker, "Bear Ropin' Buckaroo," "Jack Potter's Courtin'," and "Rain on the Range," Lawrence "Larry" Chittenden, "The Cowboys' Christmas Ball," and James Barton Adams, "The Cowboy's Dance Song," all in *Cowboy Poetry,* ed. Cannon, 12–19, 30–31.

14. Charles Badger Clark, "The Bunk-House Orchestra," in Clark, *Sun and Saddle Leather,* 57.

15. A fascinating contemporary poem using a square-dance rhythm is Wallace McRae's "Put That Back . . . Hoedown," which in both rhythm and subject depicts the greedy scramble for coal-mining leases as an ironic square dance: "So everybody swing." See *Cowboy Curmudgeon* (Salt Lake City: Gibbs Smith, 1992), 86–88.

16. Curley Fletcher, "The Flyin' Outlaw," D. J. O'Malley, "D-2 Horse-Wrangler," and Bruce Kiskaddon, "When They've Finished Shipping Cattle in the Fall," all in *Cowboy Poetry,* ed. Cannon, 59–63, 28–29, 35.

17. Baxter Black, "A Time to Stay, a Time to Go," in Black, *Coyote Cowboy Poetry* (Brighton, Colo.: Coyote Cowboy Co., 1986), 80.

18. Black, "A Time to Stay, a Time to Go," 79.

19. Bruce Kiskaddon, "The Cowboy's Dream," in *Cowboy Poetry,* ed. Cannon, 38–42.

20. T. J. McCoy, "Alkali Pete Hits Town," in *Cowboy Poetry,* ed. Cannon, 19–20.

21. Charles Badger Clark, "The Rains," in Clark, *Sun and Saddle Leather,* 145.

22. "The Zebra Dun," "Windy Bill," and "The Gol-Darned Wheel," in *Cowboy Poetry,* ed. Cannon, 8–11, 26–27.

23. "Murph and McClop," in *Cowboy Poetry,* ed. Cannon, 49–51.

24. See Warren Miller's essay on Gail Gardner in this volume (chapter 7).

25. Georgie Sicking, "To Be a Top Hand," in Sicking, *Just Thinkin'* (Fallon, Nev.: Loganberry Press, 1985), 8.

26. Seymour Chatman, *A Theory of Meter* (The Hague: Mouton, 1965), 224.

27. Wallace McRae, "Reincarnation," in *Cowboy Poetry,* ed. Cannon, 185–86.

28. Vern Mortensen, "Range Cow in Winter," in *Cowboy Poetry,* ed. Cannon, 152–53.

29. Nyle Henderson, "How Many Cows?" in *Cowboy Poetry,* ed. Cannon, 72.

30. Yula Sue Hunting, "Dear Sirs," in *Cowboy Poetry from Utah,* ed. Carol A. Edison (Salt Lake City: Utah Folklife Center, 1986), 42.

31. Vess Quinlan, "Sold Out," in *New Cowboy Poetry: A Contemporary Gathering,* ed. Hal Cannon (Salt Lake City: Gibbs Smith, 1990), 98.

32. Rod McQueary, "A Joker's Pay," in *New Cowboy Poetry,* ed. Cannon, 40–41.

10

Poems and Songs on the Rodeo Trail

Glenn Ohrlin

I suppose I could say that I've collected poems and songs literally all my life, as my folks claimed I knew one hundred songs by the time I was six years old. For the first forty years or so my collecting consisted of soaking up songs and poems I liked from people I liked to fill the great empty spaces between my ears. My first guitar chords I learned from an aunt. She played in the old way with the fingers of the right hand. I can't even remember the first poems and songs I learned, but I know that I got a lot from my family. My father, the late Bert Ohrlin, was a great singer who also composed a lot of popular songs, although he never had any success with them. He wrote one cowboy song, "I'm a Working Cowboy," and I also learned from him some humorous songs like "The Swede from North Dakota."[1]

Growing up in northwestern Minnesota, I heard a lot of songs and poems about cowboys. I recall in my teens that a lot of cowboys' singing was much like recitation. Of course, like anyone who lived with a rich oral tradition I also gathered poems and songs from printed sources—booklets of cowboy songs and poems that radio singers sold over the air (I think that's where I got "Cowboy in Church").[2] One of the most popular radio singers when I was growing up was George B. German, who broadcast from Yankton, South Dakota, on WNAX. He used to sing Curley Fletcher's "The Strawberry Roan," which he heard Fletcher sing in Arizona in the 1920s. German had worked there on cattle and sheep ranches, and his program was responsible for getting a lot of southwestern cowboy songs into circulation in the upper Midwest. German also wrote a lot of poems, including one he gave me in Yankton in 1968 called "Windy Bill's Famous Ride" about a bragging bronco rider who tried to drive a limousine.[3] As a kid, I had one of the folios of cowboy songs that he sold over the air—it had a picture of a bucking horse on it, which probably started my interest in rodeo—and my Aunt Irene also had a bag of cowboy and hillbilly songs which she had learned from folios and copied down from the radio. Another book had a recitation in it called "Hanky Dean." I saved those books mainly if they had pictures of bucking horses so I could figure out a scientific way of riding them.

It seems as if it was real easy to memorize what I heard or read when I was young. I'd remember the words almost instantaneously—sort of a memory feat. After I started performing at folk festivals and such, people started sending me tapes and words written out to stuff I liked. Now it's slower for me to memorize poems and songs, but they form together out of bits and pieces—a narrative is easiest.

As long as I can remember, I wanted to be a rider. When I was about twelve, I started working and hanging around stables, dude ranches, stockyards, and what have you just to get experience. Sometimes I'd get a dollar a day, sometimes just the rides. By the spring of 1943, when I was sixteen, I was buckarooing in Nevada. When July Fourth rolled around, all the cowboys went to Caliente for the annual rodeo, and I decided to try the bareback bronc event. It must have been one of the last places in the country where broncs were ridden with a loose rope instead of the rigging they use now. That first horse bucked like the dickens, but I stayed on him all right—if he'd bucked me off it might have saved me twenty-three years of knocking big holes in the ground. So I started rodeoing then, riding bareback broncs for $2.50 a head mount money. During 1943 and 1944 I cowboyed on ranches in Nevada, Arizona, Montana, Wyoming, and California, entering an occasional rodeo whenever possible. In 1945 and 1946 I was in the army; from 1947 through 1950 I rodeoed full-time as a contestant in the bareback riding and, starting in 1949, in the saddle broncs. One little poem of advice to bronc riders I learned from Chip Morris, who liked to recite it when he was announcing rodeos:

Take a deep seat and a faraway look,
Keep him between your knees.
The higher he goes, the sweeter the breeze.
Keep your mind in the middle and let both ends flop![4]

Later on I made up a verse of my own:

Turn your toes out, jerk your knees.
The higher he goes, the sweeter the breeze.
The more he bucks, the more you spur.
All I want to see is flying fur![5]

I finally quit riding saddle broncs in 1965. After too many years you are a slowed-up wreck, fixing to happen; I was ranching more by then anyway.

I've been collecting sayings and rhymes like these, and poems and songs, ever since I can remember, especially the hard-core cowboy songs and poems. By "hard-core" I don't mean obscene, although they can be, but they are what "civilians" (non-cowboys) seldom know or have heard of. Because I've loved everything about the cowboy life since year one, I was happy to find that lots of cowboys still knew a bunch of this stuff when I started my own working life. In Tucson, Arizona, in 1944 I met Powder River Jack Lee, a great performer of real cowboy songs. He seemed to know them all, so I learned early on it was possible to know a hell of a lot of songs. Once in Tucson about 1977, an elderly gent stepped up to me during intermission of a concert and said he recalled songs that Powder River Jack had sung at his ranch near Sasabe. He said that he gave Jack his brother's address in New York, and that eventually Jack looked him up. His brother hauled Jack down to the New York Stock Exchange for a look-see, and Jack stopped everything with an ear-splitting holler, "Powder River, let 'er buck!" So he couldn't have been all bad.

In the summer of 1943 in Kingman, Arizona, I worked at the Rabbit Ears ranch with a young fellow who sang, Jack Mullins. When we rode it was alone, but we swapped some songs when we worked together, like one day when we hauled fence posts about a hundred miles. Ben Fancher was well known in that area as a poet and reciter. The Diamond Bar, where the great cowboy poet Bruce Kiskaddon worked, was about fifty miles north by northeast of us, but he was then long gone from that country so I knew him mainly from mention in *Hoofs and Horns* magazine, which all the rodeo cowboys read. Will James may have worked at the Diamond Bar, too.

I picked up a lot of old tunes at dances. I first heard "Put Your Little Foot," which is also called "Varsouvienne," at a dance in a one-room schoolhouse somewhere on the east side of the Superstition Mountains in Arizona late in 1943. I was working on a ranch belonging to the Clemons Cattle Company, which was headquartered at Florence, Arizona, and I went to the dance with the ranch manager and his wife and son and daughter-in-law. All the people at the dance were ranchers with their families and cowboys. I remember that some miners from either Globe or Miami showed up, and after the dance there was a great fight. I remember standing near the porch after the dance and seeing my boss's son knock one of the miners plumb off the porch. All the *non*-fighters seemed to enjoy it very much.

I also heard "Varsouvienne" at Kinsley's ranch between Tucson and the Mexican border. I think the place was called Amado. I don't remember what instruments they had besides fiddle and guitar, but I remember it was kind of simple, kind of nice. I remember once at Kinsley's ranch, a Mexican cowboy from California, Johnny Quijada, took great delight in dancing that number. I knew Johnny real well, and he sang a lot, both Mexican and hillbilly. I have met people from New Mexico and Colorado who also knew the music and the dance steps.

Back in California in May of 1944 I was working with horses in the Riverbottom section of Burbank, an enclave of horsemen, pro rodeo hands, and movie stuntmen, a world of its own. There were over a thousand horses in the Riverbottom at that time, so there were always riding jobs like breaking colts, putting a rein on green horses, and wrangling dudes. The riders were a jolly, sporting crew, funny as hell; some knew songs and stories until the end of time.

An old Arizona range cook, Hercules Kennedy, better known as "Kenny," fed most of us at his El Rancho Café. Kenny was as salty as they come, a top cook, a genuine fighting man who could handle the unruly, a collector of old songs, rare songs, and bawdy songs who also recited a lot of bawdy poetry. Claimed he had five hundred songs and poems. "Pretty good," I thought.

Cafes like Kenny's and bars in Burbank like the Hitching Post—owned by the Olmstead brothers—and the Pickwick—owned by Jerry Ambler and Wag Blessing, two of the best rodeo riders of that time—were at that time on the pro rodeo circuit, and you could hear songs and poems there almost any time. These bars didn't hire entertainers, but there was always a microphone and guitar available in case someone felt the urge to sing. Tommy Coates, a bartender at the Pickwick—a cowboy, stuntman, and ex-rodeo hand—would sing or semi-recite "Ace in the Hole" in a Broadway wiseguy accent while standing on the bar.

One of the best reciters I got to know in those days was the late Slim Pickens, who was a rodeo hand long before he got into pictures. He was real good at reciting and had a phenomenal memory. He knew the entire "Open Book" or "Open Ledger," which he shocked some guests with at a party at my ranch house one night years ago.[6] Quite a number of rodeo riders knew that one, too, like Bud Linderman and Fighting Jack McCuellar. Johnny Quijada, whom I first met in Arizona, knew a lot of bawdy verses, too. There was a woman in Burbank, Fighting Joan Edwards, who owned good horses (one a great bulldogging mare) who also knew "The Open Book." She'd fight men if they weren't too darn tough.

The obscene poems were probably the commonest ones I heard during that time. In fact, I associated poetry with bars and tough people. One of the horse guys in Burbank's Riverbottom who also made saddles had a song called "Blue Ball Shanker Blues" that he learned from Barbara Stanwyck while working as her horse groom. Curley Fletcher often had both bawdy and straight versions of his poems; I got the straight version of "The Wild Buckeroo" (that's how he spelled it) out of his book *Songs of the Sage* and the bawdy verses from Nevada Slim (Dallas Turner).[7] Fletcher himself wrote a parody of "The Strawberry Roan" called "The Castration of the Strawberry Roan," and there have been a lot of other bawdy parodies as well.[8]

Another place where I found a lot of poems was the old *Hoofs and Horns* magazine out of Tucson, which ran poetry sent in by cowboys and also carried words to songs in a column. When a rodeo cowboy lost his life there were often poems sent in about him, such as "Fritz Truan, a Great Cowboy" by Larry Finley.[9] Larry Finley was bareback champ in 1948 and as tough a man as ever wore boots. Other poems that I found in *Hoofs and Horns* later on were "Heelin' Bill," "Powder River Jack" by "Colorado Bill," and "Starlight," about a great bucking horse in the late 1930s and early 1940s. In 1940 only Fritz Truan was able to make the whistle on him. The author of this poem, Noah Henry, was a fine all-around rodeo contestant. The poem is about a young rider who had the bad luck to draw Starlight. Here's how it ends:

> For quicker than a lead balloon
> The cowboy landed—splat!
> "I've had enough of him," he groaned,
> "He sure don't travel flat."[10]

Quite a few of the poems that I learned out of *Hoofs and Horns* and other places I found tunes for so that I could sing them. Sometimes I figured out that the words would fit a tune that I already knew. In 1953 there was a raid on a colony of polygamists in Short Creek, Arizona, that inspired me to start writing down some verses a few years later, using the tune of an old cowboy song by D. J. O'Malley, "When the Work's All Done This Fall." I finally finished the song in 1967.[11] Other poems that I found tunes for were "The Stray," which was called "The Estrays by Pecos the Ridgerunner" when it was published in *Bit and Spur* in 1948, and "My Stetson Hat," from *Hoofs and Horns*.[12]

At a Yankton, South Dakota, rodeo in 1949 or 1950, where I was entered in the bareback and saddle bronc riding, I heard the old champion steer roper Ike Rude recite "Windy Bill" right in front of the bucking chutes. There were cowboys all over the place but maybe half a dozen listening to him. When some youngster asked, "Gosh, where did you learn that?" Ike said, "Well I was raised as sorta half a cowboy, you know." I had first learned "Windy Bill" as a song from Powder River Jack Lee in Arizona in 1944.[13] Even though movies and TV shows are full of gunfights, most of the poems that cowboys recite and most of the stories they tell in bull sessions concern roping wrecks like Windy Bill's, or tough horses, or outfits they worked for.

A comical song that I first saw as a poem in a book or a magazine—I forget which—was "The Gol-Darned Wheel." This was another one that Powder River Jack sang. I read in Dane Coolidge's *Texas Cowboys* that Coolidge got a cowboy named Jess Fears to write the words down for him in 1909, also in Arizona.[14] Not all the poems that I learned were about cowboy life, though. I got a lot of mileage out of "The Face on the Barroom Floor" by Hugh Antoine D'Arcy, which I originally learned in the army in 1945 or 1946. There was a guy I knew in the military who recited Kipling's "Gunga Din," but I always thought the dramatics detracted from the spellbinding words.

Some other recitations that I picked up along the way were "Cincinnati Jim," which was in criminal argot, which I knew from my lowlier friends. Hub Willis, my late neighbor in Arkansas, showed me a book of recitations that had "Cincinnati Jim," "The Face on the Barroom Floor," and some others. Also, the Canadian cowboys that I worked with on the chuck-wagon races in Alberta in 1968 knew a lot of poetry. Alan Nixon, a Canadian who now ranches in the Ozarks, does the same Gaelic version of "Reincarnation" that Wally McRae told me was the genesis of *his* poem.[15] From Nixon I've also learned songs like "Saskatchewan." Another Canadian who winters in Arkansas, Jack Lauder, has given me poems like "Chuck-Wagon Races," "The Days of the Past Are Gone," and an untitled poem by J. K. Trout that I call "Canuck's Lament."[16] In the early 1950s I picked up a copy of *The Complete Works of Robert Service,* which is another favorite of the northern guys from Canada and Montana.

When Joe Cavanaugh of Chambers, Nebraska, and I were rodeoing in 1950, traveling in a 1932 Plymouth, I picked up a lot of Irish songs because Joe and most of the ranchers in his part of Nebraska were Irish. Joe once dyed a horse green and rode it in the St. Patrick's Day Parade in the streets of O'Neill, Nebraska. It may seem funny to think of a bunch of cowboys singing "Galway Bay" with tears in their eyes, but it seemed logical at the time. One old song I heard around those parts was "Boston Burglar," also "Twenty-One Years" and "Moonlight and Skies." Maybe it isn't necessary to mention they also knew "Barbara Allen." I almost dried all those Irish up with "The Hell-Bound Train," but a sad one sent them back to the suds again. There was one weird episode up in that country where I won a grease gun and a cold steel chisel at a rodeo. No other cowboy can make that statement.

In bars and other places Cavanaugh would often recite "The Intoxicated Rat" and "Let Old Nellie Stay." He had changed the words of "Nellie" a little to get a bull rider into it.[17] He also knew a rodeo version of "The Open Book" as well as "Kodunk" and others like "The Bloody Great Wheel." Along the way, Joe and I made up a few songs, like the parody "Bull Riders in the Sky."[18]

Another good singer and reciter was the rodeo clown Jerry Hedricks, Sr. After the rodeo was over, we'd often get together around a bottle of peppermint schnapps in Jerry's trailer, in a bar, or around a campfire on the rodeo grounds. Jerry would roar all these old cowboy songs, along with Jimmie Rodgers tunes, popular songs of the day, and poems. About the same time, I learned "The Bronco Buster" from Walter Plugge, Sr., of Bartlett, Nebraska.[19]

When I started my own ranching operation in the Arkansas Ozarks in 1954 I found nearly all my neighbors had a trove of songs or "ballets." These were mostly written down, as they hadn't heard of oral tradition either. There were also a lot of cowboys who had moved to Arkansas from other parts of the West because Arkansas had cheap land, low taxes, good grass, and open range, although not long after I moved there they passed a road law that pretty much ended the open range. One of my neighbors in Arkansas, Jim McElroy, punched cows in Texas, New Mexico, and Arizona before he came to Arkansas. He has written several songs like "Down in the Tules" and poems like "Outlaw Dummy."[20]

Later, in 1963, Archie Green and Judith McCulloh from the University of Illinois got me started performing songs and poems at university concerts and in coffee houses and at festivals. The folk song circuit reminds me of rodeoing in that you cross paths with almost everybody in the game at least once every few years. The big difference is that I don't get my head drove into the ground when I make mistakes in a song. It's lucky I learned lots of songs all through my life—singing is a lot easier on the old bones. Judy and Archie encouraged me to do a book and collect some more. So for a few years I set out with a tape recorder and collected. A lot of that was done in ranching areas I knew in the Dakotas and Nebraska. The purpose of that was to fill some holes left by my former haphazard way of going. After *The Hell-Bound Train* was finished, I went back to haphazard and still fill in holes and learn poems and songs, which are coming out of the woodwork everywhere these days. So it is mainly fun again.

The thing I liked best about working at collecting was going into little-known ranching areas and meeting folks like myself who love the cowboy songs and poems. Sometimes it turned into minor adventures, because a good place to start is the local bar or the saddle shop, if they've got one. In a small ranching town in western North Dakota in 1965 I stopped first at the saddle shop, then crossed the street to a bar where I saw a cowboy walk out backwards and fall over a car. I thought, "Now that's a shade out West!" As I went through the barroom door, a gentleman challenged me to a fight, which I ignored. I asked the bartender if anyone there knew any old cowboy songs. He said, "No, go ask at the mortuary." As I left the bar, my challenger broke a glass between my feet, which caused me to stop and look the fellow over. I said, "Know any old songs?" The fellow just shook his head and turned away. The mortician put me in touch with a ranch lady who sang and yodeled for hours.

Three years later in Buffalo, South Dakota, I taped a rancher, Dick Smith, who had thirteen children. His favorite song was "Don't Be Angry with Me, Darling." Dick taped about thirty songs for us one rainy day, and it was from him that I learned Tex Fletcher's song about the great bucking horse Tipperary, who was only ridden once in his lifetime by Yakima Canutt. Some claim that Yakima lost a stirrup momentarily and should have been disqualified. I also learned "Paddy Ryan" and "Little Joe the Wrangler's Sister Nell" from Dick.[21] Later on I picked up the words to "When Uncle Sam's Doughboy Roped a Wild Irish Rose" from Dean Tarter in Marmarth, North Dakota. It was written by Rusty Holman, who apparently wrote some other songs that have since disappeared, like "I Want to Go Back to Montana" and "Just a Cowboy's Dream."[22]

In August 1968 I met up with Jake Herman of Pine Ridge and Raymond Runnels of Batesland, both in South Dakota. Both were Sioux Indians who wrote and recited poetry. From Runnels I learned "The Fair at Batesland," a poem he wrote about a mule that bucked him off at an amateur rodeo:

I hit the town of Batesland, it was on the afternoon of the fair.
I entered in the bucking contest more for fun than on the square.
I stuck around about an hour with nothing else to do,
And every time I'd feel my nerve a-slippin' I'd go and drink a few.

Then finally I heard the band a-playin', out toward the track.
I went and threw my saddle on my old nag's back.
We rode out to the fairgrounds, a happy bunch of boys.
We seen a couple races and we heard a lot of noise.

Then finally the old judge hollered, "You riders come and line up for the draw."
I drawed an old brown mule 'bout as handsome as a squaw.
But when I stepped upon her, the crowd was mighty still.
A bunch of cowboys sat around and grinned as if they knew I'd spill.

But I pulled off my hat and hollered, and I hit her in the flank,
And I hooked her in the shoulder with a silver-mounted shank.
She left this world a-bawlin', she made one jump plumb grand.
I reached down for old safety and I grabbed a claw of sand.

Then the crowd they hollered, "Rotten, your riding's mighty cheap."
So I drifted to the mountains and got a job a-herdin' sheep.[23]

Runnels also wrote a good poem called "The Cowboy's Prayer," which is similar to Badger Clark's, and he taught me a poem called "Wild Horse Charlie" that he'd picked up in his travels.[24] I also learned a lot of poems and songs from Wild Horse Lyle Cunningham of Miles City, Montana. His wife Mary Lou had a collection of songs and poems that had been written by a guy called Diamond Spike, including "Ace in the Hole" and "Two-Dollar Girl."

I'm glad to see things like the Cowboy Poetry Gathering in Elko. The old music and poetry are coming back, and cowboys from all over are discovering that people are interested in what they know. To steal a line from Badger Clark, "Slim was the treasure we gathered and scattered, / But can you measure the wind and the sky?"[25] That's what cowboying amounts to, and nobody who knows what it's like would trade it.

Notes

Parts of this essay are adapted from "Glenn Ohrlin: Cowboy Singer," *Sing Out!* 15 (May 1965): 40–44; from the liner notes to my album *The Wild Buckaroo* (Rounder 0158); and from Ohrlin, *The Hell-Bound Train: A Cowboy Songbook* (Urbana: University of Illinois Press, 1973).

1. See Glenn Ohrlin, *The Hell-Bound Train: A Cowboy Songbook* (Urbana: University of Illinois Press, 1973), 20–21.
2. "Cowboy in Church," in Ohrlin, *The Hell-Bound Train,* 18–19.
3. George B. German, "Windy Bill's Famous Ride," in Ohrlin, *The Hell-Bound Train,* 172–75.
4. "The Sweeter the Breeze #1," in Ohrlin, *The Hell-Bound Train,* 205.
5. "The Sweeter the Breeze #2," in Ohrlin, *The Hell-Bound Train,* 206–8.
6. See Guy Logsdon, *"The Whorehouse Bells Were Ringing" and Other Songs Cowboys Sing* (Urbana: University of Illinois Press, 1989), 108–17.
7. Curley Fletcher, *Songs of the Sage* (1931), reprinted as Fletcher, *Songs of the Sage: The Poetry of Curley Fletcher,* ed. Hal Cannon (Salt Lake City: Gibbs Smith, 1986), 68–69.
8. "The Strawberry Roan," "He Rode the Strawberry Roan," and "The Fate of Old Strawberry Roan," in Ohrlin, *The Hell-Bound Train,* 73–79.
9. Larry Finley, "Fritz Truan, a Great Cowboy," in Ohrlin, *The Hell-Bound Train,* 88–90.
10. Noah Henry, "Starlight," in Ohrlin, *The Hell-Bound Train,* 194–95.
11. Glenn Ohrlin, "Short Creek Raid," in Ohrlin, *The Hell-Bound Train,* 117–19.
12. "The Stray" and "My Stetson Hat," in Ohrlin, *The Hell-Bound Train,* 146–47, 198–99.
13. "Windy Bill," in Ohrlin, *The Hell-Bound Train,* 12–14.
14. Dane Coolidge, *Texas Cowboys* (New York: Dutton, 1937), 104–108; *The Hell-Bound Train,* 38–40.
15. Wallace McRae, "Reincarnation," in *Cowboy Poetry: A Gathering,* ed. Hal Cannon (Salt Lake City: Gibbs Smith, 1985), 185–86.
16. "Saskatchewan," "Chuch-Wagon Races," "The Days of the Past Are Gone," and "Canuck's Lament," in Ohrlin, *The Hell-Bound Train,* 25–27, 213–19.
17. "Let Old Nelly Stay," in Ohrlin, *The Hell-Bound Train,* 109.
18. Glenn Ohrlin, "Bull Riders in the Sky," in Ohrlin, *The Hell-Bound Train,* 132–34.
19. "The Bronco Buster," in Ohrlin, *The Hell-Bound Train,* 196–97.
20. Jim McElroy, "Down in the Tules" and "Outlaw Dummy," in Ohrlin, *The Hell-Bound Train,* 182–83, 185–86.

21. Tex Fletcher, "Tipperary," and "Little Joe the Wrangler's Sister Nell" and "Paddy Ryan," in Ohrlin, *The Hell-Bound Train,* 164–71, 86–87.

22. Rusty Holman, "When Uncle Sam's Doughboy Roped a Wild Irish Rose," in Ohrlin, *The Hell-Bound Train,* 192.

23. Raymond Runnels, "The Fair at Batesland," in Ohrlin, *The Hell-Bound Train,* 188–89.

24. Raymond Runnels, "The Cowboy's Prayer," in Ohrlin, *The Hell-Bound Train,* 190; Clark, "A Cowboy's Prayer," in *Cowboy Poetry,* ed. Cannon, 69–70. "Wild Horse Charlie" is also in Ohrlin, *The Hell-Bound Train,* 191.

25. Charles Badger Clark, "Latigo Town," in *Sun and Saddle Leather, Including "Grass Grown Trails" and Other New Poems* (1915), 6th ed. (Boston: Richard G. Badger, 1922), 175.

11

Hitching Verse to Tune: The Relationship of Cowboy Song to Poetry

Charlie Seemann

Back in July of 1973, the late Dale Girdner (not to be confused with his neighbor, the better-known Gail Gardner) and I sat on the front porch of the Pioneers' Home in Prescott, Arizona, discussing cowboy songs and poetry. Dale, then seventy-four, was an old-time cowboy poet and singer who had cowboyed in northern Arizona almost his entire life. We were talking about the relationship between cowboy poems and cowboy songs and why some cowboys would sing a particular verse while others might simply recite it. Dale summed it up pretty well when he said, "Them that could sing usually did, and them that couldn't carry no kinda tune would usually just say the verses."

What Dale was saying was that one of the things needed to turn a poem into a song was somebody to sing it. The other thing necessary, of course, was a tune—a melody to set the words to. A lot of cowboy poems never got set to a tune, perhaps because their meters were unsuitable or because their themes did not lend themselves to musical performance, and so they have remained in tradition as recitations. Other poems did get attached to music and became traditional songs, whereas a great many had, and still have, simultaneous and parallel existences as both songs and recitations.

The first collections of cowboy songs focused on the words of the songs, with little or no attention paid to tunes. N. Howard "Jack" Thorp, an easterner turned working cowboy, published the first collection of cowboy songs, *Songs of the Cowboys,* in 1908. In addition to collecting cowboy songs as he worked throughout the West, he also wrote several that entered tradition and became quite well known, including "Chopo" and "Little Joe the Wrangler." His short collection of twenty-three songs contained no melodies, which suggests the preference among collectors of that era for lyrics, the "folk literature" of the people. Folklorist and ballad scholar John A. Lomax published the second major collection of cowboy songs, *Cowboy Songs and Other Frontier Ballads,* in 1910. It was a much more ambitious undertaking than Thorp's, containing 122 songs. Lomax included eighteen tunes, but the emphasis remained on song texts. There have been many important collectors and students of cowboy songs since Thorp and Lomax, including Louise Pound, Margaret Larkin, Charles Siringo, Austin and Alta Fife, Glenn Ohrlin, and John I. White. All these people have differed in their degree of interest in melodies, but the trend over the years has increasingly been to collect and publish tunes as well as texts. The first collection to include tune transcriptions for all the songs contained in it was Margaret Larkin's *The Singing Cowboy,* published in 1931.

Poems became songs in several ways. Many cowboy songs were parodies or reworkings of older traditional or popular songs, with tunes already in existence and cowboy lyrics based on those of the older song. In other cases, original poems were set to old familiar tunes, and still others had original melodies made up for them. Simple, familiar, easily sung melodies were often adaptable to several songs, leading to the often-heard observation that cowboys sang every song to the same tune. A good example of a reworked song or parody that retained the melody of the original song is the well-known "Dying Cowboy" ("Oh Bury Me Not on the Lone Prairie"), which is a parody of "The Ocean-Buried" ("Oh Bury Me Not in the Deep, Deep Sea") written by the Rev. Edwin H. Chapin, a member of the Universalist clergy, who published it in the *Southern Literary Messenger* in 1839. With music by George N. Allen, the song was copyrighted in 1850 as "The Ocean Burial."[1] Another old song that was reworked into a cowboy song with its preexisting tune intact is "The Cowboy's Lament" ("The Streets of Laredo"). It is derived from the British broadside ballad "The Unfortunate Rake," which is about a soldier who is dying of syphilis and asks for a military funeral.[2]

Another common joining of text and tune occurred when an original piece of cowboy poetry would get hooked up to an already well-known and popular melody. The poem "When the Work's All Done This Fall" was originally written by Montana cowboy poet D. J. O'Malley and published in the Miles City, Montana, *Stock Growers' Journal* on October 6, 1893 as "After the Roundup," signed D. J. White. O'Malley states that he and his friends sang it to the tune of "After the Ball," the well-known Charles K. Harris parlor song that was newly popular at the time.[3] Whatever O'Malley's intentions were regarding the tune to which he wanted his poem sung, the song eventually entered tradition sung to an entirely different melody later popularized by Carl T. Sprague's landmark 1925 commercial recording.

Another example of new words being set to an old familiar tune is Gail Gardner's "Sierry Petes" ("Tying Knots in the Devil's Tail"). Gardner, of Prescott, Arizona, wrote the words to "Sierry Petes" in 1917. He eventually published it, along with several other poems, in *Orejana Bull for Cowboys Only* in 1935. Gardner recalls: "After the war I showed that poem to some cowboy friends, among them Billy Simon. Bill decided to cook up an old tune for it and started singin' it around cow camps and rodeos. This was the first time I got the idea that a lot of my poems would do for songs."[4] The tune Billy Simon (who, like Gardner, was a long-time northern Arizona cowboy) used for "Sierry Petes" was "Polly Wolly Doodle." "Polly Wolly Doodle" was one of those tunes so familiar and simple that it was used with many different poems. It was also frequently used for "Windy Bill," a traditional song dealing with the relative merits of "tying hard and fast" and "dally roping," two competing methods of fastening a rope to the saddle horn when roping cattle. Gardner's "Sierry Petes" entered tradition and has become one of the best-loved cowboy songs, although another melody now commonly associated with it is from Powder River Jack Lee's 1930 commercial Victor recording of the song—a tune similar enough to "Polly Wolly Doodle" to suggest probable reworking of that melody by Lee.

Billy Simon was responsible for turning a number of other cowboy poems into songs, including Badger Clark's "A Border Affair" ("Spanish Is the Lovin' Tongue") and "The Glory Trail" ("High-Chin Bob"). His account of how he "rassled out" a tune to "A Border Affair" is probably typical of how many cowboy poems got original melodies made up for them and is worth giving in its entirety:

> I was workin' for the Hays Cattle Company in a line camp and there was a railroad, oh, about maybe fifteen or twenty miles from my camp. They used to call it the "Parker Cut Off," it went to California. It came from Phoenix, went through Wickenburg and turned West and went on into California. And I had about nine hundred head of steers that were camped there in that camp and there weren't many fences then, you could go clear to the Santa Maria and any old place and there wasn't any fences in the country atall there. And, of course I had a lot of ridin' to do and I'd get down along that railroad track sometime. And I didn't see very many people, no one, nobody came to my camp except when they brought me supplies, they come in with a wagon, stay overnight and go back. And I didn't have anything to read and I'd get kinda hungry for somethin', you know, just to read or anything and I'd follow that railroad line and people'd throw old newspapers out or somethin'. And somebody threw out a book. I ran onto this book of, what's the name of the man who wrote that book? Badger Clark—that's it. The book was called, what was it—*Trail Dust of the Maverick?* No. It was *Sun and Saddle Leather.* Well, I got a copy, somebody I guess dropped it or somethin', anyway I got it, and "Border Affair" was in that book. And that's where I picked it up, and when I got back to the camp I

> happened to like that little piece of poetry, ya know. And I had an old guitar there and I just fooled with it. At night I had nobody to talk to or anything and I just fooled around and fiddled around and tried chords and this 'n' that. And then when I'd ride the next day, well of course I didn't carry my guitar, but I'd try to figure out this tune, and hum and sing and what have you, and I finally wound up with somethin' that was pretty good, it sounded alright, and then I got to singin' around these cow camps and then people liked it and it just got around.[5]

In addition to the problem of poems getting matched up with workable melodies and someone who could sing them is the issue of function: Was there a practical reason cowboys may have had for singing some of their songs? Obviously, both recited poetry and singing had value as entertainment and creative outlet, but did cowboys really sing to cattle to calm them? Old-time cowpunchers and folk-song scholars alike have maintained that there was a functional use for the so-called night herding songs. Songs like "Night Herding Song," "Git Along Little Dogies," "I'm Ridin' Old Paint" and other slow, lonesome songs have long been held to have been sung by cowboys riding night guard to soothe the herd and keep them from spooking. Evidence from firsthand accounts, both oral and written, indicates that cowboys did sing, as well as talk, hum, and whistle, to cattle. Undoubtedly cowboys on night guard also sang to dispel loneliness and help pass the time, but it does seem that they also felt the cattle were calmed by their singing.

Working cowboys who kept diaries or wrote memoirs attest to the practice of singing to cattle. In his 1903 narrative *Log of a Cowboy,* one of the finest descriptions of life on the cattle trails, Andy Adams says, "Singing is supposed to have a soothing effect on cattle."[6] A more detailed and informative account comes from another working cowboy, Philip Ashton Rollins, in 1922:

> All through the darkness the men of the "night herd," working in shifts of from two to four hours, rode about the animals; and as the men rode, they constantly serenaded the beasts by crooning to them songs or chants, which, when so used were entitled "hymns." This serenading was done partly to hold the cattle under the compelling spell of the human voice, and partly to disabuse from the mind of any fearsome member of the herd the suspicion that either a puncher's silhouette against the skyline or else the noise of his moving pony might represent a snooping dragon. The rider, when "singing to the cattle," as his vocal efforts were styled, disgorged all the words he knew set to all the tunes he could remember or invent, but omitted any sound or inflection which might startle. Sacred airs were usual, for from their simple melodies they were easy of remembrance, and also they then still held the national popularity which since has passed to the tunes of the music halls; but the words set to these churchly airs well might have surprised the clergy. The proper words, accounts of horse-races, unflattering opinions of the cattle, strings of profanity, the voluminous text on the labels of coffee or condensed milk cans, mere humming

> sounds, alike and with seemingly deep religious fervor, were poured on many a night into the appreciative ears of an audience with cloven hoofs. Herded horses might wish for an occasional reassuring word, but they lacked debased operatic taste.[7]

This passage not only seems to confirm that herders sang to their charges but also illustrates yet another opportunity and motivation for cowboys to wed words and tunes. Implicit in both Adams's and Rollins's accounts is the notion that there is something especially "soothing" to cattle in the addition of some sort of music to mere words. Dale Girdner told me of another purpose for singing on night guard. Men sang, whistled, or hummed so they could hear each other in the dark and stay properly positioned around the cattle; thus they wouldn't inadvertently all wind up on the same side of the herd, leaving part of the perimeter unguarded.

Since the "golden days" of the occupational cowboy song in the late 1800s and the first two decades of the twentieth century, several major developments have had an impact on the direction of cowboy poetry and music. Real cowboys have continued to write poetry and songs, and many recent poems and songs have "gone into tradition," although now that means in print, on record, or on tape as much as in oral tradition. In reality, the print medium has always been important in the dissemination of cowboy songs. The early Thorp and Lomax collections, for example, functioned as broadsides, with many cowboys learning material from them, as did pieces like O'Malley's, published in newspapers and magazines. But the biggest impact on the relationship between song and poetry came with the onset of the commercial recording of cowboy songs in 1925, when Carl T. Sprague's Victor recording of "When the Work's All Done This Fall" sold nine hundred thousand copies and kicked off the entertainment industry's interest in cowboy music. The early recordings of cowboy songs, from the 1920s and 1930s, were made both by singers who had real cowboy backgrounds, like Carl T. Sprague and Jules Verne Allen, and by "radio" cowboys like John I. White ("The Lonesome Cowboy"), Powder River Jack Lee, and Harry K. "Haywire Mac" McClintock. Traditional cowboy songs were a feature of these recordings.

Ken Maynard initiated the motion picture singing-cowboy phenomenon when he appeared in the first singing-cowboy movie, *The Wagon Master,* in 1929. The image and exploits of the guitar-toting heroes of the silver screen like Gene Autry, Roy Rogers, Tex Ritter, and Ray Whitley were a continuation of the exaggerated mythology of the West created in the dime novels of writers such as Ned Buntline and Bret Harte. Most of the songs and music found in these movies were much more closely related to popular music of the day than to traditional cowboy song, both in content and performance style.

The second wave of "cowboy" recordings, which were made by these singing cowboys of radio and motion pictures, included many songs written by professional songwriters. These songs were very different from the often harshly realistic traditional cowboy songs, instead creating a mythic and highly romanticized portrait of cowboy life. Tin Pan Alley songwriters like Nat Vincent and Fred Howard, Nick and Charles Kenny, and Billy Hill exploited the western theme in penning many popular "western" songs such as "Gold Mine in the Sky" and "Home in Wyoming." Western singer-songwriters Tim Spencer and Bob Nolan of the original Sons of the Pioneers were responsible for some of the most beautiful western imagery of recent times, including classics like "Tumbling Tumbleweeds" and "Cool Water."

The tremendous success of commercial western music and western movies ensured that commercial lyrics, instrumentation, and performance style would have an impact on the continuing cowboy-poetry tradition. While recitation and writing poetry for recitation have continued to be thriving, vital traditions, the mid-century obsession with the singing cowboy undoubtedly created an atmosphere in which more poets deliberately created poetry with songs in mind. Certainly there has been a change in the way cowboy songs are likely to be performed. In their original context of cow camp and trail drive, songs were usually sung unaccompanied. The only instruments likely to be found were small, easily transportable ones like harmonicas, Jew's harps, and an occasional fiddle that could be rolled up in a bedroll. There were instances of guitars, banjos, and squeezeboxes being hauled around in working situations, probably in the chuck wagon, but that was not the rule.

As ranching became more important and replaced the long trail drives, the opportunity to keep instruments at the bunkhouse increased and people such as Billy Simon played guitars and even composed tunes for songs on them. But the guitar did not become ubiquitous until it was made a permanent part of the singing cowboy image by movie stars and recording artists. The same may be said of other instruments; while fiddles, banjos, and such were certainly to be found at rural and ranch dances throughout the West, it took the advent of western swing and western music played by multi-instrument combos to make such a setting for cowboy songs commonplace.

Performers like Bob Wills, the "father of western swing," combined the old-time fiddle music of Texas and the Southwest with the sounds and instrumentation of big band swing to create an exciting and popular dance music. Wills maximized his western image and Texas ranching background by performing many pieces with cowboy themes such as "Cowboy Stomp," "Ride On (My Prairie Pinto)," and "I'm Ridin' for the Rancho Tonight." Western swing instrumentation and style had a definite impact on other groups performing cowboy or western music, from Patsy Montana and the Prairie Ramblers to Bill Boyd and the Cowboy Ramblers and the Sons of the Pioneers.

As a result of these changes, tunes are rarely added today to poems intended for recitation. Instead, cowboy poets compose verse to be recited, like Wallace McRae's classic "Reincarnation," or purposely to be sung, like Gary MacMahan's "Old Double Diamond." Songs are likely to have original music and instrumental accompaniment made up for them simultaneously with the writing of the lyrics, often with formal, if not professional, performance firmly in mind.

So more than a century after the heyday of the great trail drives the best of the old-time cowboy poems and songs are still being recited and sung. Their relevance and the tradition that created those classics are still alive and vigorous although altered by changes in cattle husbandry and American society, and they are still producing literature and music that reflect cowboy life and western culture. And it's still as Dale Girdner said, some will sing 'em and some will say 'em. Regardless of whether they are recited or sung, the verses, old and new, continue to stand as a lasting tribute to the cowboys, poets, and singers who have kept this tradition alive and have lived the life they represent.

Notes

1. Jim Bob Tinsley, *He Was Singin' This Song: A Collection of Forty-Eight Traditional Songs of the American Cowboy, with Words, Music, Pictures, and Stories* (Orlando: University Presses of Florida, 1981), 81–83.

2. See James Hoy, "F. H. Maynard, Author of 'The Cowboy's Lament,'" *Mid-America Folklore* 21 (Fall 1993): 61–68.

3. John I. White, *Git Along, Little Dogies: Songs and Songmakers of the American West* (Urbana: University of Illinois Press, 1975), 85.

4. Katie Lee, *Ten Thousand Goddam Cattle: A History of the American Cowboy in Song, Story and Verse* (Flagstaff: Northland Press, 1976), 50.

5. Billy Simon, "How I Rassled Out a Tune to 'A Border Affair,'" *AFF Word* 1 (Oct. 1971): 8.

6. Andy Adams, *Log of a Cowboy: A Narrative of the Old Trail Days* (Lincoln: University of Nebraska Press, 1967), 314.

7. Philip Ashton Rollins, *The Cowboy: An Unconventional History of Civilization on the Old-Time Cattle Range* (Albuquerque: University of New Mexico Press, 1979), 267.

12

Cottonseed Cake and Pickups: Where Cowboy Poetry Comes From

Bill Lowman

I cannot reflect on why other cowboys write and recite poetry, for I cannot see into the beyond of other individuals' minds. I can only share the why's, the who's, the how come's, and the what he's made of's for myself, for I am the total authority on what drives me hard enough and moves me deep enough to record my thoughts, emotions, triumphs, failures, and visions into my own down-home cowboy rhymes. You may get a glimpse of who and what I am but may only go as far as I feel comfortable, for we all are entitled to a few deep reservations that we absolutely never will share with any other person, excluding the Lord—not even a spouse of sixty years. The more independent and reserved a person is, the more solid this is. In our way of life today, like that of a century ago, we ranchers and cowboys spend much of our work day alone. That breeds independence and guarded character. I am very much a total product of this environment.

Being born and raised in the western North Dakota badlands, a destination of many of the Texas trail drives of the 1880s and 1890s when cowboy poetry flourished, I grew up with a moderate exposure to the old classics. But it wasn't until I was a man of thirty that I ever felt the need to put on paper what had rambled for years at will in the vast unused areas of my mind. This is a common habit, I find, in today's cowboy poets. As they mature, they approach a crossroads where they begin to record their thoughts in rhyme as opposed to a looser oral communication that is used and forgotten.

In the northern states, a cowboy is pretty much raised with goals such as owning his (or her) own spread, knowing cattle bloodlines, and striving to improve the herd and weaning weight, for the calf check is the one and only payday annually. To break this down, a cowboy has to make many management decisions daily. How many pounds of supplement feed per day does each cow require throughout the winter months and what type of feed—barley cake, cotton cake, ear corn, or just hay? How much protein is there in each kind of feed per dollar spent and what percent will the cow make use of? This can go on and on to include fenceposts, liability insurance, feeding and haying equipment, easy calving bulls, the market for calves, types of mineral, and control of leafy spurge and spotted knapweed.

These pressures and decisions are what drive many to drink, but a select few are able to record the highs, lows, and unusuals of this routine into rhyme, quite often with a dry humor to smooth the rough spots in the business. Most are written not to impress the outside world but rather to amuse, entertain, and record at a personal level. Therefore, quite often they are not quite correct in meter and are not impregnated with a higher use of the English language to cause the average consumer to hold a dictionary in their free hand.

For me, the most interesting aspect concerns the different regional cultures within a bigger culture that make up the base material of any cowboy poem before an individual personality is added. The cattle industry is large, yet those in it are bonded together in the same basic effort—to make a living selling beef to the consumer. Regional culture is what adds flavor, distinction, and geographic identity. My first encounter with a western buckaroo will emphasize my thrust. In an attempt to make conversation I asked this day-work buckaroo what the calves weighed last fall when they were sold off the outfit where he was employed. I asked where they were shipped to, what feedlot they went to, what bloodlines the bulls followed, what prices the buyers were paying, and whether the buyers came to you or you went to them. These were the important things in my mind. I received a negative, blank look after each question. I soon learned that, unlike me, he took deep pride in his handmade gear (rawhide and horsehair braiding, spurs, bits, and saddles), how long he'd been with the outfit, and how many others he'd worked for in how many other states. So buckaroo poetry reflects buckaroo standards and work habits just as northern plains poetry does for us in North Dakota.

Compared to many old-time writings or works from other areas, I find my own writings to be much briefer and to the point—make a statement, corral a laugh if that is the intent, and quickly get out. That is very much a product of my region and my era, because time management is of ever-increasing importance to a ranch in the 1990s in Montana and the Dakotas compared to a half-century ago or perhaps another region. For example, an average July 1 could start before sunup, baling alfalfa to catch the dew just right for quality hay, then fighting a worn-out, third-hand swather for most of the midday, with a two-hour interruption to set a couple of posts and stretch up wire (in addition to replacing a pair of fuses at a pasture well and resetting the shut-off float) as a result of a neighbor stopping by to inform me of a hole in a fence. After supper I might check cattle and scatter bulls for a better conception rate before I ride back in by a full moon and a galaxy of bright stars, mentally and physically used.

This schedule breeds pondering and fatigue. The latter gives a person total freedom from fear of judgment by others, like the don't-give-a-damn attitude a person has while recovering from the flu. This poem, "Is There a Cathouse in Mars?" was pretty much written from the saddle horn on a note pad in one evening's ride home, transferred to a tablet the next day and jockeyed very little.

From my saddle I'm amazed by the millions of stars—
I can't help but wonder, are there others like ours?
For just beyond the sunset hangs one bright glowin' red,
So is it any wonder if the thought comes to your head,
Do they serve whiskey in honky tonks and bars?
Is there a cathouse in Mars?

Are there cattle and wild horses and the cowboy buckaroo?
Are there broken hearts and cheaters? Are there maidens that are true?
Is there eighteen-hour work days where sweat comes to your brow?
And how much money does it take to winter out a cow?
Are their social standards any different than ours?
Is there a cathouse in Mars?

Are there interest rates and mortgages? Do they have a President?
Are nerves and stress a way of life? Do preachers preach "Repent"?
Are they proud of their heritage? Do they have a National Treasure?
Are there heroes for each occasion? Is there a House of Pleasure?
Are there taxicabs a-work at night from hotels to bars?
Is there a cathouse in Mars?

Are there Malamutes and dog sleds run by the Eskimo?
If there's towns to buy supplies, how far are they to go?
If I ever ranch out there, which I hope I never do,
That the winter winds are mild, and droughts are far and few.
I'm guessin' it's top secret, when the astronauts dispute
If there's a madam in her glory at a House of Ill Repute.

Being a contemporary individual, I am constantly reinforced in the thought that the old-timers in their glory years were contemporary also. The ones that emerged the leaders of their era, that were successful and respected by their peers, didn't achieve it by being negative of mind toward change from the installed standards of their time. They were individually stable to a point that if the new way was a better way, they would adopt it against the old-timers' ways of their time. In reverse, if they felt the old way was still the better way, they'd stay with it.

Although it is simple in idea, when I was composing the next poem, I entertained many thoughts and verses over a two-week period of winter feeding in a 4x4 pickup cab before feeling I had the right message. This is when a lot of my thinking happens because my time-pressure workload is less than in the summer months. The hard-work-season poems usually happen all at once and are never added to or changed.

Old-Timers

The things we're clingin' to today
and callin' them old-timers' ways,

Remember they were once young too,
and usin' ideas that were new.

A windmill, imagine how the people fought,
and all the hard feelin's the fences brought;

Next came in the cottonseed cake—
now from all different kinds they make;

A pitchfork or shovel couldn't blow its nose
ta the work that's done through a hydraulic hose.

If they had a pickup to hay,
you think they'd use a team today,

Settin' there where it's nice and warm
next to the heater, outta the storm?

We think we'd like to live in the past—
couple of days, 'bout all it'd last.

Don't ever think to old ways they're glued—
you see, they dealt with old-timers, too.

These thoughts I hope our kids will borrow,
for we're the older timers of tomorrow.

Based on an actual event, the next poem was written swiftly with the malicious motive of condemning a growing way of handling livestock that I resist to the bone. The poem fed itself in thought so fast that I was always a stanza late with my pen. I wrote it as I rode within a half-hour after the event happened.

Motorcycle Cowboy

I'd just swung in the saddle
  from shuttin' the corral-gate latch—
I hear a roar like cuttin' wood
  or noise from the oil patch.

I rode up on a ridge
  and couldn't believe what I see:
A neighbor kid under a motorcycle,
  his ankle as big as a tree.

Said he was drivin' cattle,
  went out to turn a calf;
I looked at the wreck one more time
  then turned my head to laugh.

Didn't quite know what happened,
  had 'em about run down,
The little bugger doubled back
  and somehow put them both on the ground.

The gas tank was caved in on one side;
  he stepped back with a sigh
And said those handlebars look like
  they're almost a foot too high.

I looked away for a glance
  to see what the cattle had done;
Half a mile away, their tails in the air,
  down the draw they run.

After lots of hammerin' and bendin',
  he said it'd be alright,
Burned out throwin' dirt in the air
  to get the cattle back in sight.

I don't consider myself one
  stuck on old-timers' ways,
But certain things ain't meant for change,
  no matter how modern the days.

"Willie's Ordeal" came to me as a "fun" poem. I wrote it in three or four days, whenever the right feeling drifted my way. Again, it is a record of a true event that happened just this way to my good neighbors and their house cat, Willie.

My inspiration came as I drove home from the house of the parties involved, where I'd made a coffee stop on my way home from a 150-mile round trip to town (Dickinson) to get supplies. Cliff had just told me of the happening in his dry, humorous way, and of course Gertie was not present at the time.

Willie's Ordeal

Again there sat ol' Willie,
Square in the midst ah the yard,
On his haunches he sat so collected,
his eyes were defiant and hard.

With a tail much longer than average,
It blocked off the driver's track,
To aggravate and annoy his masters—
'Twas Willie's means of attack.

This was an ongoing happening—
for days Cliff had swung out around
With the pickup as he came in from feedin',
but his mind today was set sound.

Hell, he'd taught ugly cows lessons
and broncs that wouldn't obey;
He'd raised three kids to respect him,
now, this would be Willie's day.

He geared that Ford into low range
and this time didn't swing out.
When that Goodyear pinned down Willie's tail
the scene turned into a rout.

For the world had collapsed to a panic
on Willie, King of the Road.
He clawed and sprang for the rooftops,
but only jumped as far as a toad.

In a second the tire rolled past
and Willie made his retreat
With leaps to degrade old Kneivel
in a fashion not so secrete.

Oh, there's one thing I forgot to mention—
This feline was Gertie's cat.

That night as she rolled up the driveway,
on the porch ol' Willie sat.

He was stoved up, gimpy, and hurtin'—
perhaps he'd pulled a muscle
In the ordeal he'd experienced this morning
when forced that erratic hustle.

Now noticing Gertie's concern,
Willie played for all it was worth.
He gasped, he moaned, and he grunted
as her hand slipped under his girth.

He told her how it all happened,
the experience of death being near.
As Gertie examined poor Willie,
Cliff shed not a tear.

By morning his condition had worsened,
at least while Gertie was there.
Meals no longer impressed him,
it was hard just pullin' in air.

Not knowing the deeds of her husband,
the ordeal he'd had with her pet,
On the front seat she bedded with comfort
and headed on in to the vet.

While the X-rays were being taken
she waited, pondering his ills.
The diagnosis came as kidney infection,
"Take him home and feed him these pills."

She poked pills down his esophagus
and fed him milk in a cup.
He'd vomit them back to the surface—
Ol' Cliff, he never fessed up.

The yard stays clear at all times now,
but the memories will never grow stale,
'Cause it cost Cliff sixty-four dollars
to run over ol' Willie's tail.

I am a strong advocate of individualism, independence, and common sense. I hope that is evident in my poetry. A middle-of-the-road, moderate, non-extreme, non-radical use of mind in a crisis situation is usually the better choice. When two or more radical minds want to use the same trail at the same time, results are tragic, as opposed to a level-headed individual who can quickly adjust and adapt to each situation, using their own common sense and, if need be, lending out the rest to the adversary to smooth over an incident. As a constant reminder, I have mentally established two strong magnets in total, extreme opposition. To the far left is a whiskey bottle and to the far right lies a Bible. Common sense, independence, and individualism have worn a path square down the center. My standards reveal that both are acceptable if used in moderation. Either should be administered with plenty of fresh air and 110 cc's of common sense per hundredweight. Humor is a basic ingredient and guideline to common sense. So if it's to be in my future, something that I hope never comes to pass, that your trail would cross mine at the same time and place where I would be lying face to the earth, totally intoxicated on whiskey with a replenishing supply contained in a bottle in the grip of my left hand, and a Bible clutched in my right, mumbling quotes—please, if you are my true friend, swing from your saddle, scrape a shallow trench in the earth with your bare hands, roll me in, and replace the earth neatly. Thank you.

PART 3

PORTRAITS

Cowboy poets appear in a variety of forms: male and female, young and old, rural and somewhat urban, well educated and not so well. Although most contemporary cowboy poets are native westerners with a background of working with cattle and horses, and although they have generally grown up in ranch culture, many of the most admired classic poets were easterners who "came out West" to observe a life totally new to them. Some stayed, some eventually returned to the East, and some delved deep into ranch life, so much so that their greenhorn origins were thoroughly obscured.

John I. White, in an article originally published in 1967, gives an incisive portrait of one of the finest of old-time cowboy poets: D. J. O'Malley. O'Malley, who wrote "When the Work's All Done Next Fall" and "D-2 Horse Wrangler," grew up on the Montana rangelands near Miles City toward the end of the nineteenth century. White—a sometime singing cowboy on New York radio stations turned collector of cowboy song and poetry—discovered that O'Malley was still alive in the 1950s and began a correspondence with him that led to several articles and a chapter in White's book, *Git Along, Little Dogies.*

Henry Herbert Knibbs was another active poet during the golden age of cowboy poetry between the turn of the century and World War II. As Ronna Lee and Tom Sharpe—folklorist and cowboy poet, respectively—demonstrate, Knibbs was a native of upstate New York who migrated to California and eventually became the proprietor of a music store. But he was also a remarkably prolific writer who wrote screenplays for Hollywood during the 1920s and novels and short stories on western themes through most of his adult life. His only real knowledge of the cowboy way of life was gleaned from travels in the Southwest, but Knibbs had an acute ear and eye that made him one of the premier cowboy poets of any age.

Ray Lashley, a native of the Ozarks of Missouri, demonstrates in his career as a reciter of classic poems that cowboy poetry was popular in the frontier areas of the Midwest during the 1920s and 1930s. In his varied career as navy seaman, instrumentation specialist, and engineer, Lashley has maintained his love for horses by breeding and training them and by continuing to recite not only cowboy poetry but also poems by Benét, Kipling, and Service from the popular core of English-language literature. As folklorist Carol Edison shows in her interview, Lashley connects in his recitations complementary kinds of narrative poetry from different regions of the country and the world.

Jon Bowerman, a contemporary rancher and cowboy poet who often performs for school assemblies, grew up in an urban area but fell under the influence of an uncle who was a great reciter of cowboy poetry. From his Uncle George, Bowerman tells us, came his love of language and rhythm that eventually led him to leave the city for a life on a ranch in eastern Oregon.

This variety of backgrounds and experiences demonstrates that just as there is probably no typical cowboy poem, there is equally no typical cowboy poet. What they have in common is an affection for language, a spirit of playfulness, and some mysterious talent that draws them to express in verse their most remarkable experiences through the lenses of memory, reading, and interaction with others.

13

A Montana Cowboy Poet

John I. White

Miles City, Montana, at the confluence of the Yellowstone and Tongue Rivers, once was a rip-snortin' cow town. It boasted a real cow-town weekly newspaper, the *Stock Growers' Journal,* which devoted its news columns largely to events and statistics of special interest to cattlemen. Much of the advertising space described saddles, harness, railway cattle cars, and other items essential to the business of stock raising and included notices about horses that had strayed from home. In addition, the entire back page and a few inside columns were crammed each week with drawings of beeves displaying brands of the many cow outfits operating in eastern Montana.

Fortunately for those of us who enjoy singing or listening to cowboy songs, during the early 1890s the *Journal* had editors who liked to run poetry. It was a rare issue that failed to carry at least one, sometimes two, poems either lifted from other papers or composed by local rhymsters. In fact, the editors seem to have encouraged verse-making on the subject of cowboy life. Luckily, some of this grass-roots poetry by Montana cowhands had enough substance to catch on with range troubadours of the period. As a result, it was passed on by word of mouth from one singer to another, often being polished up in the process, and today we find variants of some of the items which originated in the *Journal*'s columns ranking high among what western historian David Lavender recently described as "America's very limited, truly indigenous folk music."[1]

The most persistent contributor of original verses to the *Journal* was Dominick J. O'Malley (1867-1943), who, at the age of fifteen, following the disappearance of his soldier-stepfather from Fort Keogh adjacent to Miles City, had gone to work as a horse wrangler for the Home Land and Cattle Company, operated by the

Niedringhaus brothers. In a very short time the young wrangler with a flair for versifying had become proficient at the cowpuncher's unique and often dangerous trade, which he followed for nearly twenty years. Three trips up the trail with Texas cattle bound for northern ranges, the last in 1891, were among his unusual experiences.

Perhaps the most famous bit of verse to which Mr. O'Malley appears to have a clear title usually is known among ballad singers as "When the Work Is Done Next Fall." When it appeared in the *Stock Growers' Journal* on October 6, 1893, its writer called it "After the Roundup" and modeled it on "After the Ball," the Charles K. Harris waltz-time song hit of 1892. Here are Mr. O'Malley's lines exactly as they were printed almost three-quarters of a century ago. The *Journal*'s compositor, apparently not up on the latest song hits, set the eight lines of the chorus flush to the left and neglected to label them "chorus." Therefore they look like a bob-tailed second stanza.

After the Roundup

A group of jolly cowboys
Discussed their plans at ease,
Said one; "I'll tell you something
Boys, if you please:
See, I'm a puncher,
Dressed most in rags.
I used to be a wild one
And took on big jags.
I have a home boys,
A good one, you know,
But I haven't seen it
Since long, long ago.
But, I'm going home, boys,
Once more to see them all;
Yes, I'll go back home
When work is done this fall.

"After the roundup's over,
After the shipping's done,
I'm going straight back home, boys,
Ere all my money's gone.
My mother's dear heart is breaking.
Breaking for me, that's all;
But, with God's help I'll see her,
When work is done this fall.

"When I left my home, boys,
For me she cried,
Begged me to stay, boys,
For me she'd have died.
I haven't used her right, boys,
My hard-earned cash I've spent,
When I should have saved it
And it to mother sent.
But, I've changed my course, boys,
I'll be a better man
And help my poor old mother,
I'm sure that I can.
I'll walk in the straight path;
No more will I fall;
And I'll see my mother
When work's done this fall."

That very night this
Cowboy went on guard;
The night it was dark
And 'twas storming very hard.
The cattle got frightened
And rushed in mad stampede,
He tried to check them,
Riding full speed;
Riding in the darkness
Loud he did shout,
Doing his utmost
To turn the herd about.
His saddle horse stumbled
On him did fall;
He'll not see his mother
When work's done this fall.

They picked him up gently
And laid him on a bed.
The poor boy was mangled,
They thought he was dead.
He opened his blue eyes
And gazed all around;

Then motioned his comrades
To sit near him on the ground:
"Send her the wages
That I have earned.
Boys I'm afraid that
My last steer I've turned.
I'm going to a new range,
I hear the Master call
I'll not see my mother
When work's done this fall.

"Bill, take my saddle,
George, take my bed,
Fred, take my pistol
After I am dead.
Think of me kindly
When on them you look—"
His voice then grew fainter,
With anguish he shook.
His friends gathered closer
And on them he gazed,
His breath coming fainter,
His eyes growing glazed.
He uttered a few words,
Heard by them all:
"I'll see my mother
When work's done this fall."

Today "When the Work Is Done Next Fall" usually is sung as a simple ballad with four lines to the stanza:

A group of jolly cowboys, discussing plans at ease.
Says one, "I'll tell you something, boys, if you will listen, please.
I am an old cow-puncher and here I'm dressed in rags,
I used to be a tough one and go on great big jags."[2]

The ending, too, has been improved as the song was passed from one singer to another over many, many years. John A. Lomax, the first collector to put it between the covers of a book, gave it this way in his notable volume *Cowboy Songs and Other Frontier Ballads:*

"Fred, you take my saddle; George, you take my bed;
Bill, you take my pistol after I am dead;
And think of me kindly when you look upon them all,
For I'll not see my mother when work is done this fall."

Poor Charlie was buried at sunrise, no tombstone at his head,
Nothing but a little board; and this is what it said:
"Charlie died at daybreak, he died from a fall,
And he'll not see his mother when the work's all done this fall."

In the original edition of the Lomax book, published in 1910, no tune was given. The revised and enlarged edition, issued in 1938 and reprinted many times, includes both words and music, the tune resembling that in Carl Sandburg's *The American Songbag* published in 1927. First to put the song on a phonograph record was Fiddlin' John Carson, who recorded it on an Okeh disc early in the 1920s.

Among the odd incidents connected with this famous western ballad was its issuance in sheet music in 1929 by the F. B. Haviland Publishing Company of New York, with words and music attributed to one R. O. Mack. When Mr. O'Malley heard about this he nearly had a stroke. All the rest of his life he saw red every time he thought of the fat profits he was certain were being made on his brainchild by someone else. Mr. Sandburg might have seen red, too, or perhaps have just been amused, had he run across Haviland's publication. The Mack version (both words and music) and that in *The American Songbag* are identical twins, even to the peculiar spelling of the words "here" and "hear" in the first and fourth stanzas respectively.

An even greater oddity is the David Guion arrangement of "When the Work Is Done Next Fall" published in sheet music by Carl Fischer Inc. in 1931. Although presented in a perfectly straightforward fashion, this carries the hard-to-believe subtitle "Humorous Cowboy Song."

An earlier O'Malley piece describing another fatal accident, this time one that occurred in daylight during a roundup, also has had wide circulation under the title "Charlie Rutledge." Mr. O'Malley stated that he and his fellow punchers sang it to an old tune, "The Lake of Pontchartrain."[3] The following verses appeared in the *Stock Growers' Journal* for July 11, 1891, with this editorial comment: "The sad and sudden death of young Rutledge on the Northside roundup is poetically described by a cowboy poet in the following obituary verses."

A Cowboy's Death

Another good cowpuncher
    Has gone to meet his fate;

We hope he'll find a resting place
    Inside the golden gate.
A good man's place is vacant
    At the ranch of the X I T,
And 'twill be hard to find one who
    Was liked as well as he.

First Kid White of the Flying E,
    Then Preller, young and brave,
Now Charlie Rutledge makes the third
    That has been sent to his grave
By a cow-horse falling on him
    Whilst running after stock
This Spring, while on the roundup,
    Where death a man does mock.

How blithely he went forth that morn
    On the circle through the hills,
Happy, gay and full of life
    And free from earthly ills;
And when they came to clean the bunch,
    To work it he was sent,
Not thinking that his time on earth
    Was very nearly spent.

But one X I T would not go
    And turned back in the herd,
So Charlie shoved him out again,
    His cutting horse he spurred;
Another started to come back,
    To head him off he tried,
The creature fell, the horse was thrown,
    And 'neath him Charlie died.

'Twas a sad death for man to meet
    Out on that lonely lea;
His relatives in Texas live,
    No more his face they'll see;
But we hope the Father greets him
    With a smile upon his face,
And seats him by his right hand
    Near the shining throne of grace.

A tune for "Charlie Rutledge" may be found in *Songs of the Open Range* edited by Ina Sires (Boston: C. C. Birchard, 1928). The words, with slight variations from those given above, appear in both the original and the revised editions of the Lomax book *Cowboy Songs and Other Frontier Ballads.* In the revised edition (1938) John Lomax stated that he first heard the song in Texas.

I was fortunate enough to meet D. J. O'Malley in 1933 and to carry on correspondence with him for a good many years thereafter. I also was able, through advertising, to obtain seven copies of the *Stock Growers' Journal* containing verses signed by him. These covered the period from August 3, 1889, to April 7, 1894. He signed his work D. J. White or with the initials DJW because at the time he went by the family name of his stepfather, Charles White. The latter was a member of Troop E, Second Cavalry, and in 1877 brought his family to the fort on the Yellowstone named for Capt. Myles Keogh, an officer who had died with Custer at the Little Bighorn the year before. In 1881 Charles White disappeared and his stepson had to go to work to help support his mother and a sister. Mr. O'Malley believed White deserted and went to Canada; a saddle mule wearing Uncle Sam's brand went AWOL from Fort Keogh at the same time.

Throughout his life Mr. O'Malley liked to be known as Kid White. In 1934, when he attended a big cowboy reunion at Miles City, the other old-timers usually referred to him that way. While the record is not clear, it appears that he probably took his own father's name of O'Malley officially in 1909 when he met a girl from Eau Claire, Wisconsin, married her, and settled down there. The rest of his life was spent in Eau Claire except for a three-year period, 1921–24, when he returned to Montana to work as a guard in the state penitentiary at Deer Lodge. During his later years in Eau Claire he worked in a factory making tires for the vehicle that put the horse out of business. In his spare time he wrote more poems and many historical sketches for Montana newspapers. His last wish, which was carried out by his family, was to be buried among his old cowpuncher friends at Miles City.

I first heard of Mr. O'Malley thirty-five years ago when I was a moonlighting singer of western ballads over the radio in New York. He had written to *Western Story Magazine* (issue of January 1932) complaining about R. O. Mack having taken credit for "When the Work Is Done Next Fall." I wrote him and, in 1935, because I happened to be making a trip through the West, I arranged to visit him at his home in Eau Claire and have a look at his remarkable scrapbook. Impressed with his sincerity and the printed evidence of his work, I wrote a brief article about him for the February 1934 issue of *Frontier Times* published by Marvin Hunter at Bandera, Texas. Shortly thereafter I put together a twenty-page pamphlet titled *D. J. O'Malley; Cowboy Poet.* Most of the two hundred copies printed were given to O'Malley for distribution to his old friends in May 1934 at the Golden Jubilee of the Montana Stock Growers' Association at Miles City. A few were sent to folklorists around the country. This pamphlet was the basis for the comments on Mr. O'Malley in *Anglo-American Folksong Scholarship since 1898* by D. K. Wilgus, published in 1959.

On July 22, 1934, Mr. O'Malley wrote me that he was born April 30, 1868, at San Angelo, Texas, and I once published this information. Recently his two daughters informed me that when he attempted to obtain a birth certificate in order to qualify for an old-age pension he learned to his surprise that he had been born in 1867 at New York City. His father was a New Yorker and a member of a New York regiment during the Civil War. After the war he reenlisted and at one time was stationed at Fort Concho near San Angelo. When his son was about four years old, the elder O'Malley died while undergoing an operation for the removal of a Confederate bullet.

In 1894 the *Stock Growers' Journal* printed what has since become another well-known cowboy song, a humorous ballad for a change, titled "D-2 Horse Wrangler" and signed R. J. Stovall. Mr. O'Malley claimed credit for this one, too, maintaining that he wrote the verses but because an acquaintance who was the subject of the tale wanted to surprise his wife by blossoming out as a poet, the latter was allowed to sign his name. There was one consideration—a five-dollar hat, said by Mr. O'Malley to be the most he ever received for a set of verses.

Variants of "D-2 Horse Wrangler" have found their way into numberless printed song collections and onto numerous phonograph records under the titles "The Horse Wrangler" or "The Tenderfoot." According to Mr. O'Malley, it was written to be sung to the tune of an old Irish-American comic ballad called "The Day I Played Baseball." Incidentally, making up new western poetry to fit the tune of a well-known song was by no means unique with Mr. O'Malley. Back in 1904 the late Joseph Mills Hanson wrote the famous cowboy song "Railroad Corral" to be sung to the Scottish air "Bonnie Dundee."[4] The unknown ranch poet who composed "Whoopee Ti Yi Yo, Git Along Little Dogies," first recorded in 1893 by Owen Wister at Brownwood, Texas, almost certainly had "The Rose of Tralee" in mind.[5]

The model for "D-2 Horse Wrangler" began this way:

My name it is O'Halloher,
    I'm a man that's influential,
I mind my business, stop at home,
    My wants are few and small.
Some blackguards 'tother day did come,
    They were full of whiskey, gin and rum
An' they took me out in the broilin' sun,
    To play a game of ball.[6]

Here is the *Stock Growers' Journal* offering for February 3, 1894:

D-2 Horse Wrangler

One day I thought I'd have some fun,
And see how punching cows was done;
So, when the roundup had begun,
I tackled a cattle king;
Says he: "My foreman is in town;
He's at the MacQueen, his name is Brown;
Go over, and I think he'll take you down";
Says I: "That's just the thing."

We started for the ranch next day,
Brown talked to me most all the way,
He said cowpunching was only fun,
It was no work at all;
That all I had to do was ride,
It was just like drifting with the tide,
Geemany crimany, how he lied;
He surely had his gall.

He put me in charge of a cavard
And told me not to work too hard,
That all I had to do was guard
The horses from getting away.
I had one hundred and sixty head,
And oft times wished that I was dead,
When one got away Brown he turned red.
Now this is the truth, I say.

Sometimes a horse would make a break
Across the prairie he would take
As though he were running for a stake,
For him it was only play.
Sometimes I couldn't head him at all,
And again my saddle horse would fall
And I'd speed on like a cannon ball
Till the earth came in my way.

They led me out an old gray hack
With a great big set fast on his back,
They padded him up with gunny sacks
And used my bedding all.

When I got on he left the ground
Jumped up in the air and turned around.
I busted the earth as I came down,
It was a terrible fall.

They picked me up and carried me in
And rubbed me down with a rolling pin:
"That's the way they all begin,
You are doing well," says Brown.
"And tomorrow morning if you don't die,
I'll give you another horse to try."
"Oh! won't you let me walk?" says I.
"Yes," says he. "Into town."

I've traveled up and I've traveled down,
I've traveled this country all around,
I've lived in city, I've lived in town,
And I have this much to say:
Before you try it go kiss your wife,
Get a heavy insurance on your life,
Then shoot yourself with a butcher knife,
It's far the easiest way.

Considering the general excellence of the rhyming in the above, the poor rhyme in the third line of the second stanza probably can be blamed on an unpoetic printer who had to decipher a handwritten manuscript. Obviously the writer intended "He said cowpunching was only play."

The MacQueen mentioned in the opening stanza was Miles City's leading hostelry and headquarters for stockmen. Its *Journal* advertising of the day played up its electric lights, electric bells, and steam heat. A news item on November 18, 1893, read: "The bathrooms at the MacQueen have recently been renovated, and to those who bathe, Mr. Tracy will be pleased to explain the valuable properties of the artesian water used for that purpose." The old landmark went up in smoke in 1897.[7]

"Cavard" (third stanza) is a corruption of a Spanish word meaning a herd of horses. A "set fast" (fifth stanza) was a saddle sore that never quite healed.

Mr. O'Malley's scrapbook yielded one other newspaper clipping that could well be part of the history of another very famous song, one commonly known as "The Cowboy's Dream" or "Grand Roundup" and sung to the tune of "My Bonnie Lies over the Ocean." Before describing the O'Malley contribution, I should point out that the authorship of "The Cowboy's Dream" has been ascribed to more people than any other song I ever heard of; also that any reader interested in going into its ramifications will find an entire chapter devoted to it in a scholarly new book, *Songs of the Cowboys,* by Austin and Alta Fife of Logan, Utah.

The O'Malley clipping, unfortunately, has no date and the verses are not signed. However, the editors inserted this one small clue at the top in capital letters: BY ONE OF THE COWBOYS OF MONTANA, FORMERLY OF LYNN.

In 1934, when Mr. O'Malley and I were preparing the pamphlet already described, he wrote me concerning his recollection of the song.

> This was written in 1887 while our wagon was working the North Fork of Sandy Creek. I was wrangling horses for the outfit. One of the boys at the wagon whose name was Tom Phelps was a great hand for singing old Sunday School songs. About three fourths of the time he was singing "The Sweet Bye and Bye" and often he would finish a verse with "I wonder if ever a cowboy will get to that sweet bye and bye?"
>
> One night after supper I had unrolled my bed and was lying on it and that line of Phelps's kept running in my head and I began to try to add enough to it to make a verse, which I did before I rolled in. It was the first verse, and the next day I kept at it, and in three or four days I had written all of it. Tom Phelps was the first to sing it.
>
> At the request of some of the boys I sent it to the Miles City paper but wouldn't let them put my name on it as I was afraid I'd be joked at by the boys. We got mail for a while at a ranch P.O. called Lynn and the editor credited the poem to "one of the cowboys of Montana, formerly of Lynn." Lynn had been discontinued in the fall of '86. I had written a couple of other pieces before I did this but never got up courage enough to have them printed.

Here are the stanzas Mr. O'Malley claimed he wrote in 1887 at the age of twenty.

Sweet By-and-By Revised

To-night as I lay on the prairie,
 Looking up at the stars in the sky,
I wonder if ever a cowboy
 Will go to that sweet by-and-by.

For the trail to that bright mystic region
 Is both narrow and dim, so they say,
While the broad one that leads to perdition
 Is posted and blazed all the way.

Now I wonder whose fault that so many
 Will be lost at the great final day,
When they might have been rich, and had plenty
 Had they known of the dim narrow way.

I hear there will be a grand roundup,
    When the cowboys, like others, will stand,
To be cut by the riders of judgment,
    Who are posted and know every brand.

Then perhaps there may be a stray cowboy,
    Unbranded, unclaimed by none nigh,
To be mavericked by the riders of judgment,
    And shipped to the sweet by-and-by.

Another extremely interesting chapter in the history of this same song was contributed by Will C. Barnes—cowboy, author, forester, legislator, and holder of the Congressional Medal of Honor for bravery in action against the Apaches. The Barnes version, which conceivably could have been a working over of Mr. O'Malley's, was widely circulated almost three-quarters of a century ago. I quote it below for comparison with the verses given above and because interested scholars will not find it in the Fife book just mentioned.

In an article "The Cowboy and His Songs" in *The Saturday Evening Post* for June 27, 1925, Mr. Barnes, who had never heard of Mr. O'Malley, had this to say:

> I first heard this song in 1886 or '87 on the Hash Knife Range in Northern Arizona. A half-breed Indian boy from Southern Utah sang about four verses which he had picked up from some other singers. He knew nothing of the authorship. I wrote these four out in my calf-branding book one evening. Later on, a boy from down Pecos way drifted into our camp and sang the four with slight variations with two new ones, one of which he claimed as his own work. I wrote another and eventually picked up three more, until I finally had ten verses in all.
>
> With the idea of using it as the motif for a cowboy story, I rewrote two or three verses, changed the words of several, added the chorus, and cut the ten down to six verses. These were published with one of my earliest Western stories—The Stampede on the Turkey Track Range. So far as I have been able to run it down, this was the first time the words ever appeared in print. Since that time the song has been printed in almost every volume of cowboy songs which has been published.

In his short story, printed in *Cosmopolitan* for August 1895, author Barnes has his verses being sung by a cowboy on night guard circling a herd of cattle. The chorus he mentions is missing.

Last night as I lay on the prairie,
    And looked at the stars in the sky,
I wondered if ever a cowboy
    Would drift to that sweet by and by.

The trail to that bright, mystic region,
    Is narrow and dim, so they say,
But the one that leads down to perdition
    Is staked and is blazed all the way.

They say that there'll be a great round-up,
    Where cowboys like dogies will stand,
To be cut by those riders from Heaven,
    Who are posted and know every brand.

I wonder was there ever a cowboy
    Prepared for that great judgment day,
Who could say to the boss of the riders,
    I am ready to be driven away.

They say He will never forsake you,
    That He notes every action and look,
But for safety you'd better get branded,
    And have your name in His great tally-book.

For they tell of another great owner
    Who is nigh overstocked, so they say,
But who always makes room for the sinner,
    Who strays from that bright, narrow way.

Shortly before Mr. Barnes died in 1936 he wrote to me and added an amusing sidelight to his *Saturday Evening Post* account of his song: "Several years before it appeared in the *Cosmopolitan* I had sung it in public during the first political campaign I was in, in Arizona in 1888. I and another cow person made the campaign with a buckboard and a little folding organ. I played and we sang cowboy and Mexican songs all over northern Arizona, and were terribly defeated. However, in 1890 we came back with the same organ and songs and were both elected."

Like D. J. O'Malley, Will C. Barnes obviously was a cowboy who liked to sing—which leads to an interesting question: was there a great deal of singing by the rough, tough men who followed the longhorn cow? For years I have saved clippings and references on the subject, and I would say the answer is "yes." As to evidence from a real, live ex-cowboy, my files show that on December 29, 1934, I stirred up Mr. O'Malley on this with the following: "Some day when you haven't anything better to do, I wish you would write me a paragraph or two on just how much and what kind of singing was done in the old days by cowboys on roundups or when driving cattle up the trail. A man from West Texas once told me that in his outfit they didn't sing at all. After a day's work, all they wanted was some sleep."

He came right back on January 6 with the following, written in the present tense although the events described took place half a century before.

> I can't imagine what sort of an outfit that man from West Texas worked with who told you cowboys didn't sing on the roundup or trail. Maybe they were all dummies. Why, there is more singing on the trail than on the roundup. The boys all sing on night guard, and almost every evening until first guard comes off some will be around the fire singing. I'll admit that on the general or spring roundup there isn't as much of it as on the beef work for the reason that breakfast usually is about 4 A.M. and from daylight till dark it is just work, and then two hours guard, and a hand does usually catch a few snores whenever he can. There is a big circle in the morning, dinner along about 9 A.M., then the roundup is to be worked, cows and calves to be cut out and all the calves to be branded. But on the beef work there are not many calves to be branded, the moves are not as long, and beeves have to be handled slowly. The herders go on at noon and all the boys but the herders are in camp till late in the afternoon when camp is moved just far enough so the beef herd can feed in to the bedground. And then the boys gather around and sing a lot, play the mouth harp, too, and maybe a banjo, but seldom a guitar as all the radio cowboys do now. Maybe that man [from West Texas] worked on only one general roundup and thought the whole works was the same.

When I thanked him and said I was surprised to hear about banjos being so popular in cow camps, he sent this additional comment on January 14:

> I never saw a bunch of cowhands at a camp where there wasn't someone singing unless it was on the Spring work when days were so long and so much work. There would often be nights when the boys were too tired to sing in camp, but you'd sure hear the night guards at it, tired or not. Yes, the banjo was in the majority on the range. I think the guitar came into use on the radio and phonograph from the fact that the cowboy was associated in the minds of the people with Mexicans. And it is well known the guitar is their instrument. But I can honestly say that where I saw one guitar in a cow camp I saw twenty banjos and about double that number of mouth harps, and once in a while a violin.

Two other signed O'Malley poems in the *Journal* that appear never to have been taken up and perpetuated by rangeland troubadours are worth quoting as early portraits of cattle-country life painted by a genuine working cowboy. These were called "The Cowboy Wishes" and "Cowboy Reverie." The former appeared on April 7, 1894. According to its composer, it was written during a meeting of the Stock Growers' Association when Miles City was full of young fellows seeking jobs as cowhands: "They were all dressed up with no place to go. Big hats, spurs, leather cuffs, six-shooters. And 95 per cent of them had never punched a cow in their lives unless it was some old milk bossie in the barn they had punched with a pitchfork handle while they were feeding her."

Mr. O'Malley explained that to make a "Winter play" was to keep busy in sight of the boss in order to be considered when the scarce off-season jobs were handed out. To "catch a regular" meant to take a nap on day herd while the cattle were lying around on water. The word "rep" (last stanza) was an abbreviation for "representative," a highly responsible cowpuncher who often worked outside the home range, checking on stray cattle and otherwise looking after his company's interests. Mr. O'Malley was just a mite proud of his own long service as a "rep" for the Home Land and Cattle Company, whose principal brand was N-Bar-N.

The Cowboy Wishes

I want to be a cowboy
And with the cowboys stand,
With leather chaps upon my legs
And a six-gun in my hand.
And, while the foreman sees me
I'll make some Winter plays,
But I will catch a regular
When the herd's thrown out to graze.

I'll have a full-stamped saddle
And a silver-mounted bit,
With conchos big as dollars,
And silvered spurs, to wit;
With a long rawhide reata
And a big Colt's forty-five
I'll be a model puncher
As sure as you're alive.

I want to be a tough man,
And be so very bad,
With my big white sombrero
I'll make the dude look sad.
I'll get plumb full of bug juice
And shoot up the whole town
When I start out to have a time,
You bet I'll do it brown.

I want to be a buster
And ride the bucking horse,
And scratch him in the shoulders
With my silvered spurs, of course.

I'll rake him up and down the side,
You bet I'll fan the breeze.
I'll ride him with slick saddle
And do it with great ease.

I want to be a top man
And work on the outside
So I can ride within the herd
And cut it high and wide.
Oh, a rep is what I want to be,
And a rep, you bet, I'll make.
At punching cows I know I'll shine;
I'm sure I'll take the cake.

The following stanzas appeared in the *Journal* over Mr. O'Malley's name on May 14, 1892.

Cowboy Reverie

Tonight as I rode 'round my cattle
I thought of my once cozy home,
So full of the little one's prattle,
And wondered how I came to roam.

To leave the dear home of my childhood
Cost my poor heart a great deal of pain,
But now my mind's fixed on one happy thought,
I'll soon see my dear ones again.

No more will I be a wild cowboy
But I'll live like a man ought to do,
And sit by the stove when the chilly winds blow
And not freeze myself through and through.

No more will I ride on the night guard
When loud Heaven's thunders do roar.
No. I'll pound my ear down on a goose hair
And think me of third guard no more.

No more will the cook's call to "grub pile"
Cause me from my hard bed to creep.
No. I'll wait till the gong sounds at seven—
To rouse from my innocent sleep.

No more festive calves will I wrestle
  So close by the hot branding fire.
I'll have no hide knocked off my knuckles,
  For that always did rouse my ire.

When the rain's coming down, my slicker I'll have
  And not leave it lying in camp.
For in herding without one when Fall rains are here
  A cowboy most always feels damp.

Now look at that long-horned son-of-a-gun,
  Up that draw, now he's going to sneak.
I wish I could run him plumb off that cut-bank
  And break his blamed neck in the creek.

Get back in the bunch, blame your trifling hide,
  Or with you it will go mighty hard.
What's that, Jim? Ten minutes of twelve did you say?
  Well, go in and call up the third guard.

In his autobiography, *Adventures of a Ballad Hunter,* John A. Lomax, in discussing the famous song "Whoopee Ti Yi Yo, Git Along Little Dogies," stated: "So far as I can discover, the word 'dogie' was first printed in *Cowboy Songs*" (the noted Lomax collection of western ballads first issued in 1910). Author Andy Adams could have disputed this, for seven years earlier on page 313 of *The Log of a Cowboy* he quoted two lines from the same song and used the word "dogie." True, an eastern typesetter who must have thought the animal referred to was canine rather than bovine spelled it "doggie." And Mr. Barnes, of course, put it in the third stanza of "The Cowboy's Dream." But D. J. O'Malley was several jumps ahead of all of them. On November 28, 1891, the *Stock Growers' Journal* printed "Cowboy's Soliloquy," signed by him, which mentioned "dogies" in both the first and third stanzas.

In 1934 Mr. O'Malley supplied me with this account of the circumstances that inspired the verses printed below.

> I was with a trail herd from the Texas Panhandle in 1891. We left the Canadian River in early March and crossed the Yellowstone onto the N-Bar-N range the middle of September. We were to drive them to the Little Dry and turn them loose, but two days before we got to where we were to ride off from them we got word to hold them along the Dry until further orders. We didn't get away from them until the 14th of October—just about eight months looking at the same dogies. Every day grew so monotonous we scarce knew what to do with ourselves. Just day herd and night guard.

Half a dozen writers have given half a dozen explanations of the origin of the word "dogie." It all seems to boil down to this: dogies were range cattle, usually young range cattle.

Cowboy's Soliloquy

I am a cowpuncher
From off the North Slide,
My horse and my saddle
Are my bosom's pride;
My life is a hard one,
To tell you I'll try
How we range-herded dogies
Out on the Little Dry.

The first thing in the morning
We'd graze upon the hill,
Then drive them back by noontime
On water them to fill.
Then graze them round till sundown,
And I've heaved many a sigh
When I thought "two hours night guard"
After night fell on the Dry.

The next day was the same thing
And the next the same again,
Day-herding those same dogies
Out on the Dry's green plain;
Grazing them, then bedding them,
One's patience it does try
When you think "now comes our night guard"
After night falls on the Dry.

They're all right in the daytime,
But our Autumn nights are cold,
And the least scare will stampede them,
And then they're hard to hold.
How many times I've "darned" the luck
When dusk I would see nigh,
And say, "I wish you were turned loose
E're night falls on the Dry."

For a large bunch of cattle
  Is no snap to hold at night,
For sometimes a blamed coyote howl
  Will jump them in a fright,
Then a man will do some riding,
  O'er rocks and badlands he will fly;
A stampede is no picnic
  After night falls on the Dry.

Then should my horse fall down on me
  And my poor life crush out,
No friendly hand could give me aid,
  No warning voice could shout;
They'd hardly give one thought to me
  Or scarcely heave a sigh,
But they'd bury me so lonely
  When night fell on the Dry.

Lomax, by the way, thought enough of Mr. O'Malley's claims to authorship to correspond with him for several years and to mention him three times in the 1938 edition of *Cowboy Songs.* Fellow Texan J. Frank Dobie, on the other hand, took a dim view of the whole thing, insisting in correspondence with me during 1934 that D. J. O'Malley was a Johnny-come-lately, that the songs discussed here originated much earlier. The late Mr. Dobie had very positive ideas on the origin of "When the Work Is Done Next Fall," based purely on hearsay. He spoke his piece at least twice in print. A comparison of his statements reveals a striking inconsistency.

In 1927, when writing in *Texas and Southwestern Lore,* a publication of the Texas Folk-Lore Society, Mr. Dobie quoted a Confederate veteran, W. W. Burton of Austin, Texas: "We had in our company during the Civil War a fellow named Marshall Johnson from Waco, who was the greatest hand to make songs and speeches that I have ever known. Poor fellow, he got killed in a stampede one fall early in the seventies, up on the Bosque River, and the well known cowboy ditty 'When Work is Done This Fall' was made on the occasion."[8]

Thirty-two years later, in *Western Folklore* for October 1959, Mr. Dobie stated that W. W. Burton told him Marshall Johnson made up the song to commemorate the death near Waco of a cowboy known as Arkansaw.

There are two other rather interesting pieces which, like "D-2 Horse Wrangler," Mr. O'Malley claimed but could not supply positive proof of authorship. One of these, "A Busted Cowboy's Christmas," was printed in the *Stock Growers' Journal* on December 23, 1893, signed with an obviously fictitious name, Iyam

B. Usted. The same issue of the *Journal* stated that the town's "tin horn gamblers" also were having a rough Christmas, twenty of them having been told by the chief of police to leave Miles City or else. The editor must have been up against it, too, because he announced that the office would be open on Christmas day to receive delinquent subscriptions.

A Busted Cowboy's Christmas

I am a busted cowboy
    And I work upon the range;
In Summer time I get some work
    But one thing that is strange,
As soon as Fall work's over
    We get it in the neck
And we get a Christmas present
    On a neatly written check.

Then come to town to rusticate,
    We've no place else to stay
When Winter winds are howling
    Because we can't eat hay.
A puncher's life's a picnic;
    It is one continued joke,
But there's none more anxious to see Spring
    Than a cowboy who is broke.

The wages that a cowboy earns
    In Summer go like smoke,
And when the Winter snows have come
    You bet your life he's broke.
You can talk about your holiday,
    Your Christmas cheer and joy;
It's all the same to me, my friend,
    Cash gone—I'm a broke cowboy.

My saddle and my gun's in soak,
    My spurs I've long since sold;
My rawhide and my quirt are gone;
    My chaps—no, they're too old;
My stuff's all gone, I can't even beg
    A solitary smoke.
For no one cares what becomes of
    A cowboy who is broke.

Now, where I'll eat my dinner
    This Christmas, I don't know;
But you bet I'm going to have one
    If they give me half a show.
This Christmas has no charms for me,
    On good things I'll not choke,
Unless I get a big hand-out—
    I'm a cowboy who is broke.

The other, according to Mr. O'Malley, was written in 1897 at the request of a cowpuncher friend named Green Johnson who had suffered a hip injury. Because he could no longer ride, Johnson had become a sheepherder. To quote Mr. O'Malley:

> He was camped about eight miles from where I was camped holding some bulls for my outfit, and I rode over to see him on several occasions. He was a good cook and neat about his camp. One day I found him pretty grouchy. He said he didn't care who came to his camp nor how much they ate of what he had cooked up but he'd be damned if he didn't think they ought to clean up the dishes they dirtied and not leave them for him to do after he'd been with the sheep all day. And he said, "Kid, write me a verse to leave in sight; maybe it will do some good." I said I'd try, and when I came to see him again I had written these verses. Green sent them to the *Stock Growers' Journal* in Miles City, saying he had found them on his mess box. Ed Butler, one of the editors, asked me if I wrote them, as they sounded like me, and I told him I did and why. He wrote quite an article in his paper on passers-by at a camp leaving dirty dishes after feeding themselves.

I am sorry to say I never have found the issue of the *Journal* said to have carried Mr. Butler's comments and the following gem of Western Americana.

Found on a Sheep Herder's Mess Box

You stranger, who comes to my tent,
I hope you'll ride away content.
Eat all you want, my only wishes
Are, when you're through you'll wash the dishes.

The fare is plain, I will allow,
But you are in a sheep camp now;
So bacon fried you'll have to go,
With flapjacks made of sour dough.

There's coffee made and in the pot,
Placed on the stove 'twill soon get hot.

You cannot ask for pie or cake,
For they take too much time to make.

So, stranger, please be kind enough,
Don't try to treat the herder rough;
Eat all you want, eat all you can,
But tie my tent and wash the pan.

Yes, stranger, of a sin beware,
Don't make the poor sheep herder swear;
But please respect his only wishes,
Eat of his grub but wash his dishes.

Notes

This essay was first published in the *Journal of American Folklore* 80 (April–June 1967): 113–29. A few changes have been made to regularize spelling, punctuation, and citation forms. Reprinted by permission of the American Folklore Society. Not for further reproduction.

1. David Lavender, *The American Heritage History of the Great West* (New York: American Heritage, 1965), 353.

2. D. J. O'Malley, "When the Work's All Done This Fall," in G. Malcolm Laws, Jr., *Native American Balladry: A Descriptive Study and Bibliographical Syllabus,* revised ed. (Philadelphia: American Folklore Society, 1964), 134.

3. For a sample stanza and list of references to "The Lake of Pontchartrain," see Laws, *Native American Balladry,* 234.

4. Anonymous, "A Folk Song of Recent Origin," *Literary Digest,* April 25, 1914, 985.

5. For Wister's version of this famous song see Owen Wister, *Owen Wister Out West: His Journals and Letters,* ed. Fanny Kemble Wister (Chicago: University of Chicago Press, 1958), 153.

6. "The Day I Played Baseball," in *Pat Rooney's Claribel Magee Songster* (New York: n.p., 1882), 18.

7. Mark H. Brown and W. R. Felton, *The Frontier Years: L. A. Huffman, Photographer of the Plains* (New York: Holt, 1955), 142.

8. J. Frank Dobie, "Ballads and Songs of the Frontier Folk," in *Texas and Southwestern Lore,* ed. Dobie, Texas Folk-Lore Society publication no. 6 (Austin: Texas Folk-Lore Society, 1927), 143.

14

"Some Folks Wouldn't Understand It": A Study of Henry Herbert Knibbs

Ronna Lee Sharpe and Tom Sharpe

Although "he never earned a dime as a cowboy," Henry Herbert Knibbs (1874–1945) became famous for western stories, novels, screenplays, and poems, which were his forte.[1] A few of the poems were read, enjoyed, and committed to memory by working cowboys, who passed them in verse and song along the trails. The remembered poems were generally quite humorous, although his better writing was serious. But most of Knibbs's writing fell through the cracks and disappeared until the recent resurrection of cowboy poetry, when the search for something new—or old and forgotten—rekindled interest in his work.[2]

It is not often that writings by non-cowboys are accepted by working cowboys. But Harry Knibbs, as his friends called him, spent a lot of time traveling in the Southwest, learning the language and the ways of those who lived and worked there. He originally intended that his travels enable him to duplicate the authenticity of locale in the works of his friend Eugene Manlove Rhodes, a cowboy, rancher, and novelist of some stature in southwestern New Mexico in the late 1800s.

Knibbs's authenticity and ability to paint with words have subsequently made him one of the most sought-after and best-accepted classic cowboy poets. It is unusual to attend a session devoted to classic poems at a cowboy poetry gathering and not be treated to at least one poem by Knibbs. It might be the camp-cook humor of "Boomer Johnson" that has been passed from campfire to campfire by generations of working cowboys, or it might be the lilting beauty and sensitivity of "Where the Ponies Come to Drink" that brings tears to the eye of the philosopher as well as the grizzled cowhand.

In his seventy years, Knibbs told hundreds of stories. In thirteen novels and hundreds of poems and short stories, he explored every aspect of the historical West.[3] But perhaps the most moving story of all was the one he began to tell at the end of his life in his unpublished autobiography, "A Boy I Knew." Rich in facts about his childhood, the memoir also holds the key to understanding Knibbs's origins, his past popularity, and the tragedy that resulted from a single, career-ending factual error (the length of a mare's gestation period). Details of Knibbs's life, gathered from his autobiography as well as from published biographical sketches, his personal and professional papers, and interviews with his close friends, provide some context in which to interpret his ability to write so effectively about western life and his recent rediscovery as one of the finest of western writers.

The small town of Clifton, Ontario, Canada (later known as Niagara Falls) may seem an unlikely birthplace for a western writer. Nevertheless, it was there that Henry Herbert Knibbs was born, on October 24, 1874, to his American parents, Sara and George. His childhood revolved around several factors that would deeply influence his later life and work: adventure, curiosity and independence, family, poetry, horses, and "Fiddle."

Many contemporary cowboy poets and musicians have observed that they can hear music in the lyrical words and rhythm of a Knibbs poem. Several, in fact, have been put to music, including "Boomer Johnson," "Where the Ponies Come to Drink," "The Bosky Steer," and "Walkin' John." It is also worth noting the titles that Knibbs chose for some of his volumes of poetry: *Songs of the Outlands: Ballads of the Hoboes and Other Verse, Songs of the Trail, Saddle Songs and Other Verse,* and *Songs of the Lost Frontier.*

By the time he was five, Harry was preoccupied with music—with one violin in particular. He had noticed a beautiful instrument in a shop window but had never heard one played. In his third-person autobiography, Knibbs recalled a memorable church garden party when "the boy [Knibbs] even forgot the ice cream when Mr. Colethurst began to play" his violin. "Just how well he played the boy never knew. But even today his spine can still feel the thrill that went up it when he first heard the sound of Mr. Colethurst's violin."[4]

The boy gazed later, with new admiration, at the violin in Howarth's window, for he had learned that "it wasn't just a fancy box made of wood. It was a passport to another world." Still wearing the dresses that young boys wore at the time, Harry craved to own the violin. Unfortunately, his life's savings, stored in an old cowhide trunk in the woodshed, totaled considerably less than half the stiff purchase price of $3.50. He devised several schemes to amass the fortune. Some were brilliant, some less than honest, and most made for intriguing stories. The strain of acquiring and saving nickels, dimes, and quarters, without his parents' knowledge or consent—and the fear that his prize would be snapped up by someone else—"used up a lot of boy."

At last, lacking only 25 cents, he visited his father at the bank and asked for the additional money to buy something special. His father asked offhandedly if he planned to buy a horse. "More than a horse," Harry replied. "But not so big." Mr. Howarth was a gruff shopkeeper and suspicious of little boys. But when cold hard cash materialized he realized that Harry, now a mature seven-year-old, meant business. Softening a bit, he replaced a broken string, then surprised Harry by playing "Annie Laurie." Harry's fears redoubled when Howarth noted that it was a better violin than he had thought and mused that perhaps he was selling it too cheaply. Harry collected his treasure and raced home via back alleys to avoid curious neighbors and unsuspecting parents.

Harry now had the fiddle but dared not play it, for the instrument was too precious to suffer under his unskilled fingers. He also feared discovery and imagined the enforced return of the unnecessary luxury to Howarth's shop. So Harry kept Fiddle hidden in the woodshed, safely tucked away in the same cowhide trunk where he had hidden his coins, taking it out only to hold and admire.

When at last he overcame his fears and put bow to string, he was overheard. It was the groom across the street who first discovered Harry's secret. At the groom's request, Harry reluctantly handed over the fiddle and was amazed as the sweet sound of "Sailor's Hornpipe" flew from the strings: "Jarvey the roustabout, who fed horses and shoveled manure for a living, had become a person of influence. He could play the violin."

Jarvey demonstrated the playing of fifths and was the first to teach Harry "to hear—actually to hear—the voice of [my] Violin." For only a dime a lesson, Jarvey offered to continue the instruction. Although he was a "person of influence" to the aspiring musician, Harry knew his parents had little respect for the man and so avoided him in the future. But Jarvey had given him the basics: "Each day Fiddle meant more to me. It wasn't just a varnished box with four strings. It was something alive and filled with voices. Occasionally it would sing."

Eventually George and Sara discovered not only the fiddle but also their son's passion for it. Fiddle was moved from the cowhide trunk to a place of honor beneath his bed, but until winter arrived Harry's practicing was limited to the woodshed studio. Formal lessons proved to be of some value, but Harry continued to rely on his ear and his instinct—"something told me inside when the fiddle sounded right." He heard, played, and owned many fine fiddles and eventually operated the Farthing Hub Violin Shop in Banning, California. How could there not be music in the poetry of a man who at the age of seven had a best friend named Fiddle?

Several stories in Knibbs's autobiography indicate that as a child he was not only curious and adventurous but also mischievous and often in trouble. At the age of four, for example, young Harry found a frozen cat behind his house. He had never seen a dead cat and thought it was only sleeping. He took it to the woodshed, laid it on the chopping block, and began petting it, trying to make it purr as any good cat should. Confused when his attentions were not rewarded with the cat's sound of contentment, he tried talking to it but still it did not respond:

> I picked kitty up and shook her. Kitty did not wake up. I shook her harder. Still no response. I tried to move her legs. They were stiff, unmovable. Her tail stuck straight out. I was puzzled. Kitty's eyes were open, and yet she was asleep. The wheels that should have gone round didn't go round. I wanted very much to find out why. . . . I laid kitty on the chopping block. I took the handle of the hatchet in both hands, raised it high and brought it down. It was a fairly heavy hatchet, and father always kept it sharp. Half of kitty remained on the chopping block. The other half fell to the floor. I felt just a bit queer, but I was still curious. I picked up the fallen half and looked at it. It is fortunate that kitty was frozen. Even so, what I saw was not any too encouraging. . . . Perhaps the something which made cats go was in one of the parts I had not yet chopped. So I chopped some more. When I finished there was a dismembered tail, a pair of hind legs, several cutlets of frozen midsection, a pair of front legs, and a head on the floor of the woodshed. . . . As a cat, kitty no longer had any appeal.

Despite his mischievous streak, Knibbs remembered his family with fondness and reverence. Even the arrival of a baby sister, although viewed at the time with some skepticism, was remembered with humor: "I thought that life was just right. It never occurred to me that it could change. And then my baby sister was born. . . . Some people never think about earthquakes happening to *them.* I had never thought much about babies. And now one had happened to me."

His mother Sara was a homemaker and suffered from migraine headaches; Harry recalled his disappointment when one such spell kept mother and son from attending a much-anticipated picnic. Nevertheless, he remembered her fondly, proclaiming that "Mother was an angel." Harry's love and respect for his family is portrayed in the following passage that describes his punishment for stealing 50 cents for his fiddle fund from their hired girl's purse:

> But to be sent upstairs to bed, not alone supperless, but deprived of the warm feeling of companionship and well being you had when you sat at the supper table with your father and mother, hungry for the food which smelled so good, and unaware that you hungered quite as much for love and sympathy and understanding—and praise if you had earned it; when you eagerly unburdened your heart of the day's triumphs or failures (omitting to mention little indiscretions and mistakes), and your mother was going to read to you after the supper things had been cleared away and you had done your lessons; to be deprived of all this, to know that you were in dis-

> grace, an outcast whom your father and mother no longer loved, was a punishment so bitter you felt you could never survive it.

Knibbs credited his early exposure to and appreciation of poetry to his father: "How many of the grace notes of existence I owe to my father! His spriteliness could lift the dullest hour to a frolic. The works of Longfellow, Lord Byron, Whittier, Tennyson, Edgar Allen Poe and other then popular poets gave father a fine chance to disport himself for the amusement of the family."

Another influence was Wib, the hired man on his grandparents' farm who first taught young Harry about the power of language: "He had a dry ornate way of talking that was fascinating to a small boy, and his admonitions were a great deal more impressive to me than if he had used ordinary country language. When he told me that Grandmother's fields and pasture lots were 'densely populated with rattlesnakes,' it really made me want to watch out where I was going, when an ordinary grownup warning would have sounded like a lecture and put my contrary back up."

In a chapter he entitled "My Grandma Was a Thoroughbred," Knibbs notes, "The man who hasn't spent at least a portion of his boyhood on a farm has missed the best part of his life." Harry spent every summer vacation of his first fifteen years on his grandparents' Pennsylvania farm. Between ages one and five he was escorted there by his mother, but "when I was five years old father took me to the station, fastened a tag on my coat lapel, put me on the Erie train, and shipped me to Grandmother's all by myself." During these childhood train rides Harry became increasingly independent and fond of travel. He dreamed of becoming a railroad conductor and did in fact spend time later in life as a hobo.

At Grandma's farm, Harry became acquainted with his extended family and acquired a great respect for his ancestors' pioneer spirit and hard work. His great-grandfather "was a neat workman" who impressed Harry with his ability to carve ornaments and utensils from wood and horn; to make ox yokes, bows, and flails; to sole and mend cowhide boots; to make rawhide; and to build a well-constructed house from wood by hand.

Like his poetry, Knibbs's recounting of childhood farm memories is characterized by deep emotion, acute observation, and detailed description: "It is more than half a hundred years since I last saw the old farm. The family has long since scattered, most have died. But I have not forgotten one little corner of Grandmother's place . . . every fence post and clump of petunias. I can see Grandma herself, now rosy with vexation at some misdeed of that dratted boy, now beaming with the loving kindness her heart was full of. I am glad to keep such memories in that one spot where they will never fade."

Harry developed his love of horses during these summers: "Of course fiddles were the most important things in the world. Except when I was looking at horses." In a chapter entitled "Fiddle and Four Legs," Knibbs explains his love, respect, and understanding of horses and their relationship to people. This aspect of Knibbs's early years helps to explain his ability to speak so well through his later poetry to the cowboy and horseman.

He couldn't pinpoint the exact moment when he "first loved horses" but suspected that "it was probably the first time I ever saw one." It was in his blood to love fine horses, for his Pennsylvania relatives were not only farmers and teachers but also horsemen and horse breeders. Great-uncle Smith bred horses, and Aunt Lib "was the only person, man or woman, who could handle Frank, her beautiful black gelding." Of his grandmother he said, "If I hadn't admired her for anything else, I would have had to admire her for the way she had with horses. Grandmother was a notable horsewoman. I shall never forget the authority, the daring, and the good hard sense with which she handled her favorite mare." He continued:

> Even when I was in short dresses, whenever there was a fence with a horse on one side of it, you could see me on the other, pressing as close as I could get to see all there was to see. After I graduated into short pants I spent my time in Uncle Smith's barn whenever I could, pestering the hired men when they hitched up or fetched in the work teams. I wanted to help unharness. I wanted to feed and water the horses. I wanted to do everything but keep out of the way when the men were working around the horses. I'm surprised I didn't ask to sleep with them.

Occasionally, Henry was allowed to ride on the "front seat of a hack driver's carriage," and he wanted nothing more than to grow up quickly, have his own horses and buggies, and go into business as a hack driver. From this perfect observation point he was able to note each and every detail of the horses' actions, and he stored these scenes away in his exceptional memory. Several decades later he called upon his remarkable skill to fashion vivid, poetic images from those detailed memories: "I could see all around and I could see the backs of Tom Riley's horses gently move up and down like the shafts of our sewing machine. I could watch what they did with their heads and keep track of their ears. I loved to see how those ears moved, like little men, stood still, listened, moved sidewards or forwards again."

From these family and farm experiences during the first fifth of his life, Knibbs gained a great deal of useful knowledge and a keen intuition about people as well as horses: "There on the farm I could see with my own eyes what it meant to breed a strain for courage, endurance and spirit. Gradually I came to see that it applied just as well to people as to horses." Armed with these insights, a spirit of adventure, an unquenchable thirst for knowledge, and a love of horses, poetry, and fiddles, he was ready to embark upon adulthood.

Although Knibbs never graduated from college, he was well educated by the standards of the day. At fourteen, he attended Woodstock College in Woodstock, Ontario, and at fifteen, Bishop Ridley College at St. Catherine's, Ontario, spending the next three years there. Upon leaving Bishop Ridley College, Knibbs migrated to Buffalo, New York, and found employment as a wholesale coal salesman with a Michigan-Ontario territory. He left that position to clerk for the Lehigh Valley Railroad. A short time later he took off for a two-year stint as a hobo in the Midwest. Completing that tour, he married and went to work as a stenographer in the Division Freight Office of the BR&P (Buffalo, Rochester, and Pittsburgh) Railway in Buffalo. When he was summoned to the Rochester office to become private secretary to the traffic manager, he built a house but never lived in it. At the age of thirty-four, he decided it was time to go to Harvard University.

Little is known about the time he spent at Harvard—he did not receive a degree—but two years later, in 1910, he moved to California and wrote his first western novel, *Lost Farm Camp*. When it was accepted for publication by Houghton Mifflin, he embarked on an extensive trip through California, Arizona, and New Mexico. Knibbs absorbed plenty during his travels, learning enough about the West and cowboy life to be considered an authority who was highly respected by other western writers.

In 1899, soon after his hoboing days, Knibbs had married Ida Julia Phiefer. Thirty years later he left Ida to live with Turbesé Lummis Fiske, whose father—Charles Fletcher Lummis, historian, novelist, and editor—he had known before he left the East. Ida refused to divorce Harry and wrote to him daily for the first year, then weekly, and eventually annually, begging him to return and denouncing the woman with whom he was living. The reasons for the separation are speculative, but Turbesé, eighteen years younger than Knibbs, no longer lived with her husband. She and Knibbs wrote a novel together and she edited much of his work, including his autobiography, which she attempted to have published several times. After Knibbs's death, Ida went to court to gain the copyrights owned by Henry and claimed by Turbesé. Ida lost.

Among the people with whom Knibbs associated in California were Turbesé's father and Frank King, a writer for the *Western Livestock Journal*, who told Knibbs about cowboy poet Bruce Kiskaddon. Whether Knibbs and Kiskaddon ever met or corresponded is unknown. Like Charles Lummis, Eugene Manlove Rhodes had become a friend of Knibbs before he left for the West; they had met while Knibbs was working for the BR&P. At one point the friendship between them became strained when Knibbs used Rhodes as a character, somewhat unflatteringly, in *The Ridin' Kid from Powder River*, but he made up for it in *Partners of Chance*, in which the hero is based completely on Rhodes.[5]

Harry published six books of poems during his lifetime. *First Poems* was published in a limited edition of three hundred copies, signed and numbered, under the pen name of Henry K. Herbert. The remaining five books were written in a less formal, more familiar style, with topics ranging from the sentimental ("Where the Ponies Come to Drink") to the hilarious ("Boomer Johnson"). The topics of these poems take readers from the sea to the plains and through the mountains, both on horseback and on foot, with the stars and dogs for companions. "Where the Ponies Come to Drink," once lost and forgotten about, has only recently been rediscovered. It is the final poem in Knibbs's second collection, *Songs of the Outlands: Ballads of the Hoboes and Other Verse.*

Where the Ponies Come to Drink

Up in Northern Arizona there's a Ranger-trail that passes
Through a mesa, like a faëry lake with pines upon its brink,
And across the trail a stream runs all but hidden in the grasses,
Till it finds an emerald hollow where the ponies come to drink.

Out they fling across the mesa, wind-blown manes and forelocks dancing,
—Blacks and sorrels, bays and pintos, wild as eagles, eyes agleam;
From their hoofs the silver flashes, burning beads and arrows glancing
Through the bunch-grass and the gramma, as they cross the little stream.

Down they swing as if pretending, in their orderly disorder,
That they stopped to hold a pow-wow, just to rally for the charge
That will take them, close to sunset, twenty miles across the border;
Then the leader sniffs and drinks with fore feet planted on the marge.

One by one each head is lowered, till some yearling nips another,
And the playful interruption starts an eddy in the band:
Snorting, squealing, plunging, wheeling, round they circle in a smother
Of the muddy spray, nor pause until they find the firmer land.

My old cow-horse, he runs with 'em: turned him loose for good last season;
Eighteen years' hard work, his record, and he's earned his little rest;
And he's taking it by playing, acting proud, and with good reason;
Though he's starched a little forward, he can fan it with the best.

Once I called him—almost caught him, when he heard my spur-chains jingle;
Then he eyed me some reproachful, as if making up his mind:
Seemed to say, "Well, if I have to—but you know I'm living single . . ."
So I laughed. In just a minute he was pretty hard to find.

Some folks would n't understand it,—writing lines about a pony,—
For a cow-horse is a cow-horse,—nothing else, most people think,—
But for eighteen years your pardner, wise and faithful, such a crony
Seems worth watching for, a spell, down where the ponies come to drink.

Knibbs was also the author of thirteen novels, which most critics consider to be lacking in originality. He always seemed to allow the good guy to win, and the heroine always ran off with the hero. He often included a character who was a wanderer and had a violin. But his portrayals of the landscape were filled with detail and remarkably accurate, as were his descriptions of horses, equipment, and cowboy work.

Knibbs wrote both poetry and fiction for various popular magazines of the time, including *The Saturday Evening Post, Red Cross Magazine, Current Opinion, West, Western Stories,* and *Adventure.* Most of his novels were printed serially in these magazines before they were published in book form.

As a writer of the West in the early part of the twentieth century, Knibbs was closely watched by his contemporaries, and their interest proved fatal to his career. In a series of short stories for *The Saturday Evening Post* about a horse called Pericles, he inadvertently stated that the gestation period of a mare was nine months instead of eleven. His peers defamed him for the error. It was a shocking blow to Knibbs. He tried many times to explain the error, but the damage had been done and none of his stories was ever again accepted for publication.

Knibbs turned back to his first love, Fiddle, and spent his remaining years running a violin shop in Banning, California. "Certain words," he wrote, "can be ridden like horses. One word carries me farther than any horse has ever done. That word is violin." The only writing of consequence Knibbs accomplished during his last few years was an autobiographical manuscript that remains unpublished and obscure. It will be a great loss if "A Boy I Knew" does not find a publisher, for captured within its nearly three hundred typewritten pages are some of the finest examples of personal history ever written. It is a story of late-nineteenth-century small-town life and the childhood adventures of a special man.

On May 17, 1945, Knibbs died in California from a respiratory illness from which he had suffered most of his life. His companion Turbesé wrote: "I too knew a boy. Though he was ailing and slender and gray then, and in the grip of his last illness, he would often grin at me from his pillow, and that grin would bridge more than sixty years and he was once again the boy who had yearned over old man Howarth's violin."[6]

Appendix: The Publications of Henry Herbert Knibbs

All information regarding printed work is from *Twentieth-Century Western Writers,* ed. James Vinson (Detroit: Gale Research, 1982), 461–63; information on films is from *Encyclopedia of Frontier and Western Fiction,* ed. Jon Tuska and Vicki Piekarski (New York: McGraw-Hill, 1983), 202–4.

Novels

Lost Farm Camp. Boston: Houghton Mifflin, 1912; London: Constable, 1912.
Stephen March's Way. Boston: Houghton Mifflin, 1913; London: Hodder and Stoughton, 1913.
Overland Red: A Romance of the Moonstone Cañon Trail. Boston: Houghton Mifflin, 1914; London: Hodder and Stoughton, 1925.
Sundown Slim. Boston: Houghton Mifflin, 1915; London: Hodder and Stoughton, 1917.
Tang of Life. Boston: Houghton Mifflin, 1918; London: Melrose, 1922. Also published as *Jim Waring of Sonora Town.* New York: Grosset and Dunlap, n.d.
The Ridin' Kid from Powder River. Boston: Houghton Mifflin, 1919; London: Hodder and Stoughton, 1921.
Partners of Chance. Boston: Houghton Mifflin, 1921; London: Hutchinson, 1922.
Wild Horses: A Novel. Boston: Houghton Mifflin, [1924]; London: Hutchinson, 1924.
Temescal. Boston: Houghton Mifflin, 1925; London: Hutchinson, 1925.
The Sungazers. Boston: Houghton Mifflin, 1926; London: Hutchinson, 1926.
Sunny Mateel. Boston: Houghton Mifflin, 1927; London: Hutchinson, 1927.
Gentlemen, Hush! With Turbesé Lummis. Boston: Houghton Mifflin, 1933.
The Tonto Kid. Boston: Houghton Mifflin, 1936; London: Hutchinson, 1937.

Uncollected Short Stories and Poems

"Rancho in the Rain." *Red Cross Magazine* (New York), July 1920.
"Broncho Shod with Wings." *Current Opinion* (New York), Dec. 1922.
"Lee of Rimrock." *Adventure* (New York), 1 April 1928.
"An Old Fashioned Sheriff." *Adventure* (New York), 15 April 1928.
"Tonto Charley." *Adventure* (New York), 15 Aug. 1929.
"Head Money." *West* (New York), 25 Nov. 1931.
"Crow Bait." *Western Story* (London), March 1932.
"Three Swinging Shadows." *West* (New York), 30 March 1932.
"Three of a Kind." *West* (New York), 31 Aug. 1932.
"Why, Pericles!" *Saturday Evening Post* (Philadelphia), 1 April 1933.
"That Colt Pericles." In *Horses, Dogs, and Men,* ed. C. W. Gray. New York: Holt, 1935.
"Pericles' Honeymoon." In *Gallant Horses: Great Horse Stories of Our Day,* comp. Frances E. Clarke. New York: Macmillan, 1938.
"Shot in the Dark." In *Great Tales of the American West,* ed. Harry E. Maule. New York: Modern Library, 1945.
"Mebbyso a Thousand Dollars." *West* (Kingswood, Surrey), Aug. 1946.
"The Rat's Nest." In *Gun Smoke Yarns,* ed. Gene Autry. New York: Dell, 1948.
"Road Runner." In *Western Stories,* ed. William MacLeod Raine. New York: Dell, 1949.
"Young Pete Pays a Bill." In *Selected Western Stories,* ed. Leo Margulies. New York: Popular Library, 1949.
"Thunder Mountain." *Zane Grey's Western* (New York), Feb. 1949.

Screenplay

Tony Runs Wild, with Edfrid Bingham and Robert Lord, 1926.

Verse

First Poems (by "Henry K. Herbert"). Rochester: Genesee Press, 1908.
Songs of the Outlands: Ballads of the Hoboes and Other Verse. Boston: Houghton Mifflin, 1914.
Riders of the Stars: A Book of Western Verse. Boston: Houghton Mifflin, 1916.
Songs of the Trail. Boston: Houghton Mifflin, 1920.
Saddle Songs and Other Verse. Boston: Houghton Mifflin, 1922.
Songs of the Lost Frontier. Boston: Houghton Mifflin, 1930.

Films Based on Knibbs's Work

Overland Red (Universal, 1920), directed by Val Paul. Remade as *The Sunset Trail* (Universal, 1924), directed by Ernst Laemmle.
Sundown Slim (Universal, 1920), directed by Val Paul. Remade as *The Burning Trail* (Universal, 1925), directed by Arthur Rosson.
The Ridin' Kid from Powder River (Universal, 1924), directed by Edward Sedgwick. Remade as *The Mounted Stranger* (Universal, 1930), directed by Arthur Rosson.
Knibbs also contributed the original story for the film *Tony Runs Wild* (Fox, 1926), directed by Thomas Buckingham.

Notes

1. The quotation is from Keith Lummis, friend of Henry Herbert Knibbs, son of Charles F. Lummis and brother of Turbesé Lummis Fiske, as told to Ronna Lee and Tom Sharpe in an interview in September 1991.

2. Cowboy poetry never really died, but, like the cowboy, you just couldn't see it from the interstate.

3. See the appendix for a list of Knibbs's novels, uncollected short stories and poems, collections of verse, and a screenplay, as well as a listing of films based on Knibbs's works.

4. From the unpublished manuscript of Henry Herbert Knibbs's autobiographical "A Boy I Knew." All quotations are from this manuscript unless otherwise noted. The manuscript is housed in the Henry Herbert Knibbs Collection, Special Collections, Stanford University Library, Palo Alto, Calif.

5. Jon Tuska and Vicki Piekarski, eds., *Encyclopedia of Frontier and Western Fiction* (New York: McGraw-Hill, 1983), 203.

6. Turbesé Lummis, "Editor's Farewell," in "A Boy I Knew."

15

Ray Lashley: An Interview with a Frontier Reciter

Carol Edison and Ray Lashley

Reciter Ray Lashley is the product of a community, of a place in time, and of an artistic tradition that led him to cowboy poetry as naturally as it taught him to be self-sufficient. Born in 1923 into a rural Ozark Mountain community abounding in large families and livestock but shy on roads, electricity, and interactions beyond the county line, Ray wasn't raised on a ranch or even in the West. But he grew up in a region that identified with the West and the frontier experience—in Missouri, the point of departure for exploration of the far West, the heart of the American fur trade, and an area that still proclaims itself "The Gateway to the West."

In Ray's home region, the lifestyle of the frontier persisted long after the frontier had moved westward, especially during the Great Depression. Like the generations that preceded him, Ray fed, tended, and moved the cattle, sheep, and hogs that his family and neighbors all raised. He cared for, broke, and rode the horses they depended upon to move both people and things. He cut timber for fences and firewood, hunted wild game for its meat, and helped his neighbors harvest grain. And like the other young people in his community, Ray mastered the skills needed to feed a family and to provide cash for those necessities that came from beyond their isolated valleys.

Ray attended country schools, where he developed a passion for words that led him to appreciate those in his family and community who shared a story, a song, or a stanza of verse during long winter evenings. And he read and dreamed about the land beyond the rolling crests of the Ozark Mountains.

As times changed, Ray took opportunities as they developed—first in the navy in World War II, then as an instrumentation and testing specialist in California and Utah—opportunities that ultimately led him to the West of his boyhood dreams. There he sought out those who understood his love of the land, livestock, and the lifestyle of the frontier. Around the campfires of hunting and fishing trips or while working with his horses on his country places, first in northern Utah and now in western Colorado, Ray shared his view of the world and the poetry of his childhood, especially the tales of the frontier past expressed so eloquently by America's nineteenth-century narrative poets. And he subsequently became known as one who recites the same words that were undoubtedly spoken around the fires of cow camps a hundred years earlier.

America's nineteenth- and early-twentieth-century cowboys were also born into a community, a place in time, and an artistic tradition that led them to these forms of expression. Many of them had attended school, where memorization was considered an important skill and where they were taught not only reading but also public speaking and elocution—skills often practiced by reciting poetry. Out on the range, with only each other to provide entertainment, it is no wonder that recitations, like storytelling and singing, became popular evening entertainments, just as they were at indoor gatherings in Victorian parlors.

Like their urban counterparts, cowboy reciters either learned poems by listening to other reciters or memorized them from written sources. Some undoubtedly even memorized poems from books published by early collectors of cowboy lore, bringing the poems full circle to their folk origins. As poems were passed from one reciter to the next, verses were frequently altered and refined to emphasize the most vital aspects of the material. Among the early favorites were those narrative poems that recorded the frontier experience or dealt with the human struggle against the elements. Poems that the reciters took time to memorize, and which they continued to pass along, must have had special resonance for those who lived on horseback, must have communicated something that was real and true about their collective experience and shared heritage.

Like the cowboys of long ago and many of their successors, Ray Lashley has a love and a talent for expressing important thoughts and stories through rhymed and metered verse. He shares that tradition by reciting classic American verse such as "The Ballad of William Sycamore" by Stephen Vincent Benét and by writing poems like his own narrative piece "A Ride with Chief Joseph," which provide insight into the lives of those who created America's history. Perhaps it is because he was born in an isolated, frontierlike place where change came slowly that he developed a view of the world and a way of expressing that view that parallel the experiences of many contemporary western cowboys. But more important than the circumstances of his birth is the fact that the poetry Ray Lashley recites and writes eloquently illustrates a continuity of feeling and experience that links him with the western lifestyle and the rich frontier heritage of the American past.

[The following is an edited version of an interview with Ray Lashley conducted by Carol Edison on Thursday, 20 October 1988, at his home in Syracuse, Utah.]

I was born on the first of August 1923. It was a really hot day. I can depend on that being true because August is always hot in Missouri. I was born near a place called Des Arc, Missouri. Des Arc—the name comes from the fact that the railroad had a big bend in it there. That's down in Iron County, Missouri, in the Ozark Mountains. Most people there lived on farms where they raised vegetables, fruit, and stock. Our family never raised any sheep to amount to anything, but others raised them. We raised mostly hogs, cattle, horses, and mules. That part of Missouri was considerably behind the time curve—I'd estimate something like fifty years. I had three brothers and six sisters. I'm the third child in the family. The rest are all scattered out at about two-year intervals behind me.

There was not a whole lot of money. We were poor; we knew we were poor because everybody said we were, but everybody else was too. It may sound like we were living in some sort of hardship. If we were, we never knew it because it was a standard. That's the way everyone was. Looking back, I feel fortunate to have grown up there. I had available to me unlimited country to run in as I grew up. There was game in the woods, and there was a good reason for catching it. All the game that we caught we used. We had one period there that was nearly two years long when probably 75 percent of the meat that was put on the table was game that we took out of the woods, so it was quite fortunate that we had it. That doesn't mean that hunting was a chore. We enjoyed it. In fact, there's an incentive in hunting—when you really need the meat—that is missing to me now.

Everyone had cash crops of some sort. It's called diversified farming. They'd raise a number of different things, including things they needed for food themselves. There were still people spinning wool when I was a child. They raised hogs, cattle, chickens, and sheep for food. The cash was not normally from the crops out of the field. It would result from the sale of milk, wool, lambs, beef, or hogs that ate those crops. Hogs were probably the most widespread money crop.

As I was growing up I liked the work that there was to do on the farm. That was not cattle ranching as one thinks of it in connection with the West. Only a few families were dependent solely on cattle, but nearly everyone raised some. There was an open-range law, which meant you could graze your stock on any land that was not fenced. At that time, you marked and branded your cows and turned them loose, and they strayed wherever the graze was, and then you went to look after them yourself or gathered them and brought them to be sold or to be doctored or whatever was required. We'd usually bring them in during the winter months and keep them on the place where we could feed them. As soon as the graze started to come in the spring, we'd turn them out on the open range again. So we had the same chores that the men out on the western range had, on a smaller scale: searching for the cattle, bringing them in, doctoring them, helping the cows calve, seeing to the breeding, branding them, ear-marking and cutting calves, and all the other things that go along with raising cattle.

I liked best the handling of horses, and so I would make any excuse to use a horse to do anything at all. That stayed with me. That's why I've been in the horse-raising business for some eighteen years on this place. All of our farm work we did with horses. We used the horses to handle stock, to plow the ground, to haul logs, to go to church on Sunday, and for whatever needed to be done. Horses were the main source of power and transportation. Besides being ridden or driven, horses were even used to power many of the mills, like sorghum mills or grist mills.

As a kid I'd seen just how hard work can be on a farm. The other choices that I had were to work in the woods, cutting and hauling timber, working in a sawmill, or working in one of the mines. But I dreaded the idea of ever having to take a job in a mine. I didn't like the idea of being underground. I'd always wanted to do anything where I could see the sun. Even if I had to get rained on and all of the other things that go with it, I much preferred that. So it seemed to me that the key to my survival was to get some education and training so that I wouldn't have to work as hard as the folk I knew were required to work.

My dad knew that I wanted to go to high school. He told me that he could provide me with a place to sleep and something to eat but for anything beyond that—like clothing and books or any extracurricular activities—for the most part he'd be able to provide very little. It even pleased me, as I remember, for him to stand there and express confidence in me and to give me the opportunity to go out and help myself. The high school was in town. We lived about a mile and a half from the bus line, and then I had a two-mile ride to school. During the bad part of the winter sometimes I would stay with a family that lived in town within walking distance of the school. I'd do chores for them in exchange for my room and board.

In my last year of high school, when I would have been in the twelfth grade, I joined the navy. That was in September of '41, just as school was starting. My brother was already in the navy, so I joined, and in December of that year World War II started. My brother and I were on a destroyer-minesweep during the first two years of the war. I went from there to a gyro-compass and navigation-equipment school. I became an electrician's mate. I found working with electricity kind of fun and easy. I was stationed for two years in Panama, where I worked on navigation equipment, for the most part on gyro-compasses.

When the war was over and I got out of the navy, I went back home. I could see the country had changed completely during the war. Farms that had always been operating farms and had supported big families were vacant and were growing up in underbrush. The farming effort had dropped to something less than 10 percent of what it had been when I'd left. People were buying the farms, as many adjacent farms as they could, usually people from another state like Texas. They recognized the potential as a cattle-raising country. Out here in the West it takes twenty-five to forty acres to support one cow unit. Back there you can support a cow unit on one or two acres, and when it's improved it is even better than that. They get a lot more rainfall and have plenty of water and lush, easy growth with good grasses to feed the stock. A lot of those combined outfits are still in place and doing well now.

After seeing that my choices remained the same at home, I decided that I needed to get more school. I wound up in California, where I'd served in the navy and worked toward an engineering degree. I got interested in instrumentation, the work of measuring things, determining how hot something gets and how fast it gets hot, or how loud a noise it makes, or measuring just about any physical phenomenon by various electronic, optical, or mechanical means, recording and analyzing the data and presenting it to someone for use. I decided that I wanted to get into that work.

As soon as my certification as an engineer came through in '64 I had three bonafide job offers. One was at Deseret Test Center at Fort Douglas in Salt Lake City. So I took that because it sounded like a very interesting job. It was testing classified weapon systems—chemical and biological weapon systems for the most part. I was there for two years and then a job opened up at Hill Air Force Base as a technical advisor to their testing operation there. I applied and got that job, and that's where I spent the rest of my career.

Now all of this time, it sounds like I didn't do anything but technical work. But there's almost no period of time when I didn't manage to work with stock of some kind or other, usually horses. When I was in the navy and at sea there was very, very little opportunity to ride. But in Panama, almost the first thing that I did when I was stationed there was find a riding stable. At the riding stable they had a riding club for anyone who wanted to join. My job with the club was to take the barn-spoiled horses and beat the hell out of them when they acted up and make them go where they didn't want to go. What I did was to take them and teach them that it was in their best interest to go wherever the rider wanted to go. So I spent all the time I could out there. It was a lot of fun. I also helped them with the young horses they were breaking. They used a little Spanish Barb, which is an interesting horse. It's kind of a homely-looking horse, but for his size he's almost as tough as an Arabian.

When I went to California it just seemed natural to get acquainted with people that came from ranches and had worked stock. I had friends who had ranches around southern California. During vacations and as I had time to do it, I'd help at these places doing whatever needed to be done. When I came to Utah I was able to buy twenty-three acres, and from the day that I moved onto this place I knew that I was going to raise horses. I thought I was going to raise Arabians, but I'm raising Appaloosas.

I'd always read everything, from the Sears and Roebuck catalog to the Bible. There was something about reading that I just liked, that I seemed to have an insatiable appetite for. I even read John Bunyan's *Pilgrim's Progress* when I was about nine or ten years old. I couldn't tell you now what that was all about. I have a vague notion because I remember it to be one of the most boring things I ever read, but I read it anyway. I read it because my grandmother had a copy of it and there weren't any magazines or any good new catalogs that I hadn't already read. When I got down to that, I read it one winter. What I remember more than anything else is that there were woodcut prints in it—pictures of terrible angels who were about to tear somebody up or about to save somebody or terrible devil figures that were about to get the pilgrim in one situation or another. In any case, I evolved into a reader. But to tell you the truth, as a kid I didn't pay a whole lot of attention to poetry, even though my grandmother recited some poetry and my father recited poetry at the family gatherings now and then.

My grandmother was a fairly well-educated woman. She had a sense for poetry and she liked it, and so she would recite things. The poems she would recite were usually tragic things. I remember the one that she seemed to like the best because she recited it several times. She would do it while she was standing over the stove if there was anyone to listen to her. It was "The Gypsy's Warning." I did that out at Elko in '87, in one of the classic poetry sessions.[1]

I learned most of it from her reciting it, but then other people at one time or another would sing it. I have no idea who wrote this poem—it comes from somewhere back in antiquity. It sounds like it might have been written in the 1850s or '60s or somewhere along in there.

Gentle lady, do not trust him
Though his voice is low and sweet.
Listen to this gypsy's warning,
Gently pleading at your feet.
Now your life is in its morning,
Cloud not this your happy lot.

Listen to this gypsy's warning,
Gentle lady, trust him not.

Do not turn so coldly from me,
I would only guard your youth
From his stern, withering power.
I would only tell the truth.
I would shield you from this danger,
Save you from this tempter's snare.
Do not trust this dark-eyed stranger,
I have warned you, now beware.

Lady, once there lived a maiden,
Pure and bright, and oh so fair,
Until he wooed her and he won her,
Filled her gentle heart with care.
Then he heeded not her weeping,
Nor cared he her life to save.
Soon she perished, now she's sleeping
In a cold and silent grave.

Keep your gold, I do not want it,
Lady, I have prayed for this,
For the hour when I might foil him,
Rob him of expected bliss.
Gentle lady, do not wonder
At my words so cold and wild.
Lady, in that green grave yonder,
Lies a gypsy's only child.[2]

That was my grandmother's favorite.

My father recited some poems—when there were only men around. Some were a little bit on the dirty side. He never was a man to recite really raunchy stuff, although some of it was a little bit on the shady side. But they were usually about some tragic event that had happened. There was one about a man and a sawmill where he'd gotten sawed and killed. There was another one, but I couldn't remember it all so I made up the parts that I couldn't remember and thought I was following the theme until I saw a copy of the original in John Lomax's *Cowboy Songs and Other Frontier Ballads.*[3] It was about some trappers—Jim Bridger was involved in it, rescuing a trapper's daughter from the Indians and that sort of thing. The original name of it was "California Joe," the name of the main character in it. There are two ways it starts—the way the original starts and the way

I've been doing it for a number of years since I rewrote it as I remembered it. This is my version:

I used to run with Bridger,
I guess you heard of him.
He's the first one that I think of
when they talk of mountain men.
We took many a beaver
in the western mountains blue,
and I'm proud I shared his campfire
and have been one of his crew.

Close to what's now Fort Reno,
a trapper used to dwell.
They called him old Pat Reno,
we scouts all knew him well.
He'd a lovely daughter, Hazel,
dark hair and hazel-eyed.
It was my secret that I loved her,
for her I'd gladly died.

It was in the spring of '50
and we'd camped on Powder River,
we'd killed a calf of buffalo
and fried a slice of liver.
We were eating quite contented
when we heard three shots or four,
put out our fires and listening,
we heard a dozen more.

We knew that old Pat Reno
had moved his traps up there,
so catching up our horses
and fixing on our gear
we mounted quick as lightning
to save was our desire.
Too late, the painted heathens
had set the house on fire.

We led our horses quietly
and waded up the stream,
there among the willows
I heard a muffled scream.

There among the bushes,
my darling Hazel lie,
I picked her up and whispered,
"I'll save you or I'll die."

There was near a hundred Indians
within an arrow's flight.
Our best hope to live
would be a dash into the night.
We led my pony quietly
across to the other side,
Then both mounted on his back
to make our desperate ride.

Then spoke up Jim Bridger,
"We'll cover your retreat,
no time for any palaver now,
just rattle that pony's feet."
We burst out of the willows
in a clawing, tearing run.
Behind we heard Jim Bridger's band
as each man warmed his gun.

We heard the war bows thumping,
the arrows to each side.
War cries and crashing guns,
as red and white men died.
In the moon and starlight,
we gained a little hill,
then dashed along a brushy ridge
and across a rocky rill.

Then out onto the sagebrush flats
as fleeing pronghorns go
a good five miles before we dared
to let that tired horse slow.
Then we stopped to breathe him,
and he stood with feet apart.
We thank God for his strong legs
and thankful mighty heart.

Then on we went, and when we were
far from the battle line,

we stopped and made a fireless camp
beneath the friendly pine.
It was a fierce ride and Bridger
had covered our retreat.
That night my Hazel whispered
in a voice low and sweet,

"They sent Papa to heaven
to Mama up above,
there's no one left to love me
and no one left to love."
The little girl was sixteen
and I was twenty-two.
I said, "I can't be your Papa,
but I'll love you just as true."

She nestled closely to me
and with her hazel eyes so bright,
looked up and made me happy,
though we'd rode through hell that night.
Now in this church where we're to wed,
I make my prayers to Him,
and thank God for that gallant horse
and Bridger and his men.

That was the sort of thing that my dad did. It was the way that we entertained at any kind of a gathering there was—anyone who could play an instrument, or thought they could, tried to play an instrument, and anyone who had the same qualifications for singing might sing, or if you could wiggle your ears or anything else that was amusing. Those people who could recite recited. There was appreciation, I guess because of the lack of competition, for almost anything that anyone could do, so reciting poetry was an ordinary thing that happened when a group of people got together.

I think that maybe half of them learned their poems from having seen them written somewhere, but at least as many learned them as I learned them, from hearing someone else recite them. The first time that I heard "The Strawberry Roan" a young lady by name of Jenny Hawks recited it. I remember it very well, the event of her reciting it. It was at a gathering—by gathering, I mean a group of people who happen to be together, two families or maybe a church gathering or school gathering or community gathering of some kind or another. But later on, about six months or a year, I suppose, I heard her singing the same words she had recited. She was a pretty good country singer, and she sang "The Strawberry Roan." From then on, although I heard the thing mostly sung, it was always one of my favorite cowboy poems, and I like to recite it yet.

To get some understanding of why people did the kinds of things they did, remember that there weren't even radios around for the most part then. I suppose what people had been doing over the centuries when they got together was they talked to each other about the things they knew to talk about, about the news, and then "what if's" might come up. When they started to run out of those things, they started to do whatever else might be done to communicate with each other some more. They worked hard enough then that they didn't want to waste an opportunity to be involved with the people that they knew around them, their friends and their families, and to communicate to them in some method. Poetry certainly is communication. So is music.

We were at a point in social development where we were not that far from the people who fought the Indians. The stories of the Indian fights were still known firsthand by some of the grandfathers. Of course, from day to day, the things that might happen with cattle or stock were constant things. They were things that people related to—they knew those experiences. They knew what it was like to get a rope on a steer and have him get your horse off balance and get the advantage and jerk the horse down, or tangle you up in a fence, or run into a tree or something else like that. They empathized with people in the poems and in many cases had direct or similar experiences somewhere.

One Friday afternoon in my little two-room country schoolhouse, my teacher, Mr. Long, read Alfred Noyes's "The Highwayman"—you've heard that dramatic poem about an English highwayman. When Mr. Long got up and did that—you see, he was patriarchal-looking, tall, six foot two or so, fine baritone voice and a beautiful way of using words. That voice of his just seemed to roll around that whole room as he talked and did that poem. I don't know if it was conscious or subconscious, but I had not paid much deliberate attention to poetry until that point. The way that he did that thing impressed me; it was like someone had run a Technicolor movie. I could see everything that was happening in my mind's eye as he read that poem. That was when I started to be interested in poetry. I guess I was about ten or eleven or so.

A little before that time, I had discovered a medium called the western magazine. All of the heroes in there always did right by the girls, whether the girls deserved it or not. The girls always turned out to be wonderful people. The heroes were always flawless heroes, and they used their six-guns to right all sorts of wrongs. The typical "dime western," they were called. There was one company that put out something called *Street and Smith's Wild West Weekly.* You could buy that sucker for a dime, and it had $10 worth of entertainment in it. In the back, they had a section where in nearly every issue they would publish one of the old cowboy poems, stuff by Curley Fletcher, Gail Gardner, and folks of that kind. So I memorized the ones that took my fancy. I've always had a fairly easy ability to memorize anything that I'm particularly interested in. It's little more than that—it isn't really very difficult. Lots of people remember songs. They hear a song a few times and then they know the words to the song. Memorizing poetry is really the same thing. They memorize a song because they have an interest in it, because it touches something in them and it sticks in their head. I think that's true of poetry too. A poem touches the heart and then it's easy to memorize. Those were probably the main sources of my western poetry.

In our area we had a number of young men who'd catch a freight train out west somewhere and get a job on a cattle ranch, which was an easy thing. They knew the work already, but they wanted to get out and experience a different country—a big wide-open country—and work on the big ranches, and there were a number of those that did that, and that feeling was around all the time. These guys came back and told about a country where you could ride for maybe a hundred miles without seeing another person. That was one of the differences in Missouri: The country was heavily wooded, and that kind of openness simply wasn't available. There were lots of places then where you could have easily ridden a hundred miles without having to go through any fences, but you would have had to pick your way. You couldn't have just taken a straight line like you might do in many cases around here.

We felt like we were, I guess, next to the West. That would be the most honest way to put it. We didn't feel that we were what a full-blooded cowboy ought to be because we had to take care of hogs as well as cattle, you know. Cowboys don't do that stuff. They don't do anything they can't do from a horse, you know. It says right there in *Street and Smith's Wild West Weekly.* Yes, we felt a strong kinship to the cattle country, to the West. Southwest Texas was probably the big place that we thought about, and Oklahoma to a lesser extent, but it seemed that a great number of people who went to find a ranch to work on headed directly to Texas, bypassed Oklahoma, where of course there were some big cattle operations. Others went up into the Dakotas and Wyoming and that area up in there.

I think the feeling of the frontier was closer to us than the West because we were closer to that time in our period of development. Methods of doing things were pretty much the way they were done on the frontier. Gathering in meat out of the wilds was normal for nearly every family, so we were very likely closer to that than we were to the western experience as it pertains to cattle ranching.

I expect that if I had not gone in the navy when I did, and if world history hadn't developed the way it did, I would very likely have gone to Colorado and found a ranch because I would have known what I was doing. I knew how to use a rope, and I was at least as good a rider as an average rider. I was one of those people who was not particularly worried about getting thrown. That was one thing where my size was an advantage, because I had light upper body weight. It was pretty hard for a horse to loose me, let alone throw me. I could get one to do whatever I wanted. I thought that shooting was more important than what it is, and I was always a good rifle shot, but I was always a lousy shotgun shot and still am. I could probably come closer to hitting a pheasant with a .22 rifle than I can with a 12-gauge shotgun, for some reason that I don't quite understand.

Poetry has been a constant part of my life. Since Mr. Long read "The Highwayman" to me I've read lots and lots of poetry. When I was in Panama in '44 I stole a book out of the library because I liked that collection of poems. I've carried it with me everywhere. You can see its condition—it was a brand-new book when I pilfered it. One of the other poems I think is in here had a lot to do with my life, and Mr. Long was the first one who read that poem to us, and it's Kipling's "If." It's probably had as much, or possibly more, influence on me than any other single piece of literature. There's also one of Robert Service's things. He's written a lot of stuff; some of them are pretty well written. I think the best and most beautiful piece he wrote is a thing called "The Spell of the Yukon":

I wanted the gold and I sought it,
I scrabbled and mucked like a slave,
Were it famine or scurvy I fought it,
And hurled my youth into the grave.
I wanted the gold and I got it,
Come out with a fortune last fall
But somehow life's not what I thought it
And somehow the gold isn't all.

No, there's the land, have you seen it?
It's the cussedest land that I know,
From the big dizzy mountains that screen it
To the deep death-like valleys below.
Some say God was tired when he made it,
Some say it's a fine land to shun.
Maybe, but there's some who would trade it
For no land on earth, and I'm one.

You come to get rich, damn good reason,
You feel like an exile at first,
You hate it like hell for a season
And then you're worse than the worst.
It grips you like some kind of sinning,

It twists you from foe to a friend.
It seems it's been since the beginning,
It seems it will be to the end.

I've stood in some mighty-mouthed hollow
That's plumb full of hush to the brim
And watched a big, lusty sun wallow
In crimson and gold and grow dim.
Then the moon set the pearly peaks gleaming
And the stars tumbled out neck and crop
And I thought that I surely was dreaming
With the peace of the world piled on top.

The summer, no sweeter was ever,
The sunshiny woods all a-trill.
The grayling, a-leap in the river,
The bighorn asleep on the hill.
The strong life that never knows harness,
The wilds where the caribou call,
The freedom, the freshness, the farness,
Oh God, I'm stuck on it all.

The winter, the brightness that blinds you,
The white land locked tight as a drum,
The cold fear that follows and finds you,
The silence that bludgeons you dumb.
The snows that are older than history,
The woods where the weird shadows slant.
The silence, the moonlight, the mystery,
I'd bid it goodbye but I can't.

There's a land where the mountains are nameless,
Where the rivers all run God knows where,
There are lives that are erring and aimless
And deaths that just hang by a hair.
There are hardships that nobody reckons,
There are valleys unpeopled and still,
And the land, how it beckons and beckons
And I want to go back, and I will.

They're making my money diminish,
I'm sick of the taste of champagne,

Thank God when I'm skinned to a finish
I'll pike to the Yukon again.
I'll fight and you'll bet it's no sham fight,
It's hell but I've been there before.
It's better than this, by a damn sight
So it's me for the Yukon once more.[4]

I think there's one more verse, but it seems like a dangling verse, so I don't intend to do it. It seems to me that the poem ends where I ended it. One of the things my uncle used to say is, "You've got to know when the job's done."

Notes

This essay is based on an edited transcription of an oral interview with Ray Lashley; transcript and tape recordings are in the archives of the Utah Arts Council's Folk Arts Program.

1. Ray refers to the annual Cowboy Poetry Gathering, produced by the Western Folklife Center in Elko, Nevada, every year since 1985.

2. Another version of the anonymous poem "The Gipsy's Warning" was published in *Best Loved Story Poems,* ed. Walter E. Thwing (1941), (Garden City: Halcyon House, 1949), 693–94.

3. "California Joe," in John A. Lomax and Alan Lomax, *Cowboy Songs and Other Frontier Ballads* (1910), (New York: Macmillan, 1986), 346–53. The book attributes the poem to Capt. Jack Crawford, "Indian scout and hunter."

4. Robert W. Service, "The Spell of the Yukon," in *The Complete Poetical Works of Robert W. Service* (New York: Barse and Hopkins, 1921), 1:15–18.

16

THE MAKIN'S OF A COWBOY POET

Jon Bowerman

Uncle George never had a show to be normal. His family was too rich, and he had too much outlaw blood in his veins. Not the robber-killer type outlaw. More like the Willie Nelson type, I'm-gonna-do-it-my-way-and-if-the-rest-of-the-world-doesn't-like-it,-t'-hell-with-'em sort of outlaw. And he is one of the main reasons I'm a cowboy poet today.

Some folks probably figured him for spoiled, and he may have been—but not for long. At fourteen he was kicked out of prep school for chewing tobacco and using profanity. Before the family could get him into another school he lit out for Alaska. The year was 1901. In the Yukon the last great gold rush was in full swing; men were getting rich overnight. At least that's what he'd heard. But Alaska wasn't sympathetic to a fourteen-year-old who'd known nothing but chauffeur-driven limousines and yachting off the coast of Massachusetts.

He nearly froze to death. He almost starved. He barely survived. He worked his way back to the continental U.S., where he found work as a cowboy in Oklahoma, Kansas, and Nebraska for "forty a month and found."[1]

He sweated in summer, froze in winter, chewed tobacco, and cussed constantly. The cow ponies were about as different from the horses he'd known on Cape Cod bridle paths as a Texas double rig was from the pancake saddles he'd ridden before.[2] In a way, the start of his cowboy career may have been tougher than prospecting. But if the wages weren't much at least he was being fed, and he stuck like a cockleburr in a cow's tail.

He was in his mid-thirties when he was broken up in a horse wreck. There was no workmen's compensation, unemployment, or welfare. Too crippled to do physical labor, he got a job in a bank, making agricultural loans.

He was well suited for his new calling. He knew livestock, land, and people, and he had a strong belief that the only good deal was one where both parties had a chance to make some money. Years later he was still proud of the fact that "I never made any big killings like some of those shysters from Chicago, but I had damn few people default on a loan, either."

When the depression hit he was managing a chain of midwestern banks. Banks were closing all over the country. There was no money. You can't run a bank with no money. But Uncle George did. Like a good horse wrangler, he didn't lose a single bank in his string. They stayed open. He just switched to the barter system he'd learned in the goldfields and perfected in the cow camps.

Every one of his banks had a corral somewhere on the edge of town. They'd swap horses, cows, chickens, spuds, whatever. The bank buildings themselves probably looked more like pawn shops than banks, but they stayed open and kept folks in business somehow.

As the country slowly worked its way out of the depression and toward World War II, Uncle George moved to Chicago, where he was president of a bank. He was a small man, but even in Chicago he stood out. A Hopalong Cassidy–style hat made him look a lot bigger than he really was. He wore a three-piece suit with pants shotgunned into knee-high riding boots. A walrus mustache and the ever-present chew of tobacco completed the outfit. If one of his old cowboy buddies hit town, they say he'd go on a binge that might last for days. Stories of his activities somehow reached clear out to Oregon, where the remains of his family had taken refuge after the depression. They'd lost everything and never really recovered.

Well, according to Uncle George, they didn't lose everything. They still had "that blue blood runnin' through their brains that makes 'em think they're smarter'n ever'one else just 'cause they inherited a bunch of money. But they never learned that if you're gonna buy stock, buy livestock. At least you can eat it if the market goes to hell. All that paper they had wasn't any better than a sand castle at high tide."

His talk and his attitude didn't help mend the fence he'd cut when he'd left home. His occasional visits were tense at best. On one occasion when my mother was in high school, he made her a present of *Sun and Saddle Leather* by Badger Clark, a book that I still have. Before she could even open it, her mother snatched it away with the comment, "Nothing but the mutterings of a common cowboy!" To which Uncle George replied, "Ain't no such thing as a common cowboy."

It was with mixed emotions that the family received the news that Uncle George planned to join them in Medford, Oregon, after his retirement. On the way out he picked up a new Chrysler convertible. It was top of the line and made every other car look like a draft horse plug next to a Kentucky Thoroughbred. Then he detoured down to Hollywood, where he picked up a nineteen-year-old starlet and an English sheepdog that smelled like a wolf den.

To say he created a scandal when the outfit hit town would be an understatement. This was the 1940s. The family begged him to change his lifestyle or move someplace else. He did neither. He did change girlfriends though, and when the first one left she took the sheepdog, which he soon replaced with a mongrel that was hell on cats and flower beds, not to mention giving the town an overabundance of puppies that were about as welcome as Uncle George.

His love of poetry had come long after he left school. He quoted Robert Service, of course, from his Alaskan adventures, along with Clark, Knibbs, and a few others from his cowboy days. He could recite for hours. He had a strong feeling that schools ruined most people's chance to develop a liking for poetry: "They start kids on poetry too young and shove too much at 'em at one time," he'd sputter. "It's like forcin' a man to eat a whole turkey at one settin'. Before he's halfway through he's sick of it and even if he gets it all down he'll never want any again. You need to see some of the world to really appreciate poetry. Then it's the language of the gods."

Folks sometimes ask me how I got to be a cowboy poet. It's a fair question, considering I sure wasn't born to it. My father was a school teacher turned college professor, Olympic coach, and running shoe inventor.

But I came by it naturally. My great-great-grandfather on Dad's side started ranching in Wheeler County, Oregon, in the mid-1800s. Visiting the ranch at about age eight, I made up my mind that someday I'd have a ranch in Wheeler County, but even before that I wanted to be a cowboy.

The Saturday matinee had a lot to do with it. Roy Rogers, Gene Autry, and all the others made every kid want to be a cowboy. It was the early 1940s. Everyone's dad was away fighting the war. But because of our matinee heroes it never crossed our minds that some of our dads might not come home. Those Saturday movies taught us that good guys fought fair, told the truth, and always won. Only bad guys lied, cheated, or got killed. Our dads were the good guys, so they were safe.

I still recall those early days
When we went to the Saturday matinee.
There was Roy and Hoppy and Lash LaRue,
Gene Autry and a lot of others, too.
They rode good horses and they all packed guns
But it seems they never killed anyone.
When threatened by a rustler band
They shot the guns from the outlaws' hands.
They never ran from a stand-up fight

But they always fought fair and did what was right.
They had truth and honor and all the traits
That makes a hero really great.
And after the Saturday matinee
When we all went outside to play,
We lived by "The Code" and could understand,
Only shoot at the guns in the bad guys' hands.
Back when playin' cowboys was all in fun
And heroes never killed anyone.[3]

The matinee should have been required viewing for mothers. They didn't share our confidence. Back then, word of fatalities came by telegram. When the Western Union messenger came pedaling his fat-tired bike up the street, anxious wives would hold their breath until he passed their house. Then necks would stretch to see if the dreaded message might be for a neighbor. Thankfully, they never stopped on our block.

Of course, the kids could have told them that. Our dads were the good guys. Just like Hopalong Cassidy, they couldn't be killed. Is it any wonder we wanted to be cowboys?

But in Medford we got an extra push when Uncle George hit town. Here was a real cowboy, not just someone in a movie! Kids just didn't believe it when parents pointed out that he was a banker, not a cowboy. We knew what a banker dressed like. And we knew how a cowboy dressed. Uncle George was a cowboy.

He hadn't been there a month before it was a spanking offense for just about any kid in town to be caught at Uncle George's place. He was famous. Perhaps infamous is the word. Anyhow, it was worth the risk, and we took it at every opportunity. Forbidden fruit is sweet.

The stories he told! The profanity! Along with the whippings, there were a lot of mouths washed out with soap for using words that we thought sounded good but didn't know the meaning of.

And the poetry! It may have been at Uncle George's that I first heard "The Glory Trail," "The Legend of Boastful Bill," or any of the dozens of cowboy poems I can recite today. I can't remember which poems they were, but I sure remember that they were as packed with colorful vocabulary and action as any Saturday shoot-'em-up.

That summer Uncle George offered to take a bunch of us kids to the set of a western movie being shot at Crater Lake. Well, our parents were horrified, and the upshot for me was that my dad made me a deal. Every year his mother and sister went to Wheeler County and spent the summer on the ranch where they'd grown up. If I'd quit fightin' my head over this movie idea, I could go with them. To a real ranch with real cowboys and horses and cows.

So Uncle George went to Crater Lake to be a movie star, and I went to the ranch to be a cowboy. But you don't take an eight-year-old kid from town and put him on a horse and make him a cowboy any more than that same kid could flap his arms and turn into an astronaut. I didn't make a hand that summer. Seems like every time I went out ahorseback, I came back afoot. But I never gave up, and I didn't get homesick. I knew where I belonged.

At the end of the summer I didn't go back to Medford. Dad had taken a job at the University of Oregon, and the family had moved while I was away. He'd turned the job down a year earlier. I wonder if Uncle George hadn't had something to do with him finally accepting.

Anyhow, I never saw Uncle George again. He'd lived his life and fulfilled his dreams. That winter he told his last story, recited his last poem. But teller of tales, reciter of poems, banker, cowboy, or whatever, he'd planted the seed.

Thirty years later I was on a small cow-calf outfit about twenty-five miles out of Kalispell, Montana. It was a hard winter, with temperatures forty below zero and colder for weeks at a time. Cows started calving during the worst of it. We rode through those cows every hour around the clock. The owners lived eight hundred miles to the south. Their boy, just out of high school, took the day shift. I had the night duty.

As soon as a calf hit the snow we took it in the cabin to get it dry. We couldn't take a chance on the cow getting it licked off in time—just made a run for the wood stove. We leppied a few calves that winter, but at least they didn't freeze to death.[4]

Then one night a chinook hit—warm wind and rain. By morning three feet of snow had turned to three feet of mud the consistency of pancake batter. And with the mud and warm weather came scours. For people not too familiar with livestock, scours is a form of diarrhea in calves.

We couldn't take the sick ones to the corral; it was muddier than the pasture. We just roped 'em where we found 'em and poked pills down their throats. After the first calf the rope was covered with mud. Catch a calf, dismount and slog through knee-deep mud, throw the calf, doctor it, and turn it loose. Catch another sick one and start over again. It was the messiest job I ever had. Somewhere there's a poem waiting to be written about that spring. But it hasn't come to me yet.

Spring brought green grass and the urge to follow the rodeo circuit again. I rolled my bed, drew my time, and headed down the road. A few days later I was in Lewistown, Montana. Someone had brought in a bunch of big, stout broncs out of the Missouri River Breaks for a rodeo school. There's a lot of good bronc riders in Montana, and the school had a fair sprinkling of them. Maybe they weren't there so much to learn as to get tuned up for the start of the rodeo season.

One stood out from the rest. He was old enough to be the father of most of the kids there. He wore silver-inlaid spurs with his jeans stuffed into red boots. And red chaps. The second day it was purple boots and purple chaps. Talk about colorful. He'd make a peacock look like a mud hen. It was Billy Stockton, who had been riding bucking horses for some twenty-five years. Riding really tough broncs was his life's passion. That winter he'd gotten a flower-carved bronc saddle and had come to the school to get on a few head and "get the leaks out of that new saddle before the season starts." That saddle didn't leak very much at all. But when he did hit the ground he came up with a grin from ear to ear. Whether he rode to the whistle or got bucked off, he put on a whale of a show in the arena, but it was only a warm-up for that night in the bar.

Even kids under twenty-one were drinking. When Billy walked in and ordered a soda pop, the bartender asked if he was sure he didn't maybe want a shot of something in it. "Nope," was Billy's reply, "I learned my lesson last time I went on a thirty-day drunk. The first three days it's a luxury. After that it's a necessity. Besides, then I couldn't remember my lines." Lines? What lines? Billy began: "'At a roundup on the Gila one sweet mornin' long ago, / Ten of us was throwed quite freely by a bronc from Idaho. / And we 'lowed he'd go to beggin' . . .'"

He went from Clark's "Legend of Boastful Bill" to Gardner's "Sierry Petes." Seemed like maybe I'd heard them somewhere before. Couldn't remember for sure, but they sounded familiar. On and on he went, one poem after another, with an occasional story to boot.

I don't think he ever ran out of poems. All of a sudden it was closing time, and the bartender was herding the whole bunch of us out the door. I knew a couple of poems he hadn't done, but the few that I knew were like a busted flush compared to what Billy laid on us. I kept quiet and listened.

We listened to Billy recite for three nights running. We couldn't get enough. I think everyone there made up his mind he was gonna learn some of those poems that summer. I don't know if the other guys did or not. It just turned out that I had a lot of free time that year.

Traveling between rodeos, I prowled the bookstores looking for cowboy poems. The books by Kiskaddon, Gardner, and Knibbs had been out of print for years. Badger Clark's *Sun and Saddle Leather* wasn't available in the shops I visited. Finally, at the Buffalo Bill Historical Center in Cody, Wyoming, I found John White's *Git Along, Little Dogies.* It didn't have "The Legend of Boastful Bill" and only part of the poem about High-Chin Bob ropin' the mountain lion, but it was a start.

A cowboy's winter wages don't last long on the rodeo circuit, so I took a three-week job riding colts during spring roundup. Then, with White's book on the seat of the pickup, I worked on learning a few new poems while driving to the next rodeo. They may not have been the ones Billy Stockton recited, but they were still worth learning.

Seems like every rodeo season starts out like a gambling trip to Reno. You win a little bit early on and think you're on a hot streak. You go for broke. And suddenly you are broke. In Sheridan, Wyoming, I got bucked off a good horse and didn't have enough gas to get out of town. But I had good broncs at the next couple of rodeos, so I just parked the pickup and started hitchhiking. Nearly ten years later that hitchhiking trip provided the material for a poem:

One summer up in Wyoming I was hittin' some rodeos;
I was drawin' poor and missed one out and a couple o' times got throwed.[5]
You couldn't say I was short of cash. There just wasn't any more.
They'd take my check for an entry fee but the restaurants barred the door.

For three days straight I tried to ride without a thing to eat.
I didn't think I'd lost my lick, but I was feelin' kinda weak.
You read about Walt Garrison and his Copenhagen can,
But I tell you, friends, a pinch won't do to fill a hungry man.[6]

I got piled again in Sheridan and was feelin' kinda low
As I hitchhiked down the highway toward the Jackson Rodeo.
The farmer boy that picked me up said he's only goin' part way
But was grateful for the company to help him stay awake.

The hunger pains were all but gone after the second day.
There was just that pounding in my head as I tried to figure a way
To get myself a meal to eat, most anything would do
So long as it had more calories than a Copenhagen chew.

Well there wasn't a doggone thing where that fellow finally left me,
Just a crossroad and more highway for as far as I could see.
But I guess the Lord was with me, as they tell us in The Book,
'Cause it was on a stretch of roadkilled rabbits, big jacks wherever I looked.

Now when a cowboy's ridin' good he can eat steak and pay the check,
But when he's hitchin' rides and hungry he'll take anything he can get.
So since beggars can't be choosers, into my gear bag I quickly loaded
Several of the best ones that weren't too squashed or bloated.

Then I went off beside the highway and built a sagebrush barbecue,
Skinned 'em with my pocket knife and tossed 'em on to stew.
They were awful tough and stringy, marinated with hair and dirt,
But I ate 'til I nearly foundered and stuck the leftovers in my shirt.

Then I hitched on into Jackson, in time for the rodeo.
I'd drawed a bronc to win on if I could stick 'til the whistle blowed.
I spurred him mane to cantle for the full eight-second ride,
Kickin' like the rabbit on which I was fortified.

I rode him tall and shiny, there wasn't any doubt.
That day I beat the magpies out of their rabbit meat, but I missed that
saddle bronc out.[7]

When I got back to Sheridan I'd won enough money to make it to Oregon. I hadn't seen the folks for a couple of years. I figured I could visit for a few days, make a few more rodeos, and get a riding job when the fall roundup started.

I was hungry when I pulled up to the Long Beach arena—hungry for a win. For two weeks I'd drawn some pretty sorry horses, broncs that bucked just hard enough to get a marking from the judges but nothing you could win any money on. I'd be hitchhiking again if I didn't win something here.

As I walked up to the rodeo office, a cowboy stopped me with "hey, you've got the top horse in the string. All you've got to do is ride him and you'll win the bronc ridin'." It's not always that easy.

You measure the rein one more time and ease over the side of the chute and into the saddle. As you work your feet into the stirrups the bronc squats and starts to tremble. He's like a powder keg with a short fuse. He's ready and so are you. You holler "Outside!" and the latch pops. The gate swings open. The horse explodes into the arena as both spurs catch him high in the neck. A quick, snappy horse. And powerful! There's no time to think "charge the front end, lift on that rein." Those things just happen or you're in trouble.

You are in trouble. The horse is too quick. He's half a jump ahead of you, and you can't catch up. Thrown forward against the swells of the saddle, you try and hook your spurs in the cantle and ride for a jump 'til you can get back in time with him, but he's too strong. The horse has too much power, and you can't hold on. There's not even time to get your hands out to break the fall. Head first into the arena dirt, then waiting to feel your body smashed into the earth. But it doesn't happen. You feel like an arrow buried point first, shaft projecting skyward from the direction of flight. No pain but there's an uncomfortable feeling in your neck.

And then you realize you're staring up at the sky. Not like an arrow that's stuck in the ground—more like a tree felled by lightning or toppled by old age, lying there, no movement.

Ambulance, hospital, X-rays. Seven vertebrae cracked, broken, crushed. I had to be transferred to a bigger hospital, where they put me in traction and fed me on un-cowboy-like vegetable soup. One day, with the sun pouring in through the hospital window, I began to feel some sensation in my extremities—pins and needles. My toes wiggled, my fingers moved. Not out of the woods yet, said the doctor, but progress. Progress? Yeah, progress. So, positive attitude. And beef (no more vegetable soup). And poetry.

From traction to a body cast, from the body cast to a neck brace, and all that time learning poems, writing poems. I was in traction when someone brought me a magazine with a story about Freckles Brown's ride on Tornado. Two days later I'd completed "A Tribute to Freckles Brown and Tornado," which was later published in *Cowboy Poetry: A Gathering.*[8]

About that same time I finished learning "The Glory Trail" by Badger Clark. Since the only copy I had came from the book *Git Along, Little Dogies,* with the second and third verses missing, I wrote my own to fill in what White had omitted. I still recite it that way today.

From the hospital it was home to the folks' place. I was reciting "The Glory Trail" for some visitors one day when Mother walked over to the book case and came back with *Sun and Saddle Leather* by Badger Clark, the same book that Uncle George had given her nearly fifty years before.

Long before I was out of the body cast I'd memorized every poem in Clark's book, plus written a few more of my own. No student ever looked forward to graduation more than I did the day the doctor turned me loose. He tossed the neck brace I'd been wearing into the trash can and fitted me with a foam-rubber collar with the words, "Well, you can do just about anything you want except ride a horse."

I told him that Monday morning I'd be starting to ride for the Butte Creek Company, and he replied, "I thought you probably were. But you ought to know that your spinal cord is just held together by a thread. Your next headfirst fall will be your last."

You don't quit cowboying just 'cause you've broken a few bones. Freedom's what cowboying's all about. If you give up riding you give up your freedom. There's no other job where a hired hand has as much freedom as a cowboy does.

The Butte Creek Company was a good example, about a dozen miles back in the hills on a four-wheel-drive road that's impassible most of the winter. No one bothers you. You just do your job. Saddle in the dark, ride all day, unsaddle in the dark, seven days a week. Freedom. Ride anywhere you want, any way you want, just so the work gets done.

You can make up a dozen poems during a day's ride. So what if you've forgotten 'em all by the time you get back to camp. There'll be a dozen new ones tomorrow about cows at the salt lick at dawn, like regulars who line the counter at the town cafe for their morning cup of coffee. Or the mad dash down a frozen hillside in a foot of fresh snow to head a bunch of yearlings before they can escape. It crosses your mind: "Your next headfirst fall will be your last."

But you pull all the stops. Pell-mell down the hill, dodging rocks and sagebrush. Then suddenly you crash—head over heels, horse over cowboy. There's a burning sensation on your cheek as your face plows snow all the way down to frozen ground and bunchgrass.

Lost 'em. You're limping. So's your horse. But you survived. Those yearlings'll be there tomorrow. Call it job security. You lead your horse back to camp in the gathering dusk.

Once in a while you get a few lines written down at the end of the day, but mostly you forget 'em and start again the next day with a clean slate. The few poems that you get on paper you can use to entertain the crew while you're riding out on the morning circle come springtime. How would you know that there'd be something called a "Cowboy Poetry Gathering" comin' up in a few years? But about ten years later folks are calling you a cowboy poet. You find out you can make more money in an hour reciting poems at a convention than you could make in a month as a cowboy working for wages. It looks like a chance to make some big money. You give it a try, and it's kind of fun—for a while.

But one night you get home after a performance and realize that you're not doing it for fun anymore. You're doing it for money. You've sold that freedom you worked so hard to keep over the years. Is it worth it? Well, maybe to some it is, but it wasn't to me.

There's a lot of folks say it's all over. There's no need for cowboys anymore. But as long as there are cows there'll be outfits needing cowboys. There's a lot of country out there that's too rough for a pickup, too rough for a motorcycle. Cow country. They'll have to have hired men on horseback—cowboys. Freedom!

You'll still be able to recite those poems riding out on circle in the morning or at dinnertime while the crew's waiting for the cook to holler "come and get it." And somewhere down the road maybe there'll be a few kids come around and go to pestering you the way you used to do to Uncle George and to Billy Stockton. Then you treat 'em. Poems, stories, and freedom.

You followed rodeo from Calgary to El Paso,
Ridin' the broncs and the bulls,
Knew the hunger and pain before every win
Like the rest of those hard-riding fools.
You paid all the costs to be your own boss
And seen about all this big land.
Then you found the life of the buckaroo
Beats everything else in the end.
At four hundred a month, grub and a bunk,
Ridin' from morning till night

Through the wind and the snow and the forty below
And sometimes you ask yourself why.
When there's jobs with more pay and a much shorter day
Workin' inside where it's warm,
You still chose the life of the buckaroo
Out there in the cold and the storm.

. . . .

It's either too hot, or too cold when it's not,
But you're out every day just the same.
Glad you can be where the wind's blowin' free
With the smells of the wide-open plain.
In this land that God saved for the juniper and sage
And critters and drifters like me,
He set it aside for the buckaroo,
Where everything's still wild and free.[9]

Notes

1. That is, $40 a month plus food.

2. "A Texas double rig" refers to the double cinches on a saddle often preferred by Texas cowboys.

3. Jon Bowerman, "The Saturday Matinee," in Bowerman, *Mustang Bulls and Milksnakes* (Antelope, Ore.: Antelope Free Press), 28.

4. A leppy is an orphan calf, so "to leppy" is to break the bond between a calf and its mother, after which some cows may disown the calf.

5. The rules state that cowboys must have their spurs touching the horse's neck ahead of the break of the shoulders on the first jump out of the chute. Failure to do so is called "missing him out" and results in disqualification.

6. Walt Garrison is a former professional football player and rodeo cowboy who advertised Copenhagen snuff, which is packaged in a round can.

7. Jon Bowerman, "Road Kill," unpublished.

8. Jon Bowerman, "A Tribute to Freckles Brown and Tornado," in *Cowboy Poetry: A Gathering,* ed. Hal Cannon (Salt Lake City: Gibbs Smith, 1985), 81–83.

9. Jon Bowerman, from "For Jeff," in *Cowboy Poetry,* ed. Cannon, 79–81.

Part 4

Themes

Despite the posters and book jackets depicting lone cowboys scribbling verses by the campfire or in a deserted bunkhouse, the fact remains that cowboy poetry has been as much a group effort as an individual one. Just as dozens of anonymous cowboys must have contributed verses to the frequently bawdy, never-ending "Old Chisholm Trail" in the nineteenth century, so too have individual reciters modified verses of poems to fit local settings or changing times. More recently, as cowboy poets have become acquainted at gatherings and have begun communication by letter, telephone, fax, and even e-mail, new poems have been subjected to a rigorous review and revision process in which other poets read, comment on, and suggest revisions. As cowboy poet Sue Wallis suggests, these relationships within the cowboy poetry community build from a sense of family tradition and have the net effect of improving the quality of new poems. At the same time, these friendships and family connections become a major theme in contemporary cowboy poetry.

Folklorist Craig Miller examines another universal theme in cowboy poetry: that of human relationships to the natural world. Miller discovers a progressive change in cowboy poetry over the years as poems reflect values and attitudes of their authors, from an antagonistic relationship with nature to a tolerant acceptance to an admiration for nature as an alternative to the urban civilization that threatens the cowboy way of life.

Another recent development in cowboy poetry has been the increased participation of women. Not only are more women writing poetry and participating in gatherings but they are also developing new forms and subjects. Independent folklorist Elaine Thatcher shows how a group of women writers have fashioned new approaches to cowboy poetry in the subjects they cover, their description of gender roles, and their adaptation of open forms. Rancher-poet Peggy Godfrey in particular uses her poetry to explore multidimensional aspects of ranch life and investigate topics men rarely explore.

Writer Teresa Jordan, who assembled the first anthology of poetry by ranch women (*Graining the Mare: The Poetry of Ranch Women* [Salt Lake City: Gibbs Smith, 1994]), here adapts her introduction to that volume to explore the rich variety of poetry now being written by women in the West. Like men, women write of horses, cattle, the landscape, and weather, but as Jordan demonstrates, they write as well of "the interior landscape of family, community, and self." These new subjects and the women writers' determination to find poetic forms appropriate to their expression are leading cowboy poetry in directions that continue to surprise participants and observers alike.

17

Families, Neighbors, and Friends: The Tradition of Cow-Country Poetry

Sue Wallis

> Then in the evenings there'd be songs, old trail-herd songs that some used to sing. There was even poetry at times, made right there at the cowcamp. It'd always be about some cowboy and some bad horse, and the whole outfit chipped in or suggested a word to make it up.
>
> —Will James, "The Breed of 'Em," 1927

> Once again she returned to the kitchen, and this time, as she looked at the sky, she found herself repeating poetry: "Wake! For morning in the bowl of night / Has flung the stone that sets the stars to flight."
>
> —Alice Marriott, "The Round Up," 1953

Ranching and cowboying are lonely occupations; they are and always have been conducive to reflection, reflection that shows in the poetry that folks commit to memory or the words they piece together to share with their families, neighbors, and friends around cow camps and barrooms and ranchhouse kitchen tables—words that string them together as a unique people, a cattle culture.

In the country I come from, the words of "A Cowboy's Prayer" were invoked just as often and with the same kind of reverence and patriotism as "The Star-Spangled Banner." No cowboy's funeral was complete without it. Bob Laramore, a northeastern Wyoming rancher and rodeo announcer, never failed to recite the entire poem as part of the Grand Entry—that familiar bit of tradition that begins every rodeo—when the rodeo hands circle the arena riding hard, flags waving and banners flying, to pull up and face the grandstand knee to knee in a long horseback line, face to face with the crowd. Every hat on both sides of the arena fence covered a heart, and we'd all raise our voices to sing the national anthem, then bow our heads to honor the Almighty to the powerful ring of Laramore's voice and Badger Clark's words over the rodeo sound system:

Oh Lord, I've never lived where churches grow.
    I love creation better as it stood
That day You finished it so long ago
    And looked upon Your work and called it good.
I know that others find You in the light
    That's sifted down through tinted window panes,
And yet I seem to feel You near tonight
    In this dim, quiet starlight on the plains.[1]

I've traveled to those rodeos from a cattle ranch in the rugged, lonely Powder River Breaks of northern Wyoming where I was raised. My mother's folks came down from the big cattle country of Montana when she was a girl and established the home ranch of the Greenough outfit on S A Creek. When my mother brought her new "bronco-twistin'" husband home from college, they settled on the Bitter Creek side, about eight miles over the hills or twenty miles by country road from the home ranch. That rodeoing husband, my father, was born on the Wallis brothers' ranch on the high plains of southern Wyoming beside the Big Laramie River. Dad's grandfather first came to Wyoming Territory about 1869; Wyoming finally got around to becoming a state twenty-two years later. We've been in cow country a long time—five generations—and we're not alone. There are families all over the West who can say the same.

About the time I was traveling the fifteen miles to Recluse School for the fifth grade, my folks were feeding a thousand heifers on Bitter Creek. They accomplished this with a good team of Belgian work horses and a hay sled, and it took two days to get everything fed—up the creek from the house one day and down the creek the next—all day long, day after day, until winter was done.

There was a lot of intellectual slack time inherent in this task, and my father took up the memorizing and recitation of poetry to fill in the empty spaces from one hay corral and bunch of hungry Herefords to the next. I believe he picked up the idea from a neighbor, a man prone to spontaneous outbursts of incredible memorization—Keats, Coleridge, Robert Service, and Badger Clark—accented by obscure cowboy tunes and little jokes of various sorts. Anyway, Daddy soon settled on Kipling as his poet of choice and for the rest of that winter he spent his time at the dinner table reciting over and over the particular stanza he was inserting into long-term memory that day. We got pretty sick of it.

On the weekends, home from school, I would sit at the back of the empty sled on the way to yet another bunch of bawling, hungry livestock, watching and listening as the tracks of horses and sled hissed and swished and crackled through the snow between my dangling legs. Daddy would stand tall and spraddle-legged in the very middle of the flatbed, bracing himself lightly and easily against the lines running over the hay rack and through his gloved fingers. He didn't have to do much driving—Grant and Lee already knew where they were going—so Dad would bellow out "The Ballad of East and West" for the enjoyment of us kids and the cows: "Oh, East is East, and West is West, and never the twain shall meet, / Till Earth and Sky stand presently at God's great Judgment Seat." I can hear him still.

The Powder River cow country I grew up in was, and is, a place layered with tradition. I have traveled half a life, lots of miles, through a lot of really rough country to a place where I can begin to understand the significance of those traditions. Somewhere along the way I developed an almost religious reverence for the ways of my raising—the way we rode our colts, and built our gear, and threw our ropes, and tried to live our lives. A few years ago I rediscovered the tradition of oral recitation in the form of cowboy poetry. Like many of my fellow poets, that reconnection literally turned my life around, allowed my creative instincts to explode in unexplainable, unforeseen directions, and tapped me directly back to the places and people and philosophies from which I have always been able to make the most sense.

And somewhere along the way I discovered that lots of ranching families, including my own, have pieces of heirloom poetry that their cowboy granddaddy or ranch-wife ancestor wrote, tucked away in cedar chests, or in bibles, or just as often only in their memories. In my mother's family nearly everyone has a copy of the poem my great-grandfather, Packsaddle Ben Greenough, wrote down in his shaky hand while working on a cow outfit years and years ago. It's called "Punching Cows":

I've worked at almost everything, since I was a small boy
    And everything I've tackled, boys, I did it with great joy.
I've worked upon big vessels, from the stern unto the bows
    But the hardest job that I've struck yet, is that called punching cows.

You're up ere daylight in the morn, and after dark at night
    And when it rains and thunders, why then you're in a plight
You swear when you reach town, you'll quit, so each makes his vows
    But still you stay and work away, and keep on punching cows.

Some blankets spread upon the ground is what you call your bed
    And when it comes to food, my boys, upon the plainest you are fed
Black coffee, fried potatoes, and the bosom of a sow
    But still a job you'll rustle boys to go and punch the cow.

You're coming up the trail again behind an ornery herd
You swore you'd never make two trips, yet this one makes your third
You drive along the prairie, the sweat rolls down your brow
Mind what I say, you'll curse the day that you first punched a cow.

When you turn loose you'll go to town and there blow in your roll
And 'ere you've been there many a day you'll find you're in the hole
Your saddle and your gun in hock, you've had a short carouse
Yet in the spring, you'll gaily sing, and go out punching cows

Now when the last day's work is done and you are called away
You're drove into that Great Roundup and cut out for a stray
The roundup foreman looks at you, and then he knits his brow
He knows that you're not much account for there they

. . . Don't Punch Cows.

Ben's handwritten copy contains a note along the bottom: "This song was written by a cowboy called McGinty and Ben Greenough during a spring rainy spell at a roundup camp on Powder River Montana fifty years ago." Ben died in the 1950s. Kenn Lee heard it and realized that it fit perfectly the tune of "When the Work's All Done This Fall," which D. J. O'Malley wrote around Miles City, just over the divide, in the 1880s.[2] "Punching Cows" was probably written in the 1890s, so it all seems to fit together. Who knows?

On the Wallis side we had a great-aunt, Jessa Eula Wallis, who ranched with her husband Oliver outside of Laramie, Wyoming. She published a small book of verse, *Wyoming Breezes,* full of poems about the Laramie Plains, the Johnson County range war, outcast rustlers, hard winters, "The Passing of the Range," and the coming of barbed wire and homesteaders. One of my favorite pieces to recite is her "Snowman":

We like the days when the snow drives in,
From every way, and shuts us in
The House. For then we have good eats,
Like pop-corn balls, and mixed nut meats
In fudge, and cakes and other sweets.

We'll watch the snow as it floats past,
We'll make that man of snow at last;
So fat and sleek, and the cold clear through,
He'll look just like our bankers do.[3]

My friend Jan Wood in South Dakota, who is a fine poet like her husband Bill, can quote bits of verse, never written down but passed down from her great-grandfather, Jake Palmateer, who according to Jan was a man who "would just walk up to somebody on the street and carry on a conversation—all in rhyme." The first time I ever heard Kenn Lee sing, he played one of the most beautiful cowboy songs I've ever heard, a song he calls "Beauty in the Moonlight." The words come from a poem that his grandfather, Frank G. West, wrote in Kansas. I've also heard Gary McMahan sing a lovely piece that he put to music from words written by his grandmother in Colorado, "My Husband and I." Jayne Harris, who runs an outfit just over the divide from my folks' place on Bitter Creek, has the tally book that her daddy, Glen Morse, kept as a young man. It contains not only cattle counts and neighbors' brands but also a number of his own poems, the words to popular songs like "Hell-Bound Train," a whole Bruce Kiskaddon poem written down from memory as prose, and a pretty good recipe for rye whiskey. Some of the poems, Jayne says, "You can't publish, 'cause they aren't fit to be printed," meaning they're a little on the bawdy side.

Ranch country used to be (and in some places still is) full of old-fashioned drifting cowboys, the kind who break out in rhyme as easy and as often as they tell a joke or crack a smile. Our old neighbor Blitz Nelson still comes and goes around our part of the country. Like lots of others he knows little bits and pieces of a bunch of real classics—Coleridge's "The Rime of the Ancient Mariner," Poe's "The Raven," and Robert Service's "The Shooting of Dan McGrew"—which, in between singing little cowboy ditties, he will spill out for anybody who will listen. Mama smiles and says fellows like Blitz have probably "spent too many winters in line camps with good bookshelves."

Cowboys like Blitz, Dad, Great-Aunt Jessa, and their contemporary counterparts have always respected and loved classic poetry. Many of today's poets will recite a few lines of Robert Frost or Poe when the mood strikes them, but by far the largest share of what they store in amazingly extensive memories is the traditional cowboy poetry of Bruce Kiskaddon, S. Omar Barker, Curley Fletcher, Badger Clark, Gail Gardner, Henry Herbert Knibbs, and a few others, as well as contemporary poems by friends and poets whose works they have admired.

One of the real benefits of the rise of cowboy poetry gatherings is the tearing down of regional fences so that the work of real great poets is being shared across the West. Bruce Kiskaddon was as revered in the big Nevada buckaroo country as Badger Clark was in the Black Hills of South Dakota. Listening to someone like Waddie Mitchell recite Kiskaddon's "When They've Finished Shipping Cattle in the Fall" shows that it doesn't matter whether we hail from northern Montana or southern Arizona, Canada, or Mexico. Anybody who's ever followed a bunch of cows, been around the seasons of a working ranch, or gone out with the wagon recognizes the feeling, those times when we pause to reflect and remember:

Though you're not exactly blue,
Yet you don't feel like you do
In the winter, or the long hot summer days.
For your feelin's and the weather,
Seem to sort of go together,
And you're quiet in the dreamy autumn haze.
When the last big steer is goaded
Down the chute, and safely loaded;
And the summer crew has ceased to hit the ball;
When a feller starts a draggin'
To the home ranch with the wagon—
When they've finished shippin' cattle in the fall.[4]

Kiskaddon can keep anybody's attention through the whole 108 lines, with every line chock-full of words and images that create a whole vision for anyone who has ever been close to being there. That slow and easy rhythm, kind of lazy, and the sentiments expressed—they'll even come across to someone who doesn't know the difference between a chuck wagon and a cattle car.

Not so long ago, before the first Cowboy Poetry Gathering in Elko, Nevada, in 1985, those who still memorized and recited the old cowboy classics were seemingly few, barely numerous enough to catch the attention of a folklorist or two or entertain a bunch of working cowhands from time to time. The Elko Gatherings, and the many local and regional gatherings that followed, were enough to lay the foundation for a cultural niche that the far-flung ranching community could call its own—a place to preserve and revive the old traditions, to celebrate a precariously precious lifestyle, and to socialize with a much broader selection of true cow-country colleagues than most had ever imagined possible. In turn, this renaissance in cowboy poetry has led directly to the most significant phenomenon to arise from the gatherings: an intimate, exhilarating, widespread, and demanding community of poets, writers, and musicians that appears to have no borders and no limits and is tied together by an integral appreciation for the livelihood that spawns it. We have become family.

We call, we write, and we check on each other. Scattered across the United States from Georgia to Oregon, a writing community has emerged as intense and personal as any that ever existed in London, bohemian Paris, or New York. We have the telephone bills to prove it. Most of us send and receive a volume of correspondence practically unheard of in this century. And for many of us, that ready access to approval, constructive criticism, and shoulders to cry on when we need them has become an essential part of our writing process. We wonder how we ever lived or wrote successfully before.

Like most families, we squabble. No longer can a poet slide by with finagled rhyme, twisted syntax, or sloppy meter without being called on it. Some have insisted that cowboy poetry is limited to "rhymed and metered verse." Others say that definition is far too narrow to accommodate the diversity of the contemporary scene. But nobody will say that rhyme and meter can be summarily dismissed, for even the most experimental open forms still retain a lyricism, a cadence, or an expressive rhythm that harks back to that structured tradition and does not lose sight (maybe I should say hearing) of the oral recitation that remains central to the art.

And like a big, far-flung, freewheeling family, cowboy poetry is essentially a leaderless movement with no gatekeepers, no experts, no associations, and no competitions to decide who is or isn't a cowboy poet. The grandest achievement of cowboy poetry is its ability to remain undefined and unfenced. That is a good glory. And that is part of what maintains such vitality and excitement in this intoxicating realm of creativity. As a poet, you either ride with the herd because something in your work speaks to the heart and soul and essence of cattle people or you don't. It's a quirk deeply embedded in the independent nature of folks who will not tolerate anybody riding fence on them.

Probably this one attribute has caused more consternation and internal conflict, a little of which has spilled out into the open air, than any other problem within cowboy poetry. The off side of not allowing anybody to ride fence on you is how in hell to deal politely with some gunsel who doesn't know the difference between a steer and a heifer, who is embarrassing everybody except himself by trying to pass himself off as a cowboy poet, and who knows he has the absolute authority to do so because he watched a lot of John Wayne westerns when he was a kid. Confronting such folks would be a breach of etiquette that would spark an instant fistfight in any honorable cowboy crowd. But at the same time it concerns us that such folks, left alone, might possibly be mistaken for "real" cowboys by an unknowledgeable audience.

That kind of romanticized poetry perpetuates the false and phony perceptions of cowboys and ranching fed by myths of dime novels and B movies on one hand and by the most radical anti-rancher environmental rhetoric on the other. Both extremes are myths that most respectable contemporary poets go to great lengths to dispel. The glorified, unreal, Hollywood-style cowboy has been a perennial American folk hero and one that plenty of us are occasionally guilty of playing up to, but the real cowboy is something else entirely and fairly rare. If you gathered all the ranching folk from all over the American West together in one big roundup, you wouldn't come up with enough people to make a decent town by today's standards, yet those few folks have the stewardship of more land than anyone outside of the federal government. Cowboy poetry is about the working cowboy, the ranching family, the folks who are out there raising the beef that goes on your table, taking care of the earth they own or lease or just doing the best they can while working for "the other guy," who far too often is some faceless, nameless, mega-monster corporation. It is a lifestyle challenged on all sides.

Cowboy poetry is seen by many as a survival tool, as a way to communicate with and educate an urban population now generations removed from the land. We need to continue writing about the realities of work and the environmental sensitivities of a valuable and increasingly distinct culture that remains intimately connected to nature. Writing and reciting are our best opportunities to create a new myth of the modern cowboy and instill in American culture the concept of rancher environmentalism. The *Dry Crik Review*'s environmental issues, the increasing influence of Allan Savory and holistic resource management, and sessions about the survival of ranching culture and the future of the western environment at poetry gatherings are all prominent examples of this new direction, not to mention the blizzard of continuing dialogue and correspondence, telephone calls, letters, and manifestos flying between poets all over the West.[5] Out of these developments have arisen some extremely promising, although tentative, communications and overtures between previously polarized ranchers and environmentalists who are both becoming more aware of the tie that binds in the love of the land, regardless of whether you call it "good grass" or "a healthy ecosystem."

A common theme runs through these new developments that points to a shift in cow-country philosophy—something that was always latently there but has recently started to bubble to the surface. You can find it in Ray Hunt's *Harmony with Horses,* in Savory's research and writings, and in contemporary cowboy poetry.[6] It has something to do with being aware, spiritual, and in tune and of being or needing to be a people who see every little sign and stay constantly in touch with all that is—something to do with a rural reality and maintaining a strong sense of what is happening around us. At the root is what Teresa Jordan has called "that ancient self-sufficiency" and the ties that bind people together across the West.

This sudden sense of connectedness is most startling and satisfying to ranch-country individuals used to being alone and being different. Now we've suddenly discovered a whole world of like-minded folks with the same backgrounds, the same traditions, and the same concerns that so many assumed did not exist outside of our families or ranch communities. It is a theme you hear over and over again until it almost rings of cliché—statements like "poetry gatherings are spiritual reunions," "Elko feels like coming home," and "we will never be alone again."

It all has a lot to do with the genuine love and concern that Vess Quinlan says give us a platform on which to stand. It is a platform that we all support, from which we build and establish a level of trust that allows us to experiment with, modify, and jostle ideas. Teresa Jordan challenges us to reach even further from this platform, to see beyond the narrow conflicts and use our savvy, our "ancient capacity for self-reliance . . . to create a West that can endure and satisfy."[7]

This sense of connectedness, the closeness and security of family within cowboy poetry, has germinated a broadening and expanding spirit in the genre. There is unquestionably an upsurge of strong, clear, positive female voices speaking to and for women's concerns in ranching culture. And there is a growing willingness to address serious issues, although not without difficulty. The first dangerous water to cross is a private and collective struggle with unaccustomed openness, for ours is not a culture that speaks easily or comfortably about deep things or difficult emotional experiences. At the same time, we are not a culture that shies from reality. These two characteristics set up a touchy dichotomy that has begun to be addressed in creative work. Consider Waddie Mitchell's "Sold Your Saddle," Audrey Hankins's "Relapse," Wallace McRae's "Things of Intrinsic Worth," and the Vietnam poetry of Rod McQueary, Bill Jones, Joe Bruce, and Lisa Quinlan—poetry that looks the hard, uncomfortable topics of war, divorce, alcoholism, and greed straight in the eye and does not flinch.[8]

So we use our words to stretch and share and explore experimental forms of expressing ranch-country experience. And we cling to tradition, returning again and again to the lyric, to these tried and true forms of oral poetry. That recitation of easily memorized, rhymed and metered verse reaches back through the generations—through our great-grandfathers' Montana roundup ballads and our great-aunts' Laramie Plains blizzard verse; back through the Texas punchers that came singing up the trail; through the boys who rode the big, bad broncs east from Oregon; through the Spanish vaquero's love of silver, flash, and drama; over the seas, through the Irish bards; all the way back, I suppose, to the ancient seafaring, singing Greeks—one long, long intangible rope that we hope to throw straight and true and soft as a hoolihan through our children and our children's children and beyond.

Gatherings

We Gather
To scatter and toss deep, honed, thoughts
Between good friends with . . . Clear minds . . . Bright eyes
Over and over again

And an invisible genesis of incredible proportions
Spews forth a far-flung country
That contains us all

How can this be so?

Like a magnetic, mystical, instrument that we just barely
Know how to play

Reach up and tentatively twang a string
That smiles and send it on to California
Hum a tune on the phone in Nevada
A memory sings through Montana
Drifts down a wailing Wyoming wind
Creates a waltzing lament in Laramie

We've damn near made a telepathic symphony
A new and eerie, partly scary, mental energy

Pluck a painful healing chord in Ruby Valley
And a jester weeps, and writes, riding the Wind Rivers
A bear spirit rises, raging and roaring, in a Colorado cowboy
And a woman in Alamosa, too young, too female
To understand . . . does

The music swells to communal crescendo
In Durango
But Durango cannot contain it . . . or us
Leaps the peaks
Echoes haunt us all home

Still, we seek the way
Gather again
Tune our collective instrument
Scatter again
To practice and play

My God . . . what have we done? What have we made?[9]

Notes

1. Charles Badger Clark, "A Cowboy's Prayer," in Clark, *Sun and Saddle Leather, Including "Grass-Grown Trails" and Other New Poems* (1915), 6th ed. (Boston: Richard G. Badger, 1922), 50–51.

2. D. J. O'Malley, "When the Work's All Done This Fall," first published in the *Stock Growers' Journal,* 6 October 1893 (chapter 13).

3. From the author's collection. Reprints available from Laramie Plains Museum, Laramie, Wyoming (original publication place and date unknown).

4. Bruce Kiskaddon, "When They've Finished Shipping Cattle in the Fall," in *Rhymes of the Ranges: A New Collection of the Poems of Bruce Kiskaddon,* ed. Hal Cannon (Salt Lake City: Gibbs Smith, 1987), 115.

5. *Dry Crik Review* 1 (Fall 1991), and 2–3 (Fall 1992–Winter 1993); Allan Savory, *Holistic Resource Management* (Covelo, Calif.: Island Press, 1988).

6. Ray Hunt, *Harmony with Horses: An In-Depth Study of Horse/Man Relationship,* ed. Milly Hunt (Fresno: Pioneer Publishing, 1978).

7. Teresa Jordan, "Beyond Conflict," *Dry Crik Review* 2 (Spring 1992): 22.

8. Waddie Mitchell, "Sold Your Saddle," in *New Cowboy Poetry: A Contemporary Gathering,* ed. Hal Cannon (Salt Lake City: Gibbs Smith, 1990), 57–59; Audrey Hankins, "Relapse," *Dry Crik Review* 2 (Winter 1992): 17; Wallace McRae, "Things of Intrinsic Worth," in McRae, *Cowboy Curmudgeon* (Salt Lake City: Gibbs Smith, 1992), 131; Rod McQueary and Bill Jones, *Blood Trails* (Lemon Cove, California: Dry Crik Press, 1993); Joe Bruce and Lisa Quinlan war poetry, unpublished, from the author's collection.

9. Sue Wallis, "Gatherings," *Dry Crik Review* 2 (Winter 1992): 6–7.

18

Nature and Cowboy Poetry

Craig Miller

The culture and way of life of cowboys and the cattle industry in the American West are inextricably linked to nature and the physical landscape. It is a relationship that has always been at the very soul of the cowboy's existence, for his occupation, cultural heritage, and often personal identity are built upon day-to-day, long-term associations with nature.

Just as cowboying as an occupation has evolved since the early days of the western frontier, the cowboy's relationship to nature has also evolved. Evidence of change is everywhere visible; the cultural landscape is increasingly marked by technology as the pickup truck and other machinery have partly replaced the horse and rider, and the physical landscape is also greatly altered. The unbroken plains and mountains have given way to patterned rows of fencing, lushly irrigated pasture lands, overgrazed sand barrens, and even resort communities.

Not so obvious are the changes that have taken place in the ranching culture's perception of its interaction with nature. Although it is rare to find historical documentation of this kind of perceptual change, the strong oral tradition of cowboy poetry clearly reveals a shifting relationship. It also provides a rare opportunity to trace the evolution of a culture's perceived relationship with nature. Cowboy poets are great expressive chroniclers, and with the perspective of insiders completely fluent in their idiom are able to document, interpret, and reflect upon cowboy life.

Cowboy poets use their relationship to nature to generate metaphors and allegory, color the mood and setting of narration, and symbolize personal identity and cowboy culture. A review of cowboy poetry since the early twentieth century reveals an evolutionary development in its references to nature that correlates with the historical development of the American West. That development seems to occur in three stages:

1. *The Old Paradigm: Nature Equals Chaos, Civilization Equals Order.* The cowboy's encounter with nature became a metaphor for the human struggle for life and for the struggle to civilize the West. Poems of this period are characterized by enormity of landscape, natural disasters that test individuals and groups, and a correlation between nature and the devil.

2. *A New Paradigm: Nostalgia Ushers in a Growing Respect for Nature.* As the West was tamed, cowboy poets reflected upon old ways of life—times of unfenced range and long trail drives. Around 1900 they began to chronicle a growing respect for nature and describe personal identity in terms of the relationship between the cowboy's way of life and the natural environment. Major themes of this stage include nostalgia, regional patriotism, and nature separating westerners from the cultured East.

3. *The Old Paradigm Inverted: The Chaos of Civilization Becomes the Major Threat to the Environment and to Cowboy Culture.* During the 1980s and 1990s, civilization in the form of government, laws, regulations, and population pressures threatened the cattle industry in the West and the foundations of the cowboy lifestyle. The cowboy code expanded to include a responsibility to maintain the natural order and act as steward of the natural landscape. Poets began to correlate the decay of the natural environment with the erosion of cowboy culture.

These developments constitute a clear evolution in the relationship between cowboys and nature. At first the natural environment was seen as a threat to the pioneer cattle industry in the West. The forces of nature contained uncontrolled powers at odds with the destiny of humans. According to their poetry, early cowboys struggled to defeat nature, survive in a harsh world dominated by natural forces, and build a future for western culture. Just as their ancestors had domesticated cattle for the benefit of humanity, they believed their destiny was to tame the landscape and introduce civilization.

As cowboys worked to tame the forces of nature, cowboy culture became intimately wedded to the natural landscape. Indeed, cowboys' personal and occupational identity grew out of the day-to-day interaction between personal experience and the natural environment. Similarly, their cultural identity grew from the cumulative acceptance of nature as an integral part of his heritage and lifestyle. Work in harmony with nature has become an important theme in cowboy poetry that endows the cowboy with the power and wisdom of the environment.

Increasingly, cowboys have recognized that the relationship between the natural environment and the civilized landscape parallels the relationship between their culture and the increasing complexity of civilization—urban society—itself. In almost completely reversing their predecessors' relationship to nature, contemporary cowboys align themselves with nature to do battle against outside forces of government and civilization that threaten to destroy both the natural environment and their culture. Nature is no longer cowboys' rival, for they see it as a part of their identity, an inseparable component of their way of life. Indeed, the perceived threat to lifestyle and traditions is the same force that threatens the natural environment: the insatiable encroachment of civilization in the form of laws, taxes, regulations, economic constraints, the increasing expropriation of natural resources for national development, and the degradation of the landscape due to pressures of industry and population growth.

Cowboy poets are the chroniclers of this constantly changing West—how the landscape and environment have changed, how humans have adapted their lifestyles to accommodate or accelerate those changes, and how their cultural perceptions have evolved. Fortunately, the tradition of writing poems and songs has accompanied the occupation since its earliest days; consequently, the interpretive cultural record stretches back for more than a century. Cowboys and ranchers have chronicled their lives and occupations and, in parallel, their relationship to the natural landscape. Exploring this relationship between natural and cultural environments can provide insight into the interactive changes of environment, lifestyle, and perceptions of cowboys as a cultural group.

The Old Paradigm: Nature Equals Chaos, Civilization Equals Order

Dating back to the commentaries of the first European-Americans to enter the region, the West has been consistently described in exaggerated terms greater than reality. The awesome expanse of the Great Plains is frequently compared to the vastness of the ocean. The Rocky Mountains are described as barriers to civilization. The weather is extreme, summer and winter, and danger is everywhere. The enormous extremes of western landscape as depicted in the paintings of artists such as Albert Bierstadt are still mirrored in cowboy poetry and recitation.

Early on, the poets and balladeers of the nineteenth-century West adapted the occupational songs of other cultures to the rigors of life on the frontier. The cowboy's struggle with the wild and untamed environment found resonance in the oral traditions of other occupational groups who risked their lives and fortunes in a struggle against nature. Songs of sailors, for example, were adapted to cowboy life. The sailor's vast ocean became the cowboy's rolling prairie, the herds of buffalo a living tide. In "Bury Me Not on the Lone Prairie," burial at sea became death on the desolate western plains; "The Cowboy's Lament" is a funeral march down the streets of Laredo.

The poems of Robert W. Service, whose popularity peaked during the 1920s and 1930s, are clearly very different in their Yukon settings from cowboy poetry, yet they have entered the repertoire of many cowboy poets through recitation. Service's popularity suggests the lasting appeal of his themes of nature's power and humanity's struggle to survive. Although set in a land far from cattle country and replete with unfamiliar occupational references, the poems resonate with cowboys because they conjure up the primeval struggle between people who work in the elements and the natural environment.

Like the ancient sailors and the characters of the Service poems, early cowboy poetry demonstrates the struggle to calm the wild, uncontrolled, unproductive aspects of nature and to channel those resources into building a bucolic, safe environment where nature would exist under the control and to the benefit of humanity. The early cowboy poets knew well the terrors unleashed by nature in a land out of their control, and scores of poems attest to the hostility presented by the landscape. In "The Desert" (1914), E. A. Brininstool warns:

Sun, silence, sand and dreary solitude;
    Vast stretches, white, beneath a glaring sky;
Where only those stout-hearted may intrude,
    With Death to harass them and terrify.[1]

A poem by Homer W. Bryant, "He Rang the Devil's Knell," portrays nature as the devil himself as a cowboy endures a windy night: "The wind so long, made an eerie song, as it followed the first guard's trail," and then "he saw a light in the darkened night and he thought of the fires of hell." Bryant continues, "The restless herd and the eerie wind, it carried a deathlike song. . . . / That seemed to keep time with the beat of his heart, like the devil was tagging along."[2]

"The Llano Estacado" is an old cowboy song that describes the fate of a cowboy who ventured across Texas's Staked Plains and died of thirst.[3] Here and elsewhere, as in Bryant's poem, the West is portrayed as a living hell or worse, as described in the anonymous "Hell in Texas." In that poem, the Lord tricks the reticent devil into taking excess Texas property off his hands, whereby the devil adds a creative flourish:

He began to put thorns in all of the trees,
And mixed up the sand with millions of fleas;
And scattered tarantulas along all the roads,
Put thorns on the cactus and horns on the toads.[4]

The literature also contains a large body of poems from the early twentieth century that describe the terrible forces of nature in terms of natural disasters that dwarf the presence and action of those on the landscape. In the anonymous "Wrangler Kid," for example:

The grass fire swooped like a red wolf pack,
    On the wings of a west wind dry.
Its red race left the scorched plains black
    'Neath a sullen, smoky sky.[5]

Furthermore, unpredictable extremes of weather represent an ever-present danger. Many poems relate the loss of whole herds of cattle to blizzard conditions; Hamlin Garland's "Lost in a Norther" compounds the danger of becoming lost on a featureless prairie with the life-threatening conditions of a two-day blizzard.[6]

Whether bound in print or maintained in the repertoire of oral recitation, few collections of cowboy poetry exist without reference to that dreaded occupational hazard, the stampede—a topic especially popular in the nineteenth century because eastern readers were so unfamiliar with it. In these poems, herds of domestic cattle represent raw energy ready to explode at the slightest spark, whether caused by man, as in "Utah Carroll"; by wild animal, as in Freeman Miller's "The Stampede"; or by the weather, as in "Lasca" by Frank Desprez.[7]

Many cowboy poems both past and present contain ominous descriptions of darkening skies and heavy, humid air that foreshadow approaching disaster. The lightning storm, representing the rawest energy of nature, can conjure up the most primeval animal powers feared by humans. It can ignite what little remains of the wild ancestry of the cattle and transform a calm, domestic, humanly controlled herd into a savage tidal wave of deadly energy. Melvin Whipple's "Electric Storm" begins with the Frankenstein-like transfer of energy that takes place between lightning and monster: "Did you ever see the fire on the tips of the cattle's horns, / A-dancin' and a-playin' in a fierce electric storm?"[8]

This romantically adventurous and dangerous relationship between nature and man has become one of the symbols of the cowboy. Nature's challenge to the cowboy can be presented in two ways. Individuals pitted alone against the forces of nature must develop skills and acumen to combat nature on its own terms. But if the challenge is presented to cowboys as a group, their hope of survival lies in the ability to work as partners, each contributing their share to overcome natural adversities. Nature presents those challenges, which in turn identify the danger, the adventure, and the rewards of the occupation. According to tradition, a successful cowboy could meet each of nature's tests and wear each accomplishment as a badge converted into a poem, story, song, or recitation. With each repetition the individual and group connection to nature and the occupation itself was reinforced. Contemporary cowboys still work with the powers of nature every day, so tales of old adventures and dangers are well understood and relevant.

A New Paradigm: Nostalgia and a Growing Respect for Nature

As European-American farmers and merchants moved west of the Mississippi and began settling the plains and mountains around the turn of the century, cowboy poets increasingly began mentioning a growing distaste for the complications of civilization in the forms of barbed wire, railroads, towns, restrictive laws and institutions, domestic culture, and conflicts with other groups. The cowboy lifestyle had changed substantially from the days of the great cattle drives, when cowboys could ride from Texas to Montana in one season, to the days when they would work at a single ranch for an entire season or a lifetime. Poetry began to highlight the distinction between the old days when the West was untamed and uncontrolled and the new era of fenced grazing allotments, towns within a day's travel occupied by diversely employed people, a whirl of technological advancements, and growing pressures on tamed but limited resources.

Unlike the early songs and poems that depict the cowboy struggling against nature, poets of the late nineteenth and early twentieth centuries began chronicling their nostalgia for the old days and the old ways just as the Old West slipped from their grasp. Their former relationship with nature was now described as a part of the working life they loved, and in many ways that perceived relationship formed the core of their identity. "The Last Longhorn"—which the Lomaxes attribute to Judge R. W. Hall of Amarillo—uses a nostalgic, talking longhorn steer to symbolize the passing of the Old West and the end of the old cowboy life:

"I remember back in the seventies,
Full many summers past,
There was grass and water plenty,
But it was too good to last.
I little dreamed what would happen
Some twenty summers hence,
When the nester came with his wife, his kids,
His dogs, and his barbed-wire fence."[9]

As cowboys developed these new themes in their poetry, they also explored their relationship to nature and the land. With nostalgia they reflected upon their feelings and eloquently refined their stand regarding the landscape. More frequently now, nature was described with respect and referred to lovingly in terms of home and native land. Cowboy poets joined the ranks of other westerners in writing what amounted to patriotic poems dedicated to the natural environment. That in itself set them apart from Americans living and writing in the crowded, urban East. Examples of what might be called regional patriotism include Brewster

Higley's "Home on the Range," E. A. Brininstool's "Where the Sagebrush Billows Roll," and Charles A. Siringo's "Way Out West."[10]

As cowboys began separating themselves from cultured easterners, a closeness to nature became the symbol of that difference. The intimate relationship with nature is sometimes expressed in personal, down-to-earth terms. In deliberate contrast to what they perceive as a highly refined and overly sophisticated urban population, cowboy poet–humorists enthusiastically approach the subjects of breeding and bodily functions in direct and natural terms. Although that repertoire is not completely free of vulgarity and tastelessness, it includes outstandingly clever gems of wit and tongue-in-cheek allegory that will undoubtedly remain a permanent part of the literature. No poet has ever delivered a cleverer friendly insult than Wallace McRae in "Reincarnation," in which he elaborately develops the cycle of birth, death, and decomposition on the range simply to call a friend a pile of horse manure—but in much more eloquent terms.[11]

In cowboy poetry, nature is also depicted as a worthy adversary, something that brings out the best in a man or woman. It is an opponent to be respected and negotiated with, and in those negotiations, even if cowboys do not gain material wealth they are always rewarded with a greater self-understanding or an appreciation for the human relationship with the land. Gary McMahan's song "The Old Double Diamond" tells of a cowboy who at first "was a damn poor excuse for a man." He credits nature for its role in making him a good cowboy and a mature man who concludes "I'm moving on, but I'm leaving with more than I came":

> I fought her winters and busted her horses,
> you know, it took more than I thought I could stand.
> But the battles with the mountains and the cattle
> seemed to bring out the best in a man.[12]

Respect for nature is often represented by the cowboy's relationship with horses and cattle. These animals—often wild, independent, and proud-spirited—are frequently described with human traits of bravery, individualism, perseverance, devotion, loyalty, innocence, and purity. Indeed, the most domesticated animals may be portrayed with the worst characteristics of over-civilized humans who create their own problems because they ignore innocent, honest, and pure natural instincts for the patterned, ingrained, and inbred responses of civilization. The careful breeding that humans employ to domesticate animals and improve stock is ironically responsible for the animals' stupidity and loss of individuality (as numerous poems making fun of chickens, turkeys, and sheep attest), dooming them to a destiny of eternal and inescapable subjugation and dominance. Modern cattle breeds, for example, are nearly incapable of surviving unassisted, and if left to the ravages of nature their demise would be immediate.

That situation is often contrasted in the stories and poems of cowboys by accounts of nature calling a formerly domesticated or renegade animal to return to its natural state, a theme made popular by Jack London's *The Call of the Wild* (1903). The animal regains its individuality, virility, cunning, and inventiveness, sometimes becoming magically invincible, as in "Windy Bill," "The Strawberry Roan," and "The Flyin' Outlaw," all from the early twentieth century.[13]

In some poems, the renegade animal is characterized as a paradoxical combination of good and evil, as if all the wild and pagan powers of nature have gathered strength to defy the domination and control of humans. Some poems present this as a clear struggle between good and evil in which humanity (although somewhat reluctantly) performs its duty of domination because that is how it sees its role in the plan of life. The reluctance to dominate rises out of sadness and the realization that victory heralds the fall of free will and wildness. Even when the wild mustang is the personification of evil, the image of a self-determined mustang running free and wild, the wind in its mane, is far more attractive and alluring than the well-trained steed that obediently bends to command or spur.

"The Buckskin Mare" by contemporary poet Baxter Black develops this theme further than usual. In this poem, the narrator becomes obsessed with conquering a wild mare, which, over a period of years, has become legendary among local cowboys for her strength and independence:

Some attributed her prowess
to a freak in Nature's Law.
    Still others said
    she was the devil's spawn
        So the incident that happened
        at the top of Sheepshead Draw
            Served notice hell's account
            was overdrawn.[14]

His obsession drives the narrator to hunt her down and capture her, but instead of taming her in the traditional way, the cowboy submits to the base instincts of fear, anger, and frustration. In total disrespect, he shoots the wild mare dead. As the poem ends, other cowboys reject him for essentially murdering that symbol of nature incarnate and for acting like a traitor, betraying their culture and the Code of the West.

The tragedy of "The Buckskin Mare" is more apparent when one realizes her similarity to cowboys, who often see themselves as individuals who have managed to break away from the herd of modern civilization to establish identity and exercise free will. A closeness to nature has sharpened their wits and reflexes and provided the skills to maintain their independence and control their destinies.

Like the wild mustang, they can draw upon the powers of nature to fortify their resolve to defy encroaching civilization, which in several different ways threatens cowboy culture and traditional lifestyles.

The Old Paradigm Inverted: The Chaos of Civilization, the Environment, and Cowboy Culture

The stresses and complications of modern society are increasingly reflected in cowboy poems, especially those written in the 1980s and 1990s, and the stakes are getting higher as the rate of encroachment on traditional ways of life increases. In some of these poems more than just personal identity and self-determination are at risk. In the direct and poignant "Ode to LAX," for example, Montanan Mike Logan contrasts the worst aspects of urban America with the pristine nature of his home state.[15]

Although cowboy poetry has always reflected disdain for the ways of city life, the assaults on one's senses—the noise, polluted air, crowds, and clutter of material things—are increasingly mentioned by contemporary poets. Indeed, Montana poet Wallace McRae, Texas poet Buck Ramsey, and other poets throughout the West have identified and condemned the encroachments of civilization that threaten traditional lifestyles. In "The Mines, from the Strip Mines," McRae shows the direct connection between the loss of natural resources and the end of the cowboy life when a strip mine feeds the nation's insatiable appetite for energy at the expense of the local cattle industry and cowboy culture.[16]

Ramsey uses political satire in the previously unpublished "The Man for Our Time" to illustrate an unscrupulous rancher's abandonment of traditional values. "He prayed to the money god, pledged to a flag and / made sure all the newshounds were lookin'," Ramsey writes.

> He dug up his pastures for all they were worth with
> no mind for the livin' to follow,
> Left poisons and sludge and the leavin's of greed
> till his creeks would catch fire and run yellow.

This poem is an apocalyptic warning of what could happen if traitors to the land and culture abandon the cowboy code and despoil nature in the process.

McRae's collection of poems, *It's Just Grass and Water,* also focuses on the cowboy's changing relationship to the land. In belligerent terms, he rails against those causing the environmental crises that threaten land-based occupations and turn Mother Earth into a prostitute ("The Land"). In "Our Communion," he likens the earth to Christ, reminding us that what we do to the land we are doing to our bodies; in "Things of Intrinsic Worth," he blasts the materialistic values of the present.[17]

Many other recent poems, although not strictly environmental criticism, portray the natural landscape and a healthy environment as integral parts of cowboy life and an equilibrium in which the good evens out the bad. The harshness of nature is at times what actually nourishes the land and the cowboy. In such circumstances nature and humanity become one, as in McRae's "Rain" and "Signs."[18]

It's a long-standing practice for cowboy poets to reflect nostalgically on the changing West, but the poets of today are registering a powerful alarm at the rapidly increasing pace of urbanization and environmental degradation. Ernie Fanning's "The Vanishing Valley" describes neighbors driven from their land only to see it replaced with smog and grey concrete.[19] Other poets lament the pressures of population growth and the loss of individual freedom; Gordon Eastman, for example, wrote "Buckskin Flats" after being cited for riding his horse through the town square of Livingston, Montana.[20]

In poem after poem, the old paradigm that civilization brings order and nature equals chaos is being inverted. More and more contemporary poets are writing of the order and simplicity found in nature as opposed to the chaos of modern society. They express frustration at what they perceive as encroachments of an outside order in the form of government taxes, laws, and restrictions that force them to make accommodations that benefit the faceless and nameless in places far away. They fear that this outside order chaotically threatens the internal order of the natural cowboy lifestyle.

Cowboy poets register these fears and frustrations in numerous poems that question the rationale behind a governmental system they fear will ultimately drive them from their land and pervert their reputation and standing in the national community. Yula Sue Hunting, for example, satirically signs a letter-poem to the tax commission "criminally yours."[21] Although long-time ranchers have always considered themselves to be caretakers of their land, journalists, writers, and politicians have ironically pitted them against the conservation movement, painting the ranchers as cultural intruders who seem to be working against the environment.

At stake is the cowboy's cultural identity, which to a large extent is based on his or her relationship to the natural environment, the physical landscape of the West. As Buck Ramsey points out in the unpublished "Names and Callin's," a lot of people are called cowboys, from presidents to hillbilly singers, but the term is much more than just a name. It is an occupation, a lifestyle, and a continuing relationship with the land involving far less disruption than the tame gardens of a New England farm, the humid monocultured plantations of the South, the acrid feedlots of the Midwest, or the suburban sprawl of the West Coast. Cowboy poetry shows a positive relationship to the natural environment, at times in awe of its enormity and power and at other times merely a constant if mundane reminder of the trials of the occupation, whether as spring mud and manure, sweltering summer heat, constant autumn drizzle, or bitter winter cold.

There is a maturity to cowboy poetry now that is championed in poems such as Buck Ramsey's "Anthem." Like Longfellow's "Hiawatha," the rhythm of Ramsey's poem adds solemnity and an apocalyptic ominousness that warns against the abuse of nature and Mother Earth. Its haunting beauty suggests that modern cowboys may unwittingly be following the ideology of outsiders who have no regard for nature, the land, or their heritage. In the process, perhaps they are fooled—or bribed—into abandoning the old cowboy code, thus betraying nature and themselves. "Anthem" builds in tension:

We knew the land would not be ours,
That no one has the awful powers
To claim the vast and common nesting,
To own the life that gave him birth,
Much less to rape his Mother Earth
And ask her for a mother's blessing,
And live in peace with her,
And, dying, come to rest with her.

The tragedy of the poem lies in the realization that moneyed outsiders are paying cowboys to do their bidding. The cowboy boasts, "But in the ruckus, in the whirl, / We were the wolves of all the world." And, in solemn reflection, he finally admits:

Some cowboys even shunned the ways
Of cowboys in the trail-herd days,
(But where's the gift not turned for plunder?)
Forgot that we are what we do
And not the stuff we lay claim to.[22]

In "Anthem," Ramsey brings the chaos of outside civilization home to the cowboy individual, warning that chaos exists as an inherent characteristic of humankind and that threats to nature and cowboy culture can come from within that same culture, from within themselves.

If cowboy poets are cultural barometers, recording and interpreting the changes and concerns of society as a whole as well as those of a relatively small occupational group, then it appears that stewardship of nature has become, finally, a part of the cowboy code as well as the nation's. We have arrived at an unspoken acknowledgment that one path to maturity and self-knowledge is through contact with nature, with its challenges and its solace, its power and its quiet. That code is expressed in terms of respect for individual integrity and for the rights of privacy and self-determination. Similarly, nature has earned cowboys' respect, and increasingly their cultural identity has come to depend upon a strong, close relationship with the natural environment. If the physical environment is to continue to nourish cowboy culture as it has in the past, it must be given the same respect and a delicate balance of recognized integrity, the right to privacy, and self-determination. In recognizing that relationship, cowboys are learning to care for nature and guard it from harm as if their lives and culture depended upon doing so—as indeed they may.

Notes

1. E. A. Brininstool, "The Desert," in *Trail Dust of a Maverick* (New York: Dodd, Mead, 1914), 19.

2. Homer W. Bryant, "He Rang the Devil's Knell," manuscript copy.

3. "The Llano Estacado," in John A. Lomax and Alan Lomax, *Cowboy Songs and Other Frontier Ballads* (1910), (New York: Macmillan, 1986), 313–15.

4. "Hell in Texas," in Lomax and Lomax, *Cowboy Songs,* 319.

5. "The Wrangler Kid," in *Best Loved Poems of the American West,* ed. John J. Gregg and Barbara T. Gregg (Garden City: Doubleday, 1980), 278–80.

6. Hamlin Garland, "Lost in a Norther," in *Best Loved Poems,* ed. Gregg and Gregg, 21–24.

7. "Utah Carroll," in Lomax and Lomax, *Cowboy Songs,* 125–28; Freeman Miller, "The Stampede," in *Best Loved Poems,* ed. Gregg and Gregg, 186–88; Frank Desprez, "Lasca," in John A. Lomax, *Songs of the Cattle Trail and Cow Camp* (1919), (New York: Duell, Sloan and Pearce, 1950), 23–26.

8. Melvin Whipple, "Electric Storm," in *Echoes of the Past: The Cowboy Poetry of Melvin Whipple,* ed. Jim McNutt (San Antonio: University of Texas Institute of Texan Cultures, 1987), 14.

9. R. W. Hall, "The Last Longhorn," in Lomax and Lomax, *Cowboy Songs,* 326.

10. Higley's authorship of "Home on the Range" is documented in Jim Bob Tinsley, *He Was Singin' This Song: A Collection of Forty-Eight Traditional Songs of the American Cowboy, with Words, Music, Pictures, and Stories* (Orlando: University Presses of Florida, 1981), 212–15; E. A. Brininstool, "Way Out West," in *Trail Dust of a Maverick,* 51; Charles A. Siringo, "Way Out West," in Lomax and Lomax, *Cowboy Songs,* 333.

11. Wallace McRae, "Reincarnation," in *Cowboy Poetry: A Gathering,* ed. Hal Cannon (Salt Lake City: Gibbs Smith, 1985), 185–86.

12. Gary McMahan's "The Old Double Diamond" has been recorded by a number of other singers, notably Ian Tyson, *Old Corrals and Sagebrush* (Columbia FC 38949).

13. The anonymous "Windy Bill" and Curley Fletcher, "The Strawberry Roan" and

"The Flyin' Outlaw" are all in *Cowboy Poetry,* ed. Cannon, 26–27, 57–59, 59–63. A contemporary example is Lucky Whipple, "Buckin' Horse Ballet," in *Cowboy Poetry,* ed. Cannon, 137–38.

14. Baxter Black, "The Buckskin Mare," in Black, *Croutons on a Cow Pie* (Brighton, Colo.: Coyote Cowboy Co., 1992), 2:190.

15. Mike Logan, "Ode to LAX," in Logan, *Bronc to Breakfast and Other Poems* (Helena, Mont.: Buglin' Bull Press, 1988), 62.

16. Wallace McRae, "The Mines, from the Strip Mines," in McRae, *It's Just Grass and Water* (Spokane: Shaun Higgins, 1979), 5.

17. Wallace McRae, "The Land" and "Our Communion," in McRae, *It's Just Grass and Water,* 16, 26; Wallace McRae, "Things of Intrinsic Worth," in *New Cowboy Poetry: A Contemporary Gathering,* ed. Hal Cannon (Salt Lake City: Gibbs Smith, 1990), 54.

18. Wallace McRae, "Rain" and "Signs," in McRae, *It's Just Grass and Water,* 24, 25.

19. Ernie Fanning, "The Vanishing Valley," in *Cowboy Poetry,* ed. Cannon, 95–96.

20. Gordon Eastman, "Buckskin Flats," in *Cowboy Poetry,* ed. Cannon, 139–40.

21. Yula Sue Hunting, "Dear Sirs," in *Cowboy Poetry from Utah,* ed. Carol A. Edison (Salt Lake City: Utah Folklife Center, 1985), 42.

22. Buck Ramsey, "Anthem," in *And as I rode out on the morning* (Lubbock: Texas Tech University Press, 1993), 3–6. The poem is also in *New Cowboy Poetry,* ed. Cannon, 99–102.

19

Women and Cowboy Poetry

Elaine Thatcher

The cowboy life is defined by the work to be done—raising cattle for the beef market. Until only recently in the popular mind this has been man's work, and woman's role has been considered peripheral. Men have been the ones to ride the horses through miles of rough western terrain, moving, doctoring, and gathering cattle. The reality, however, is not so clear-cut. Women have always played a variety of roles in ranch life, from bookkeeper and cook to cowhand on horseback, and they were a featured part of early Wild West shows as trick riders and trick-shot artists.

Cowboy poetry, like cowboying itself, started out being perceived as a man's art. Students of the genre have so far uncovered little evidence of women poets in the early history of ranching, although the Arizona collector, scholar, and poet Sharlot Hall is a major exception. Yet from the beginning of the modern cowboy poetry movement, marked by the first Cowboy Poetry Gathering held in Elko, Nevada, in 1985, women poets have been a part of the scene.

Like other ranching arts (leatherwork, silverwork, and rawhide and horsehair braiding), cowboy poetry carries evidence of the values of its creators. Ultimately, the test of whether a poem is "cowboy" or not is whether the poem is accepted as such by cowboys and ranching people. Its content and language will make it expressive of the values of the group. To listen attentively to cowboy poetry is to discover a strong sense of community and the love of a way of life.

More women than ever now write cowboy poems and participate in cowboy poetry gatherings.[1] Women's cowboy poetry has increased in sophistication and complexity of content and form over the years, just as men's poetry has. Many cowboy poets participate in writers' groups, and many have experimented with blank and free verse as well as using traditional rhymed and metered forms. Women's poems express the same sense of community and commitment to the ranching life that men's poems do. Women, however, sometimes bring a different perspective to their work. Just as a poem's subject and tone often make it easy to tell whether the author is a hired hand or a landowning rancher, so can it be said for women's cowboy poetry—the female perspective frequently shines through. At times female writers assume a male or genderless voice in their poems. In those cases, their unity of purpose and interest with male peers on horseback is most obvious and their poems are least differentiated from those written by men. But when these women write with a feminine voice, their traditional roles are thrown into greater relief against the backdrop of ranching in general.

Many women discuss the varied roles they play on the ranch, as in Gwen Petersen's "A Working Ranch." Petersen, who lives in Big Timber, Montana, describes her life juxtaposed against that of city friends who say they'd like to have a working ranch for the fun of it. She lists the day's trials, from a hen pecking her hand, to falling in a cow pie, to cows eating the fruits of her carefully nurtured garden:

I fix the fence and enter the house
As a neighbor phones to say
That my horses have wandered into his field
And are eating his prime cut hay.

And do I want my registered saddle mare bred
To his workhorse stud, asks he.
"No, no!" I screech, and filled with dread
I move with alacrity.

My city friends wear designer jeans;
My city friends eat quiche;
They have a courtyard full of flowers
And poodles trained to leash.

But they yearn for a working ranch, they claim,
To experience its joys and its fun.
Another day like this has been
And, hell—I'll give 'em this one.[2]

Georgie Sicking was one of the few women working as a cowboy before World War II. She was respected by her fellow Arizona punchers as a top hand. Later she owned ranches in Nevada and California and, having raised her family, still identifies most strongly with the working cowboy. She expresses her feelings about the life in "To Be a Top Hand," using a voice that could be male or female except, perhaps, for her willingness to share the touching naiveté of youth and speak the unspoken ethics of being a good hand:

When I was a kid and doing my best to
Learn the ways of our land,
I thought mistakes were never made by
A real top hand.

He was never in the right place at the wrong
Time or in anybody's way.
For working cattle he just naturally knew
When to move and when to stay.[3]

Women can bring unique perspectives as mothers to bear on the life-and-death experiences of ranch life. Peggy Godfrey, for example, ranches in southern Colorado:

I did a poem about mother sounds because the first sounds that a cow makes to her calf or a ewe makes to her lambs are not the "moo" sounds. They're just kind of a grunt or a hum sound, and anybody who's worked around livestock and paid attention knows that, but nobody's ever thought about it and you don't know what to call it, so I called it "mother sounds," and I wrote a poem about it. And one of the Gathering coordinators asked some of the ranchers, "Is that true?" And one guy said, "Yeah, but I never thought about what to call it." And another guy said, "I been calvin' for years, and I don't think I ever even noticed." But several of the people said, "Yeah, it's true." And afterward, the guy said, "You know, I think that's something that women bring to cowboy poetry that is unique, that they have a different way of looking at it, and they have a way of expressing the way they look at it that makes it pleasing to all of us to know." And he said, "I really appreciate that. I think women will always have a place in cowboy poetry."[4]

Mother Sounds

The calving lot is silent now
No lazy chewing sound
No restless, sleepless heifers
Standing up and laying down.

No panting, sighing, straining
Only day sounds fill my ears
No deep and chesty bovine hum
To comfort newborn fears.

My lambing shed holds memories:
Of heavy-bodied ewes

Sighing, resting, waiting
For daybreak's rosy hues.

When one by one their time came
Labor's insistent demand
Softly they changed to mother sounds
Encouraging weak legs to stand.

A vulnerable time, and reverent
Set apart by the process of birth
No wonder the accompanying sounds
Are more pleasing than any on earth.[5]

Although many women work as cowboys, the occupation remains male-dominated and male-defined. In spite of the fact that most ranch women contribute meaningfully to the well-being of the outfit, they often do not feel appreciated for all they do. A strong theme in women's ranch poetry has to do with the relationship of women and men as they work side by side at the traditionally male ranch jobs women can also do. Jo Casteel of South Dakota, for example, good-naturedly chides her husband about how he treats her on their family ranch:

The critter that he let on through
Was not his first or last,
But naturally 'twas my fault,
For I pushed it up too fast.

That gate that got left open
Surely wasn't done by him,
For the chance it being his mistake
Is *always* mighty slim.[6]

Some men have expressed discomfort with this I-can-do-it-and-I-can-do-it-just-as-well-as-any-man type of poetry.[7] But many women tell stories about how men condescend to them or make fun of them at work. Peggy Godfrey says:

> There's still a lot of jabs, even at the poetry gatherings, there are some gut punches made at women, heaven only knows what reason. . . . The men whose wives and daughters have kept them in business as being their right-hand people, come forward so fast, they come to the front of the room and grab us and hug us and say, "It's about time somebody tell what the women have to go through. My son will go down the road to help a neighbor, and the neighbor pays him. My daughter goes down the road to help the same neighbor do the same thing, and he doesn't even thank her. It's about time somebody say it." So there are an awful lot of men who respond warmly to even the sassy-mouth cowboy poetry coming from women.

Several of Godfrey's early poems dealt with old-time ranchers' perceptions of her as a woman who ranched alone:

I Tried

Seven barely-yearlin' bulls
Was chasin' Punkin 'round
She didn't "take" on her second calf
I'd have to haul her to town.

Ralph and Vogal worried
'Bout ol' Punkin's sorry plight
She'd stand chin-deep in a muddy ditch
Watchin' the yearlin's fight.

I gathered my horse and trailer
To see what I could do
'Bout gettin' her moved to a home corral
Away from that seven-bull zoo.

Between ol' Ralph and Vogal
Lay a hundred 'n fifty years
Of cowboy life and ranchin'—
Respected among their peers.

The two of them sat in the truck
Watchin' this girlie show
While Horse and I crawled in the mud
Persuadin' that cow to go.

There's lots of women cowboys
Scattered out across the West
Darn few of us have ever caught
A glimpse of all the rest.

Sometimes I get to "prove myself"
And earn my reputation
By performin' ranchin' duties
For this older generation.

I knew that I had ridden well
My efforts they'd endorse
These two old codgers sat there
Finally one said, "Damn good horse."[8]

Although such poems express anger and frustration with men's unfairness and arrogance, most of them have a distinctly non-strident tone. The poets generally use humor to express their feelings. That may be partly to cushion the message, but it also may indicate a sense of willingness to put up with such things for the sake of the life-style. These women like the ranching life and accept most of its values and mores. They may wish to change a few things, but they also know that if they do their work well they will be accepted. Stories abound in ranching communities about greenhorns/strangers/women who are treated with skepticism at first but gain the respect of other cowboys by proving their worth on the job. "The Zebra Dun" is a classic poem that tells such a story; it ends, "One thing and a shore thing I've learned since I've been born, / Every educated feller ain't a plumb greenhorn."[9] Ultimately, acceptance in the ranching community is based on the ability to do the work. Regardless of gender, race, class, creed, or origins, if a person can make a hand he or she is respected and welcomed. The same is true of poets. As Godfrey says:

> The thing I am most honored by is when people in the San Luis Valley . . . want to hear the poetry. These are the people who know the names of the people I'm writing about, they know the names of the places—they know what autumn is like, they know what cattle work is like, and if I'm telling any stories, they're the ones that are going to catch them, and if I'm telling any truth, they're the ones that are going to know. They're the ones whose responses mean the most to me because they are saying "Yes, you caught it, you've got it, you've put it into words, you've named it for me, you're my poet, you speak my heart."

There are many kinds of work to be done if a ranching operation is to succeed. These include the expected calving, branding, herding, doctoring, moving, fixing fence, and so forth that most people think of. But they also include bookkeeping, fixing equipment, feeding workers, tending orphaned animals, running errands, and raising the next generation of cowboys. Women and men both are capable of fulfilling any or all of these roles. Strong ties to land and community are what sustain people in the difficult and often heart-breaking work. Virtually every woman who writes cowboy poetry also writes about how much she loves her way of life. Jo Casteel, in "It's Been a Long Day," tells of a hard day of branding with her husband and neighbors. Then,

We're headin' for the home ranch,
The day has gone right well,
But if ya think my day is over,
Well, it's a cold day in hell.

For there's horses need a grainin',
And supper yet to cook,

Kids that need a washin',
And recordin' in the book.

Yeh, I'm hired man and mother,
Kettle-washer, cook and wife,
I'm damn tired, but I'm happy,
With our cowboy kind of life.[10]

Peggy Godfrey expresses the visceral pain she would feel if she had to quit ranching in "Thoughts of Leaving the Land":

Ornaments of my life
Are the invisible
Unrecognizable to the world
Qualities embodied in the life
I have orchestrated:
Fields, meadows, streams, reservoirs
Cow herds, flock of sheep, remuda
Interwoven community relationships
With people, pets, wildlife
WHO I AM is part of that
Mostly invisible tapestry of wealth
Inter-relationships with life and death
Land, season, weather, one another
And the spirit of the land.
Without land and flocks and herds
My blood dries up.
Irrigating, walking the fields
Mending fences
Standing among my livestock
Observing, tending—
These are the organs of my body
Searching for toxins, expelling them.
Those activities are the breathing
Digesting, pulsing life that wakes me up
And puts me to sleep KNOWING I live.
    Thoughts of leaving make me
  Waver between weeper and warrior.[11]

The cowboy poetry movement in the late twentieth century has provided a forum for a whole community to tell its own story and to be heard—a story whose popular telling has been previously dominated by mythmakers in urban centers on the East and West Coasts. Cowboy poets have been able to express themselves on diverse topics, helping the broader public to see cowboys and ranching in a more realistic light. Ranching women, like their male counterparts, have been able to make use of this new forum to tell the truth as they see it about their roles in the cattle business and the culture that surrounds it. Today's ranching women have helped to shape the modern tradition of cowboy poetry, reflecting a much more diverse world than that expressed in the old-time poems. In its late-twentieth-century incarnation, cowboy poetry, including women's cowboy poetry, is a more active—even activist at times—tradition that illustrates the diversity of life among ranchers and cowboys. Women's cowboy poetry has been growing in artistry and conviction, expressing the values of women who tend to both embrace and shatter traditional gender roles at the same time. It is a voice that is important to hear, both in the world of raising cattle and in the larger American scene.

Notes

1. The term *cowgirl* is used in a limited way in ranching culture, depending on the region and the individual. "Cowboy" is a word describing a type of work, and people who work cattle use it more frequently as a verb than as a noun: "I've cowboyed for three different ranches." When a noun is required, "cowboy" may be used, but "hand" is a frequently heard alternative: "She's one of the best hands I know." Similarly, the term *cowgirl poetry* does not exist in general usage, although one sometimes hears the term *lady poets* at gatherings. In this essay I use variants of *women's cowboy poetry.*

2. Gwen Petersen, "A Working Ranch," in Gwen Petersen and Jeane Rhodes, *Tall in the Sidesaddle: Ranch Woman Rhymes* (Big Timber, Mont.: P/R Press, 1986), 8–9.

3. Georgie Sicking, "To Be a Top Hand," in *Cowboy Poetry: A Gathering,* ed. Hal Cannon (Salt Lake City: Gibbs Smith, 1985), 76–77.

4. All quotations from Peggy Godfrey are from an interview conducted by the author on 19 March 1997, in Moffatt, Colorado; tape is in author's possession.

5. Peggy Godfrey, "Mother Sounds," in Godfrey, *Write 'Em Roughshod: Life 'n' Such Like* (Crestone, Colo.: Media Chaos Books, 1994), 5.

6. From Jo Casteel, "He Ain't Never Made One," in Casteel, *Pardners* (Newell, S.D.: Jo Casteel, 1987), 22.

7. This phrasing is courtesy of Peggy Godfrey, from the interview with the author.

8. Peggy Godfrey, "I Tried," in Godfrey, *Write 'Em Cowboy!* (Lake City, Colo.: Peter Carlyle Elliott Publishing, 1993), 40.

9. "The Zebra Dun," in *Cowboy Poetry,* ed. Cannon, 8–9.

10. Jo Casteel, "It's Been a Long Day," in Casteel, *Pardners,* 35–36.

11. Peggy Godfrey, "Thoughts of Leaving the Land," in Godfrey, *Write Tough!* (Crestone, Colo.: Media Chaos Books, 1995), 41.

20

A New Wind Out of the West: The Poetry of Contemporary Ranch Women

Teresa Jordan

There is a new wind blowing out of the American West—the poetry of ranch women. It is a fresh poetry, nourished by both beauty and crisis. Born out of intimate relationships to land and animals, to weather and seasons, and to friends and family, it is true to the heart, close to the earth, and unflinching. It has a raw intensity that comes when voices emerge where there has been only silence before. Rural women have only recently begun to write this honestly about their lives.

The truth is, rural women have only recently begun to write about their lives at all, at least for publication and in any number. When I was compiling the bibliography for *Cowgirls* (1982), an oral history of women on ranches and in rodeo, I could find fewer than three dozen first-person narratives by women in ranch culture, and those had been published over a period of eighty years. Only three—Elinore Pruitt Stewart's *Letters of a Woman Homesteader* (1914), Agnes Morley Cleaveland's *No Life for a Lady* (1941), and Nannie Alderson's *A Bride Goes West* (1942)—were well known. I located only one ranch novel that had realistic women characters and was written by a woman: Peggy Simson Curry's *So Far from Spring,* which was based in part on the lives of women she had known growing up on a ranch in North Park, Colorado. There were books that I didn't learn about until later—Mary Clearman Blew's collection of short stories, *Lambing Out* (1977); Marguerite Noble's novel *Filaree* (1979); and Gwen Petersen's humorous *Ranch Woman's Manual* (1976), to name a few—but women's voices were rare and hard to find.

I wasn't looking for poetry at that point, but had I been I would have found the pickings leaner yet. Several horse and cattle magazines carried occasional poems by women, and I might have been lucky and stumbled upon Martha Downer Ellis's *Bell Ranch Glimpses* (1980), a compilation of four earlier books of her poetry. I knew of Peggy Simson Curry's *Red Wind of Wyoming and Other Poems* (1955), which had been republished so many times it had become something of a legend in my home state of Wyoming. But there was no tradition of women's poetry parallel to that of cowboy poetry. There were no ballads women recited to each other over coffee or on the long rides to distant pastures, and certainly most of the ranch women I knew would not have considered the dailiness of their lives as material worthy of verse.

If I had been particularly acute, I might have picked up rumblings that this was about to change. If I had lived in South Dakota, I might have heard about the poetry of ranch woman Linda Hasselstrom, which was just beginning to appear in literary magazines. If I had still lived in Wyoming, I might have run across a slim volume of poems by Gretel Ehrlich, a documentary film maker who had moved to the state and started working as a ranch hand, or I might have heard about the appointment in 1981 of Peggy Simson Curry as Wyoming's first poet laureate. And if I had followed Peggy Curry's story and had fully understood it, I might have known that women's voices were just beginning to burst forth in new and powerful ways and that when they did they would be met with surprising acceptance by both women and men.

The day of Peggy Curry's appointment, a reception was held for her at the governor's mansion with the members of the Wyoming legislature and their spouses. Curry was asked to read some of her work. "She had planned to read some of her favorite landscape and nature poems," wrote Mary Alice Gunderson in the introduction to *LandMarked,* a collection of Peggy Curry's short stories, "but overcome with the emotion of the day and the honor she had received, she lost her voice." Her friend, the poet Charles Levendosky, agreed to read for her, and she indicated to him her selections. Then, at the last minute, she nudged him and whispered for him to include another, "Jack Patton":

Jack Patton, Commander of rakers in the hay field,
Jack Patton, General of my thirteenth summer,
Jack Patton cursing me on hot afternoons when I
stop to gulp tepid water from a canvas bag.
Jack Patton scolding me to make another round
while others leave the field, making me drive
the old gray team until I scream in tears and rage.

"If you do it, do it right," he says.

Stuck it out all summer, face burned black,
behind numb from rake seat, arms stiff tugging lines,
stuck it out too tired to eat at noon, too tired
to wash for supper, stuck it out and hated him.

"If you do it, do it right," he said.

Wished him all manner of evil:
Lord, give him loose bowels squatting in a ditch
before the President of the United States.
Lord, make him have pimples on his face the size of horse turds.
Lord, let his penis fall off, be eaten by a million flies.

All my life remembering, "If you do it, do it right."[1]

Later, Peggy Curry would say that she didn't know what got into her. This was not, after all, language that nice ladies used before the Wyoming legislature. But the assembly burst into enthusiastic applause, and "Jack Patton" was the poem people wanted to take home afterward.

Since that time, a whole new literature has sprung forth from women on the land. Some who were just beginning to write in the early 1980s have gained national recognition. Since 1984 Linda Hasselstrom has published three volumes of poetry and three of essays, including *Windbreak: A Woman Rancher on the Northern Plains* (1987) and the award-winning *Land Circle: Writings Collected from the Land* (1991); Mary Clearman Blew has published a second collection of stories, *Runaway* (1990), and a memoir of her Montana ranch family, *All but the Waltz: Essays on a Montana Family* (1991), both to great acclaim; and Gretel Ehrlich's *The Solace of Open Spaces* (1985) has become a classic and she has since published several more books. But nowhere has the proliferation of women's voices been more pronounced than in poetry.

When the first Cowboy Poetry Gathering was held in Elko, Nevada, in 1985, only six out of twenty-eight featured poets were women. Several of them recited cowboy classics, and with a few exceptions their original work tended to be patterned after traditional male poems, both in style and content, or to be humorous, often self-deprecating tales of a woman's particular folly in a mostly male domain. None of this was surprising. The tradition of reciting poems drawn from men's stories and performed by men dates back more than a hundred years in the American West; its roots, grounded in Anglo-Saxon and other balladeering cultures, are much older. There was no such tradition for women. In addition, ranch women shared with other women the muteness about their real knowledge and concerns that Tillie Olsen described as "the silence of centuries as to how life was [and] is."[2]

Cowboy poetry has enjoyed a renaissance, and there are now more than 150 gatherings a year in a dozen western states. Although recitation of classic poems is still important, a phenomenal number of ranch people are writing new poetry, and much of it, particularly the poetry by women, is breaking new ground. At the Elko Cowboy Poetry Gathering—still the largest one, with an attendance each year of more than eight thousand—the all-women sessions are among the most popular, and women are well integrated into the rest of the program as well. Some, such as Gwen Petersen, whose work was featured at the first Gathering, write traditional rhymed and metered verse; others, such as Marie Smith (another early participant) and Sue Wallis, write both rhymed and free verse; and some, such as Thelma Poirier and Linda Hussa, write free verse only. All are drawing on their experiences and ways of seeing to develop a poetry that is decidedly female and alive with energy, freshness, and courage. The cowboy poetry movement did not give birth to this body of work, but it has nourished it, providing a climate for deep friendship, inspiration, and experimentation.

When I look back on my childhood and young adulthood on a ranch in southeastern Wyoming, I realize that I knew early that women inhabited secret territories. I often had the sense of living in two worlds, a sense that is shared by many ranch women I know. There were few girls in the neighborhood my age, so I mostly played with my older brother and his friends. I was a consummate tomboy: I played cowboys and Indians, I wrestled, and I swore. As much as I annoyed the boys, I made sure they could never say I was a quitter or a 'fraidy cat. I hated dolls and dresses, and one Christmas I cried all day because my great-grandmother—who *knew* that the only thing I really wanted was a bazooka—had given me a handcrafted doll carriage.

But when I had girls for company, the play was altogether different. I never grew to like dolls, but I loved the camaraderie of girls in the great outdoors, where we inhabited a separate and quite magical world. When I was with boys, we rode horses. When I had girls to play with, we actually *became* horses.

With girls, it didn't matter if we played in the front yard, galloping and neighing as we chased each other in circles, or if we saddled up real horses and headed out from the house. Our horses were not just vehicles, they were intimate friends. We sometimes forgot entirely that we were human or that a saddle separated us from the huge beasts that carried us, and I can still remember that magical moment of transcendence when we first would nudge our horses into comfortable lopes. Suddenly my own chubby awkwardness would fall away, and I would be sleek and strong and graceful. It would be *my* neck straining forward, *my* hooves that were striking the ground. I knew we could run forever.

Inside the house I had a similar sense of living by two sets of rules. Our home was often full of people as the community gathered after a branding or weaning or other shared labor, and I remember standing in the dining room, listening to the deep rumble of the men's voices in the living room and the softer murmur of the women in the kitchen, trying to decide which world to step into.

No men ventured into the kitchen, but some women found places in the living room. These were the women who worked outside, who could handle a rope and knew how to treat diphtheria or poisonweed. I was proud to be one of them, to have earned the right to sit in, and I liked the men's hard, clear stories of adventure in the outside world, of horses they had ridden or bullies they had stared down. Sometimes the women who sat in the living room told stories, too, but we were careful to say nothing that might endanger our place among the chosen; we kept our secrets. We might talk about horses, but we didn't talk about our separate ways of seeing them. And when we joined the women in the kitchen, we entered into another secret territory, the interior landscape of family, community, and self.

Much of the energy of this new poetry from ranch women comes, I suspect, from its charting of those mysterious lands. Although the work is still evolving, much of it clusters around three topics, none of which were considered the stuff of literature in the 1980s: women's particular and sometimes transcendent identification with nature, their relationships with family and community, and their roles, both contemporary and historical, in ranch culture.

In Judy Blunt's "Sisters," two girls watch from the corral fence as the men rope an unbroken colt for the older sister. When the horse is thrown and tied, the older girl is

> . . . beside herself in love
> with the shine of sun tan flanks, snowy
> stockings tied in a bunch, the bay fringe
> of mane and tail to match. When she reached up
> and drew me off the fence, her hands shook
> like the colt's own hide and I forgot
> the unfair edge of luck and age she held
> eight years over my head. We hunkered
> down close enough to touch, our faces
> and the clouds behind us mirrored
> in the dark, wild eye of her colt.
> Cream Puff, she said, glancing back
> for fear the men would hear and laugh,
> I'm going to name her Cream Puff.

The connection that many women feel to animals is transcendent yet seldom sentimental. In Linda Hussa's "Under the Hunter Moon," the narrator stalks a coyote that has ravaged her flock:

Slain lambs, guts ripped open
Magpies and blow flies
Blatting ewes with swollen bags searching the flock

A lamb a day for two weeks
    I grip the rifle tighter

The narrator comes upon the coyote at play:

I watch her snatch mice out of the grass
    flip them up like popcorn,
    down the hatch. She is a comic
    this coyote, playing, laughing
    making her way steadily toward me
    my finger soft on the cold steel trigger

The narrator and the coyote lock eyes on each other, and the final three lines of the poem compress the whole complexity of the natural world, where one life often weighs against another:

Coyote stops
    looks directly at me
Her eyes hold me accountable

Linda Hasselstrom's "Beef Eater" draws on a related complexity, that of eating the animals you love. The narrator's preparation of a beef heart is unflinching and yet filled with tenderness, echoing the rancher's cycle of nurture and slaughter:

I split the smooth maroon shape
lengthwise,
open it like a diagram, chambers exposed.
I cut tough white membranes off valves,
. . . .
Gently,
I lift the full heart
between my hands,
place it in the pan
with its own blood, fat, juices.
I roast that heart
at three hundred fifty degrees

for an hour or two.
Often I dip pan juices,
pour them lovingly over the meat.

When the heart is ready, the poet smiles as she takes it to the table:

My friends have begun to notice my placid air,
which they mistake for serenity.
Yesterday a man remarked
    on my large brown eyes,
    my long eyelashes,
    my easy walk.

I switched my tail at him
as if he were a fly,
paced
deliberately
away.

Edith Rylander acknowledges in a different way the transcendence of a life that takes full responsibility for the cost of its survival: "We can sleep through the whole night now," she writes at the end of "Out to Grass," the last of a series of poems that captures the exhausting work of lambing season. "We can study to make our lives / Worthy of what they eat."

Ranch women also draw parallels between the lives of the animals they love and their own. In "Graining the Mare," Jo-Ann Mapson sympathizes with a mare:

It was less than a thrill
watching the stud do his work:
chains, hobbles, both horses panic-eyed,
handlers turning sheepish, her tail
stiffly arced in defiance.

March sky: empty, gray,
barren as this horse.
Whatever do we expect, falling
for mustaches like shades of lipstick?
"Honest, he's different, this time for sure,"
the chorus we sing in any weather.

The more interior worlds of family, community, and self make up a second hidden territory explored in these poems, one that may be even more difficult to map, often hiding the secrets we were raised never to reveal. Marriage has long been the source of humor in rural culture, as when Jeane Rhodes describes her husband's reaction to the chokecherry jelly she labored for hours to make in "Berry Me Not":

This morning my husband beamed over his plate
Of sausage and pancakes, and said as he ate,

"The best thing about this syrup to me
Is that these nice berries are utterly free."

To show that I'm tolerant and kind and forgiving—
The man that I live with is still with the living.

But these women are not afraid to write also about the depth of love, and of loss. "Love, my love, you are not gone from me, / for I see you in the face of all the land" writes Marie Smith in her lovely poem of grief, "Finding." Elizabeth Ebert describes a moment of love's recognition in "Song from the Day the Pump Broke":

I watched him through the dusty plumber's glass:
The mud-caked jeans, unshaven face,
The squinting eye. He looked so very tired
—and *old*! My heart caught in my throat
And through the quick hot tears I saw
My life's one verity, the pivot point
On which my world revolves:
I love you, and I always will, my dear.

Other poems deal with the inner workings of family and the rituals of generational teaching, as when Sue Wallis describes in "Mama Lessons" how her mother (Myrt Wallis, also a poet) taught her about calving:

Thus my Mama's mother taught her, and then my Mama taught to me
The important things of birthing and of Life and Nature's ways—
Of the knowledge wise and female—first so given to me free
By my mother in a pasture on those long-passed calving days.

Nevertheless, the passing of information from one generation to another is not always easy, and Thelma Poirier captures the pain of father and son in "sorting cattle":

your son shouts, move out
move out of the way
. . . .
you should have known you could not build a
corral large enough for both of you

This poetry mentions, too, the desperation and despair that were rarely spoken of in rural communities—alcoholism, abuse, and the marriages that don't work. In Doris Bircham's "leaving," a woman hangs out wash and thinks about a neighbor who left her husband; "could it have been . . . that night / he came home drunk / the burden of his anger / clenched inside his fists," she asks.

I continue this simple task
of hanging clothes thinking
how little I know
about where they go
between one wash and the next
how there's no place to hide
the worn places, the three-cornered rips
how no bleach has been made
that can remove all the stains

Sometimes these women write about the difficulties of their own lives—the broken loves, the unrealized dreams, and the loneliness. Some of these poems are painful; others are salty. Here's a fragment of Sue Wallis's "Coyote Bitch":

I feel like a Coyote Bitch
(in heat)
Do not annoy me, tempt me, or toy with me
I have been lonely too long.

The final territory mapped in these poems may have been the most secret of all until recently, and that is the landscape where we view ourselves and where we are viewed as women—a territory that has shifted tremendously over the past few years. Peggy Godfrey captures the frustration of many ranch women who see their skills discounted in her description of "Old Vogal":

He assured me I was lucky
That my bales were done up tight
Lucky that I caught the dew
And chanced to bale it right.

. . . .

I clenched my jaw and held my tongue
Red anger 'round me swirled
If I was a man, he'd say I was good,
But "lucky" 'cuz I'm a girl.

This short poem is light and humorous, easy to digest, but it is also the work of a quiet revolutionary. It has been reprinted in several publications and is magneted to refrigerators all over the West.

Hand in hand with a more open claiming of their own place, ranch women have claimed their female ancestors. As Zelda Fitzgerald's biographer Mark Shorer has suggested, the "ultimate anonymity" is to be storyless.[3] Anglo women in the West were storyless until the the latter part of the twentieth century. As late as 1976, a major textbook on the history of the West was published that listed only three women in its index. There has been, of course, a tradition of reverence for generalized female pioneers, sometimes taking the form of sentimental paeans to the "backbones of the West," carved into statues of sunbonneted madonnas or read at historical celebrations. But only recently, with the publication of hundreds of pioneer women's diaries, letters, and memoirs—and the searching out of other records that many women have undertaken on their own—have individual lives come into clear enough focus to provide the stories we have hungered for. These stories in turn have inspired a poetry that is deeply empathic and fascinated with particulars. In "Flowering Almond," Jane Candia Coleman recalls a visit with a neighbor:

. . . I read your diaries,
sixty years of valley history recalled . . .

The white leghorns laid today. First time.
The eggs were fine.
Went up the creek, cut wood, drove the wagon down.
Bought 18 dozen clothespins at the store.
The baby died. Ground so hard we dug all day.
The paint mare foaled a brown stud colt.
My almond tree put out a flower.
Two dry years and cattle dropping.
I lug water to the tree and pray . . .

What lies in my lap is the coming and going
of lives and seasons; a ritual,
as the twilight whirling of wild babies,
as the branch of your almond tree
laid lightly down along the split rail fence
each spring for years.[4]

◇◇◇◇

"How do we tell the truth in a small town?" asked North Dakota author Kathleen Norris in the *New York Times Book Review.* "Is it possible to write it? . . .

A writer who is thoroughly immersed in the rural milieu . . . faces a particularly difficult form of self-censorship. . . . [She] must either break away or settle for producing only what is acceptable at a mother-daughter church banquet or a Girl Scout program."[5]

Anyone who has lived in the country or in a small town knows what Norris is talking about, and I suspect that most contemporary women poets of the West have struggled with it to greater or lesser degree. Yet ranch women have broken through, if only in the last few years of the twentieth century, to a startling honesty. "If I left," writes Penelope Reedy,

the gals at the supermarket
over coffee and a smoke
would say they knew it
would come to this
" . . . her, with 'the big head and all.'"

. . . .

And if I stay
until he shoots me,
catches me in the act of poetry,
barricaded behind a wall of books,
the Women's Auxiliary would say,
"She drove him to it."

As Norris suggested, some women have to break away to tell the truth, and Penelope Reedy had to leave rural culture in order to claim her own life. Other women have not, although they might have been able to write about personal difficulty only after their situation had changed. Peggy Godfrey describes humorously the "Perfect Wife" her second husband and she could use to get their life in order and then notes:

I've chopped away her personhood
To get this "perfect wife"
It makes me sick to realize
This joke was once my life.

On occasion, these poems can be harsh, but the purpose is not to dwell in bitterness but to acknowledge difficulty and move on. The greater urge is to regain—or perhaps to create for the first time—harmony. The poetry of contemporary ranch women looks at the realities of rural life in all its joy and pain—truly, honestly, and without elaboration or denial. And through that keen look, we gain the ability to live more fully, to tell the truth and survive. "I'm quite prepared to leave old cruelties behind," wrote Thelma Poirier in a recent letter, "but not 'old beauty.'"

Notes

A version of this essay first appeared as my introduction to the anthology *Graining the Mare: The Poetry of Ranch Women* (Salt Lake City: Gibbs Smith, 1994). All of the poems quoted without citation are from this collection. As I note in the book's introduction, the thirty-six poets included in the anthology "range in age from their early twenties to their nineties. Nearly two-thirds . . . make all or most of their income from raising some combination of cattle, sheep, and crops on ranches in the western United States and Canada, or they did so for a substantial part of their adult lives. Some of these were born to the work; others came to it on their own or married into it. Of the remaining third, most were raised on ranches but left at adulthood or after a first marriage—some departed with great reluctance; others fled. A couple of the women featured here were raised in town but grew up close to the land because of grandparents or other relatives. A few have been involved more exclusively with horses than with cattle or sheep."

1. Peggy Curry, "Jack Patton," in Curry, *Summer Range* (Story, Wyo.: Dooryard Press, 1981), 36.

2. Tillie Olsen, *Silences* (New York: Delacorte/Seymour Lawrence, 1978), 10.

3. Quoted in Carolyn Heilbrun, *Writing a Woman's Life* (New York: Ballantine, 1988), 12.

4. Jane Candia Coleman, "Flowering Almond," in Coleman, *No Roof but Sky: Poems of the American West* (Glendo, Wyo.: High Plains Press, 1990), 34.

5. Kathleen Norris, "A Crowded Writer on the Lonely Prairie," *New York Times Book Review*, 27 Dec. 1992, 1, 16–17.

Part 5

Connections

As Alan Lomax has pointed out on a number of occasions, oral poetry seems to be the common property of humans engaged in outdoor occupations, whether logging the woods, sailing the seas, or riding the range. Indeed, says Lomax, early herders in Britain developed and maintained a rich corpus of oral poetry.

That tradition is especially clear in comparative studies. Cynthia Vidaurri, a Texas-based folklorist now working out of the Smithsonian Institution in Washington, D.C., has researched the expressive culture of Mexican American cowboys in south Texas, a culture that includes song, poetry, and storytelling. Because most of the gear, stock-handling techniques, and even the vocabulary of cowboy work is ultimately derived from Spain by way of Mexico ("vaquero" became "buckaroo," for example), the potential influence of Mexican and Mexican American folk arts on contemporary cowboy life makes for fascinating speculation and opportunities for further research.

Clearer similarities are to be found in the poetry of loggers in the Pacific Northwest, as independent folklorist Jens Lund demonstrates. Not only do loggers and cowboys share parallel poetic traditions, but some logger poems also refer directly to the better-known cowboy tradition as a source for ironic humor.

William Katra, a scholar who has a strong background in the arts and literature of Argentina, demonstrates that the oral traditions of the gaucho diverged from those of the cowboy. As with cowboy song and poetry, gaucho traditional arts became popular with the media and with the public, being transformed as they became part of popular culture. In the case of Argentina, however, urban-centered arts movements, which Katra calls "nativist" and "gauchesque," developed in an attempt to revive what artists thought of as the traditional culture of the gaucho.

In another culture, the cattle-and-sheep industry of Australia, the drovers of the bush have maintained a strong poetic tradition similar in many ways to North American cowboy poetry. Folklorist Keith McKenry shows that as with the ranching areas of the Western Hemisphere, Australians have both poetry and song as well as an urban-based revival movement that provides publishing outlets and annual competitions.

These comparative essays suggest that other grazing cultures may have an equally rich and various repertoire of folk arts that express the difficulties and mysteries of the herding life.

21

Levantando Versos and Other Vaquero Voices: Oral Traditions of South Texas Mexican American Cowboys

Cynthia L. Vidaurri

Ranches in south Texas in the first half of the twentieth century were very different from those found today. Spanish-speaking vaqueros from both sides of the border lived and worked on ranches that functioned as independent entities separate from the rest of the community. Some had their own commissaries, chapels, and schools. Contact with the rest of the world was limited to a few free days a month when vaqueros would go into town for a haircut, purchase those things unavailable on the ranch, and sometimes catch a bit of diversion at a local bar.[1]

Work was difficult, dangerous, and intensive, with the typical workday beginning and ending with the sun's rising and setting. It was not unusual for a *corrida* (work crew) to be out on the open range for weeks at a time. Meals were prepared by a camp cook out of a chuck wagon. Creature comforts were limited to what vaqueros could carry on horseback.

The nature of the work kept vaqueros from recreational conversations while actually working cattle. They would sometimes congregate at lunchtime, but generally socializing was done at the end of the workday. Men would sit or lie around a campfire, consuming large quantities of coffee. On some ranches, younger vaqueros would have a separate fire, where they would not intrude on *los mayores* (the elders). At some camps, boys as young as twelve worked alongside older vaqueros, but women were rarely found at cow camps even though area vaqueros reported that some women did work cattle. Conversations would go late into the night until everyone fell asleep or until the *caporal* (foreman) ordered them to sleep with a reminder of the long workday ahead.

It was in these camps, where vaqueros relied on each other for work support as well as entertainment, that oral traditions flourished. Unfortunately, many men who experienced this variety of ranch life are no longer alive. When asked about vaqueros in a community, people now often advise one to go to the cemetery to find "real" vaqueros. That comment is usually followed by an explanation that the term *vaquero* is not merely the Spanish word for cowboy but that historically it was more of a title to be earned over a long period of apprenticeship while novices learned and honed their skills. The title was accorded only after the mayores deemed one worthy. The oral traditions discussed here originated in a time when vaqueros were Vaqueros with an upper-case *V.*[2]

Corridos

Perhaps the most romantic element of vaquero life portrayed in popular culture is the cowboy sing-along around the campfire. Many corridas had a few vaqueros who were musicians. Commonly found instruments were portable, such as a guitar, *música de voz* (harmonica), and occasionally an accordion or violin.

The preferred music was *música ranchera* (ranch music) or *música de conjunto* (literally, music of a group but specifically the accordion-dominated polkas and other tunes popular in south Texas). Also popular was *música mexicana,* composed of songs from the Mexican revolution ("La Adelita" and "La Rialera") and romantic songs made popular in Mexico's golden age of cinema ("El Rancho Grande," "Las Gaviotas," "Las Golondrinas," and "Una Noche Serena y Oscura"). This type of music was also referred to as *música vieja* or *canciones viejas* (old music or songs).

The most common musical form was the *corrido* (Mexican folk ballad), the most popular of which were about horses or *tragedias* (tragedies). Horse corridos generally paid tribute to a horse's qualities and included "El Caballo Bayo," "El Alazán y El Rocío," "El Caballo Prieto Asabache," and "El Caballo Blanco."

Tragedia corridos documented unfortunate events that happened to usually innocent individuals, making the stories all the more tragic. Other favorites told of just men who acted upon just causes or innocent men who stood up for their rights or those of others. Some were of tragedies that resulted from being involved in a not-so-legal activity, such as running contraband. Those most commonly recalled included "El Carro Rojo," "Gregorio Cortez," "El Hijo Desobediente," "El Contrabando," "Los Tequileros," and "Juan Charasciado."[3] Vaqueros recalled tragic ballads in the context of similar events that happened in their communities or remembered their own involvement in the event. When telling about "El

Corrido de Gregorio Cortez," Ramiro Ramírez of Uvalde recounted how his grandfather gave Gregorio Cortez a gun with which to defend himself in Cotulla.[4]

Some vaqueros were known to compose and perform corridos, and the south Texas vaqueros identified at least two regional ones. "El Corrido de Alejo Sierra" documents the story of a man who died in a Piedras Negras bar across from Eagle Pass, Texas, but no one was able to recall its words or the specifics of the event. The other, "El Corrido de un Toro Morro," was written in 1926 or 1927 by Miguel de Luna on the Norias Division of the King Ranch and describes a bull with an attitude. In true vaquero fashion, the inability of the men in the ballad to manage the bull is attributed not to their own lack of skill but to the horse itself. Alejandro Soliz of Orange Grove recalled portions of the song, and Omar Galván of Hebbronville remembered the entire ballad:

Aquí me siento a cantar
En el nombre sea de Dios.
Voy a cantarle los versos
De la corrida del Dos.

[Here I sit myself to sing
In the name of God.
I will sing for you these verses
Of the cow camp at El Dos.

Aquí me siento a cantar
Con todito mi decoro
Voy a cantarle los versos
Del mentado toro morro.

Here I sit myself to sing
With all my respect.
I will sing for you these verses
Of the famous cross bull.

Este es un torito morro.
Tiene el espinazo bayo.
No lo han podido lazar.
Le echan la culpa al caballo.

This was a cross bull.
His back was colored bay.
They could not lasso him.
They placed the blame on the horse.

Lo lazaron de dos años
Y lo vieron toditos
Tomás Stacey lo lazó
En su caballo Espejito,

They lassoed him when he was two.
Everyone saw it.
Thomas Stacy lassoed him
On his horse, Mirror,

Cuando andaba en los cerritos
A la edad de unos dos años
Ahora anda en Los Marcelinos
Completando los ocho años.

When he was in the hills
At the age of two.
Now he is found in Los Marcelinos
Going on about eight years.

Una tarde muy temprano
Se lo hallaron dos compadres
Se pusieron a echar trazas
Y allí se les hizo tarde.

Early one afternoon
Two friends found him
They began to make plans
And there it grew late.

Eugenio es muy buen vaquero
Primerito de la Gostadera.
Nomás oyó el primer grito
Y se le hizo al corredero.

Eugenio was a good vaquero
First at La Gostadera.
He heard that first yell
And headed after him.

Iba por toda la brecha
Una fuerte polvareda.
Era La Changa diciendo
—He perdido la carrera.

He was headed through the path
In a heavy cloud of dust.
It was La Changa saying
"I have lost the race."

Eugenio lo divisó
Y brincando las nopaleras,
Y luego, luego se apuró
A su yegua Pesenera.

Eugenio spotted him
And jumping through the cactus,
He quickly headed
To his dark mare, Pesenera.

Eugenio se lo lazó
Por no verlos batallar.
Y en el Plan de la Cantera
Allí se los fue a amarrar.

Eugenio lassoed him
So no one would have to struggle.
And at La Cantera
There he took the bull to be tied.

Cuando supo Don Juvencio
De gusto aventó la capa.
Y le dijo a su compadre
—Vaya y doble otra reata.

When Don Juvencio heard of this
He threw his cap up in joy.
He told his friend,
"Go and double up another lariat."

Y allí se aventó Macario
Iba al trote y al galope
En busca del toro morro
Para doblarle un calabrote.

Macario took off
Trotting and galloping
In search of the cross bull
To double up the cable.

Y decía Don Juvencio
—El la orilla del papalote
Se lo encuernan a La Colcha
Y lo echan en el Tecolote.

And Don Juvencio said,
"At the edge of the windmill,
Yoke him to the ox
And take him to the Tecolote trap."

Ahora sí torito morro
Ya no te vamos a ver
Ya te vamos a embarcar
Derechito a Fort Wer.

And now little cross bull,
We are no longer going to see you.
We are going to ship you
Straight to Fort Worth.][5]

With the exception of a few isolated cases, self-accompanied vaquero corrido singers have not remained a living tradition, although corridos are still popular because contemporary singers such as Los Cadetes de Linares, Los Tigres del Norte, and Vicente Fernández continue to record them. Even younger vaqueros recognize old corrido titles but associate them with contemporary recording artists. Of course, they also listen to country-western music stars such as George Strait, Garth Brooks, and Clint Black.

Versos

The poetic tradition of *versos* (verses) includes the composing and reciting of poetry. The actual composing was referred to as *"levantando versos"* (to erect or raise verses), implying that the procedure was a deliberate construction of words related to ranch events. The poems could either be recited or sung and often are similar in structure to corridos. Often camp cooks became known for this skill because their work, unlike that of the vaquero, did not require undivided attention and they would have time to create poems. Poems could document single events or could be accounts combined from several different events in order to make the story more interesting. A number of area vaqueros were known for their ability to *levantar* versos, and one Hebbronville vaquero was remembered for his distinct brand of obscene poetry. Unfortunately, little remains of these creative works.

Some vaqueros do recall and recite isolated pieces of poetry, however. Ramiro Ramírez, for example, remembered a portion of a poem by Manuel Castor of La Bonita ranch about a *remudero* (cowboy in charge of the horse herd) named Chavarría. The sounds he made enclosing the horse herd would signal the camp cook to proceed with the evening meal:

Por hay viene Chavarría
Por hay viene ya llegando
Ya se escucha los encierros
Y el cocinero aquí está
Calentando los aceros
Para hacerle de comer
A toditos los vaqueros.

[There comes Chavarría
He is about to arrive
The gates can be heard
And here the cook is
Heating the cooking pans
So he can prepare food
For all the vaqueros.][6]

Julián Dimas of Hebbronville recalled the following verse from a poem by

Vicente Guerrero of Rancho La Partición when an unusually hot summer was documented:

En ese mes de septiembre
El aire no corría.
Se calmó La Partición
San Pedro y Jesús María.

[In the month of September
The air did not stir.
La Partición was in a dead calm
Along with St. Peter and Jesús María.][7]

Omar Galván was able to recite still other poems. One was written by his brother Julio Galván about a bucking horse that escaped the corral while vaqueros were able to lasso only the saddle:

Decía Juan Galván en la puerta del corral
—Si a Juvencio lo ha tumbado yo lo monto completar.
El caballo brincó la cerca y corrió con rumbo a
La Pita y llegó un poco asustado.
Nomás a brincar la cerca Tomás Rangel lo ha lazado;
Nomás la silla pescamos.

[Juan Galván said at the door of the corral,
"If the horse has thrown Juvencio, I will mount him."
The horse jumped the fence and ran towards
La Pita and arrived a bit frightened.
Upon jumping the fence, Tomás Rangel lassoed him;
We only captured the saddle.][8]

A poem by Sifredo Guerra of the East brothers' ranch documents his brother Alejandro's riding skills:

Un día 10 de noviembre, esto fue lo que pasó
Una yegua reparando, con Alejandro se azotó.
Cuando la yegua cayó, toditos nos asustamos.
Tomás como caporal dijo,—ahorita la lazamos.
Dijo—ahorita la lazamos—y se montó en su yegüita.
Y como bueno lazador, la fama no se le quita.
Y luego, luego, la lazó. No anduvo con caranzadas.
La silla se le lidió, porque no estaba apretada.
La cosa se puso feo, se puso poco tirante.

No había ni quien le entraba y quien le aventara el guante.
El que no le quiera creer, que monte arranque al galope.
Que vaya al Rancho del Blanco y se lo pregunte a López.
Si López no da razón y quiere desengañarse,
Que se pasen a La Perla y le pregunten al Niño Arce.

[On November 10 this is what occurred.
A bucking mare with Alejandro broke loose.
When the mare fell, we were all frightened.
As foreman, Tomás said, "We'll lasso her."
He said, "Now we lasso her," and he mounted his mare.
And like a good man with a lasso, his fame wouldn't be lost.
And quickly, quickly he lassoed her. He didn't waste any time.
The saddle slid because it wasn't tightened.
Things got ugly, it got a bit tight.
There was no one who would enter, no one to lend a hand.
Whoever does not believe this can mount their horse at a gallop,
Go to Rancho del Blanco and inquire of López.
If López does not respond and you want to erase all doubt,
Go on to La Perla and ask Niño Arce.][9]

The most complete and elaborate piece of poetry found was composed not by a vaquero but rather a vaquero's wife. Melesia Galván Ramírez wrote the following poem on July 8, 1929, at Rancho San Antonio Viejo to express sorrow at her cowboy husband's death due to a ruptured appendix. She was left pregnant at the time of her husband's death, and her son later died at the age of two.

Lágrimas de Ausencia Eterna

Negra la sombra de mi triste vida,
Tristes recuerdos de mi bien pasado,
Pasajero dolor cubrió la dicha
Del aquel hogar feliz y hoy desolado.

Aquella humilde casa sin tristezas,
Aquel grande corazón lleno de amores,
El era mi querer y mis grandezas
Y hoy cambiaron mis dichas por dolores.

¿Por qué perdí el amor que fue un tesoro?
¿Por qué acabaron mis bellas ilusiones?
¿Por qué estoy siempre triste? ¿Por qué lloro?
Adiós amor, adiós dulces pasiones.

Tristes horas de angustia y de dolores,
Cuando al verlo en un lecho moribundo,
El ya no conocía los amores
Que lo hicieron feliz en este mundo.

¿Por qué quedé a llorar su eterna ausencia?
¿Por qué sentía amargas decepciones?
Aquel hombre llenaba mi existencia
De risueñas y bellas ilusiones.

Ya nunca volveré a apoyar mi frente
Sobre aquel pecho que por mí latía.
Esto me hace sufrir intensamente
Y tener su recuerdo noche y día.

Yo no puedo olvidar aquellas horas.
Yo no puedo olvidarte amor perdido.
Oigo su voz que me dice—¿por qué lloras?
No soy yo. Es el destino quien te ha herido.

Yo transporto mi mente donde él se halla.
Y le cuento lo mucho que he sufrido
Y parece que me dice—Amada, calla.
Mi fe y mi amor se han desvanecido.

¿Por qué mi calma se tornó en locura?
¿Por qué sentí en mi alma un dardo fijo?
Sentía inmensa y amarga desventura
Porque aquel hombre me dejaba un hijo.

Huérfano quedaba el hijo de mi alma.
Yo su madre lloraba sin consuelo.
El quedaba a volver aquella calma
Que pocas veces se halla en este suelo

Así pasaron los terribles días
Noches y horas de dolor profundo.
Y sin consuelo en mis brazos lo mecía
Porque su padre no estaba en este mundo.

El inocente crecía cada día
El volvía el recuerdo del ausente.
—El será mi porvenir—decía,
Y volvía la calma ya a mi mente

Así llegó a cumplir un año y ocho meses
Su alma inocente y pura—¡cuál delirio!
El que fue mi consuelo tantas veces
Ya que borraba de mi mente aquel martirio.

Hoy ya sin él, sin ti, hijo del alma.
Hoy es mi vida dolorida y marchitada.
Ya no tengo un ser que me dé calma
Y mi senda es oscura y desgraciada.

Lágrimas vierto cada día por vos.
Mis miradas están al cielo fijo
Ya nunca volveréis a oír mi voz.
Adiós amante esposo y noble hijo.

[*Tears of an Eternal Absence*

Black the shadow of my sad life,
Sad memories of my good past,
Passing pain covered the good fortune
Of that happy home today ravaged.

That humble home without sadness,
That grand heart filled with loves,
He was my love and my greatness
And today exchanged my happiness for pains.

Why did I lose that love that was a treasure?
Why did my beautiful illusions end?
Why am I always sad? Why do I cry?
Goodbye love, goodbye sweet passions.

Sad hours of distress and pain,
When upon seeing him on his deathbed,
He no longer knew the loves
That made him happy in this world.

Why was I left to cry his eternal absence?
Why did I feel bitter deceptions?
That man filled my existence
With smiles and beautiful illusions.

Now I'll never place my forehead
On that breast that beat for me.

This makes me suffer intensely
And hold his memory night and day.

I cannot forget those hours.
I cannot forget you, lost love.
I hear his voice say, "Why do you weep?
It is not I, it is destiny that has wounded you."

I transport my mind to where he is found
And I tell him how much I have suffered,
And it seems that he says, "Hush, loved one."
My faith and love have vanished.

Why did my calm turn to insanity?
Why did I feel in my soul a fixed dart?
I felt an immense and bitter misfortune
Because that man left me with a child.

The child of my soul was left orphaned.
I his mother cried without solace.
He stayed to return that calm
That few times is found on this earth.

Like that passed those terrible days,
Nights and hours of profound pain.
Without solace in my arms I rocked him
Because his father was not in this world.

The innocent child grew every day.
He returned the memory of the absent one.
"He would be my future," he said,
And the calmness returned then to my mind.

He came to be a year and eight months old.
His soul innocent and pure. What delight!
The one that was my solace so many times
Since he was erasing from my mind that martyrdom.

Today without him, without you, son of my soul,
Today my life is aching and withered.
I no longer have that one that will give me peace,
And my path is obscure and adverse.

Tears I pour each day for you,
My gaze is to the fixed sky.

You'll never again hear my voice.
Goodbye, beloved husband and noble son.][10]

These few surviving examples provide insight into the types of stories that became themes for vaquero poetry. Examples of outstanding horsemanship, lack of horsemanship that provided comic relief on the ranch, nature, family relationships, and general ranch life were other themes commonly reported.

Conclusion

Songs, poetry, and other folklore provide insight into vaquero daily life. They are the personal and social histories of the men who were the foundations for the great American mythic hero and of the ranching institution that became one of the economic cornerstones of the American Southwest. One vaquero observed, "They always come to interview the owners, never us. We're the ones that made them rich, we were the ones that showed them how to work. These are our stories and our history."

Changes in the ranching industry have had devastating effects on vaquero oral traditions. Increased labor costs, reduction in ranch sizes, and advances in technology have changed the nature of the ranch structure. Helicopters and pickup trucks have replaced the full-time, live-in vaquero. Many workers find jobs on a daily or seasonal basis and return home at the end of the workday. Younger cowboys do not have the opportunity to train under the same rigorous conditions as their predecessors and do not get to experience the camaraderie developed in collective ranch living. Those end-of-the-day campfire storytelling sessions are no longer a routine part of the vaquero experience, causing a dramatic decrease in the more creative oral traditions of poetry and music. Traditions such as jokes and narratives, requiring only retelling rather than specialized skills, have not suffered as drastically.[11]

Sadly, the Mexican American vaquero of the early twentieth century had no anthropologist or folklorist or interested layperson to document this rich body of information; it is impossible to tell how much of it has been lost. The growing interest in vaquero traditions among academic circles and at folklife festivals provides hope for the survival of some. In these new public forums, individual names and dates are lost, and perhaps the stories themselves become greatly embellished, but what remains important is that the contributions and experiences of these men are being retold and remembered by their children and grandchildren. At long last, vaquero voices are being placed within the greater American cowboy experience.

Notes

I would like to thank the Western Folklife Center of Elko, Nevada for funding the fieldwork for this study as part of the 1993 Cowboy Poetry Gathering. I am indebted to Ricardo Palacios for the support and enthusiasm expressed for this project and to Olivia Cadaval, Nilda Villalta, and Marcelo Argotty for reviewing the Spanish portions of the text. I am especially grateful to Omar Galván, Ramiro Ramírez, Alejandro Soliz, Jr., and Alberto "Lolo" Treviño, four South Texas vaqueros who have been wonderful teachers and friends. During the fieldwork, I interviewed twenty-five different vaqueros ranging in age from fifteen to ninety-one. They collectively represent more than 875 years of ranching experience on more than forty ranches. The terminology used in this essay reflects those terms used by the interviewees and does not necessarily conform to terminology and genres as they have been designated by scholars.

1. See Arnoldo De León, "Rancheros, Comerciantes, and Trabajadores in South Texas, 1848–1900," in *Reflections of the Mexican Experience in Texas,* ed. Margarita B. Melville and Hilda Castillo Phariss (Houston: Mexican American Studies Center, University of Houston, 1979); and Arnoldo De León, *The Tejano Community, 1836–1900* (Albuquerque: University of New Mexico Press, 1982).

2. Jovita González, "Folklore of the Texas-Mexican Vaquero," in *Texas and Southwestern Lore,* ed. J. Frank Dobie (Austin: Texas Folk-Lore Society, 1927), 7–22; also see J. Frank Dobie, *A Vaquero of the Brush Country* (Dallas: Southwest Press, 1929); and Jovita González, "Social Life in Cameron, Starr, and Zapata Counties," M.A. thesis, University of Texas at Austin, 1930.

3. Américo Paredes, *"With His Pistol in His Hand": A Border Ballad and Its Hero* (Austin: University of Texas Press, 1958).

4. Personal interview, 5 Sept. 1993. Original audio tapes, annotated transcripts, and field research reports are housed in the archives of the Western Folklife Center, Elko, Nevada; other documentation is in the author's possession. All translations are by the author.

5. Personal interview with Alejandro Soliz, 30 Aug. 1992, and with Omar Galván, 7 Sept. 1992.

6. Personal interview, 5 Sept. 1992.

7. Personal interview, 13 Sept. 1992.

8. Personal interview, 7 Sept. 1992.

9. Interview with Omar Galván, 7 Sept. 1992.

10. Personal interview with Omar Galván, Sept. 1994, author's possession.

11. Roberto M. Villarreal, "The Mexican-American Vaqueros of the Kennedy Ranch: A Social History," M.A. thesis, Texas A&I University, 1970; Joe S. Graham, *El Rancho in South Texas: Continuity and Change from 1750* (Dallas: University of North Texas Press, 1994).

22

Cows and Logs: Commonalities and Poetic Dialogue among Cowboys and Loggers in the Pacific Northwest

Jens Lund

Logging and ranching in the American West share a heritage of narrative occupational poetry. Both are associated with predominantly male outdoor occupations that involve working close to nature with raw natural resources. Both types of work have traditionally been performed by small groups of men in remote, rural locations and involve considerable discomfort and danger.

The most typical cowboy and logger poems are usually structured as rhymed couplets arranged in stanzas and narrated in linear chronology. Common themes include humor, tragedy, love, and the details of work, the latter often exaggerated or expressed as bragging. Cowboy poetry's capture of mass-media attention since the mid-1980s is at least in part a manifestation of the American love of nostalgia. The persistence of composition in these two genres, however, reflects something much deeper than mere nostalgia for a lost way of life. That is especially true of logger poetry, which has seen little public attention. Logger and cowboy poetry are both typical of folk poetry as discussed by Roger DeV. Renwick. They are "explicitly situated in the poet's bounded and knowable world."[1]

Cowboys and loggers have lived and worked in remarkably similar ways, especially during the earlier decades of the twentieth century. Verbal culture flourished in the cow camp and the logging camp. Isolation, danger, camaraderie, and machismo were forces that shaped verbal artistic expression.[2] Old-time loggers and cowboys were often migrant men, who, if they had any schooling, might have been taught to recite the work of such school favorites as Coleridge, Tennyson, or Housman and who, if they liked poetry, probably read the "manly" verse of Rudyard Kipling and Robert W. Service.[3]

Workers in the ranching and logging industries—cowboys and loggers—were and still are highly visible members of "high-context" occupations, meaning they share a large amount of experience and cultural knowledge that bind them together.[4] Both groups have been romanticized in popular culture. In the case of cowboys, the image has persisted for more than a century and is international in scope. The romanticization of loggers is localized to those areas where logging is or was an important local industry. Both loggers and cowboys share certain values associated with exaggerated masculinity and the celebration of man's dominance over nature.[5]

Loggers and cowboys wear their respective professions proudly, especially in the face of battles with governmental bureaucracies and meddling outsiders. Logging towns like Forks, Washington, and cattle towns like Pendleton, Oregon, are unmistakably stamped by their occupational cultures. The logger's tin hat, calk shoes (always pronounced "cork"), suspenders, Old Hickory shirt, and stagged "tin pants" are as much a folk costume as the cowboy's Stetson, bandanna, boots, yoked shirt, and chaps.[6] Each profession also has its own jargon, often unintelligible to the outsider.[7]

Cowboys in the open-range trail-driving days had to make their own entertainment or do without, as did loggers in the days of isolated logging camps. Thus, it is not surprising that similar expressive traditions developed. In fact, logger song and poetry predate those of cowboys, going back to the "shanty boys" of Maine and eastern Canada. "Lines upon the Death of Two Young Men" (1815) and "The Falling of the Pine" (1825), both from Québec, may be the oldest known North American logger poem and ballad.[8] By the 1930s, extensive collections of northeastern and Great Lakes lumber ballads had been published.[9]

As logging moved west, so did the poetic tradition. Charles Dinsmore, a Maine logger who came to Washington in 1900 and lived and worked in logging camps in the North Cascades, brought along traditional northeastern lumber ballads.[10] The full flowering of the singing and reciting tradition among northwestern loggers was never fully chronicled, however, because the Northwest never had a corps of folklorists and ballad collectors until the radio and the phonograph supplanted homemade entertainment. Nonetheless, there is little doubt that a recitation tradition existed. A "camp bard" might parody Kipling or Service, poetically featuring people in the camp itself and notable or humorous incidents familiar to listeners.

It has been said that logger song never developed in the Northwest to the point that it had in eastern North America.[11] Northwest song collections do include songs about logging, however.[12] Carl Sandburg recalled being present at a logging camp song-swap involving a Salem, Oregon, logger poet, Charles Olaf Olsen, and James Stevens, a millworker-writer and author of "The Frozen Logger," the best-known Northwest logger song.[13] Some accounts of logging camps mention singing as a popular activity, at least among loggers who came to the Northwest from the Northeast.[14]

Logger and cowboy poetry are strongly influenced by specific individuals whose poems have been accepted into tradition. Among cowboys, Bruce Kiskaddon, Badger Clark, Curley Fletcher, S. Omar Barker, and Gail Gardner were the best-known poets, and cowboys still recite their verse.[15] Among Northwest loggers, the two poets most quoted are Buzz Martin and Robert E. Swanson. Martin was from Five Rivers, Oregon, a tiny community in the Siuslaw National Forest.[16] In the 1970s he distinguished himself by setting his works to music and performing them in a Johnny Cash–influenced country-western style. Martin also recited other poems to musical accompaniment, notably his three classics "Used Log Truck," "Since They Repossessed My Used Log Truck," and "(Where There Walks a Logger) There Walks a Man." Although usually thought of as a logger, Martin actually drove log trucks in Oregon and southeastern Alaska. Since his death in 1982, several other Northwest logger poets have married their verse to the country-western musical idiom, although with less success than Martin.[17]

Robert E. Swanson, a retired logging engineer and government safety inspector from Vancouver Island, died in 1994. A radio raconteur during the 1940s and a friend of Robert Service, he published six books of poetry. The first five were printed in small, inexpensive editions on both sides of the U.S.-Canadian border, and older loggers perhaps still own a cherished but worn copy of one of Swanson's volumes.[18]

Some cowboy poetry has been traced to its appearance as filler in ranching newspapers.[19] The persistence of logger poetry in the Northwest, despite a decline in recitation, is due mainly to publication in timber industry newspapers.[20] Over more than forty years, *Weyerhaeuser News* and *Weyerhaeuser Magazine* published numerous logger poems, as did the company's official history.[21] So did Simpson Timber Company's *Simpson Lookout* and the Loyal Legion of Loggers and Lumbermen's *4L Bulletin.* They also appeared in labor newspapers such as the International Woodworkers Association's *Timber Worker* and *International Woodworker.*

When Finley and Jean Hays were publishing *Loggers World, Log Trucker, Timber Cutter,* and *Christian Logger,* they usually included at least one poem in each issue as filler; in addition, their book-length anthologies of logger prose and folklore contain much poetry.[22] The Hayses have also published anthologies of poetry, so their efforts have kept the tradition of logger poetry alive for their readership, which constitutes a significant proportion of the Northwest's timber industry at all levels.[23] Bill and Vi Iund's *American Timberman and Trucker* features even more poems and not surprisingly, for both are accomplished logger poets. Hank Nelson, a logger poet who is also a singer and songwriter, is the Iund's roving reporter and associate editor. *West Coast Logger,* out of Vancouver, British Columbia, also occasionally publishes logger poems, as did *Chain Saw Age* when it was published in Portland, Oregon.

Ironic humor is one of the major features of both logger and cowboy poetry, and it is often based on jargon confusion. The Northwest's geography helps to effect this in the examples offered here. In the Pacific Northwest (British Columbia, Idaho, Oregon, Washington, and parts of Alaska, California, and Montana), logging country and ranching country are in close enough proximity that many individuals may know at least a smattering of both trades' vocabularies. Some individual poets, such as Sunny Hancock, Bill Iund, and Ray Iund, Sr., have worked in both industries.

That cowboy and logger poets would write poems aimed at each other was perhaps inevitable in the Northwest. Bisected by the Cascades range, the Pacific Northwest includes two very different climatic, vegetative, and economic regions. Logging occurs in forests on both sides of the mountains, but ranching is important only to the east.[24]

In 1975 Lon Minkler, then of Woodland, Washington, inadvertently began a dialogue of folk humor between loggers and cowboys when he submitted "Cow Punchin'" to *Loggers World* editors Finley and Jean Hays, who published it as filler between articles on contract logging companies and advertising for logging equipment and trucks. Minkler, a yarder engineer or "donkey puncher" for almost forty years, wrote "Cow Punchin'" as a joke.[25] He imagined the problems that the word *branding* might cause to a logger who tried to brand cattle the way he was used to branding logs. Logs are branded for the same reason as cattle, to show ownership. A log is branded by hitting its end once with a long-handled branding hammer, to the surface of which is welded a steel plate embossed with the company's brand. The hammer is never heated like a cowboy's branding iron.

Cow Punchin'

The year was in November,
Bob and I decided to have a fling.
Every outfit was snowed out,
So we'd try punchin' cows 'til spring.

For a couple of old loggers
To take on such a chore,

They've got to be plumb crazy,
And that's for damn shore.

The foreman looked down at our shoes
With the bottoms full of calk,
And his lip curled back in a half-assed grin,
As if we couldn't walk.

He asked if we'd ever branded
Anything as big as a cow.
Bob said, "Son, that's right down my alley.
I used to brand[26] for Weare and Howe."

He gave us a bunch of chokers,[27]
The damn things were made of rope,
And told us to choke[28] a brindle cow
And brand him on the rump.

We found that cow in the corner
Of a pasture to the north,
And thought we were lucky to find him,
Until we heard him snort.

He pawed the ground and bellered
I looked at Bob and said,
"We're not going to choke the butt,[29]
So we'll have to take the head."

The cow lowered his big head
And came at us like a runaway train,
And the first time he got branded
Was right across the brain.

If I'd had a heavier branding hammer,
We'd have finished the job right there,
But he wheeled around and charged again
And Bob choked a leg from the rear.

I branded him again beside the head
To sorta slow him down.
Ol' Bob timber-hitched[30] him to the fence,
There was nothing else around.

Then he kicked him where it hurt
The cow let out a beller.

I finally got my choker on up front
And put a roll on 'er.[31]

We both got on the front choker
And give 'er a sideways haul,
And got the limbs a-pointin' up
All the cow could do was bawl.

And then we got to figgerin'
How to give that rump a brand.
We bruised it up quite a bit,
When the foreman decided to give us a hand.

He said, "You boys are crazy.
You can't brand a cow like that.
You've got to stick it in the fire
And heat the end of it."

Right then and there we bunched[32] 'er.
Bob called him a fool.
Although we'll do most anything,
Neither one of us is cruel.[33]

When he wrote "Cows and Logs," Harold Otto was a retired "fruit-rancher" (the local idiom for an orchardist or fruit-grower) from Pateros in central Washington's Methow Valley. The Methow Valley, east of the Cascades, is an area that has changed since irrigation from open-range cattle-ranching to apple-growing. Otto was born in the logging town of Getchell in Snohomish County, west of the Cascades, where his father had been a logger. While Otto was a boy, his family moved east of the mountains. He worked for years as a cowboy, mule wrangler, and deckhand on a Columbia River steamboat. After World War II he started working in the region's orchards, eventually becoming a grower himself.[34]

Harold Otto's son Earl, who worked for Weyerhaeuser in Tacoma, saw "Cow Punchin'" in *Loggers World* at work and passed it on to his father. Minkler's poem tickled Otto, especially the misunderstanding of branding. He remembered such confusions from his own youth. Soon afterward, he sat down and wrote "Cows and Logs."

For many years I herded cows
Upon the dusty trail.
I've throwed my rope around their horns,
And twisted on their tails.

I've cussed them in the spring and fall
And in winter's freezing days,
And wound up broke by Christmas time
In a line shack feeding hay

To a bunch of cows that seemed to know
Just how to make me mad,
And anything that bothered me
Just seemed to make them glad.

Then I heard about a logger's life
In the woods of Puget Sound;
Of the money paid for little work,
And of the girls in town.

So I threw my saddle on my horse
And bid the cows good-bye.
I sang a song as I rode away
To the land of timber high.

One summer day I reached my goal
Not far from Snohomish town.
Getchell is what it was called
And the boss I soon had found.

He said that he would put me on,
As help was rather short
But as he looked my outfit o'er,
I thought I heard him snort.

He eyed my spurs and my high-heeled boots
My Stetson and my jeans.
Then said, "My boy, when morning comes,
You'll see just what I mean."

When morning came and breakfast o'er,
I soon appeared for work.
A logger's strife my aim in life,
No duty would I shirk.

The boss soon took me in tow
He said I'd work on foot, of course.
I wondered what a man could do
Without a saddle-horse.

He took me to a pile of rope;
The stuff was made of steel.
Too stiff to braid a hondo in
Or rope a critter's heel.

He said, "Just take a coil of that
To the donkey in the woods.
But first you should take off your spurs;
In the brush they are no good."

With rope in hand, I walked awhile,
But no donkey could I see;
Just a big iron thing, blowing smoke,
Fastened to a tree,

With steel ropes going ever'where.
What an awful racket it made.
I couldn't've heard the donkey,
Even if he had brayed.

I walked around the woods 'til noon,
And then I saw the boss.
He said, "My boy, where have you been,
Or were you only lost?"

He said, "The donkey needs that line;
You take it there right now."
I said, "Where is that donkey at?
I will rope him like a cow."

He looked amazed and pointed
To the iron thing blowing smoke.
Then said, "My friend, I only hope
You are not playing a joke."

I said, "No, sir. It is no joke.
Of that you have no fear.
The only kind of donkey I know
Has four legs and long ears."

And then I saw him kind o' grin.
He seemed all right, somehow.
He said, "You sure don't know the woods,
But I never saw a cow."

We shook hands, then parted friends.
I threw my saddle on my horse,
And started back to the bunchgrass hills
To punch more cows, of course.

So, punchers, just take my advice.
Don't yearn for pastures green,
And don't believe the stranger's tales
Of places he has seen.

Just stay at home where you belong
For riches do not hope.
You'll find in life, there's things much worse
Than cow dung on your rope.[35]

Harold Otto at this time was already an established "occasional poet"—a term folklorist Suzi Jones used in a personal communication to me to denote folk poets who specialize in commemoration of such community events as funerals, graduations, and the like. Folk poems are often context-specific expressions associated with family celebrations, workplace gatherings, and workers' clubs and meetings.[36] Like many cattle-country occasional (or context-specific) poets, much of Otto's verse concerned ranching and the cowboy life, although other examples were about apple growing and picking. He was aware, however, of a tradition of cowboy poetry from older cowboys he had known during his youth in the Methow and upper Columbia Valleys.

Both "Cow Punchin'" and "Cows and Logs" share a familiar theme in occupational folklore, the initiation of the greenhorn.[37] Cowboys think they know all about rope until they see some "made of steel." A "donkey" in the woods is even less familiar. In "Cow Punchin'," the two loggers think that being sent out to brand will be easy because log branding is one of the easier tasks in the woods. The irony is that neither the cowboy nor the two logger protagonists are really greenhorns. All are presumably experienced workers in their respective trades. When they are removed from familiar contexts and moved a few score miles east or west into a contrasting climate, much seems at first to be the same, including jargon and equipment, until the differences become apparent and confusion reigns. In "Cow Punchin'," additional irony comes from the fact that the two loggers quit in protest over being asked to do something cruel ("You've got to stick it in the fire / And heat the end of it"), when repeatedly clobbering a cow with an unheated branding iron is far more punishment for the poor beast than a quick singe.

In 1987 a handwritten copy of "Cows and Logs" was submitted to *Loggers World* by a friend of Otto's, together with a brief note describing how it had first been written in response to a poem seen there. *Loggers World* printed the poem as a facsimile in Otto's own handwriting. Since 1976 "Cows and Logs" has appeared in several newspapers and books and on a cassette-tape anthology.[38] Otto was invited to the first Cowboy Poetry Gathering in Elko, Nevada, in 1985 (he declined) and soon after was honored by being proclaimed Cowboy Poet of the State of Washington by the state's House of Representatives.

"Cow Punchin'" received less notice but was also republished in an illustrated collection of Minkler's work.[39] The collection includes another poem alluding to cow-punchers, "Cowboy," a humorous sketch of a Stetson-wearing former cowboy turned inept woods boss (foreman). After an unpleasant encounter with a choker cable, he leaves the woods: "They say he's punchin' cows now, over near the town of Roper."[40] Minkler takes his poetry seriously and has studied writing at Lower Columbia College in Longview, Washington.

Harold Otto had a number of opportunities to recite "Cows and Logs" around Washington, including at the Omak Stampede (a large rodeo held on the Colville Indian Reservation) and at Seattle's Northwest Folklife Festival. Minkler did not recite at all until 1986 but has since performed at company banquets and industry meetings, at gatherings of a local literary society, on local television in Longview, and at the Elko Cowboy Poetry Gathering. He worked as a cowboy, mule wrangler, fruit rancher, and campfire entertainer for a tour company in Longview, Washingon.

Ten years after "Cow Punchin'," in 1985, Minkler wrote another poem, "Greener Pastures," about dissatisfied loggers who try to make it as cowboys. Once again, he lampooned the plight of the greenhorn via the loggers' unfamiliarity with cowboy work. He also satirized the popular image of the cowboy as starlight crooner:

I'll quit the woods (I've heard them say),
For lots less work and better pay.
Those sawmills ain't so bad, you know
And walls protect you from the snow.

Those sawmill-dogs all drive new cars,
And smoke big fancy cigars,
And factory workers got 'er made
With holiday vacations paid.

These stories you've all heard, I'll bet,
Some afternoon, plumb full of sweat.
'Twas such a day, Bob says to me,
"Let's leave the gloom of this here tree."

We hitched a ride upon a freight,
And headed for another state,
And left the timberland behind,
Seeking work of another kind.

"We can punch cows," said Bob, "of course.
All cowboys do is ride a horse,
And plunk upon an old guitar,
Sing lonesome verses to a star."

We took a job where we could see
Away out on the lone prairie,
And took a mighty cut in wage,
And smelled the bloom upon the sage.

The ranch was run by a cowhand,
Full six foot three and quite a man.
Was rawhide tough and skin and bone.
He worked the ranch there all alone.

He hired us to help castrate,
And brand some calves and vaccinate.
He'd bought those bulls down at the sale.
They was out in the old corral.

Now this corral was kinda round,
With slimy stuff upon the ground.
The bulls about four-hundred pounds,
And acting like a bunch of clowns.

The cowboy looked at us and grinned,
This here show's about to begin.
I'll need one of them on the ground,
And then you'll have to hold him down.

We charged what looked the weakest bull,
And about then I lost my cool,
And called upon the mighty Eck,[41]
And grabbed that sucker by the neck.

And then I felt Bob's body hit,
The calf about to have a fit.
We wrestled him the corral around,
Before we got him on the ground.

The cowboy came then at a trot,
The branding iron smoking hot.
The bull then gave a mighty flip,
And I got branded on the hip.

The cowboy seemed to like his job.
He laughed and grinned at me and Bob,
With sweat and grit, we held him there,
The smell of blood and burning hair.

The cowboy was doing his best,
But he was careless, nonetheless.
The dust so thick you couldn't see.
And we got vaccinated free.

For bangs and hoof-and-mouth disease.
And blackleg. How I missed the trees.
And logging camps and riggin' men.
I was glad when that day was in.

About dark, we washed our blisters,
He fed us on mountain oysters.
We liked cowboyin', all right, but,
We headed back for the tall uncut![42]

Although "Greener Pastures" was first published in a Seattle literary magazine, the transition from folk logger poetry to literary logger poetry is most prominent in the work of Peter Trower, a British Columbia logger poet who is read all over Canada.[43] Even more surprising is that Gary Snyder, a Beat poet of the 1950s who is now best known for environmentalist poems, first started writing poetry as a young man when he worked as a logger and lived in a logging camp, where he was inspired by older traditional poets.[44]

One of Oregon's most recognized cowboy poets and reciters, Sunny Hancock, recites at rodeos and cattle auctions and works as a rodeo and cattle-show announcer. His home near Lakeview is east of the Cascades but surrounded by the Fremont National Forest, near both timber and rangeland. Originally from Arizona, he was "buckaroo boss" at the ZX ranch near Paisley, Oregon. In the early 1980s, Hancock, who owns a small ranch, started driving a log truck. He soon began writing logger poetry as well as continuing with his cowboy verse and has begun to recite logger poems although he says that the opportunities are not as frequent as they are with cowboy material. One of his favorites is Robert E. Swanson's "They'll Do It Every Time," which Hancock calls "The King of All,

Both In- and Outdoor Sports," a poem about braggart "bunkhouse casanovas."[45] One of his most recited poems is "Ode to the Spotted Owl," a scathing criticism of environmentalists from a logger's perspective.[46]

Since the 1980s the ironies of "Cow Punchin'," "Cows and Logs," and "Greener Pastures" have delighted many northwesterners. (Minkler recites "Greener Pastures" in preference to "Cow Punchin'," considering it a better poem.) The three poems evoke amusing images of the logger, the cowboy, and especially the perennial greenhorn. A somewhat similar example is the traditional cowboy poem (and song) "Zebra Dun," which reminds its audience that "every educated feller ain't a plumb greenhorn," and Minkler's "The Greenhorn," which ponders "how many times these kinds of battles are won / By some ignorant damn fool kid because he didn't know it couldn't be done."[47]

The state of being a greenhorn, according to all five poems, is relative. The logger is glad to be sent to brand: "I used to brand for Weare and Howe." Then he discovers that he is not as worldly as he thought, just as the cowboy who is handed a piece of steel rope "too stiff to braid a hondo in / Or rope a critter's heel" starts to realize that he is out of his element. In "Zebra Dun" and "The Greenhorn," greenhorns best old-timers. In "Cow Punchin'" and "Cows and Logs," old-timers find out that they are greenhorns in new surroundings. Minkler's "The Greenhorn" is comparable to the cowboys' "Zebra Dun" in that the apparent greenhorn is able to show up his harassers. In this case, he figures out how to straighten out kinked chokers, a chore the old-timers set him to do as a prank because they believe it cannot be done.

"Cow Punchin'," "Cows and Logs," "The Greenhorn," and "Greener Pastures" suggest another traditional cowboy poem/song, "The Gol-Darned Wheel." The bragging cowboy "can ride the wildest bronco in the wild and wooly West" and "handle any [critter] ever wore a coat of hair," but he meets his master when he is shamed into trying to ride a bicycle for the first time, which "really made [him] squeal." Again, the seasoned veteran turns greenhorn when confronted with an unfamiliar situation.[48]

"Cow Punchin'," "Greener Pastures," and "Cows and Logs" are fiction. But that is not entirely the case with Minkler's "Cowboy," or "The Greenhorn," or with yet another cowboy-goes-logging poem, "Powder River Ray," written by Ray Iund, Sr.

Old Cherokee Bill told a story one day,
While standing around the dinner fire,
About some guy called Powder River Ray,
A dude you should never hire.

He wore an eighteen shirt, a number four hat,
And looked like the kind of a guy
That could shoulder the butt-riggin',[49] pull his own slack,
And wade through a brush-pile, waist-high.

The name seemed strange, or so old Bill felt,
For a fellow who was making claims
Of logging experiences under his belt,
Powder River's on the Wyoming plains.

Their suspicions rose more as they watched this recruit,
He said he wore spurs every day,
Putting climbing hooks on cowboy boots,
With the gaffs pointing out the wrong way.

They asked if he could punch a donkey or a cat,[50]
And he said, "Well, not as good as a cow,
But you show me the herd and I'll bet my hat
That I'll get the job done, somehow."

The bullbuck[51] nearly keeled over dead,
When he asked, "Do you know how to fall?"[52]
"Why, sure," Ray replied, with a nod of his head,
"Just relax and it won't hurt at all."

They whisked him off on the rigging crew;
The chokermen[53] went plumb wild.
The slinger,[54] he was mighty blue
And his language wasn't too mild.

"We'll have to choke that sapling there,
And let the yarder[55] pull it down.
Now get your fingers out of your hair,
Or I'll send the whole crew back to town."

They caught old Powder River headed out,
And asked him what was wrong.
He said, "Boys, this ain't no place for me.
My belly just ain't that strong.

That guy down there in that old tin hat,
Has ideas much too hard.
He said they were going to choke a sap,
Somewhere out there in the yard.

It just ain't my idea of fun.
Choking people ain't my game.
'Specially when you're four to one,
So I'm going to quit this claim."

Now if someone doesn't chuck this down the well,
You might hear more someday,
Because this isn't all there is
To tell about old Powder River Ray.[56]

"Old Cherokee Bill" and "Old Powder River Ray" refer to the brothers Bill Iund and Ray Iund, Sr., respectively, of Winlock and Stanwood, Washington. Both men are Cherokee from Oklahoma, raised on the Powder River in Wyoming cattle country; they came to western Washington during the 1940s and learned the logging trade.

"Powder River Ray," unlike "Cow Punchin'," "Greener Pastures," and "Cows and Logs," is based on reality. Although the events themselves are fictional, they refer directly and autobiographically to the Iunds' inexperience not only in the logging woods but also in new physical and cultural environments, far removed in both distance and character from their native Oklahoma. Both Iund brothers grew up on working ranches in Wyoming. "Powder River Ray" was, in fact, a nickname given to Ray because it struck loggers as funny that a former Wyoming ranch hand was now yarding logs instead of cows. Ray's older brother Bill, who had been a cowboy in Wyoming and Montana, came to Washington in 1937 and soon began working in the woods. In 1945 Ray joined him, having just been discharged from the service. Ray began working in the woods and, being slight of build, had a harder time in the beginning than Bill. Twenty years later Bill wrote a humorous tall-tale poem, "Powder and the Bear," about Ray's experiences as a greenhorn and an encounter he had with a bear in the woods. Amused by "Powder and the Bear," Ray then wrote "Powder River Ray," exploiting the humor of jargon confusion in "donkey," "cat," "fall," "choke," and "sapling." Bill submitted both poems to *Loggers World,* and they were published together, on the same page, in the anthology *World of Loggers!* Bill Iund later republished his poem in *American Timberman and Trucker.*[57]

A different example of a cowboy-logger dialogue is "Ballad of the St. Helens Ape Man." Logger poet Otto Oja of Detroit, Oregon, wrote it in the early 1960s and submitted it to Courtland Matthews, editor of *Chain Saw Age* in Portland. Matthews and Oja sent it back and forth, with the editor making various suggestions, some of which Oja followed. Matthews also wanted to shorten it but finally published a long version.[58] Oja, who now lives in Cathlamet, Washington, is a second-generation Finnish-American who grew up in northwestern

Oregon and worked as a bucker and faller most of his life.[59] Now retired, he is a skilled woodcarver and chainsaw sculptor as well as a poet, and he also draws cartoons and writes about logging history. A piano-playing friend of Oja's, Clarice Staats of Redland, Oregon, set "Ballad of the St. Helens Ape Man" to music in 1964. She and her husband helped Oja find a singer who recorded a demo tape of it that was never released. Oja and his friends have, however, circulated copies. Soon afterward, Oja submitted the ballad to the Hayses, and it appeared in *Loggers World* in 1965.

High up on Mt. St. Helens' crags,[60]
Up where the thunder rolls,
There dwelt a monster ape man,
Who gathered loggers' souls.

At night he roamed the logging roads,
Howling wild with glee,
While tall and lonely firs did keep
Him silent company.

He played around the yarder sleds,
And scattered rigging wide,
And banged a hundred diesel drums
Far down the mountainside.

The lightning flashed one early morn,
Made light the forest gloom.
The loggers saw the ape man's tracks,
And felt the pall of doom.

They swiftly turned the crummy[61] 'round,
And headed back for home,
And swore by all things holy,
They'd let the ape man roam.

But two there were who chose to stay
And take a look around,
A pair who never turned for home,
'Til timber hit the ground.

Big One-Eyed Jim, a chainsaw man,
Whose name all loggers knew,
For he had traveled far and wide,
Wherever timber grew.

And Slabwood Bill, a bucking fool,
From somewhere on the Sound,
Whose chainsaw roared a hungry tune
And logs did roll around.

They'd take on any foe they'd meet,
And fight with knuckles bare.
No ape man roaming logging roads
Could stay the famous pair.

They gathered up their gas and oil,
And buckled on their packs,
And heading up the mountainside,
Spit snoose[62] upon the tracks.

High upon the rocky slope,
Along the right of way,
Big One-Eyed Jim looked down his sights,
To where the tree he'd lay,

When suddenly he stiffened
And a chill went up his spine,
His eye had caught a giant ape,
A-comin' down the line.

Near ten feet tall, with six-foot arms,
A mass of hairy hide,
Ears like tin hats, a stump-like head
On shoulders four feet wide.

The ape let out a mighty roar
And thumped his mighty chest,
The sound boomed far across the crags,
Stirred eagles in their nests.

Jim quickly loosed the undercut,[63]
To Slabwood, he did yell,
"Hey, look who's come to visit us,
The bullbuck out of Hell!"

Slabwood Bill sprang on the stump,
From where he filed his chain,
His hat fell off, his hair stood up,
The blood froze in his vein.

Yelled Slabwood Bill to One-Eyed Jim,
"You've never missed a tree,
And if you miss what's coming there,
You've seen the last of me!"

Cried One-Eyed Jim to Slabwood Bill,
"I've never gunned[64] more true,
And if this one is off its mark
Then I'll be gone with you!"

His chainsaw screamed and ninety tons
Of timber shook the land.
The tall fir struck the mountain,
Where they'd seen the ape man stand.

They saw, while dust was settled down,
The tree had found its mark,
There, stretched out, lay the fearsome thing,
A-kicking up the bark.

Then Slabwood with his chainsaw flew,
With speed you seldom see.
The sparks were flying from his corks,
As he tore down the tree.

He bucked that gent from head to toe,
And made a long butt,[65] too.
His chainsaw roared and never hung
As fur and fire flew.

No more the ape man roams these hills,
A-hunting loggers' souls.
He lies up there among the crags,
Up where the thunder rolls.[66]

Otto Oja says he did not write "Ballad of the St. Helens Ape Man" as a conscious parody of another song or poem but rather because he was "disappointed that there were so many good cowboy songs and not very many about loggers." Oja also wrote the song in response to a spate of alleged Bigfoot sightings that were being given much media attention at the time.[67]

The ballad shows remarkable parallels to a now-traditional cowboy poem and song, "Sierry Petes" ("Tying Knots in the Devil's Tail"), which was written in 1917 by Gail Gardner of Prescott, Arizona, a ranch hand turned postmaster.[68] One of the best-known and most widely recited (or sung) cowboy poems, it is known in the Pacific Northwest. Traditional cowboy singer and reciter R. W. "Swede" Miller of north-central Washington sings it, and a localized version, "Sawtooth Peaks," exists in Idaho.[69] In summary, a couple of drunken cowboys encounter the devil while riding home to their cow camp from town. The devil is, predictably, looking for cowboys' souls. The cowboys overpower him, rope and tie him, brand him, notch his ears, tie his tail in a knot, and leave him howling in the "Sierry Petes" (Sierra Prieta Mountains).

The "ape man" is, of course, Sasquatch or Bigfoot, a wilderness wildman. The name *Sasquatch* is derived from a Salish mythological creature transformed by the media and popular culture into a tourist mascot and crypto-zoological phenomenon, complete with a following of true believers.[70] Most loggers scoff, at least if asked directly, but the actual degree of belief among rural people in the northwest woods is hard to gauge. In the area of Mt. St. Helens, Bigfoot is also a local legend, occurring even in place names (Ape Cave and Ape Canyon).[71]

Loggers often use Bigfoot as a butt of jokes. Although usually considered by believers to be merely a rare animal, to some it is a monster or devil-like creature. Despite its size and power it is no match for two loggers with chainsaws, just as the dense forests of the Northwest have shown themselves no match for the logger and his tools. The devil fares better from the cowboys; he, at least, is not dismembered. Yet fur and fire, not fur and blood, flow when Slabwood Bill bucks the ape man. The toughness of loggers, like that of cowboys, knows no bounds.

There are parallels suggesting that "Sierry Petes" might have inspired "Ballad of the St. Helens Ape Man." For example, the former begins, "Away up high in the Sierry Petes, / Where the yeller pines grow tall"; the latter begins, "High up on Mt. St. Helens' crags, / Up where the thunder rolls." Although Oja as a child owned a 78-rpm record of "Tying Knots in the Devil's Tail," he maintains that he never saw the parallels until they were pointed out to him. Confronted by the similarities, Oja observed that he had "unconsciously" copied or parodied the cowboy song.

An obvious difference between "Sierry Petes" and "St. Helens Ape Man" is that the cowboys are "some forty drinks below" when they encounter the devil, but there is no indication of drunkenness on the part of One-Eyed Jim and Slabwood Bill. Like many loggers, however, Oja explains he has never seen the legendary ape man because he "never drank that much."[72] Prodigious drinking is part of the logger stereotype in the Northwest, as it is in cowboy culture. Although the industry has tried to emphasize the logger as "family man," the old image dies hard.[73]

Even the close and obvious parallels are not as significant as what both "Sierry Petes" and "St. Helens Ape Man" reveal about qualities the cowboy and the logger see in themselves. Cowboy skills depicted include roping, tying, notching, and branding combined with the traits of pugnacity and fearlessness ("You ain't a-goin' to gather no cowboy souls / 'Thout you has some kind of a fight"). Similarly, loggers are willing to fight ("They'd take on any foe they'd meet, / And fight with knuckles bare") and possess such skills as the ability to fall a tree on a precise spot ("'I've never gunned more true'") and speed and agility in wielding a chainsaw.

Several of these poems share the theme of humor derived from the plight of the greenhorn and derive irony from the fact that cowboys and loggers, by no means greenhorns in their own trades, become such when confronted with each others' situations. In "Sierry Petes" and "Ballad of the St. Helens Ape Man," some of the self-ascribed attributes of the two occupations are treated in a parallel manner when pairs of cowboys and loggers best the apparition of evil through fearlessness, strength, and professional skills. Parallels are even more obvious between "Logger's Heaven" and "Cowboy's Heaven." Minkler, like many cowboy poets, has also written and often recites a poem lampooning vegetarians.

Among the logger-cowboy poetry parallels are content, structure, and social context.[74] Public reaction to both genres is also similar in that many people are astounded that stereotypically rough, masculine men resort to poetry, now often considered effeminate. In many ways loggers and cowboys are rivals for public adulation, yet both groups are often despised and rejected by those who profess concern for protecting the environment or reject masculine, nature-dominating ways of life. Loggers and cowboys believe in maintaining solidarity within and between their respective trades against bureaucrats, regulators, and environmentalist critics, and both groups espouse ideals of self-reliance and independence.

Changes have occurred in both ranching and logging in the twentieth century. Ranching is more dependent on the pickup truck than the horse and on the feedlot than the cattle trail. Loggers use chainsaws, log trucks, and diesel and electric yarding equipment, although logger romance still harkens to the axe and crosscut saw, ox teams, and steam-powered donkeys and locomotives.

Both ranching and logging communities celebrate their heritages with competitive sports events based on occupational skills.[75] The similarity between these two types of events is evinced by the fact that logging shows are often called "logger rodeos" and that logrolling, which involves staying on a wildly moving surface, is often a central event at logging shows. In fact, competitive logrolling events have even been called "roleos" in some places.[76] There are now even combined rodeos and logging shows, at least in Montana.

Cowboys and loggers who live and work near each other know that switching trades will give words such as *brand, choke,* and *donkey* new and contrasting meanings. That ambiguity may symbolize the many threats to both the cowboy's and the logger's livelihood. Enough northwesterners in the woods and on the range understand each other's jargon that the poems evoke humor, as in the age-old motif of the absurd misunderstanding.[77] It is possible to be an old hand in the woods (or on the range) but a greenhorn when beginning to work elsewhere.

Loggers and cowboys are also near enough to each other to be familiar with the others' traditional clothing. Three of the poems make fun of the profound differences between the two work costumes: "The foreman looked down at our shoes / With the bottoms full of calk"; "He eyed my spurs and my high-heeled boots / My Stetson and my jeans"; and, "Putting climbing hooks on cowboy boots, / With the gaffs pointing out the wrong way."

The modern composition of cowboy and logger poems is easy to dismiss as an exercise in nostalgia. But nostalgia is a polemic of reconstruction of the "good old days" that shifts, depending upon which or whose good old days are being idealized.[78] Neither logging nor working as a ranch hand has ever been steady employment. Despite high-context inside knowledge and highly developed skills, most loggers and cowboys have had to seek other work and thus perform unaccustomed tasks—in other words, become greenhorns again—often at lower pay (at least for the logger) and less prestige. The tension caused by that possibility is always present, whether work is threatened by economics, environmentalism, or weather.

All the poems considered here except "Greener Pastures," which Minkler wrote as an improvement on his earlier "Cow Punchin'," were written before serious preservation issues such as the spotted owl and ecological sabotage came to the Northwest. Vi Iund's "If the Little Owl Could Speak"; Sunny Hancock's "Ode to the Spotted Owl"; and such songs as Craig Jenkins's "Endangered Species," "Regular People," and "Middle Ground," John Barron and Nora Hanson's "Let the Yellow Ribbons Fly" and "HOOT-HOOT," and Bob Vickarious and Elmer Nichols's "Peter, Poor Peter" all address contemporary resource issues directly in a way that traditional cowboy and logger poetry and song do not.[79] It seems likely that more of this sort of material will appear as such issues continue to affect timber communities.

Ranching and logging have always been uncertain livelihoods. Before spotted owls and overgrazing controversies, there were fluctuating markets in beef and timber, labor disputes in the woods, and droughts on the range. Although it may seem out of character, some cowboys and loggers have traditionally used poetic discourse to talk about life's vicissitudes. As Pauline Greenhill has noted, "Aesthetic statements can be means by which people react to traumatic and difficult situations, assert their community's or their own individual perspective, and thereby . . . 'make their own history.'"[80] Some of the more contemporary poetry and song does that directly. The more traditional material and the older original poems, like the ones in the "cows and logs" dialogue, are indirect expressions of some of the long-standing ambiguities on the range and in the woods.

Notes

I would like to thank the following individuals for their help, including granting permission, finding sources, and offering critical comments: Finley Hays, Alice E. Ingerson, Bill Iund, Ray Iund, Sr., Vi Iund, Lon Minkler, Otto Oja, Harold Otto, Sharon K. P. Rasmussen, Charlie Seemann, David Stanley, Elaine Thatcher, Barre Toelken, and Robert E. Walls. Also thanks to the Washington State Folklife Council for making the research possible.

1. Roger deV. Renwick, *English Folk Poetry: Structure and Meaning,* Publications of the American Folklore Society: New Series, vol. 2 (Philadelphia: University of Pennsylvania Press, 1980), 5.

2. Stewart H. Holbrook, *Holy Old Mackinaw: A Natural History of the American Lumberjack* (New York: Macmillan, 1956), 130–42; Donald MacKay, *The Lumberjacks* (Toronto: McGraw-Hill Ryerson, 1978), 238–51.

3. Hal Cannon, ed., *Cowboy Poetry: A Gathering* (Salt Lake City: Gibbs Smith, 1985), x.

4. Barre Toelken, *The Dynamics of Folklore* (Boston: Houghton-Mifflin, 1979), 51–72.

5. Jack Estes, "Loggers Can't Cry and Other Taboos of the Northwest Woods," in *Forbidden Fruits: Taboos and Tabooism in Culture,* ed. Ray B. Browne (Bowling Green: Bowling Green University Popular Press, 1984), 177–82; Elizabeth Atwood Lawrence, *Rodeo: An Anthropologist Looks at the Wild and the Tame* (Knoxville: University of Tennessee Press, 1982), 217–29; Robert E. Walls, "Logger Poetry and the Expression of Worldview," *Northwest Folklore* 5 (Spring 1987): 31–34.

6. Calks—short, heavy spikes in the soles and heels of woods shoes—give sure footing on logs and are known everywhere as "corks." Old Hickory is a brand of work shirt, typically pin-striped and favored by loggers. To "stag" means to cut pants legs off short; a logger always has to be ready to jump. A tin hat is a metal or plastic safety hat; tin pants are heavy, waterproof canvas pants. Definitions in this essay are taken from Walter F. McCulloch, *Woods Words: A Comprehensive Dictionary of Logging Terms* (1958), (Corvallis: Oregon State University Book Stores, 1977). See also Finley Hays, ed., *Lies, Logs, and Loggers,* 9th ed. (Chehalis, Wash.: Loggers World Publications, [1977]), 59.

7. Ramon F. Adams, *Western Words: A Dictionary of the Range, Cow Camp, and Trail* (Norman: University of Oklahoma Press, 1946); McCulloch, *Woods Words.*

8. Fannie Hardy Eckstorm and Mary Winslow Smyth, *Minstrelsy of Maine* (Boston: Houghton Mifflin, 1927), 17–20; Edith Fowke, *Lumbering Songs from the Northern Woods* (1970), (Toronto: NC Press, 1985), 30.

9. Phillips Barry, ed., *The Maine Woods Songster* (Cambridge: Harvard University Press, 1939); Earl Clifton Beck, *Lore of the Lumber Camps* (Ann Arbor: University of Michigan Press, 1948); William Main Doerflinger, *Shantyboys and Shantymen: Songs of the Sailor and Lumberman* (New York: Macmillan, 1951); Eckstorm and Smyth, *Minstrelsy of Maine;* Fowke, *Lumbering Songs from the Northern Woods;* Roland Palmer Gray, ed., *Songs and Ballads of the Maine Lumberjacks, with Other Songs from Maine* (Cambridge: Harvard

University Press, 1924); Franz Rickaby, ed., *Ballads and Songs of the Shanty-Boy* (Cambridge: Harvard University Press, 1926).

10. Charles Dinsmore, *The Man from Maine: Charles Dinsmore, an Oral History,* ed. Peter Heffelfinger, Archives of the Skagit County Oral History Association (Anacortes, Wash.: Skagit County Oral History Association, 1980), 1:45–49.

11. Walls, "Logger Poetry and the Expression of Worldview," 26.

12. Winifred I. Knox, "Folksongs from the Olympic Peninsula and Puget Sound," M.S. thesis, Institute of Musical Art, Juilliard School of Music, 1945, 19–29; Barre Toelken, "Northwest Traditional Ballads: A Collector's Dilemma," *Northwest Review* 5 (Winter 1962): 9–18; Elmore Vincent, *"The Northwest Shanty Boy": Elmore Vincent's Lumber Jack Songs, with Yodel Arrangements!* (Chicago: M. M. Cole, 1932).

13. Carl Sandburg, *The American Songbag* (New York: Harcourt, Brace, 1927), 394.

14. Dinsmore, *The Man from Maine,* 45–49.

15. Cannon, ed., *Cowboy Poetry,* 3–7, 12–17, 32–46, 57–70.

16. Judy (Martin) Janes, "My Dad: Buzz Martin," *Loggers World* 22 (April 1986): 55; Ross West, "A Voice from Out of the Woods: The Saga of Buzz Martin, the Singing Logger," *Loggers World* 30 (Dec. 1994): 4, 7–10; see also Ross West, *A Voice from Out of the Woods,* in press.

17. Jeff Brekas, "'Bunkhouse Boys' to Perform," Silverton [Oregon] *Appeal*–Mt. Angel *News,* 26 April 1988, 6; Finley Hays, "West-Log, Inc.—Mapleton, Oregon," *Loggers World* 24 (Dec. 1988): 5–21; Finley Hays, "SWW Logging and Forestry Exhibit," *Loggers World* 25 (Oct. 1990): 32–40; Mike Thoele, "The Mill Brothers," Seattle *Sunday Times–Post-Intelligencer,* 31 July 1988, B4.

18. Robert E. Swanson, *Bunkhouse Ballads: A Third Book of Verse* (1945), (Eugene, Ore.: Finley Hays, 1962); Robert E. Swanson, *Rhymes of a Lumberjack: A Second Book of Verse* (Toronto: Thomas Allen, 1943); Robert E. Swanson, *Rhymes of a Western Logger: A Book of Verse* (Vancouver, B.C.: Lumberman Printing, 1943); Robert E. Swanson, *Rhymes of a Western Logger: The Collected Poems of Robert E. Swanson* (Madeira Park, B.C.: Harbour Publishing, 1992); Robert E. Swanson, *Rhymes of a Western Rambler* (Vancouver, B.C.: privately printed, [1940s]); Robert E. Swanson and Seattle Red, *Rhymes of a Haywire Hooker* (Vancouver, B.C.: Lumberman Printing, 1953).

19. James Griffith, "Cowboy Poetry: The First Hundred Years," program booklet for first Cowboy Poetry Gathering, 31 Jan.–2 Feb. 1985, 4.

20. Walls, "Logger Poetry and the Expression of Worldview," 26–28.

21. Alden Jones, *From Jamestown to Coffin Rock: A History of Weyerhaeuser Operations in Southwest Washington* (Tacoma: Weyerhaeuser, 1974).

22. Hays, ed., *Lies, Logs, and Loggers;* Finley Hays, ed., *World of Loggers! By Many, Many Logging Authors* (Sedro-Woolley, Wash.: Loggers World Publications, 1966); Finley Hays and Myron Metcalf, eds., *Loggers World: The First Ten Years, 1964–1974* (Chehalis, Wash.: Loggers World Publications, 1987).

23. Woody Gifford, *Timber Bind: Logger-Rhythms of the Great Northwest* (Chehalis, Wash.: Loggers World Publications, 1974); Lon Minkler and Don Graham, *The Tall and Uncut: Logging Poems and Cartoons* (Chehalis, Wash.: Loggers World Publications, 1976).

24. J. Orin Oliphant, "History of the Livestock Industry in the Pacific Northwest," *Oregon Historical Quarterly* 49, no. 1 (1948): 3–29.

25. An endless variety of steam, gas, diesel, or electric power plants—plus drums of wire rope used to haul logs from the woods, load at landings, move equipment, rig up trees, and, in the old days, lower cars down inclines—are referred to as "donkeys."

26. A brand is a log mark used to identify one operator's logs when several companies dump in one stream.

27. A choker is a short steel cable that encircles a log. When the choker is pulled, the loose circle quickly cinches tight (like a necktie), "choking" the log as it is pulled toward the landing.

28. To choke is to pass a line around a log or other object and pull it tight.

29. A butt is either the bottom of a tree or the stump end of a log.

30. A timber-hitch is formed by placing a line around a tree, placing the bight over the running line, and wrapping or twisting the cable around itself.

31. To put a roll is to sling rigging on a log in such a way as to make it roll when the main line is pulled, thus clearing some hang-up.

32. To bunch is to quit a job suddenly.

33. Lon Minkler, "Cow Punchin'," *Loggers World* 12 (Feb. 1975): 36.

34. Don Duncan, "A Poet's Life," Seattle *Times,* 8 Dec. 1984, A1, A6.

35. Harold Otto, "Cows and Logs," *Loggers World* 23 (Aug. 1987): 20.

36. Renwick, *English Folk Poetry,* 5.

37. Toelken, *The Dynamics of Folklore,* 62–64.

38. Anon., "Harold Otto: Poet of Pateros, Bard of the Methow," in *Washington's Almanac 1986: The Practical Guide to Living in Washington State,* by the editors of *Washington Magazine* (Seattle: Evergreen Publishing, 1985), 121–23; Cannon, ed., *Cowboy Poetry,* 148–51; Duncan, "A Poet's Life"; Harold Otto, *Poems: Facts and Fiction* (Palouse, Wash.: Precision Printing, 1985), 38–40.

39. Minkler and Graham, *The Tall and Uncut,* 22.

40. Ibid., 34.

41. "The mighty Eck," is, according to Minkler, an old slang term for God.

42. Lon Minkler, "Greener Pastures," *TAND* 4 (Sept. 1990): 4–5.

43. Peter Trower, *Bush Poems* (Madeira Park, B.C.: Harbour Publishing, 1978); Peter Trower, *Goosequill Snags* (Madeira Park, B.C.: Harbour Publishing, 1982); Peter Trower, *The Slidingback Hills* (Ottawa, Ont.: Oberon Press, 1986); Peter Trower, *Unmarked Doorways: Poems by Peter Trower* (Madeira Park, B.C.: Harbour Publishing, 1989).

44. Gary Snyder, interview by Terri Gross, *Fresh Air,* National Public Radio, 20 Nov. 1990. Some of Snyder's logging poems can be found in Synder, *Myths and Texts* (New York: New Directions, 1978).

45. Robert E. Swanson, "They'll Do It Every Time," in *Rhymes of a Western Logger: The Collected Poems of Robert E. Swanson,* 128–29.

46. Robert E. Swanson, "Ode to the Spotted Owl," in *The Stories We Tell: An Anthology of Oregon Folk Literature,* ed. Suzi Jones and Jared Ramsey (Corvallis: Oregon State University Press, 1984), 172–73.

47. "The Zebra Dun," in *Cowboy Poetry,* ed. Cannon, 8; Lon Minkler, "The Greenhorn," in Minkler and Graham, *The Tall and Uncut,* 3.

48. [Anonymous], "The Gol-Darned Wheel," in *Cowboy Poetry,* ed. Cannon, 10.

49. Butt rigging is a system of swivels and clevises connecting the halback and main line, to which chokers are fastened. The term also refers to short lines between the chokers and the main line.

50. A Cat is a tractor. Originally short for Caterpillar and at first used to mean that make only, now the word is often used to mean any make of tractor.

51. The bull buck is the boss of the fallers and buckers (also called the "bull bucker").

52. To fall is to cut timber; this is the woods word for "to fell."

53. Chokermen are people who set chokers.

54. The head man working on the rigging crew is called a "slinger" (short for "rigging slinger"); he spots the rigging where he wants to get the next turn and directs the chokersetters.

55. A yarder is a donkey engine used to haul logs from stump to landing or to yarding tree.

56. Ray Iund, Sr., "Powder River Ray," in *World of Loggers!* ed. Hays, 115.

57. Bill Iund, "Powder and the Bear," in *World of Loggers!* ed. Hays, 115; Ray Iund, Sr., "Powder River Ray," *American Timberman and Trucker* 2 (Sept. 1986): 38.

58. Otto Oja, "Ballad of the St. Helens Ape Man," with unsigned introduction by Courtland Matthews, *Chain Saw Age* (Oct. 1964): 4; Virginia Urrutia, "Otto Oja," *Cowlitz Historical Quarterly* [special "History in Rhyme" issue edited by Virginia Urrutia] 32, no. 2 (1990): 21.

59. A bucker is a person who cuts felled trees into log lengths; a faller fells the timber.

60. Mount St. Helens is, of course, the dormant volcano that erupted in a massive explosion in 1980, nearly twenty years after Oja wrote his poem.

61. The word *crummy* was first applied to a closed boxcar used to haul men to work out in the woods and later applied to a closed-in truck or bus used for the same purpose.

62. Snoose is Copenhagen-brand snuff.

63. The first cut made in falling a tree is the undercut. It determines the direction of fall.

64. To use a "sight gun" is to determine direction of fall; a sight gun is a triangle made of light sticks and used to determine the direction in which the tree will fall.

65. A long butt is a cull chunk that has been cut off the bottom log of a tree because of rot or some other defect.

66. Otto Oja, "Ballad of the St. Helens Ape Man," *Loggers World* (Feb. 1965): 13.

67. Matthews in *Chain Saw Age* (Oct. 1964): 4; Oja, personal communication.

68. Gail Gardner, "The Sierry Petes," in *Cowboy Poetry,* ed. Cannon, 3–5.

69. "Sawtooth Peaks," in Toelken, "Northwest Traditional Ballads," 13.

70. Marjorie Halpin and Michael L. Ames, eds., *Manlike Monsters on Trial: Early Records and Modern Evidence* (Vancouver, B.C.: University of British Columbia Press, 1980).

71. Fred Beck, *I Fought the Apemen of Mt. St. Helens* (n.p.: privately printed, 1967).

72. Otto Oja, interviewed by Pat Williams, *Channel 2 News,* KATU, Portland, July 1989.

73. Norman S. Hayner, "Taming the Lumberjack," *American Sociological Review* 10 (1945): 215–25; Hays, ed., *Lies, Logs, and Loggers,* 63, 67, 79; Buzz Martin, "Loggers Annual Party," on *(Where There Walks a Logger) There Walks a Man!* (Vancouver, Wash.: Ripcord LPM 001, ca. 1966); and Minkler and Graham, *The Tall and Uncut,* 20, 25, 27.

74. Walls, "Logger Poetry and the Expression of Worldview," 21–22, 31–32.

75. Diane M. Ellison, "Log Rolling," *Northwest Folklore* 7 (Fall 1988): 36–43; Finley Hays, "Logging Shows," *Loggers World* 18 (Nov. 1982): 63–67; Robert E. Walls, "Logger Lore," in *Washington State: Folk Life Is Half the Fun* [special supplement to the *Christian Science Monitor*], 11 March 1985, B5, B7.

76. Ellison, "Log Rolling," 42.

77. The absurd misunderstanding is a common motif in world folklore. English and North American examples are noted as motifs J1750–1849 in Ernest W. Baughman, *The Type and Motif Index of the Folktales of England and North America,* Indiana University Folklore Series no. 20 (The Hague: Mouton, 1966), 312–16.

78. Kathleen Stewart, "Nostalgia—A Polemic," *Cultural Anthropology* 3, no. 3 (1988): 227–41.

79. Vi Iund, "If the Little Owl Could Talk," *American Timberman and Trucker* 5 (April 1989): 8; Craig Jenkins, "Endangered Species," "Regular People," and "Middle Ground," on Craig Jenkins and Terry McKinnis, *Endangered Species,* audiocassette tape (Deadwood, Ore.: C&T Music, 1989); Bob Vickarious and Elmer Nichols, "Peter, Poor Peter," on Elmer Nichols, *Peter, Poor Peter,* audiocassette tape (Porthill, Idaho: Double Lazy V Music, 1988); Tigar Bell Band, Buzz Saw Band, and other artists, *Let the Yellow Ribbons Fly,* audiocassette tape (Roseburg, Ore.: Northwest Nashville Connections, 1989).

80. Pauline Greenhill, "'She Dwelt among the Untrodden Ways': Nostalgia and Folk Poetry in Ontario," *Journal of Folklore Research* 26, no. 3 (1989): 187–206.

23

The Poetic Tradition of the Gaucho

William Katra

No continent has a monopoly on cowboys and their art, for wherever a local beef industry has arisen to satisfy consumer demand a rural society and its poetic expression of life among horses and cattle will thrive. That is particularly true of the region of the Río de la Plata—the river separating Argentina and Uruguay. The area is endowed with some of the world's richest pasturelands and still preserves vast expanses of pampas, or open ranges, for its preponderant cattle industry. Accordingly, the region boasts a centuries-old tradition of gauchos (South American cowboys), gaucho verses, and an extensive repertoire of accompanying dances and music.[1]

Indeed, the gaucho poetry of the Río de la Plata region presents a case perhaps without precedent in the history of the West. Since the late nineteenth century, the poetic expression of a marginal group of sometimes illiterate ranch hands and range riders has been elevated to the status of a national literature. Poetry and song about horses, guitars, and pampa life predominate on the airwaves and at local fairs in the country's interior cities and rural areas. Based on personal observations from several trips, I suggest that the dedication of gaucho devotees in Argentina far surpasses even that of country-western fans in rural regions of the United States. In Argentina's beautiful capital city, Buenos Aires (for good reason nicknamed "the Paris of South America"), however, many individuals who have a European cultural orientation are offended by the association of their national culture with the "bumpkin" verses of one of its least progressive social groups. Yet surprisingly enough, even the most sophisticated social circles, and even the most recently arrived groups of European immigrants, contain men and women who enthusiastically celebrate the inviting sounds and symbols of rural life.

It is necessary to make certain distinctions because conceptions of who a gaucho is and what constitutes gaucho poetry have changed considerably since the 1800s. An excursion into the past can help reduce the grounds of these confusions.

First, although the history of the Río de la Plata region's export-oriented cattle industry goes back only two hundred years, its rural society and accompanying cultural expressions trace their roots at least as far back as the arrival of the Spanish in the sixteenth century. The traditional poetry of these early settlers closely followed, although in fragmented and contaminated form, the lyrical songs and short ballads (called in Spanish *romances*) then popular throughout the mother country.[2] It is understandable, then, that much of this original repertoire found comparable forms—but always with local adaptations—in the folk traditions of Venezuela, Mexico, and other former Spanish colonies with ranges and a viable cattle industry. In the central regions of Argentina, some of these compositions treated universal experiences such as love and religious devotion while perhaps the majority were inspired by the rural setting. What follows is a typical stanza that had many variants throughout northern Argentina. Note the eight-syllable lines, with the second and fourth repeating an *e-a* vowel (assonant) rhyme:

Ningún pobre puede ser	[No poor man could be rich
hombre de bien aunque quiera.	even if he chose to be so.
En faltándole el poder	Lacking the means for that change
es embarcación sin vela.	is like leaving port without a sail.][3]

In contrast to the poetry and song that would come later, these traditional poems were characterized by grammatically correct language, anonymous authorship, and oral transmission.

It was only toward the middle of the eighteenth century that a new strain of cowboy poetry began to arise that correlated with the emergence of the gaucho as a social class. The etymology of the word *gaucho,* although much disputed, is likely the corrupted form of *guacho,* the Hispanic equivalent of *wáhka* (orphan) in Quechua, the main indigenous language of Bolivia and Peru. The area of the pampas inland from Buenos Aires, with plentiful cattle and wide expanses of open ranges, gave rise to a voluntarily marginalized group of men who took considerable pride in their orphan status. Gauchos hailed from a variety of cultures and nationalities and included people of pure European descent, mestizos, blacks, and Indians. Linking all of them was a shared set of customs and values developed in response to their unstructured, egalitarian society at the margin of the law and their daily contact with physical dangers.

In the two and a half centuries since the Europeans arrived, wild horses and cattle had multiplied profusely on the open plains. Bountiful herds of unbranded animals now provided the gaucho's preferred means of transportation, a free and abundant food supply, and the bare essentials of clothing and shelter. A "gaucho ethos" characterized their attitudes as well as their songs: They were independent, courageous, haughty, defiant, and intoxicatingly free. While the more organized and better-educated rural society of Argentina's north continued singing the religious, chivalresque, and burlesque ballads that had direct links with the oral tradition of the Spanish peninsula, the gaucho's expression featured narrative ballads that exaggerated the power and ferocity of brave and clever heroes.[4]

The first documented reference to the existence of a "gaucho" poetry was in the 1770s, but it was Domingo F. Sarmiento (1811–88), writing some eighty years later, who provided the most authoritative description of what by then had become a widely practiced art.[5] According to Sarmiento, the gaucho poet was a kind of medieval bard or minstrel singer, endlessly traveling from region to region. In that primitive society his verses were almost always accompanied by dance and music, preferably of the guitar or its more primitive cousin, the *vihüela.* His arrival at a ranch was a special occasion for owner and hired hands alike, whom he would entertain in exchange for drinks or room and board. Two other sites for his performances were the postal stations and the *pulperías,* which were rural stores where menfolk gathered for socializing, drinking, and gambling at the end of the working day. Especially popular at this time was the *cielito,* which served the gaucho well as a poetic sharing of his miseries and anger over society's abuses. Note the intentionally archaic, deliberately mistaken language of the song:

Cuatro bacas hei juntado	[I wuz able to get four cows
A juerza de trabajar,	After much hard work,
Y agora que están gordas	And now that they're good 'n' fat
Ya me las quieren robar.	Someone'll rob me of 'em.
Cielito, cielo que sí,	Heavenly heaven, that's right
Oye cielo mis razones:	Listen to what I say:
Para amolar a los sonsos	To do away with such abuses
Son estas regoluciones.	We have these rebolutions.]

The gaucho singer offered to his largely illiterate public renditions of the region's anonymous poetic creations, but he was also a creator of verses in his own right. According to Sarmiento, the singer imitated medieval troubadour predecessors in reciting or singing long, balladlike compositions that chronicled "customs, history, and biography." He also possessed a repertoire of lyrical "popular poems in octosyllabic lines variously combined into stanzas of five lines, of ten, or of eight. Among them are many compositions of merit which show some inspiration and feeling." Most original of the gaucho poet's repertoire were his improvisations of "heavy, monotonous, and irregular" verse. This poetry favors the narration of adventures over "the expression of feeling" and is "replete with imagery relating to the open country, to the horse, and to the scenes of the wilderness, which makes it metaphorical and grandiose." The themes of these verses were equally original: "The Cantor [singer] intersperses his heroic songs with the tale of his own exploits. Unluckily his profession of Argentine bard does not shield him from the law. He can tell of a couple of stabs he has dealt, of one or two *misfortunes* (homicides!) of his, and of some horse or girl he has carried off."[6] Sarmiento recognized the uniqueness of the gaucho poet as a character type; other observers would praise gaucho compositions as the most original in the country's literature.

Not emphasized by Sarmiento was another aspect of the gaucho poet's craft, the *payada* (an improvised duel in verse). This form of lyrical challenge, according to wildly romanticized descriptions, was often concluded by combat with knives. A payada could be a monologue, but it was best when two versatile singers, pitted against each another, would improvise verses in the *cifra* or *milonga* forms in counterpoint fashion.[7] Although some researchers have traced the payada to remote origins in medieval Europe, others point to resemblances in the Indian traditions of Alaska, Mexico, and Argentina.[8] What is indisputable is the geographical limitation of the term and its derivatives to Argentina, Uruguay, and Chile. Also beyond argument is the relatively late popularization of the word *payada*, which was not even registered by Sarmiento in 1845. Three decades later, José Hernández (1834–86) used the verb *payamos* only once during the course of his long narrative poem *El Gaucho Martín Fierro* and avoided using the noun *payador* (improviser) as a substitute for his preferred noun: cantor.

Although both Sarmiento and Hernández were authoritative witnesses of the oral poetry recited on the Argentine pampas in the nineteenth century, they were also participants in the emergence of a new form of expression treating character types and topics relevant to the countryside but composed by society's educated elite. Now, scant written traces survive of the orally transmitted poetry of centuries past. The greater part of that known to the world as Argentina's and Uruguay's excellent "cowboy" poetry is actually works written in the *gauchesque* (imitation gaucho) style.

The emergence of the gauchesque literary tradition in the nineteenth century occurred against a backdrop of significant political, social, and economic transformations, especially the spreading hegemony of urban elites, with their mission of establishing a centralized state. In the eyes of the urban population, the customs and traditions of the rural folk, especially the gaucho, were generally the object of derision and scorn. But nationalistic politics combined with an interest in folk culture and the past derived from popular romanticism to bring other contending voices to the fore.

In the century's first few decades, Bartolomé Hidalgo (1788–1822), a soldier-poet serving the populist revolutionary movement originating in the Banda Oriental (literally the "East Bank," or today's Uruguay), composed and distributed one-page patriotic verses using the gaucho idiom. Certainly, one of his motivations was to have his poems circulate orally to "teach by entertaining" and therefore win over the illiterate classes to the emancipation cause against Spain by instilling within them a sense of patriotism. But his well-crafted, witty verses also attracted an urban readership entertained by exotic gaucho protagonists with a heavy rural dialect. Hidalgo was the first to popularize rhymed dialogue between two rural protagonists, and his represention of a perplexed gaucho's first contact with the modern city was to have many imitators. One of these poems begins:

—Y usté, ¿no jué a la ciudá a ver las fiestas este año? —¡No me lo recuerde, amigo! Si supiera, ¡voto al diablo!, lo que me pasa, ¡por Cristo!	[—An' din'cha go to the city ta see the festivals thiz year? —Don' remin' me of it, friend! The Devil wuz in on that one! If ya knew what I went through. Kee-ryst!]

Although there was a long precedent in the Spanish-speaking world of learned poets imitating rural or lower-class language and forms, Hidalgo's verses constitute the earliest printed body of gauchesque poetry in the Río de la Plata region.

Most gauchesque poets following Hidalgo continued with the practice of placing their art at the service of politics. After 1829, Juan Gualberto Godoy (1793–1864) circulated his compositions of "poesía gauchipolítica" that were flavored by his militant opposition to Argentina's dictator, Juan Manuel de Rosas. For the next thirty years the inspired poetry of Hilario Ascasubi (1807–71) dominated the literary scene. His most famous gauchesque poems, *Paulino Lucero* and *Aniceto el Gallo,* are literary masterpieces in their own right and also served the poet's objective of promoting progressive values among the rural masses and discrediting the principles of federalism, which in Argentina continued to isolate the provinces and maintain a political system based on powerful personalities. Also worthy of mention is Estanislao del Campo (1834–80), whose *Fausto* (1866), a famous gaucho rendition of the Faust legend, further popularized the genre among urban readers. Finally, José Hernández's long narrative poem *The Gaucho Martín Fierro,* published in two parts in 1871 and 1879, was not only the high point of politically inspired gauchesque verse but has also been universally acclaimed as one of the literary masterpieces of Argentina and the West.

Martín Fierro was political writing at its best. Hernández's cause was the defense of traditional rural society and its gaucho population that was threatened by encroaching modernity. His protagonist, the poor, illiterate Fierro, is a victim of such forces. During the course of the poetic narrative he becomes a *gaucho malo* after his forced recruitment and cruel treatment in the corrupt frontier army, the expropriation of his squatter ranchhouse by a justice of the peace, the dispersion of his family, and a duel in guitars and knives from which he escapes with only his life.

Hernández, like his protagonist, had heroic traits. Both struggled nobly for a cause that was destined to fail. If the poem paid tribute to the vanquished gaucho on the vanishing frontier, it also signaled this figure's ascension to major protagonist in the country's emerging national literature. The poem's first stanza majestically captures the anguish of the gaucho singer:

Aquí me pongo a cantar al compás de la vihüela que el hombre que lo desvela una pena estrordinaria, como la ave solitaria con el cantar se consuela.	[Here I come to sing to the beat of my guitar: because a man who is kept from sleep by an uncommon sorrow comforts himself with singing like a solitary bird.][9]

The poem's success resulted from its ability to straddle both the traditional and cultured literary traditions and from its appeal both to the unschooled or semiliterate rural society and to an educated, urban reading public. The poem masterfully reproduces the archaic variant of Spanish spoken in the countryside several decades earlier but without exaggerating that dialect's deformative characteristics. Its superb verses build upon the themes and forms of the region's fertile oral tradition and steer clear of theatricalized, picturesque descriptions that mar most other literary incursions by educated poets into the gaucho world. Understandably, the poem had an instant and lasting appeal. One important commentator early in the twentieth century said, "[T]here does not exist a household in the Argentine countryside that lacks a guitar and a copy of *Martín Fierro.* Those who don't know how to read learn it by ear; those who can only haltingly sound out syllables use the poem as their first reading text."[10]

The poem's reception by the region's rural population was instantaneous and fervid, and its popularity continues unchallenged even now. But three decades would have to pass after its publication before the educated groups of the region's cities would—at first belatedly, later more enthusiastically—embrace the work as the highest expression of Argentine—and, more broadly, Río de la Plata—society. Such sudden and dramatic changes in literary taste are usually responses to extraliterary factors, so to explain this gauchesque poem's definitive and universal acceptance is also to explain in large part the continuing appeal of the gaucho as a subject and symbol of Argentina's and Uruguay's national cultural expression.

In the thirty-odd years that separated the diffusion of Hernández's pace-setting verses and the canonization of *Martín Fierro,* the humid pampas that stretch three hundred miles inland from the region's great coastal cities had been definitively transformed. Modernity had arrived, with its railroads and barbed wire; sheep for the production of wool quickly displaced cattle in many areas. Changing world markets caused landowners to devote as much as a third of the region's total acreage to wheat production by 1910. In short, the proud gauchos who once rode the ranges were increasingly forced to find employment as peons or farm hands. In addition, droves of European—predominantly Italian—immigrants first crowded the cities, then displaced the old-time *criollo* population, that is the blacks, Indians, mestizos, and those of European descent who were the predominant social and ethnic groups in the countryside. These changes were especially important because the region of the humid pampas had been the principal setting for gaucho myth and history during the preceding two centuries. In this region the majority of historical figures upon whom the country's great cowboy literature and poetry had been modeled had lived, worked, and struggled.

Paradoxically, while the gaucho was being transformed from a free, itinerant range rider into a domesticated farm or ranch hand, a literature celebrating a romanticized version of the gaucho was thriving. Between 1890 and 1920, this criollo literature and its accompanying symbols were fervently embraced not only by the region's remaining rural population, now with rudimentary reading skills, but also by readers from the burgeoning cities, whose personal lives were totally unconnected to the world of the countryside. The reasons for the seductiveness of that criollo culture can only be speculated upon. First, the cities' conservative oligarchy, out of fear of losing its political monopoly, denounced previous policies that had sought the extermination of the gaucho as a social class and reevaluated its previous condemnation of any non-European forms of expression.[11] A wholly different set of circumstances affected a second urban grouping, the swollen ranks of immigrants and their recent descendants. One reseacher points to their subliminal need to embrace the symbols of a new cultural identity in the light of their own geographical and ethnic displacement.[12] The popularity of a romanticized literature built upon the anachronistic gaucho is also linked to the reading public's search for cultural roots in the face of the terrible world depression of the 1890s and the disillusionment with modernity throughout the West that both preceded and followed World War I, the "war to end all wars."

Regardless of the reasons, the enthusiasm for poetry treating the gaucho was genuine and near-universal in the Río de la Plata region. New forms of diffusion arose: dime-store novels, the phonograph, the circus, and the theater. The cities also witnessed a curious new cultural phenomenon, the rapid spread of *centros criollos* (criollo centers)—there were as many as 268 in Buenos Aires alone at the turn of the century—where primarily young people of modest means gathered to celebrate the culture of the pampas and to propagate through their dress, writing, and activities a positive attitude toward the region's old traditions. At last, gaucho poetry had arrived—or rather poetry about gauchos now figured among the predominant strains of the region's mass media discourse.

By the 1890s the term *gauchesco* ("gauchesque") was generally accepted to distinguish this new literary and cultural phenomenon from the earlier popular, often anonymous verses sung by and for gauchos. A similar distinction began to be made between folk poetry and a nostalgic and nationalistic *nativista* ("nativist") literature written in standard Spanish, like Rafael Obligado's *Santos Vega.* But there has always been disagreement in the application of these terms. For example, some critics now use the term *classic gauchesque* to give priority of date and artistry to those works written up to the time of *Martín Fierro,* whose contents supposedly reflect the linguistic, cultural, and social world actually existing at the time of composition. That distinction also assigns lower prestige to subsequent gauchesque works, described as the products of impoverished imaginations or of the will to deform and sensationalize.[13]

During the twentieth century the transformation of the Argentine countryside has been dramatic, as have been the resulting changes in the art and practice of gaucho poetry. Cattle-raising still remains the principal economic activity in the region of the humid pampas, with up to 80 percent of the land in some districts dedicated exclusively to this activity. Productive methods are largely mechanized, however, and wheat and wool production rival cattle for predominance.[14] For these reasons, it is apparent that other regions now offer an even greater claim as spiritual centers for the country's traditional cattle culture and gaucho life: the entire northwest of Argentina, which includes parts or all of the provinces of Córdoba, Santiago del Estero, Salta, and Tucumán; the vast humid plains of Entre Ríos and Corrientes; and the northern half of Uruguay. In these regions, large landholdings abound, the central role of cattle-raising in the local economy is unchallenged, and the gaucho still constitutes a distinct social grouping if not class. Not to be forgotten is the special case of Patagonia, with its vast plains in the southernmost part of Argentina, where marginal soil and cold, arid climatic conditions make grazing sheep the only feasible economic activity and where rural society and corresponding cultural expressions still prevail.

These regions still boast of large, unfenced ranges that depend upon the labor of horse-mounted gauchos; rural society thrives, although in altered forms. First, many cattle producers or ranch hands now spend as much time working on agricultural tasks—repairing farm machinery, planting, and harvesting corn or alfalfa crops—as they do with traditional tasks having to do with the care and marketing of range animals. Second, for many tasks the role of the horse has been deemphasized. Trucks and motorcycles transport hands to distant pastures, and trained dogs and movable electric fences position herds on desirable grazing. Third, readily available transportation, added to the imperatives and attractions of city living, have accelerated the march to the city and the corresponding depopulation of the countryside. Wherever possible, owners and ranch hands usually prefer to raise their families in the nearby cities and commute daily or weekly to rural worksites.

The dramatic decrease in the population of the countryside has resulted in a decreased visibility of rural culture and less artistic expression in rural society. Especially relevant is the now-marginal importance of the late fall or early winter "roundup," which usually takes place in June and July. Historically, the roundup was the most important event of the rural calendar, not only for the purposes of *apartes y marcaciones* (separating, branding, and castrating the male calves) but also for recreation and celebration of gaucho song and poetry. Accounts exist of how, a century or more ago, ranchers and ranch hands joined by itinerant gauchos would gather near a pulpería or on a very large *estancia* for eight to ten days to complete the work at hand and in their spare moments drink, race horses, throw the *taba* (a marked cow vertebra used for gambling), dance, play guitars, and recite poetry.[15] Today, fences, earmarking devices, vaccination guns, and the like reduce the complexity of the same work tasks, which are now easily accomplished in a couple of days by the owners themselves or with the assistance of a few permanent employees. The traditional occasion that served best in the past to celebrate gaucho song and poetry has all but ceased to exist.

However, this loss has been partly compensated for by the rise of new events and institutions that provide rural society with opportunities to congregate and celebrate its culture. First, each rural school throughout the region sponsors fund-raising activities on a regular basis in order to pay for building upkeep, purchase of new materials, and funding of the student lunch program. Local musicians and poets perform during the slack moments of these dances, horse races, and soccer competitions. Second, in the late summer or early fall (Holy Week is most popular in Uruguay), each city, district, or province sponsors its yearly criollo (rodeo), which features competition in bull riding and calf roping. Meanwhile, the public roams freely under the shade of the trees, indulging in savory barbequed beef and sausages and listening to the music and verses of the local performers. Third, the ever-present pulpería of yesteryear has been replaced by the *dispensa* (store), which by late afternoon and evening doubles as a bar and social gathering place for the adult male population. Here, the billiards table, *truco* (a vigorous criollo gambling game played with cards), and, in recent years, the television set are the main attractions, but on occasion a transient guitarist or a local musician will entertain the small group that enthusiastically welcomes any novelty in its otherwise routine existence. Finally, every birthday, graduation, first communion, or national holiday provides the pretext for celebration among family and friends, with extended families coming together from distant parts at least once a year.

On such occasions many rural folk still enthusiastically don the traditional garb of the gaucho of old, with the broad-brimmed hat, the bandanna, the wide leather belt with as many as two hundred inlaid silver coins, the baggy riding pants (*bombachas*), and the black leather knee-high riding boots. Lodged inside the belt at the back, they carry a silver-handled knife with a blade varying from six to fourteen inches in length, still useful for many ranch tasks and indispensable for consuming one's share of *asado* (barbequed beef). The deliberate anachronism of these gaucho admirers and imitators has limits, however. Except for planned historical representations, one rarely sees a gaucho dressed in the primitive, diaperlike *chiripá.* And only in museums and special collections have I admired the legendary *boleadoras,* the leather rope with three strands tied to round stones that was whirled and then thrown by the mounted rider. Before the advent of firearms, it was used most effectively to trip or disable the legs of a horse, steer, or *ñandú* (a small pampa ostrich).

In the great majority of rural areas dedicated to the cattle industry, in addition to the small urban centers in near proximity, gaucho and gauchesque poetry have continued to thrive. Each generation continues to produce new singers and performers who proudly reinterpret the traditional repertoire learned from their elders and attempt to incorporate the tones and themes of that tradition into their own original poetry. As might be expected, not all of the gaucho poets of today are involved in the day-to-day activity of raising cattle or riding the ranges. Indeed, it is understandable that many of the important poetic and musical interpreters of the country's rural heritage now live in urban areas where they find a means of living by their musical craft, a situation comparable to that of some American cowboy poets. Although not technically "gauchos" in their own lives, many have experienced at first hand the ways of the countryside in their youth; others are a mere generation removed from the life of horses, cattle, and the range and are active participants in gaucho culture by virtue of a close relative.

In spite of ever-encroaching urban culture and the acoustic bombardment of imported music, the allure of the gaucho, past and present, in these settings continues to dominate the collective imagination. One payador of Italian heritage, who grew up in the horse-and-cattle environment of a small town in the province of Entre Ríos, indicates that the discovery of *Martín Fierro* in the early 1950s triggered his conversion: "I felt that I was speaking through *Martín Fierro.* . . . it imaginatively transported me to rural life and its diverse circumstances, which are hardly ever happy."[16] From this experience came the purchase of a guitar, the tuning of its strings, and experimentation with gaucho-style verses. The payador spent many youthful hours in the company of cowhands and traveling minstrels while he honed his skills in the difficult craft of verse improvisation. In his case, a wealth of enrapturing childhood memories was ignited by his appreciation for gaucho literature in addition to the allure of the local song forms, the *zambas* and *cuecas* endlessly broadcast on the local radio station. All of these led to his decision to devote his creative energies toward the preservation and re-creation of traditional gaucho poetry.

Present-day *payadores* are masters of a dying form of poetic art. They take pride in their loyalty to traditions, although many have long since forsaken the traditional rural garb when they perform. The classic literature leaves the impression of a sense of rivalry existing among gaucho improvisers of old, but that is not now the case. More common is their sense of brotherhood and accomplishment when they have the opportunity to perform, especially when they "confront" one another in the fashion of the old dueling counterpoint.

Modernity has left a mark on many of these poetic duels in the form of judges and a specific rating system (normal criteria: stage presence, eloquence, knowledge and development of theme, meter and rhyme, musical accompaniment, and creative spontaneity). What remains is the payador's enthusiasm for impressing his public with the philosophical and poetic beauty of his improvised verses and the music and rhythm of the milonga, the most typical musical form, which has octosyllabic lines with a consonant rhyme scheme grouped in stanzas of six, eight, ten, or twelve lines. Being a spontaneous poetry, it generally lacks the polish of that created for a reading public. Nevertheless, some of these verses have found their way to the printed page:

Voy a cantar por decir,
en unión de tierra y gente;
porque el verso es la vertiente
de cuanto traigo conmigo:
Yo no soy más que un amigo
que habla lo que piensa y siente.

El sentir es del pensar;
y, en distintas ocasiones,
se piensan las situaciones
según sea conveniencia:
Aunque también la conciencia
toma parte en las razones.

[Singing is my means for speaking out,
in front of a land and a people;
because poetry is like a spring
gushing forth all I have within:
I'm nothing more than a friend
who talks of what he thinks and feels.

One has to feel one's thoughts;
and, on different occasions,
depending on its appropriateness
one has to think of a situation:
Although the conscience also
plays a part in one's reasoning.][17]

Whereas relatively few individuals continue the demanding art of the payada, every town or rural zone seems to have its handful of local artists. Townfolk and countryside residents continue to celebrate the ever-flowing stream of gauchesque verses about mounted protagonists and romanticized rural events of a century ago, even though a more rigorous criticism would react against the exaggerated language and stylized themes. Regardless, this type of poetry lives on, and it is the obvious choice of a large segment of the population. One contemporary poet humorously depicts a gaucho protagonist enmeshed in an unpleasant love affair:

¡La pucha que da calor	[That gol-darned hussy
esa china sinvergüensa!	has really done it again!
Le van a dejar la trensa	She deserves a whipping
como fleco di arriador.	like you'd give to 'n ornery mule.
Me parese qu'es mejor	I reckon 'twas wise to get out o' town
que rumbé ya pa otro pago,	an' stay put for a bit,
sinó v'haser estrago	if not I'd raise a ruckus
d'esa Peloche, y al hoyo	about that Peloche,
la v'a mandar algún crioyo	I'd send some dude to the grave
que s'encuentre con un trago.	if I'd caught 'im offerin' her a drink.][18]

Coexisting with the gauchesque tradition in the range areas and small towns of the interior are lyrical verses of *nativista* (local) intention. Let there be no doubt that the sentiment of present-day poets for the sights and symbols of the countryside is as sincere as it is passionate. Thousands upon thousands of poems—some good, most enjoyable, all authentic in their sentiment—have been written on a limited number of traditional themes: to honor the local town, one's favorite mount, a patriotic figure, one's mother, or a beloved schoolteacher; to celebrate youth, springtime, and love; to remember an enraptured gallop across the wild countryside; to sweetly moan the departure or absence of a loved one; and to recall aesthetically the solitude of the ranges or a favorite haunt. The best of this expression avoids sentimentality in its imaginative images. The following verses lyrically re-create the emergence of a poetic voice:

Llevo un tiempo de chicharras	[I carry hours of crickets
sobre la piel	on my bare arm
agobiada de silencios.	fatigued by silences.
Aguardo la primavera	I await springtime
al amparo del vientre de la tierra	protected by the womb of the earth
para madurar en vuelo.	my forces maturing for flight.][19]

Characteristic of almost all payada, gauchesque, and nativista poetry is its relatively small radius of diffusion; it belongs to a decentralized tradition with thousands of rural and small-town practitioners. Its themes are local, and few if any of its creators would ever aspire to more than a provincial distribution. In contrast to this is the relatively new form of gaucho poetry called *folklore* (foke-low′-ray), which is intimately tied to the rise of the radio and television industries and whose performers mesmerize national and even international audiences. A cult has grown up around this commercial celebration of horse and cattle culture and its records, radio programs, and rural festivals, with famous *conjuntos* (singing groups) like the Fronterizos and Los de Salta and especially solo performers such as Atahualpa Yupanqui, Jorge Cafrune, Mercedes Sosa, and scores of others.

Yupanqui is one of the most celebrated of *folklore* poets; his poetry and songs reflect the rural culture of Argentina's northwestern regions. The fact that in recent years he has enjoyed striking success on the concert circuit and in record and cassette sales does not diminish the authenticity of his craft. He is perhaps the region's best example of a genuine gaucho who used his musical talent and experience to become a successful popular entertainer. As he explains the magnetizing effect of the primitive countryside and its cowboy culture upon his sensitivities, "The days of my infancy passed . . . from astonishment to . . . revelation. I was born in the countryside, and I grew up before a horizon of neighs and whinnies. . . . All that world, the peace and combat in my veins between Indians, Basques, and gauchos, determined my moments of happiness and surprise, stimulated my instincts of youthful freedom, and guided me in creating a language for dialoguing with the marsh grasses and streams." Possessed with this spirit, he avidly absorbed the songs and poems of the country folk: "[W]ith the last light of the afternoon . . . the guitars of the pampas began their ancient witchcraft, knitting a web of emotions and memories with unforgettable themes."[20]

Many of Yupanqui's poems, generally accompanied by the music of his own guitar, depict the Northwest's arid, wild expanses:

Pasamos la noche
rodeándolo al fuego
Luces de esperanza . . .
sombras de recuerdos . . .
    La aurora, sangrando
    como un corazón . . .
    A ensillar de nuevo
    que falta un tirón . . . !
Canta que te canta,
camino a los valles . . .
que esta pena mía
no la sabe nadie!

[We passed the night
around the campfire
Sparks of hope . . .
shadows of memories . . .
    The bleeding dawn
    like my own heart . . .
    Saddle up once again
    only a short stretch to go . . . !
The trail into the valley
sings, it sings to you . . .
this suffering I feel
nobody else knows!][21]

The relatively crude verses of another Yupanqui poem would never find their way into the literary anthologies of a cultured urban readership. Nevertheless, the poet succeeds in communicating an authentic affection for his horses and the region of his childhood:

Tuve una majadita
de hocicos negros,
la cuidé varios años
por esos cerros
allá en San Juan.
Y por senderos criollos
con mi majada,
pastoriaba mis cuecas
y mis tonadas
allá en San Juan.
Sanjuanina—mi majada—
tu recuerdo ¡ay señora!
vivirá entre los cerros
y las quebradas
allá en San Juan.

[I had a small horse herd
all with black snouts
I raised them for several years
among those rolling hills
far away in San Juan.
And along country trails
with my small herd,
I led my cueca songs to pasture
along with my verses
far away in San Juan.
This memory—so long ago—
of my San Juan herd
will live among the rolling hills
and deep valleys
far away in San Juan.]

In contrast to the payadoresque, nativista, and gauchesque verses, the commercial medium demands a poetry of relatively accessible themes that lend themselves to a brief, memorable elaboration. Traditional themes predominate: the injustice of poverty, the beautiful solitude of a pampa setting, or the gaucho's faithful mount. Also prevalent is the age-old theme of anguished love, as communicated in a zamba written and interpreted by Horacio Guaraní:

Porque me has visto llorar
no creas que he de callar
mi guitarra también llora
y nadie pudo callar.
Porque me has visto llorar
dirás que soy un cobarde
ayer lloré por mi madre
y hoy por ti vuelvo a llorar.

[Because you have seen me cry
don't think that I wouldn't start again
my guitar is also crying
and nobody can make it stop.
Because you have seen me cry
you might say that I'm a coward

yesterday I cried on account of my mother
and today I cry again, but because of you.][22]

Over the past several decades, the cowboy poetry of South America has extended its range and broadened its practice. The gaucho of yesteryear, riding the open ranges and battling corrupt justices of the peace and marauding bands of Indians, has passed into history. But a sizable rural population still exists. They embrace the ethos of the historical gaucho with their own love of rural life and a comparable aspiration for freedom and economic justice. In moments of festivity or leisure, the singers and poets among them continue to renovate, recite, read, and celebrate the traditional forms of their region's gaucho poetry. This "popular poetry," in its nativist, payadoresque, and gauchesque variants, still thrives with the fervor of the past.

Notes

1. Studies available in English that treat the South American—but more specifically Argentine—gaucho are William Henry Hudson, *Far Away and Long Ago: A History of My Early Life* (New York: E. P. Dutton, 1918); Domingo Faustino Sarmiento, *Life in the Argentine Republic in the Days of the Tyrants; or, Civilization and Barbarism,* trans. Mrs. Horace Mann (Spanish ed., 1845; English ed., 1868), (New York: Hafner, 1971); Richard Slatta, *Gauchos and the Vanishing Frontier* (Lincoln: University of Nebraska Press, 1983); and Edward Larocque Tinker, *The Horsemen of the Americas and the Literature They Inspired,* 2d rev. ed. (Austin: University of Texas Press, 1967). An excellent bibliography of the best studies (principally in Spanish) about the gaucho and his poetry has been prepared by Rodolfo A. Borello in *Trayectoria de la poesía gauchesca,* ed. Horacio J. Becco et al. (Buenos Aires: Plus Ultra, 1977), 149–64. For a summary of gaucho literature, see also Arturo Torres-Ríóseco, *The Epic of Latin-American Literature* (New York: Oxford University Press, 1942), 133–67.

2. The Iberian medieval roots of Argentina's popular tradition have been thoroughly investigated by Argentina's great collectors of traditional poetry, Juan Alfonso Carrizo, Juan Draghi Lucero, and the musicologist Carlos Vega.

3. This translation, and the rest in the chapter, are by the author.

4. Juan Alfonso Carrizo, "Nuestra poesía popular," *Humanidades* 15 (La Plata: 1927): 241–342.

5. Sarmiento, Argentina's famous writer-editor-statesman, would serve as the country's president from 1866 to 1872. His *Life in the Argentine Republic* (1845) is a Latin American literary classic, not only on account of its unsurpassed romantic descriptions of gauchos and rural life but also for its impassioned attack against the Argentine tyrant Juan Manuel de Rosas.

6. Sarmiento, *Life in the Argentine Republic,* 51–52.

7. According to Ventura R. Lynch, *Folklore bonaerense* (Buenos Aires: Lajouane, 1953), 49, the cifra was typical of the gaucho payador who emphasized serious recitations, whereas the milonga offered greater rhythmic and musical possibilities to the more educated singer. In both, the eight-syllable line predominated. But while the cifra had no determined stanza length or rhyme, the milonga featured a variety of strophes (six, eight, four, and ten lines were the most frequent) in which assonance (vowel rhyme) predominated, with consonance on occasion.

8. Respectively, Ismael Moya, *El arte de los payadores* (Buenos Aires: Berruti, 1959), and Marcelino M. Román, *Itinerario del payador* (Buenos Aires: Lautaro, 1957).

9. José Hernández, *The Gaucho Martín Fierro,* bilingual edition, trans. C. E. Ward (New York: State University of New York Press, 1967), 2–3. English translations also exist by Henry Alfred Holmes (New York: Hispanic Institute in the United States, 1948) and Walter Owen (London: Blackwell, 1933).

10. Leopoldo Lugones, *El payador* (1916), (Buenos Aires: Huemul, 1972), 185.

11. Rodolfo Borello, "Introducción a la poesía gauchesca," in *Trayectoria de la poesía gauchesca,* 68. The essays in this volume by Becco, Borello, Adolfo Prieto, and Félix Weinberg provide perhaps the most concise and comprehensive overview of the topic.

12. Adolfo Prieto, *El discurso criollista en la formación de la Argentina moderna* (Buenos Aires: Sudamericana, 1988), 98, 131.

13. Carlos Alberto Leumann, *La literatura gauchesca y la poesía gaucha* (Buenos Aires: Raigal, 1953), 7, 29; Emilio A. Coni, *El gaucho: Argentina, Brasil, Uruguay* (Buenos Aires: Solar, 1986).

14. Preston E. James, *[Geography of] Latin America,* 3d ed. (New York: Odyssey Press, 1959), 341–45. This source reveals that at least fifty mid-century families in the Province of Buenos Aires—which coincides more or less with the area of the humid pampas—owned more than seventy-five thousand acres each.

15. Juan Carlos Vedoya, *Fierro y las expoliación del gaucho* (Tandil: Universidad Nacional del Centro de la Provincia de Buenos Aires, 1986), describes one such gathering as remembered by an eighty-four-year-old man in an interview in 1916 (43).

16. Adolfo F. Cosso, *Camino del payador (memorias y versos)* (Gualeguay: n.p., [1983]), 10.

17. Cosso, *Camino del payador,* 99.

18. Guillermo Cuadri, *Entre volcano y las musas* (Minas: Waldemar M. Cuadri, n.d.), 218.

19. Roberto A. Romani, *Aurora del canto (poemas)* (Santa Fe: Colmegna, 1985), 13.

20. Atahualpa Yupanqui, *El canto del viento* (Buenos Aires: Honegger, 1965), 13, 15.

21. This and the following poem, entitled "Camino a los valles" and "La majadita," are from the pamphlet *Ritmos del Ande: Cancionero Popular* (Buenos Aires: Bona, 1975), 24, 46.

22. Horacio Guaraní, "Porque me has visto llorar," in the pamphlet *Grandes canciones folklóricas,* no. 4 (Buenos Aires: Continental, 1986), 16.

24

Australian Bush Poetry

Keith McKenry

It is just two hundred years since the first European settlements were established in Australia as toeholds on the fertile east coast of the continent. Those toeholds today are major cities, within which resides the great bulk of the continent's eighteen million population. Outside these and other cities on the coastal fringe lies the bush, and in the far reaches of the bush, "beyond the black stump," lies the outback, the Never Never, altogether some three million square miles of grassland, forest, desert, and semidesert, the locale of Australian legend.

The legend is personified by the cattle drover, the stockman driving vast herds long distances through arid, dangerous country. In times past, drovers were true pioneers, opening vast tracts of land to a burgeoning new industry. In many cases the open rangelands they sought were thousands of miles from settled districts, and the movement of stock overland was a task that beggars the modern imagination. In March 1883, for example, the MacDonald brothers left Goulburn in New South Wales with five hundred head of cattle on what was to become the world's longest overlanding exploit; three years and 3,500 miles later they reached their destination in western Australia's remote northwest, where they established Fossil Downs Station.[1]

By the late 1880s, cattle and sheep stations—a station is equivalent to a large ranch—had been established across the continent. Some, like Wave Hill in the Northern Territory, were huge, ranging over six thousand square miles, their homesteads lonely outposts hundreds of miles from the nearest township. Others, in the comparatively fertile southeast, where rivers flowed all year round and crops could be grown, were small and capable of being traversed on horseback in less than a day.

These days, ownership of many outback stations has passed from individual families—descendants of the pioneer settlers—to large corporations and banks. Cattle are no longer driven overland to market along mighty stock routes but rather travel in huge road trains (cattle trucks) on a network of beef roads. Even on the stations themselves, stockmen and boundary riders sometimes prefer motor bikes (or even ultralight aircraft) to horses. But still the legend survives.

Australia is one of the most urbanized and (following migration from Europe and elsewhere) culturally diverse nations in the world. That, however, hasn't lessened the maintenance among large sections of the community of a national myth based on idealized images of the bush and of the men and women who live there. Nowhere is this more evident than in the enduring national affection for the poetry and poets of the bush and in ordinary Australians' continuing use of the simple rhyming forms of bush poetry as a means of self-expression. The nation's joys and disappointments, loves and loathings, frustrations and aspirations, humor and social and political opinions, they're all there in verse. It's the tradition, and the tradition's strong.

Beginnings

The early poets of the bush cleave neatly into two groups. First, there were those who sought the high road, aspiring to produce fine poetry in the shadow of the English masters. Their efforts were often, if nothing else, grotesquely elegant, as ill-fitted to the Australian environment as were the early attempts by colonial artists to depict Australia, its colors and its light, with an English palette.[2]

The second stream of verse also took some time to adapt to the new setting, but the transition was less difficult. These were the broadsides, the street literature, printed ballad sheets about current events that were hawked about the streets of the infant colonies and recited or sung to popular tunes of the day. This group included many of the earliest Australian folk ballads, such as "The Convict Maid," "Van Dieman's Land," and "Bold Jack Donahue."[3]

There were in fact many ballads about the bushranger (highwayman) Jack Donahue, an Irish convict who in 1828 took to the bush around Sydney and evaded capture for nearly three years before being shot dead in a police ambush.[4] Several of these ballads traveled to the Northern Hemisphere, and two have been collected in oral tradition in the United States.[5]

At least one of the Donahue ballads was the work of the convict Francis MacNamara, better known as Frank the Poet, a prolific and fearless rhymester renowned for his capacity to extemporize, who never let self-interest or survival stand in the way of a good line. Frank was a true folk poet, a number of his works passing around in handwritten form and entering the oral tradition. He is best known for his magnificent Swift-like satire "The Convict's Tour of Hell," which he wrote in 1839 while working as an assigned servant shepherding stock in the bush of the Hunter Valley, and for the ballad "The Convict's Arrival." This latter piece circulated widely and was eventually transformed by the folk process into one of the finest and best-known Australian folk ballads, "Moreton Bay."[6]

The gold rushes of the 1850s transformed colonial society, attracting fortune hunters from all over Europe as well as from China and the United States. Business boomed; there was wealth (and its bedmate poverty) everywhere. All of a sudden the goldfields and cities attracted professional entertainers from northern climes, veterans mainly of the music-hall circuits, in a gold rush of their own.

These entertainers brought to Australia popular melodies, songs, and recitations from overseas, which having landed often took hold, some serving as rootstock for Australian adaptations, others providing melodies for new texts or models for entirely new works. Some entertainers commented in song and verse on colonial society, and their best compositions circulated rapidly through word of mouth, printed sheets, periodicals, and songbooks. The most notable of these performers was the inimitable Charles Thatcher, a master entertainer and humorist. A number of his compositions entered the oral tradition, not only in Australia but also in New Zealand.[7]

Thus, by the early 1860s there was firmly established in Australia a body of (mostly execrable) colonial verse modeled on the style of the "major" English poets along with popular verse and songs evolving from the broadside and folk traditions of Britain and Ireland and reinforced by the repertoire of the music hall. This occurred at a time when literacy among adult white Australians was becoming nearly universal and when the boundaries of settlement were spreading into the country's inhospitable interior along a rapidly expanding pastoral frontier. The scene, therefore, was set for the emergence of a truly naturalized school of Australian verse, the bush ballad.

The Bush Ballad

The ballad is, of course, an ancient form, and in the mid-1800s even such eminent English poets as Tennyson and Browning used it. Small wonder, then, that colonial poets, even in respectable circles, tried their hand as balladists. They soon discovered the racy, narrative style and rhythmic, easily memorized form fitted colonial life, especially bush life, splendidly.

Further inspiration came from across the Pacific in the form of contemporary poetry and stories by Bret Harte and others about the California goldfields and the American West. A few early bush ballads even contained Wild West–inspired ideas and language. Witness, for example, the following account of mayhem at an Australian outback station:

> Then he started to go ratty, and began to fancy that he
> Was an Injun on the warpath; so he plaited a lassoo,
> Shaved and smeared his face with raddle, and knocked up a greenhide
>   saddle,
> After creeping on his belly through the grass a mile or two.
>
> Then he decked himself in feathers, and went out and scalped some
>   wethers—
> Just to give himself a lesson in the sanguinary art;
> Sammy then dug up the hatchet, chased a snake but couldn't catch it,
> Killed his dog, lassooed a turkey, scalped the cat and made a start.
> . . . .
> Next, the wood-and-water joey fell a victim to his bowie,
> And the boss's weeping widow got a gash from ear to ear,
> And you should have seen his guiver when he scalped the bullock driver
> And made openings for a horse-boy, servant-maid and overseer.[8]

This poem, so indebted to the most sensational treatments of the American West, exhibits its misunderstanding by rhyming "joey" with "bowie"—to American ears a nonrhyme that calls attention to an uncomfortable intermixture of Australian and American idiom. In any event, the words *bowie* (knives), *Injuns,* and *scalpings* are foreign to Australia and Australian terminology, but then the author clearly was using some poetic license. The ballad is also richly larded with Australian slang and occupational terminology. "Ratty" here means "mad"; raddle is a colored ochre used for marking sheep; "knock up" means to construct hastily; a greenhide saddle is one built of fresh, untanned leather; wethers are rams castrated when young; a joey is a young kangaroo but here refers to a child who fetches wood and water; "guiver" means fantastic talk or explanations; and bullocks are steers used for plowing or pulling wagons.

In another instance, the early bush balladist John Farrell had his unhappy hero use his last bullet to spare his loving wife a fate worse than death when their remote homestead was attacked by savages—and if the setting was the Australian bush instead of Wyoming and the homestead's attackers Aborigines rather than Indians, you still could clearly hear in metaphor the bugle of the cavalry in the distance. (In a cruel twist, Farrell's hero was then hung as a wife-murderer by his rescuers, the moral being that he should have had faith and trusted in the Lord's salvation. These were Victorian times.)[9]

Such borrowings of foreign idiom and ideas were rare, however, and the bush ballad—temper democratic, bias Australian—quickly became established as an acknowledged literary form, the epitome of Australia's emerging national consciousness. Although the bush ballad had no single parent, it is perhaps fitting that the honor of leading the new ballad school should fall to an expatriate Englishman, a skilled horseman named Adam Lindsay Gordon. Gordon was a reckless youth who, banished to the colonies by despairing parents in 1853, tried his hand as a mounted policeman, steeplechase rider, land speculator, member of Parliament, and horsebreaker; by the late 1860s he had also established a minor reputation as a poet.

Although most of Gordon's work harked back to English themes, he did write a small number of ballads set in Australia; one in particular, "The Sick Stockrider," blazed a trail many would follow in its effective use of the bush setting. In this long, somewhat maudlin piece, the hero looks back on the characters he has known:

There was Hughes, who got in trouble through that business with the cards,
    It matters little what became of him;
But a steer ripp'd up Macpherson in the Cooraminta yards,
    And Sullivan was drown'd at Sink-or-Swim;
And Mostyn—poor Frank Mostyn—died at last a fearful wreck,
    In "the horrors," at the Upper Wandinong,
And Carisbrook, the rider, at the Horsefall broke his neck,
    Faith! the wonder was he saved his neck so long!

Ah! those days and nights we squandered at the Logans in the Glen—
    The Logans, man and wife, have long been dead.
Elsie's tallest girl seems taller than your little Elsie then,
    And Ethel is a woman grown and wed.

. . . .

The deep blue skies wax dusky and the tall green trees grow dim,
    The sward beneath me seems to heave and fall,
And sickly, smoky shadows through the sleepy sunlight swim,
    And on the very sun's face weave their pall.
Let me slumber in the hollow where the wattle blossoms wave,
    With never stone or rail to fence my bed;
Should the sturdy station children pull the bush flowers on my grave,
    I may chance to hear them romping overhead.[10]

Gordon was, alas, subject to fits of deep depression. On June 23, 1870, the day his book *Bush Ballads and Galloping Rhymes* was published, he quietly carried his rifle into the scrub along the shore at Brighton near Melbourne and killed himself. He was just thirty-six.[11]

In the years that followed Gordon's death, his reputation as a poet grew immensely, spurred on no doubt both by the dramatic, melancholy nature of his demise and the yearning of the Australian colonies for a national poet of their own, one who could find acceptance among the haughty literary establishment of the mother country. His work was recited both around bush campfires and in the drawing rooms of high society, and it was published in serious poetry anthologies as well as in popular "reciters" (books of poetry intended for memorization and recitation). Indeed, homage to the dead Gordon became a cause célèbre for generations, culminating with the erection of a Gordon statue outside Parliament House in Melbourne in 1932 and the unveiling by His Royal Highness the Duke of York of a memorial bust of Gordon in the Poets' Corner of London's Westminster Abbey on May 11, 1934.

The trail blazed by Gordon and others rapidly became a highway as Australians everywhere, inspired by the new Australian ballads and burning to give expression to their experiences and literary aspirations, took up the muse. By this time many rural towns had their own newspapers, which were eager for contributions, however rustic. For the more ambitious rhymsters there were the larger city publications like *Bell's Life* and the *Australian Town and Country Journal.*

The establishment in 1880 of the Sydney *Bulletin* gave new impetus to this trend. Rapidly becoming known as the "Bushman's Bible," the weekly actively encouraged a new generation of bush balladists and provided them with an audience that stretched from Maoriland (New Zealand) in the east to western Australia and to every bush homestead, cattle camp, and township in between. Many of the balladists it nurtured far surpassed Gordon both as poets and as apostles of bush life.

One of the finest was Will Ogilvie, a Scot who came to Australia as a twenty-year-old in 1889. He spent twelve years on outback stations droving, mustering (rounding up stock), and horse-breaking, his prolific pen providing *Bulletin* readers with a constant flow of finely crafted, rhythmic ballads romanticizing bush life. His work is still widely recited in the bush. These stanzas from "From the Gulf" are representative of his skill:

Store cattle from Nelanjie! They're mute as milkers now;
But yonder grizzled drover, with the care-lines on his brow,
Could tell of merry musters on the big Nelanjie plains,
With blood upon the chestnut's flanks and foam upon the reins;
Could tell of nights upon the road when those same mild-eyed steers
Went ringing round the river bend and through the scrub like spears;
And if his words are rude and rough, we know his words are true,
We know what wild Nelanjies are—and we've been droving too!

Store cattle from Nelanjie! Around the fire at night
They've watched the pine-tree shadows lift before the dancing light;
They've lain awake to listen when the weird bush-voices speak,
And heard the lilting bells go by along the empty creek;
They've spun the yarns of hut and camp, the tales of play and work,
The wondrous tales that gild the road from Normanton to Bourke;
They've told of fortune foul and fair, of women false and true,
And well we know the songs they've sung—for we've been droving too!

Store cattle from Nelanjie! Their breath is on the breeze;
You hear them tread, a thousand head, in blue-grass to the knees;
The lead is on the netting-fence, the wings are spreading wide,
The lame and laggard scarcely move—so slow the drovers ride!
But let them stay and feed to-day for sake of Auld Lang Syne;
They'll never get a chance like this below the Border Line;
And if they tread our frontage down, what's that to me or you?
What's ours to fare, by God they'll share! for we've been droving too![12]

Ogilvie lived to a ripe old age, dying in 1963 at ninety-four. Not so some of his contemporaries. Harry Morant, whose horse-breaking skills earned him the nickname "The Breaker," gained fame far beyond his poetic station through the dubious distinction of dying by British firing squad in 1902 during the Boer War in South Africa, having been convicted by court-martial of shooting Boer prisoners.[13] And Barcroft Boake, a youthful balladist of real promise, so loved droving and boundary riding that a forced return to his family in Sydney filled him with melancholy and despair; he hung himself with his stockwhip at the tender age of twenty-six. His "Where the Dead Men Lie" uses an unusual stanza form and rhyme scheme to express the class antagonisms so common in bush poetry:

Out on the wastes of the Never Never—
    That's where the dead men lie!
There where the heat-waves dance for ever—
    That's where the dead men lie!
That's where the Earth's loved sons are keeping
Endless tryst: not the west wind sweeping
Feverish pinions can wake their sleeping—
    Out where the dead men lie!

Where brown Summer and Death have mated—
    That's where the dead men lie!
Loving with fiery lust unsated—
    That's where the dead men lie!

Out where the grinning skulls bleach whitely
Under the saltbush sparkling brightly;
Out where the wild dogs chorus nightly—
    That's where the dead men lie!

Deep in the yellow, flowing river—
    That's where the dead men lie!
Under the banks where the shadows quiver—
    That's where the dead men lie!
Where the platypus twists and doubles,
Leaving a train of tiny bubbles;
Rid at last of their earthly troubles—
    That's where the dead men lie!

East and backward pale faces turning—
    That's how the dead men lie!
Gaunt arms stretched with a voiceless yearning—
    That's how the dead men lie!
Oft in the fragrant hush of nooning
Hearing again their mothers' crooning,
Wrapt for aye in a dreamful swooning—
    That's how the dead men lie!

Only the hand of Night can free them—
    That's when the dead men fly!
Only the frightened cattle see them—
    See the dead men go by!
Cloven hoofs beating out one measure,
Bidding the stockman know no leisure—
That's when the dead men take their pleasure!
    That's when the dead men fly!

Ask, too, the never-sleeping drover:
    He sees the dead pass by;
Hearing them call to their friends—the plover,
    Hearing the dead men cry;
Seeing their faces stealing, stealing,
Hearing their laughter pealing, pealing,
Watching their grey forms wheeling, wheeling
    Round where the cattle lie!

Strangled by thirst and fierce privation—
    That's how the dead men die!

Out on Moneygrub's farthest station—
  That's how the dead men die!
Hardfaced greybeards, youngsters callow;
Some mounds cared for, some left fallow;
Some deep down, yet others shallow;
  Some having but the sky.

Moneygrub, as he sips his claret,
  Looks with complacent eye
Down at his watch-chain, eighteen-carat—
  There, in his club, hard by:
Recks not that every link is stamped with
Names of the men whose limbs are cramped with
Too long lying in grave mould, camped with
  Death where the dead men lie.[14]

Thankfully, not all the balladists shared Boake's bleak outlook. Thomas Spencer, for example, was a master at bush humor and delighted *Bulletin* readers with well-crafted comic ballads, a number of which remain popular as recitations.[15] W. T. Goodge satirized Australian lingo while having fun with readers:

"______!"

(The Great Australian Adjective!)

The sunburnt ______ stockman stood
And, in a dismal ______ mood,
  Apostrophised his ______ cuddy;
"The ______ nag's no ______ good,
He couldn't earn his ______ food—
  A regular ______ brumby,
          ______!"

He jumped across the ______ horse
And cantered off, of ______ course!
  The roads were bad and ______ muddy;
Said he: "Well, spare me ______ days
The ______ Government's ______ ways
  Are screamin' ______ funny,
          ______!"

He rode up hill, down ______ dale,
The wind it blew a ______ gale,
  The creek was high and ______ floody.

Said he: "The ______ horse must swim,
The same for ______ me and him,
  Is something ______ sickenin',
                ______!"

He plunged into the ______ creek,
The ______ horse was ______ weak,
  The stockman's face a ______ study!
And though the ______ horse was drowned
The ______ rider reached the ground
  Ejaculating: "______?"
                "______!"[16]

Another of the early *Bulletin* poets was "Ironbark" (George Herbert Gibson). One of his poems, "Jones's Selection," describes a scientific farmer buried by a landslide after decades of plowing, draining, and fertilizing:

Bill Jones was on the lower slopes
  Of 'is long sufferin' farm,
A-testin' some new-fangled plough
  Which acted like a charm.

He'd just been screwin' up a nut
  When somethin' seemed to crack,
An' fifty acres, more or less,
  Come down on Jones's back.

. . . .

For this here land wot Jones abused,
  And harassed in the past
'Ad turned an' wiped 'im out, an' things
  Got evened up at last.[17]

An equally wry commentator on bush ways was the Catholic priest Patrick Hartigan (who wrote as "John O'Brien"). His poem "Said Hanrahan" satirizes the universal human tendency among farmers and stock people to complain about the weather, wet or dry. Rain or shine, Hanrahan and his fellow farmers predict doom and disaster. To this day, "'We'll all be rooned [ruined],' said Hanrahan" is a popular saying in the bush.[18]

Although the best-known balladists were men, many women also wrote bush verse. The best-known bush ballad by a woman was probably "Bannerman of the Dandenong," which tells a heady tale of friendship and self-sacrifice during a desperate ride to escape a bushfire; it was a certain winner in school recitations.[19] The poem was composed by Alice Werner, a remarkable woman who was born in Austria and lived for a time in New Zealand and who wrote romantic ballads about Australia before moving on to write on African mythology. In later life she became professor of Swahili and Bantu languages at the University of London.

Paterson and Lawson

While the *Bulletin* nurtured dozens of bush poets, two have an eminence that sets them apart: A. B. (Banjo) Paterson and Henry Lawson. Andrew Barton Paterson was born on a station in rural New South Wales in 1864 and developed from childhood an affinity with bush life and a love of horses and horsemanship. After a bush schooling, he tried his luck in Sydney, qualifying as a solicitor and earning a comfortable income. He contributed his first poem to the *Bulletin* in 1885, writing under the pen name "The Banjo." His first book, *The Man from Snowy River and Other Verses,* appeared in 1895 and was an immediate success both in Australia and England. It made him a national celebrity. Paterson's best-known poem, "The Man from Snowy River," tells the epic tale of a daring pursuit of a band of horses by a single horseman. The poem concludes:

He was right among the horses as they climbed the further hill,
    And the watchers on the mountain standing mute,
Saw him ply the stockwhip fiercely, he was right among them still,
    As he raced across the clearing in pursuit.
Then they lost him for a moment, where two mountain gullies met
    In the ranges, but a final glimpse reveals
On a dim and distant hillside the wild horses racing yet,
    With the man from Snowy River at their heels.

And he ran them single-handed till their sides were white with foam.
    He followed like a bloodhound on their track,
Till they halted cowed and beaten, then he turned their heads for home,
    And alone and unassisted brought them back.
But his hardy mountain pony he could scarcely raise a trot,
    He was blood from hip to shoulder from the spur;
But his pluck was still undaunted, and his courage fiery hot,
    For never yet was mountain horse a cur.

And down by Kosciusko, where the pine-clad ridges raise
    Their torn and rugged battlements on high,
Where the air is clear as crystal, and the white stars fairly blaze
    At midnight in the cold and frosty sky,

And where around the Overflow the reedbeds sweep and sway
To the breezes, and the rolling plains are wide,
The man from Snowy River is a household word to-day,
And the stockmen tell the story of his ride.[20]

There was no finer exponent of the bush ballad than Paterson. Even *The London Times* was forced to concede that his work compared "not unfavorably" with that of Rudyard Kipling, then the literary darling (and near-icon) of the British Empire. And while Kipling was indeed an influence on Paterson, as he was on other bush balladists of the time, in no way did Paterson belong in his shadow.

Paterson's ballads brought the bush to life, giving Australians characters that made them laugh and stories to excite their imaginations. He took his readers shearing and droving and to bush race meetings, and he shared with them his vision of the joys and the disappointments of bush life. Such was his importance that the compiler of one major anthology of bush ballads lamented that he could not include Paterson's *Collected Verse* virtually in its entirety.[21]

The second major ballad writer of the turn of the century was Henry Lawson, born in 1867 in a tent on the goldfields at Grenfell in New South Wales. His parents were poor and his bush childhood a far cry from that fondly remembered by Paterson. As a youth he moved to the city, met up with members of the republican movement, and, fired by revolutionary fervor, sent his first verses to the *Bulletin.* Encouraged by the journal's editor, J. F. Archibald, he became in the years that followed a short story writer of genius and a poet whose unromantic vision of the bush provided a stark contrast to the lyrical images presented by Paterson. Lawson wrote with feeling about his own circumstances and about the loneliness and hardship of bush life, topics exemplified by "Ballad of the Drover":

Across the stony ridges,
Across the rolling plain,
Young Harry Dale, the drover,
Comes riding home again.
And well his stock-horse bears him,
And light of heart is he,
And stoutly his old packhorse
Is trotting by his knee.

Up Queensland way with cattle
He's travelled regions vast,
And many months have vanished
Since home-folk saw him last.
He hums a song of someone
He hopes to marry soon;

And hobble-chains and camp-ware
    Keep jingling to the tune.

Beyond the hazy dado
    Against the lower skies
And yon blue line of ranges
    The homestead station lies.
And thitherward the drover
    Jogs through the lazy noon
While hobble-chains and camp-ware
    Are jingling to a tune.

An hour has filled the heavens
    With storm-clouds inky black;
At times the lightning trickles
    Around the drover's track;
But Harry pushes onward,
    His horses' strength he tries,
In hope to reach the river
    Before the flood shall rise.

The thunder, pealing o'er him,
    Goes rumbling down the plain;
And sweet on thirsty pastures
    Beats fast the plashing rain;
Then every creek and gully
    Sends forth its tribute flood—
The river runs a banker,
    All stained with yellow mud.

Now Harry speaks to Rover,
    The best dog on the plains,
And to his hardy horses,
    And strokes their shaggy manes:
'We've breasted bigger rivers
    When floods were at their height,
Nor shall this gutter stop us
    From getting home tonight!'

The thunder growls a warning
    The blue, forked lightnings gleam;
The drover turns his horses
    To swim the fatal stream.

But, oh! the flood runs stronger
    Than e'er it ran before;
The saddle-horse is failing,
    And only halfway o'er!

When flashes next the lightning,
    The flood's grey breast is blank;
A cattle-dog and packhorse
    Are struggling up the bank.
But in the lonely homestead
    The girl shall wait in vain—
He'll never pass the stations
    In charge of stock again.

The faithful dog a moment
    Lies panting on the bank,
Then plunges through the current
    To where his master sank.
And round and round in circles
    He fights with failing strength,
Till, gripped by wilder waters,
    He fails and sinks at length.

Across the flooded lowlands
    And slopes of sodden loam
The packhorse struggles bravely
    To take dumb tidings home;
And mud-stained, wet, and weary,
    He goes by rock and tree,
With clanging chains and tinware
    All sounding eerily.[22]

Significantly, although Paterson is universally acknowledged as a balladist of the very highest order and Lawson's verse by comparison is often demeaned, it is Lawson who has retained the greatest affection of the Australian people, the man who properly should be acknowledged as Australia's national poet. Lawson, destitute and alcoholic, struck a chord with Australians who loved and recited Paterson's ballads but knew little of the man. Lawson wore his heart on his sleeve for all to see; Paterson kept his to himself. When Lawson died insolvent, the government was shamed into according him a state funeral and tens of thousands attended; when Paterson died, in respected old age, he merely received glowing tributes. And it was Lawson, not Paterson, whose verse cried out to be sung. True,

Paterson wrote the words of "Waltzing Matilda," which became Australia's unofficial national song, and several of his other poems also acquired tunes or were set to music, but songs crafted by Australians from Lawson's verse number in the hundreds, and the list is still growing. Perhaps the best-known these days is "Reedy River," a melancholy song about the death of a frontier woman that concludes:

But of the hut I builded there are no traces now,
And many rains have levelled the furrows of my plough;
The glad bright days have vanished; for sombre branches wave
Their wattle-blossom golden above my Mary's grave.[23]

Passing of an Era

The golden age of the bush ballad was the 1890s, although for another twenty years at least the glitter was still there. But times were changing: horse-drawn buggies were being replaced by motor cars, bullock teams by trucks and railways, and draught horses by tractors. Although in time there would be odes to the Fergie (Ferguson) tractor, it just wasn't the same.

The early 1920s saw the spread across Australia of a range of marvelous new entertainment technologies—the wireless (radio), moving pictures, and phonograph recordings—and these combined with social and political change to undermine further the old ways, in particular the ways in which Australians relaxed. Like their counterparts overseas, they became a nation that increasingly expected to be entertained by professionals and less one in which family and community members entertained each other. Fewer and fewer people gave attention to maintaining their performing skills in order to be able to contribute, say, a song, piano piece, or poetry recitation to an evening's social program. In the bush itself, far from the burgeoning cities of the coast, that was less so. There, ballads of the 1890s were still committed lovingly to memory, perhaps to be recited in homes or around campfires, perhaps merely for personal enjoyment.

Australians everywhere still read for enjoyment, and the love of verse, especially bush ballads, remained, although increasingly the new crops of ballads and balladists harked back to the past, referring nostalgically to times many had never known. There was no shortage of bush poets. If anything, the number of persons writing bush verse steadily increased, although the practice was no longer primarily the province of bush-dwellers. The *Bulletin* continued to provide an outlet for publication, as did regional periodicals such as the *North Queensland Register.* A number of bush ballads from these publications gained wide distribution when they were included (without attribution) in *Bill Bowyang's Bush Recitations,* a series of six very popular booklets published in North Queensland between 1933 and 1940. One of the best of these, "Flying Kate," composed by an unknown poet, illustrates the use of the tall tale in bush verse:

It makes us old hands sick and tired to hear
Them talk of their champions of to-day,
Eurythmics and Davids, yes, I'll have a beer,
Are only fair hacks in their way.

Now this happened out West before records were took,
And 'tis not to be found in the guide,
But it's honest—Gor'struth, and can't be mistook,
For it happened that I had the ride.

'Twas the Hummer's Creek Cup, and our mare, Flying Kate,
Was allotted eleven stone two; [156 pound handicap]
The race was two miles, you'll agree with me mate,
It was asking her something to do.

She was heavy in foal, but the owner and me
Decided to give her a spin,
We were right on the rocks, 'twas the end of a spree,
So we needed a bit of a win.

I saddled her up and went down with the rest,
Her movements were clumsy and slow,
The starter to get us in line did his best,
Then swishing his flag he said, "Go!"

The field jumped away but the mare seemed asleep,
And I thought to myself, "We've been sold,"
Then I heard something queer, and I felt I could weep,
For strike me if Kate hadn't foaled.

The field by this time had gone half-a-mile,
But I knew what the old mare could do,
So I gave her a cut with the whip—you can smile,
But the game little beast simply flew.

'Twas then she showed them her wonderful speed,
For we mowed down the field one by one,
With a furlong to go we were out in the lead,
And prepared for a last final run.

Then something came at us right on the outside,
And we only just scratched past the pole,

When I had a good look I thought I'd have died,
For I'm blowed if it wasn't the foal.[24]

Bush Verse and Country Music

With the wireless and phonograph came recorded music from overseas, including early hillbilly recordings from the United States. This new country music rapidly became popular, especially in rural areas, and soon Australian hillbilly artists armed with guitar and yodel vied for an opportunity to become famous. The impact in the bush of the new musical style was profound, as Australia's country music historian Eric Watson has commented: "There can be no doubt that this influx of American recorded country music was the greatest single influence in the making of what we know today as Australian country music. It swept aside for a time the strong ballad tradition we had developed ourselves. . . . Both its music and its lyrics had an immediate appeal, and the local product was not available on radio, or discs for the old wind-up gramophone."[25]

Although the first Australian country recordings were made in the late 1920s it was not until 1936 that the country gained its first country music star, a New Zealander who gave himself the unlikely sobriquet of Tex Morton. By the late 1930s, Tex had become the best-selling recording artist in Australia, outselling all the overseas country artists put together. Like Gordon before him, he blazed a trail many soon would follow.

The new Australian country music soon began to incorporate Australian themes, with lyrics often indistinguishable in meter and content from bush verse. Indeed, in some respects it often was bush verse rendered into song. Many of the finest country music artists like Slim Dusty openly acknowledged their love of the old bush ballads and set them to music, a practice that still continues.[26]

Occasionally, too, the movement is in the other direction as reciters pick up song lyrics and render them effectively as verse. One example is Ted Egan's fine composition "The Drover's Boy." It refers to the brutal subjugation of outback Aboriginal communities and the practice of forcing Aboriginal women into cohabitation with white Australian men. Because interracial cohabitation was illegal until recently, the gender of the woman would sometimes be disguised. Egan indicates that despite the brutality of the "courtship," a caring, even loving, relationship sometimes developed:

They couldn't understand why the drover cried
As they buried the drover's boy
For the drover had always seemed so hard
To the men in his employ.

A bolting horse, a stirrup lost, and the drover's boy was dead.
The shovelled dirt, a mumbled word, and it's back to the road ahead,
And forget about the drover's boy.

They couldn't understand why the drover cut
A lock of the dead boy's hair.
He put it in the band of his battered old hat
As they watched him standing there.
He told them "Take the cattle on, I'll sit with the boy a while,"
A silent thought, a pipe to smoke, and it's ride another mile,
And forget about the drover's boy.

They couldn't understand why the drover and the boy
Always camped so far away,
For the tall white man and the slim black boy
Had never had much to say.
And the boy would be gone at break of dawn,
Tail the horses, carry on,
While the drover roused the sleeping men,
Daylight, hit the road again, and follow the drover's boy,
Follow the drover's boy.

In the Camooweal Pub they talked about
The death of the drover's boy,
They drank their rum with a stranger who'd come
From a Kimberley run, FitzRoy,
And he told of the massacre in the west, barest details, guess the rest,
Shoot the bucks, grab a gin, cut her hair, break her in,
Call her a boy, the drover's boy
Call her a boy, the drover's boy.

So when they build that Stockman's Hall of Fame
And they talk about the droving game,
Remember the girl who was bedmate and guide,
Rode with the drover side by side,
Watched the bullocks, flayed the hide, faithful wife, never a bride,
Bred his sons for the cattle runs.
Don't weep . . . for the drover's boy
Don't mourn . . . for the drover's boy
But don't forget . . . the drover's boy.[27]

Modern Times

Bush poetry is possibly as popular today as it has ever been. Certainly there is no shortage of bush poets. Every year, for example, many hundreds of Australians enter the Bronze Swagman Competition for Bush Verse. Entries come from all over the country (and even from overseas) and from people in all walks of life; they generally echo in sentiment the bush verse of yesteryear.[28]

Further evidence of the continuing propensity of ordinary Australians to gain self-expression through the writing of bush verse is easy to find. In 1985, for example, Roger Montgomery collected within a single three-month period more than three hundred original items, predominantly bush verse, from people living in the iron-mining communities of western Australia's remote Pilbara region.[29]

Unlike bush song, bush verse has never needed a conscious revival, and there is every reason to expect it to continue to prosper. Its natural habitat has never been threatened, nor has it faced serious competition from exotic forms of verse. Further, the popularity of Australian country music has, if anything, reinforced the bush verse tradition, providing it with a sympathetic and even symbiotic musical environment.

The concerns of modern bush poets are little changed from those of times past. They focus on rural themes, are tentative about love and human relationships, and are openly nostalgic and passionate about horses, the pioneer spirit, sport, and mateship. Although there is also some bawdy verse, some of which is very unpleasant, it remains a minor element of the whole.

The form of the verse—its rhythm and meter—hasn't changed either. Simple four-line stanzas are most common, although the number of lines per stanza or of syllables per line is not really an issue provided that the pattern is regular. The more adventurous and accomplished bush poets sometimes attempt more complex structures. In any event it must rhyme. Most bush verse is written in standard Australian English, without the "hath's" and "thou's" that bedevil early Australian attempts at high poetry. Local idiom, naturally, is used, although ostentatious dialect generally is avoided unless to lampoon, say, the Irishness or Germanness of a particular character.

Significantly, too, Australians don't tend to divide bush verse—or bush poets—into particular subcategories. Be it verse by or about stockmen, farmers, bushrangers (outlaws living in the bush), country schoolteachers, or truck drivers, if it has a bush setting and is cast in popular rhyming form, it qualifies as bush verse.

There are strong similarities between Australian bush verse and American cowboy poetry, and were it not for local references and idiom it would often be impossible to distinguish between the two. That ought not to be surprising; both spring from the same cultural well, albeit climatized to accommodate differing local conditions. Despite these similarities, however, few Australian reciters include in their repertoire verse from the United States, although a few poems of the Canadian Robert Service such as "The Cremation of Sam McGee" remain fairly popular. The emphasis is on Australian material, with poems by Paterson, Lawson, and other early bush balladists rubbing shoulders not only with later works by C. J. Dennis, Edward Harrington, John Manifold, Graham Jenkin, Rob Charlton, and others but also with contemporary works by the reciters themselves.[30]

The vast majority of bush poets and reciters operate largely in isolation from each other, each in his or her own community. The closest approach to a community of bush poets and reciters is found in the music-oriented folk revival and country music movements. Here reciters in particular find an appreciative audience, both when they perform alongside singers and musicians in concerts and when they give workshops and recitals on their own. The regular cycle of folk and country music festivals around Australia provides additional avenues of exposure. Some have competitions for original bush verse or for reciting, and many provide opportunities for bush poets and reciters to meet and perform informally.

Since the early 1980s the number of bush poets plying their craft on a professional or semiprofessional basis has increased notably, and in January 1984, at the annual Tamworth Country Music Festival, an Australian Bush Poets Association was formed.[31] Its monthly newsletter provides an opportunity for new works to be published and provides information about the rapidly expanding bush poetry calendar.

Despite its undeniable popularity, bush verse is openly denigrated by the literary establishment, largely (one suspects) because it is popular and therefore, by a perverse logic, subliterary. As a result, bush poets have little support from government arts funding and little chance of publication in literary journals. Faced with that situation, bush poets sometimes publish their own work, whereas others seek out commercial publishers. Good bush verse has a ready audience, and a number of publications by bush poets have been financially successful.

Finally, a contemporary poem by Claude Morris may remind American readers of "Boomer Johnson," Henry Herbert Knibbs's poem about an irascible cook. Morris entitled his poem "Trouble Brewing":

He came walking through the forest in the glaring summer sun;
In his left hand was a bottle, in the other was a gun.
His beard was wild and bushy and his hair was shaggy too;
His old straw hat was full of holes where tufts of hair poked through.

I stood and waited for him as he came with steady stride,
And I studied his appearance when he halted by my side.

He wasn't old, nor was he young, but somewhere in between,
And heavy eyebrows almost hid his eyes of greyish green.

Then he handed me the bottle—"You must have a drink," he said,
And I heard him cock the rifle, and he aimed it at my head.
"Yes, take a swig of my home-brew, and you can be the first
To have the chance of trying out my recipe for thirst."

And the rifle never wavered as it pointed straight at me,
And that close-up, gaping barrel was a nasty thing to see.
I lifted up the bottle with a very shaky hand,
And a silent prayer to Heaven as I followed his command.

I swallowed twice—and GOD ABOVE—that brew had come from Hell,
And I felt my head exploding, and it drowned my dying yell.
I fell upon the dusty ground and grovelled there in pain,
Vowing he could shoot me, but I wouldn't drink again.

When the pain and shock receded, and I staggered to my feet—
"It was AWFUL—it was AWFUL," I could hear myself repeat.
Then I heard the brewer speaking, and he said, "Yes, I agree—
Now hand me back that bottle—and you hold the gun on me!"[32]

Notes

1. Richard Appleton, editor-in-chief, *The Australian Encyclopedia,* 5th ed. (Sydney: Australian Geographic Society, 1988), 2179–80.

2. See, for example, *Bards in the Wilderness: Australian Colonial Poetry to 1920,* ed. Brian Elliott and Adrian Mitchell (Melbourne: Nelson Australia, 1970), or *The Poets' Discovery: Nineteenth Century Verse in Australia,* ed. Richard Jordan and Peter Pierce (Melbourne: Melbourne University Press, 1990).

3. See, for example, Ron Edwards's two collections of early broadsides relating to Australia: *The Convict Maid,* Australian Folklore Occasional Paper no. 16 (Kuranda, Queensland: Rams Skull Press, 1987) and *The Transport's Lament,* Australian Folklore Occasional Paper no. 17 (Kuranda, Queensland: Rams Skull Press, 1988). A more easily accessible publication, however, is Geoffrey Ingleton, *True Patriots All; or, News from Early Australia as Told in a Collection of Broadsides Garnered and Decorated by Geoffrey Chapman Ingleton* (Sydney: Angus and Robertson, 1952).

4. See John Meredith's *The Wild Colonial Boy,* Studies in Australian Folklore no. 3 (Melbourne: Red Rooster Press, 1982).

5. Duncan Emrich, in his *American Folk Poetry* (Boston: Little, Brown, 1974, 704–6), quotes a version of "Bold Jack Donahue" reconstructed from two sources: Robert W. Gordon, "Old Songs That Men Have Sung," *Adventure* magazine, 15 May 1927, 190, and

a recording by Charles L. Todd and Robert Sonkin of the singing of Cotton Davis in California in 1940 (Library of Congress AFS record 5103). A version of "The Wild Colloina [Colonial] Boy," collected from the singing of Mrs. Lyons of Michigan in 1934, was published in *Ballads and Songs of Southern Michigan,* ed. Emelyn Elizabeth Gardner and Geraldine Jencks (Ann Arbor: University of Michigan Press, 1939), 326. Sandy Ives, in a personal communication, says that the ballad is widely known in the Maritimes of Canada and in the State of Maine.

6. John Meredith and Rex Whalan have pieced together Frank's story in their delightful book *Frank the Poet: The Life and Works of Francis MacNamara,* Studies in Australian Folklore no. 1 (Melbourne: Red Rooster Press, 1979). They note that as recently as 1962 one of Frank's compositions, "McQuade's Curse," was collected in the field, having been pinned to the railway gates in the Victorian town of Tallarook by an irate swagman (an itinerant bush worker) who had been refused a drink on credit in one of the town's hotels. This piece was first published in Russell Ward, *Penguin Book of Australian Ballads* (Sydney: Penguin, 1964).

7. See, for example, Hugh Anderson's biography of Thatcher, *The Colonial Minstrel* (Melbourne: Cheshire, 1960) and his publications of Thatcher's songs in *Goldrush Songster* (Ferntree Gully: Rams Skull Press, 1958) and *Charles Thatcher's Gold-Diggers' Songbook,* Studies in Australian Folklore no. 2 (Melbourne: Red Rooster Press, 1980).

8. From Jack Mathieu, "That Day at Boiling Downs," in *The Bulletin Reciter* (Sydney: Bulletin Newspaper Co., 1901), 14–17.

9. John Farrell, "The Last Bullet," in *The Bulletin Reciter* (Sydney: Bulletin Newspaper Co., 1901), 221–29.

10. Adam Lindsay Gordon, "The Sick Stockrider," in *The Poetical Works of Adam Lindsay Gordon* (London: Ward, Lock, 1913), 131–34.

11. Of the Gordon biographies, *Adam Lindsay Gordon: The Man and the Myth* by Geoffrey Hutton (London: Faber and Faber, 1978) is the most recent.

12. Will H. Ogilvie, "From the Gulf," in Ogilvie, *Saddle for a Throne,* ed. Thelma Williams (Adelaide: R. M. Williams, 1952), 40–41. This is the definitive edition of Ogilvie's poetry.

13. No book of Morant's verse was ever published, but selections were included in several books about him, including F. M. Cutlack, *Breaker Morant: A Horseman Who Made History: With a Selection of His Bush Ballads* (Sydney: Ure Smith, 1962). Morant's court-martial in South Africa was also the subject of a successful 1980 film of the same title directed by Bruce Beresford.

14. Barcroft Boake, "Where the Dead Men Lie," in Boake, *Where the Dead Men Lie and Other Poems* (Sydney: Angus and Robertson, 1907), 140–42. This edition contains a biographical memoir by A. G. Stephens.

15. Spencer published two collections of ballads: *How M'Dougall Topped the Score and Other Verses and Sketches* (Sydney: Bookstall, 1906) and *Budgeree Ballads* (Sydney: Bookstall, 1908). He is represented in most Australian ballad anthologies.

16. W. T. Goodge, "The Great Australian Adjective," in *Hits! Skits! and Jingles!* (Sydney: Bulletin Newspaper Company, 1899), 115. The Great Australian Adjective is, of course,

"bloody," a word unaccountably too offensive to appear in print in Goodge's day. The poem was adopted—and adapted—by Australian soldiers in two world wars, and they passed it on to American troops, who substituted their own national adjective. Gershon Legman has noted two published American versions: Edgar Palmer, *G.I. Songs Written, Composed and/or Collected by the Men in Service* (New York: Sheridan House, 1944), and William Wallrich's *Air Force Airs, Songs and Ballads of the United States Air Force, World War One through Korea* (New York: Duell, Sloan and Pearce, 1957). See Gershon Legman, "Bawdy Monologues," *Southern Folklore Quarterly* 40 (March–June 1976): 90–91.

17. George Herbert Gibson, "Jones's Selection," in Gibson, *Ironbark Splinters from the Australian Bush* (London: Laurie, 1912), 21–23. "Jones's Selection" (as well as "Flying Kate" and a number of other bush poems) are recited on Alan Scott and Keith McKenry, *Battler's Ballad: Songs and Recitations of Australian Bush Life,* CD and cassette (Canberra: Fanged Wombat Productions, 1991).

18. "John O'Brien" published two collections of verse, the first of which, *Around the Boree Log and Other Verses* (Sydney: Angus and Robertson, 1921), has often been reprinted. An American edition was published in Nebraska by the St. Columban's Foreign Mission Society in 1943.

19. Alice Werner, "Bannerman of the Dandenong," in *Penguin Book of Australian Ballads,* ed. Ward, 225–26.

20. A. B. Paterson, "The Man from Snowy River," in *Collected Verse of A. B. Paterson* (Sydney: Angus and Robertson, 1932), 3–8. There are two biographies of Paterson: Clement Semmler, *The Banjo of the Bush: The Work, Life, and Times of A. B. Paterson* (Melbourne: Lansdowne, 1966), and Lorna Oliff, *Andrew Barton Paterson,* Twayne World Authors Series no. 120 (New York: Twayne, 1971). A film based loosely on "The Man from Snowy River" and bearing the same title was released in 1982. It was successful enough to produce a sequel, imaginatively titled *The Man from Snowy River II.*

21. This was Douglas Stewart who, with Nancy Keesing, edited *Australian Bush Ballads* (Sydney: Angus and Robertson, 1955), which, although somewhat narrow in scope, is the best reference in the field. Paterson's *Collected Verse* was first published by Angus and Robertson in 1932 and is still in print. A two-volume collection of his complete works (including his prose writings)—*Singer of the Bush* (1885–1900) and *Song of the Pen* (1901–41)—was issued by Lansdowne (Sydney, 1983).

22. Henry Lawson, "Ballad of the Drover," in *Selected Poems of Henry Lawson* (Sydney: Angus and Robertson, 1918), 84–86. There are a number of biographies of Lawson, among them Manning Clark, *In Search of Henry Lawson* (Sydney: Macmillan Australia, 1978), and Colin Roderick, *The Real Henry Lawson* (Adelaide: Rigby, 1982). Roderick also edited Lawson's *Collected Verse* in three volumes (Sydney: Angus and Robertson, 1967, 1968, and 1969) and a selection of verse, *Henry Lawson: Poems* (Sydney: Ferguson, 1979). A two-volume collection of Lawson's complete works—*A Campfire Yarn* (1885–1900) and *A Fantasy of Man* (1901–22)—was issued by Lansdowne (Sydney, 1984). The widely available *Poetical Works of Henry Lawson* contains a number of poems amended after Lawson's death by his editors and is to be avoided.

23. Henry Lawson, "Reedy River," in *The Songs of Henry Lawson,* ed. Chris Kempster

(Sydney: Viking O'Neil, 1989), 120–21. This delightful book draws together 230 musical settings of Lawson's verse contributed by more than fifty people operating in every musical idiom from country music to jazz.

24. "Flying Kate," in Bill Bowyang, *Bill Bowyang's Bush Recitations,* no. 6 (Bowen, North Queensland, [1940]), 16–17; republished in Hugh Anderson, *On the Track with Bill Bowyang* (Melbourne: Red Rooster Press, 1991–92), 164–65.

25. Eric Watson, *Country Music in Australia,* 2d ed. (Sydney: Angus and Robertson, 1982), 1:7.

26. Slim Dusty has set scores of poems by Lawson to music. Some, like "Ballad of the Drover" and "Sweeney," were already well known; others, like "Saint Peter," "Do You Think That I Do Not Know?" and "A Word to Texas Jack," became widely known largely through Slim's musical versions. In more recent times, he and others have set to music poems by Paterson (including "The Man from Snowy River"), Ogilvie, and Morant, among others.

27. Ted Egan's recording of "The Drover's Boy" is on his CD *The Drover's Boy: A Celebration of Australian Women;* Egan has also published words and music in *The Overlanders Songbook* (Richmond, Victoria: Greenhouse Publications, 1984). The lyrics were also published as verse in Rocky Marshall's fine compilation *Down the Track: Modern Humourous Australian Bush Ballads and Popular Performance Poetry* (Oaklands Park, South Australia: Wahratta Enterprises, 1985) and performed as a recitation on Jim Smith's *You Don't Say!* (Sidetrack TMS 015).

28. A selection of the entries appears each year in a new issue of *The Bronze Swagman Book of Bush Verse* (Winton, Queensland: Winton Tourist Promotion Association); the 1995 edition was the twenty-fourth in the series.

29. Roger Montgomery, *Pilbara Connection* (Belmont W.A.: Roger Limpid Productions, 1985).

30. See, for example, Marshall, *Down the Track,* and Bill Scott, ed., *The Penguin Book of Australian Humourous Verse* (Sydney: Penguin Books Australia, 1984). For a cross-section of less-recent bush ballads, see Stewart and Keesing, eds., *Australian Bush Ballads,* and Ward, *Penguin Book of Australian Ballads.*

31. Australian Bush Poets Association, P.O. Box 77, Drayton North, Queensland 4350.

32. Claude Morris, "Trouble Brewing," in Morris, *The Legend of Angel Creek and Other Ballads* (Devon, U.K.: Arthur Stockwell, 1979), 105.

Part 6

Developments

Cowboy poetry has had an astonishing revival since 1985, the year of the first Elko (Nevada) Cowboy Poetry Gathering. The massive impact of this festival and the hundreds of others that take place annually throughout the West has given cowboy poetry a prominence and a visibility previously unimaginable. Waves of books, cassette tapes, and compact disks are available; cowboy poets perform at state fairs, banquets, and fund-raisers; and cowboy poetry remains the darling of audio and video journalists in need of a story. Cowboy poetry, in other words, has become a tourist attraction, and it is this dimension that folklorist Jim McNutt, director of a history museum in North Carolina, explores from the perspective of a relatively new academic discipline, the anthropology of tourism.

All this publicity and attention has had mixed results. Most observers agree that the poetry has improved technically; traditionalists who stick with regular rhyme and rhythm seem to be more accurate yet more imaginative. At the same time, the influx of poets who have diverse educations and backgrounds—although they usually have in common some experience with cattle or horses—has meant a huge variety of forms, topics, and ideas. Cowboy poets and audiences have become far more receptive to poems that are pro-environment, anti-growth, pro-feminist, and even confessional. As one long-time observer commented, "Cowboy poetry looks less and less cowboy, more and more just poetry."

If that's true, the reciters and poets and audiences who have supported cowboy poetry since the mid-1980s have a challenge: how to maintain the essence of a folk tradition that stretches back almost 150 years while not binding it to restrictive forms and topics. This is the question addressed by John Dofflemyer, a working rancher who has also been active as editor, publisher, and critic of cowboy poetry. The continuing disagreement he describes between those who favor traditional ballad forms and those who advocate formal innovation is at the center of the debate over the future of cowboy poetry, a debate that recalls the "Battle of the Books" (Jonathan Swift's title) in the seventeenth and eighteenth centuries between those who favored the symmetry of classical Greece and Rome and those who argued the claims of contemporary writers.

Perhaps the continued attention of reciters and Gathering organizers to classic poetry, the continuing research and scholarship on the origins of the genre, and the playfully ironic unwillingness of poets to be slotted into clip-clop rhythms and steed/need rhymes will allow cowboy poetry to persevere. Its new role as a powerfully compelling medium by which people of cattle culture can express their politics, solidarity, and sense of community may provide a long-term focus for an evolving form of expression. From that perspective, William Kittredge—whose upbringing on a ranch in southern Oregon has provided fodder for short stories, essays, and a compelling memoir, *Hole in the Sky*—reminds us of the importance of storytelling to the human community and helps us understand the continued vitality and possibility of cowboy poetry.

25

Cowboys, Folklorists, Authenticity, and Tourism

James C. McNutt

On my first visit to Melvin Whipple's home in Hereford, Texas, in the fall of 1984, I sat across from him at the dining-room table and listened as he read several of his poems aloud. A working cowboy who had for twenty-five years been composing poems about his experiences, Melvin was eager to share his work. Born in Utah and raised on the Arizona Strip just south of the Utah border, he had come from a family of cowboy poets and had cowboyed in several states. He read his painstakingly typed and hand-illustrated poems with a sure sense of meter, even though that meter might be hard for a reader to discern on the printed page. Then he recited the twelve stanzas of "The Zebra Dun" from memory with scarcely a hitch and said he had first learned it fifty years earlier. Melvin read and talked for three hours. I recorded everything on tape, photographed him seated behind the table with his hat on, and sent the results off to Hal Cannon, who invited Melvin to the first Cowboy Poetry Gathering in January 1985 in Elko, Nevada.

Elko that year was an amazing experience filled with session after crowded session of cowboy poets reciting or reading, displays of cowboy art and books, interviews and concerts, and a crowd of folklorists and media people. Poets from most states west of the Mississippi were in attendance, and many who had only heard about other poets or read their work had the opportunity to meet for the first time. Cow people from the Great Basin area of Utah and Nevada, who formed the largest part of the audience, were intermixed with urban professionals, youthful enthusiasts of folklore and folk music, and tourists and travelers passing through Elko on Interstate 80. In a thoughtful gesture, Cannon organized a final session on the future of the Gathering and gave all concerned a chance to say how they felt about being part of the event. Before it was over, a number of cowboy poets were talking about forming a cowboy poetry association. The Elko Gatherings—now held annually—have spawned dozens of state and local events throughout the West.

The Gathering was wonderfully successful not only in terms of organization and content but also in the attention it attracted to cowboy folk poetry. Fleeting but powerful images of cowboys flashed on television news, and national magazines featured cowboy poets. *People* called Melvin Whipple a "good ole poet from Texas," and *Mother Jones* quoted him as saying, "If you can't do it on a horse, it ain't worth doin'."[1]

After visiting at Whipple's house, introducing him at Elko, and seeing his poetry through to eventual publication in book form, it was hard to avoid looking back to the work of John A. Lomax.[2] Ninety-odd years earlier he had established the image of the cowboy-song collector, lugging an outlandish Edison horn and cylinder recorder to cow camps and carrying the gleanings back to skeptical or bemused audiences. In books and lectures around the country he had promoted public appreciation for cowboy songs.[3] Occasionally, he encountered disdain from cowboys and audiences alike, but on the whole his efforts had great popular success. Recalling his work, his daughter Bess Lomax Hawes spoke for three generations of folklorists: "Ordinary men and women could and did produce beauty and truth in plain straightforward language and melody, and the nation they had built would be the poorer and the weaker if their voices were allowed to drift away on the winds of history."[4]

Although the cowboy occupation has changed a great deal since Lomax's time, its traditions have persisted and been re-created in new forms, traveling from the occupational group itself to a worldwide audience. The development of the cattle industry in the western United States, the widespread popularity of poetry recitations at public gatherings and in schools, and the acceptance of rhymed metrical verse as a popular poetic standard converged in the late nineteenth century, encouraging cowboys to create spoken and written verse about their lives and occupation. Not so illiterate as they were often portrayed, cowboys benefited, too, from cheap printing technologies and the wide distribution of periodicals. Printed versions of cowboy poems began to appear as early as the 1870s, and book-length collections followed in the 1890s.

Just as the period of the great trail drives was coming to a stormy end in the mid-1880s, folklore was emerging as a self-conscious, professionalized, academic discipline; before long, folklorists were turning their attention to preserving the verbal traditions of cowboys. Lomax first wrote about a Texas "poet-ranchman," William L. ("Larry") Chittenden of Anson, in 1896, not long after Chittenden's *Ranch Verses* was published by Putnam's in New York.[5] After studying with George Lyman Kittredge and Barrett Wendell at Harvard University, Lomax began fitting the cowboy songs he had collected to the models of folk poetry his mentors had established in their study of English and Scots ballads. His *Cowboy Songs and Other Frontier Ballads* (1910) was a popular success in which cowboys themselves joined. More than one report has come down of folklorists finding battered copies of that volume in cow camps along with N. Howard ("Jack") Thorp's *Songs of the Cowboys*, printed in limited quantity by a small shop in Estancia, New Mexico, two years earlier. Following Lomax with collections of cowboy songs were later scholar-collectors like Charles Finger, Margaret Larkin, Austin and Alta Fife, Glenn Ohrlin, John I. White, and Jim Bob Tinsley.[6] The salutary results of their research include a well-developed history of particular poems and tunes and the identification of some nineteenth-century composers and performers.

If ever folklorists had recorded, collected, and attempted to preserve a traditional American folk genre, this was it. Yet years afterward, almost as if anticipating spring roundup, collectors and scholars were again gathering up cowboys, marshaling the artifacts of their tradition, and seeking new audiences by driving the entire herd in the dead of winter to a convention center in a small town in northeastern Nevada.

Traveling to a spot like Elko to listen to cowboys recite poetry is not a traditional activity, even for the primary audience: cattle people from the region. As often as not, the cowboys who mounted the podium confessed shyness before public audiences. In the words of Charles Kortes of Wyoming: "Some poets felt uneasy when their name was called to quote, / And found their knees a-shakin', reading what they'd wrote."[7]

But there were precedents for everyone. Cowboys had their Bruce Kiskaddons and Gail Gardners, the folklorists their Lomaxes and Fifes, and many of those in the attentive, appreciative audience probably knew a lot of the poems by heart. Folklorists, for their part, were quick to point out that they were not cowboys, yet they enjoyed wearing boots and talking about cowboy gear and quoting lines from poems to journalists. Although journalists had an enormously good time creating atrocious puns about "rhyme-stoned cowboys" and other fantastic creatures, few seemed inclined to doubt the valor—or the validity—of the rhymers' performances.

No one objected to the fact that the Gathering was a performance, a public presentation far removed from the contexts of bunkhouse, chuck wagon, barroom, motel room, pickup, or rodeo arena—the usual locales for the recitation of cowboy poetry. Neither the continuing vitality of the cowboys, who had been mourned as a "disappearing breed" for more than a hundred years, nor the poetic tradition itself seemed seriously in doubt. A library of published cowboy poetry filled a display hall, and many poets were placing their verse in trade magazines directed at ranchers and horsemen or were publishing their own books.

Why all this attention to an already well-documented tradition, and why such an energetic and enthusiastic public response? At least some explanation could be found in the early rationale for the Gathering itself, which grew out of "the folkorists' sagebrush rebellion" and their feeling that "the folk arts of the West were neglected and that folk art definitions were based on the folk arts of the colonies and the old country."[8] The West's most recognizable symbol, the cowboy, was an ideal focus for a revisionary presentation of western tradition. Lomax had been similarly disenchanted with the treatment his region had received at the hands of eastern literary savants.

Further explanation lay in the continuing power of popular images of the West, which contributed, like it or not, a substantial atmosphere to the Gathering independent of any academic history. Dime novels, Teddy Roosevelt, Zane Grey's *Riders of the Purple Sage,* Louis L'Amour, and more than eighty years of films beginning with Edwin S. Porter's *The Great Train Robbery* (1903) all haunted the convention center, giving credence to Lomax's description of "that unique and romantic figure in modern civilization, the American cowboy": "The changing and romantic West of the early days lives mainly in story and in song. The last figure to vanish is the cowboy, the animating spirit of the vanishing era. He sits his horse easily as he rides through a wide valley, enclosed by mountains, clad in the hazy purple of coming night,—with his face turned steadily down the long, long road."[9]

The presentation of the poets onstage in an auditorium holding hundreds of people made it impossible to view cowboys and cowgirls as the "ordinary men and women" celebrated by Bess Hawes, and coast-based reporters sought links to a West they had seen only on screen. Offstage, the cowboys frequently performed in quasi-historical roles, some by dressing in buckaroo garb that nostalgically replicated nineteenth-century cowboy dress, others by mounting up to ride horseback for media cameras. Displays of western art, nighttime country-western dances, nostalgic songfests of popular western music, and cowboy films found niches at Elko alongside the poetry. At the same time, it was apparent that an informal star system was developing as Baxter Black and Waddie Mitchell charmed audiences. The presentation of poets and reciters on a spotlit stage in a darkened auditorium seating a thousand marked the event as something very different from the normal contexts for cowboy poetry.

The power of these popular images of the cowboy, at Elko as elsewhere, derived from the faith of performers and audiences alike that even the most outlandish representations of men on horseback had a basis in reality. The term *cowboy* has functioned richly in American language to denote everything from lowborn thieves to cosmic heroes but always with the proviso that behind the undercutting invective or romantic elaboration lay a historical figure with a fixable identity.[10] Simply put, people believe that cowboys are demonstrably authentic, regardless of popular fictions. As one cowboy poet observed, "If you got to talking to most cowboys, they'd admit they write 'em. . . . I think some of the meanest, toughest sons of bitches around write poetry."[11]

Such attitudes derive from numerous sources in American culture that have been described in such concepts as "rugged individualism," "the self-made man," and "the myth of the frontier." A belief—a faith, even—in authenticity accounts for a great deal of the popularity of other forms of western art. Frederic Remington, for example, was a romantic visionary who during his career moved from straight representational illustrations toward complex impressionist paintings. Yet he built his reputation primarily on the accuracy of physical and historical detail still considered a hallmark of his work, and his later move toward impressionism puzzled his audience and lost him commissions.[12] Louis L'Amour's attention to accuracy and historical detail attracted a huge readership worldwide, at least in part because readers responded to the claim of accuracy and the richness of detail in his novels.

Cowboy Poetry Gatherings have reaffirmed this popular faith in western authenticity by making cowboys accessible to tourists, journalists, and consumers of media productions as well as to ranchers and working cowboys. In almost all cases, media descriptions conform to readers' preconceptions about cowboys and the West, as in *People* magazine's description of the train ride from Salt Lake City to Elko: "An hour out of Salt Lake City, the quart bottle of Cuervo Gold emerged from deep within a duffel bag. As the train whistled across the night-darkened desert, the poems began and the bottle went from full to empty. On board the Amtrak special were sixty or so poet lariats. These were prairie sages heading for Elko, Nev. for the first annual convention of cowboy poets."[13] In such renditions the journalist's view of the stereotypically authentic cowboy owes more to novels and films than to the neglected folk arts of the working people of the West.

Of course journalists' and travelers' accounts of western life—often romanticized—are nothing new. Browsing through the pages of popular magazines like *Frank Leslie's Illustrated Weekly* or *Harper's Weekly* from the 1870s and 1880s can quickly reveal the popularity of the topic. Those publications, and later the *Saturday Evening Post,* gave fledgling artists like Frederic Remington and N. C. Wyeth work as illustrators. Before the trail-drive days were over, touring performing groups such as Buffalo Bill's Wild West brought cowboys and other westerners to audiences on the East Coast and even to those in Europe. Dime novels, stage plays, and eventually movies extended popular visions of cowboy life.[14] The development of national parks, dude ranches, and touring facilities such as Harvey Houses also helped make the West a destination site for people seeking authenticity.

Cowboy poetry and song have long been offered to tourists as representations of the authentic West. National park concessioners frequently dressed bellhops, bus drivers, waiters, and waitresses in cowboy garb, sometimes even hiring local men and women with ranch backgrounds who could perform cowboy songs and poetry and square dance in their spare time. Dude ranches, a major vacation destination in the first half of the twentieth century, were faced with the challenge of incorporating guests into ranch life in such a way that they could feel they had participated fully in authentic ranch work. Remarkably, "dude wranglers" were also influenced by the presence of the dudes, as Laurence R. Borne has pointed out:

> As the economic significance of dude ranching grew . . . ranchers paid more attention to their guests. Cowboys were eventually referred to more frequently as wranglers, as they had to devote more of their time and effort to the dudes. There was still plenty of ranch work to be done, but some activities were carried out primarily for the amusement of the dudes. Clothing worn by the cowboy-wrangler was occasionally more "picturesque" than before, and some westerners chided the man wearing such attire as a "diamond-pointed" or drugstore cowboy.[15]

The increasing economic and cultural impact of dude ranches also found expression in dozens of cowboy poems, most of them critical of ranch hands who had "sold out" and "gone to wrangling dudes." Best known of these are E. A. Brininstool's "The 'Dude Rancher's' Wail" and Gail Gardner's "The Dude Wrangler," in which a cowboy murders an old friend because "when a cowboy turns dude wrangler, / He ain't no good no more at all."[16]

Ironically, the chief problem with the Gatherings' increasing tourist orientation is that for many the authenticity of the performances becomes suspect. Performers go to extraordinary, untraditional lengths for non-cowboy audiences, and the visitor-tourists, nurtured on the glitter and romance of "western" images as diverse as *Maverick,* country-western singers, and the dress styles of Gerry Spence and Ronald Reagan, seem generally satisfied with sham performances that reconfirm their faith in western authenticity. Insofar as the Gatherings claim to present authentic cowboy life, art, and performance, they are likely to encourage sloppy popularization as they frustrate the public quest for authenticity by constantly lamenting the disappearing "true cowboys," who are generally pictured as an endangered species just riding off into the sunset.[17]

The enormous popularity and publicity of Cowboy Poetry Gatherings in Elko and elsewhere have each year attracted larger tourist audiences. Cowboy poets have appeared repeatedly on late-night television talk shows. Alarmingly enough, people who in 1984 had never heard of cowboy poetry, who could not identify cowboy poets in their own counties or towns, are now billing themselves as cowboy poets—and have business cards to prove it. If the mere representation or assertion of authenticity satisfies the public quest for the true West, what remains for those whose families have worked with livestock for generations, absorbed the formulaic conventions of cowboy poetry at an early age, and sacrificed comfort and financial security out of respect for this way of life?

Among folklorists, the term *authenticity* has usually denoted the quality of the relationship between a performer or artist and the traditional forms and contexts in which that person works. "Cowboy Joe is an authentic folk artist because he learned his stuff from his grandfather and is well-known in his community as the best cowboy around; Slickheels Pete is not authentic because he learned to ride at a dude ranch." Such comparisons unwittingly conform to the derivative and popularized versions of western life that folklorists have sought to overcome. Defining the relationship between the artist and the form or style or context of work is an incomplete and biased way of judging the value of that work and that artist. Information about the performance of the art and the experience of the audience is just as vital to understanding the tradition as are questions of integrity and authenticity.

The touristic experience is the key to understanding the current perplexing popularity of this traditional regional art. The journey by an audience (i.e., tourists) to a special place (Elko), the presence of special performers and performances, and the special marking and naming of those performances by folklorists, organizers, and observers conform to Dean MacCannell's analysis of tourist attractions as locales that bring together tourists, sights, and markers.[18] To MacCannell, tourists are people seeking "an *authentic* and *demystified* experience of an aspect of some society or other person."[19] In MacCannell's terms, tour guides (including folklorists and historians) "mark" performances, which thereby acquire the status of "sights" for tourists. Equally important in the character of tourist productions is providing individual tourists with an opportunity to create or accumulate their own markers—significant objects or experiences—of the sights.

As tourist productions, Cowboy Poetry Gatherings have become something larger than straightforward presentations of a limited or esoteric folk art. They combine elements of traditional life, regional and artistic identity, popular culture, and philosophical orientation in a display that invites the exchange of markers about cowboy (and, perhaps, American) life. At Elko, in front of a national audience as well as a local one, cowboys are the featured part of a display that seems to answer the quest for authentic cowboy experience through the re-creation of folk poetry performances. Individual tourists in this setting can observe and collect as many markers (whether programs, verbal introductions, or photographs) as they wish and can also create markers of their own by conversing with poets, purchasing books and tapes, and hunting autographs.

MacCannell argues that observers who concentrate on the authenticity of performances with respect to real life ignore the responses and participation of tourists in the event. It is doubtful that anyone would confuse the recitations in the Elko Convention Center with the authentic ones that occur within small groups of working cowboys. Nor do observers demean the poetry or the poets on that account. No one doubts that the Gatherings are sets of performances, public presentations of a traditional verbal art far removed from bunkhouse, chuck wagon, and barroom. Neither the continuing vitality and resilience of the cowboys, who have been mourned as a disappearing breed for a hundred years, nor the poetic tradition itself seem seriously in doubt given the number of self-published books and cassettes on the market and the ever-increasing popularity of cowboy poetry at new locales: banquets, fund-raisers, political events, and state and county fairs.

This awareness on the part of audience and performers about the created nature of these events signifies a sophistication based on the knowledge that this special experience—the heartfelt recitation of poems that contain the most important values and experiences of the group—also occurs in other contexts. The awkwardness of some cowboys in front of the microphone did not matter. Their families and friends were proud to see them onstage, even if everyone knew that podiums, sound systems, and formal introductions were not part of cowboy poetry's historical or cultural development. The folklorists' acquired knowledge about cowboy poetry and public presentations has created the Gatherings as markers of the cowboy poetry tradition for a variety of audiences, the primary one being cow-country people who have heard cowboy poetry all their lives. If the media wish to carry on about "poet lariats," that is typical and humorous but not threatening.

At Melvin Whipple's house I, as a fieldworker, came as close as a non-cowboy could to observing the performance of cowboy poetry in its presumed authentic setting, although there might have been any number of variations in physical details. All of the things I saw and heard confirmed the power and relevance of traditional cowboy poetry. As a fieldworker, I began to create a tourist attraction by marking Melvin's performance with a recording. The attraction came together at Elko when an audience witnessed his performance. Later, the publication of Melvin's book and cassette by the Institute of Texan Cultures further brought him into the tourist experience. At that point, having brought the poet to the public, my experience at Melvin Whipple's house ceased to matter. What mattered was the audience's ability and willingness to mark and absorb the performance as part of its personal experience, knowing at the same time that this experience was vastly different from Melvin's working and creative life.

Audiences are not stupid in wanting to verify the reality of other people, and tourist productions do not succeed or fail on the basis of their creators' privileged access to, or interpretation of, that reality. The solution to the dilemma of authenticity is not to dismiss authenticity but to answer the quest of tourists by encouraging the sharing of experiences rather than the acquisition of markers.

The special achievement of Cowboy Poetry Gatherings has been to make far-flung western communities aware that their poetic traditions can become vehicles for shared identity and for a discussion of the economic, social, and political questions that affect them. The complementary danger nevertheless remains that commercialized versions of that tradition will overwhelm community-based performances. Cowboy poetry, like so many other products, is growing to meet the demands of a market. The pernicious effects of popularization occur when performances presented as authentic representations of group values are copied, imitated, and multiplied only to take advantage of the market.

The real success of Cowboy Poetry Gatherings lies not in the clinching of the authentic by folklorists but in the participation in the cowboy poetry experience by an audience who, all having access to more or less the same facts, come to a consensus that the quality of the experience is vital. The makeup of that audience is no less critical a factor than the selection of the poets who participate. The choice of Elko as the site has made for a combination of artists and local audiences who can respond to each other on the basis of a common regional and occupational identity and a familiarity with cowboy life. In addition, the gatherings have reached a much wider audience whose desire for experience is expressed by reaching out for such attenuated media as a forty-five-minute cassette or a thirty-second report on the evening news. Those who watch may or may not be satisfied with their experience, but if folklorists answer their desire for authenticity only by claiming to possess better markers, those who can generate markers on a mass scale will surely exploit cowboy poetry's popularity.

Notes

My thanks to David Stanley for his help in the preparation of this paper and also to Barbara Kirshenblatt-Gimblett for sharing with me the paper she coauthored with Edward M. Bruner.

1. Deirdre Donahue and Dirk Mathison, "Out Where the Sages Bloom, 120 Rhyme-Stoned Cowboys Show How the West Was Spun," *People,* 4 March 1985, 118; Gail Pellett, "Where Seldom Is Heard a Discouraging Word and the Cowboys Write Verses All Day," *Mother Jones,* July 1985, 32.

2. Jim McNutt, ed., *Echoes of the Past: The Cowboy Poetry of Melvin Whipple* (San Antonio: University of Texas Institute of Texan Cultures, 1987).

3. For a full discussion of Lomax's early career, see James C. McNutt, "Beyond Regionalism: Texas Folklorists and the Emergence of a Post-Regional Consciousness," Ph.D. diss., University of Texas at Austin, 1982, 16–165.

4. "Statement by Bess Lomax Hawes," Cowboy Poetry Gathering program, 1985, 3.

5. John A. Lomax, "William Lawrence Chittenden—Poet Ranchman," *Texas University Magazine* 11 (1896): 112–17.

6. Charles J. Finger, *Frontier Ballads* (Garden City: Doubleday, Page, 1927); Margaret Larkin, *Singing Cowboy: A Book of Western Songs* (New York: Knopf, 1931); N. Howard ("Jack") Thorp, *Songs of the Cowboys,* ed. Austin E. Fife and Alta S. Fife (1908), (New York: Clarkson N. Potter, 1966) and *Cowboy and Western Songs: A Comprehensive Anthology* (1969), (New York: Clarkson N. Potter, 1982); Glenn Ohrlin, *The Hell-Bound Train, a Cowboy Songbook* (Urbana: University of Illinois Press, 1973); John I. White, *Git Along, Little Dogies: Songs and Songmakers of the American West* (Urbana: University of Illinois Press, 1975); and Jim Bob Tinsley, *He Was Singin' This Song: A Collection of Forty-Eight Traditional Songs of the American Cowboy, with Words, Music, Pictures, and Stories* (Orlando: University Presses of Florida, 1981) are only a few of the many books and articles in this category.

7. Charles Kortes, "Poets Gathering, 1985," in *Cowboy Poetry: A Gathering,* ed. Hal Cannon (Salt Lake City: Gibbs Smith, 1985), 110–11.

8. Hal Cannon, "Welcome to the Cowboy Poetry Gathering," Cowboy Poetry Gathering program, 1985, 2.

9. John A. Lomax, *Cowboy Songs and Other Frontier Ballads* (1910), (New York: Macmillan, 1922), xvii, xxiii.

10. Archie Green, "Austin's Cosmic Cowboys: Words in Collision," in *"And Other Neighborly Names": Social Process and Cultural Image in Texas Folklore,* ed. Richard Bauman and Roger D. Abrahams (Austin: University of Texas Press, 1981), 152–94.

11. "In Arizona: Cowboy Poets," *Time,* 25 Nov. 1985, 24.

12. William H. Goetzmann and William N. Goetzmann, *The West of the Imagination* (New York: W. W. Norton, 1986), 242–56.

13. Donahue and Mathison, "Out Where the Sages Bloom," 115.

14. An excellent overview of popular images of the West can be found in Goetzmann and Goetzmann, *The West of the Imagination.*

15. Lawrence R. Borne, *Dude Ranching: A Complete History* (Albuquerque: University of New Mexico Press, 1983), 112.

16. E. A. Brininstool, "The 'Dude Rancher's' Wail," in Brininstool, *Trail Dust of a Maverick* (Los Angeles: Gem Publishing, 1926), 67–68; Gail I. Gardner, "The Dude Wrangler," in *Cowboy Poetry,* ed. Cannon, 5–7. See also Borne, *Dude Ranching,* 112–17; and Joel H. Bernstein, *Families That Take in Friends: An Informal History of Dude Ranching* (Stevensville, Mont.: Stoneydale Press, 1982).

17. A surprising number of cowboy poems from all periods echo this notion. See E. A. Brininstool, "The Disappointed Tenderfoot" and James Barton Adams, "A Cowboy Toast," both in *Songs of the Cattle Trail and Cow Camp,* ed. John A. Lomax (1919), (New York: Duell, Sloan and Pearce, 1950), 182–83, 176–78; and J. W. Beeson, "Last of a Breed," in *Coolin' Down: An Anthology of Contemporary Cowboy Poetry,* ed. Phil Martin (Tulsa: Guy Logsdon Books, 1992), 8–9.

18. Dean MacCannell, *The Tourist: A New Theory of Leisure Class* (New York: Schocken Books, 1976), 109–10.

19. MacCannell, *The Tourist,* 94, emphasis in the original.

26

Cowboy Poetics at the Millennium

John C. Dofflemyer

In 1994 alone, no less than six new anthologies of cowboy poetry became available to the book-buying public, all preceded by Phil Martin's *Coolin' Down: An Anthology of Contemporary Cowboy Poetry* (Guy Logsdon Books, 1992) and Ted Stone's *Riding the Northern Range: Poems from the Last Best-West* (Red Deer College Press, 1993). These followed Hal Cannon's groundbreaking collections for publisher Gibbs Smith, especially two cowboy poetry anthologies published in 1985 and 1990 that sold fifty thousand copies each and demonstrated the lucrative, bottom-line possibilities for adventurous publishing houses.[1]

Considering that contemporary cowboy poetry has only been widely recognized since 1985 and that only two or three magazines regularly print more than two or three cowboy poems per issue, the enormous popularity of an oral, entertainment-oriented poetry tradition breaks all literary precedent. Some poets even label cowboy poetry an oxymoron and view their own existence as a conundrum, like the trickster of Ian Tyson's "The Coyote and the Cowboy."[2] What a paradoxical and fertile mindset this is for a genre's rebirth. And when scholars and academic poets cringe as self-published print runs of what they call "doggerel" outsell their own dusty inventories, all of these things that "don't seem right" seem to nurture the growth of cowboy poetry.

After the publication of Cannon's second anthology, it was whispered at poetry gatherings that the cowboy poetry craze would surely weaken and wither, that few gatherings could break even consistently, and that only a few poets could afford to attend regularly. In 1990, though, approximately sixty poetry gatherings were held across the West. Three years later, according to the Western Folklife Center, there were 150.

What's more, none of the new poetry anthologies repeat each other. Each emphasizes a different cultural slant, theme, and poetic form from the others. The debate over traditional rhymed and metered poetry versus new, free-verse, open-form styles has broadened the genre to encompass a variety of styles and forms and encouraged individuality through the examples of such poets as Baxter Black, Waddie Mitchell, Wallace McRae, Buck Ramsey, and others who have created niches for themselves. That individualism is confirmed again in their musical counterparts—such originals as Ian Tyson, Red Steagall, and Don Edwards—who have worked within the tradition yet trusted in their uniqueness and where it might lead.

Conformity and nonconformity have always been part of the fluctuating, cyclical tension within artistic expression. Whether "cowboy poetry" as a folk art is strictly tied to continuing the forms of the classic examples of Bruce Kiskaddon, Badger Clark, Gail Gardner, and Curley Fletcher or whether the remnant cowboys at the end of the twentieth century are so contaminated by modern living that they are no longer capable of matching these purer, traditional strains, it is apparent that contemporary poetic expression from this work culture is evolving—and rapidly. Meanwhile, most advocates of traditional form fall short of their classic models; fewer yet attempt to build upon or improve the form—with a few notable exceptions.

Of these exceptions, Wallace McRae enhances the traditional form, tightening the meter from easy prepositional phrases to alliterative adjectives and cacophonous adverbs to drive his message home. This move from the light anapestic metrical foot of the traditionalists to stronger iambs and spondees seems consistent with the state of affairs of contemporary cowboy culture. Many of McRae's more powerful works forge his outrage over environmental destruction and his ethical narratives into a shorter, more urgent line. McRae may base his work in the tradition of regular meter and rhyme, but his innovations in developing more imperative metrics and subject matter break trail and buttress the foundation in cowboy poetry for the more contemporary free-versers. In "Put That Back . . . Hoedown" he takes the ballad form and makes it a square-dance rhythm:

Right hand across to the MX pad,
    Tell Ivan, "Howdy-do."
Left hand back with lead gloves on
    and, "General, how are you?"
Shimmy down in a Texas Star,
    with a chain saw in your hand,
And clear-cut trees two centuries old
    To McCulloch's Ragtime Band.

Hum, hum, uranium,
  Oh hear them Geigers rattle.
This beats to hell, any-old-day,
  them days with longhorn cattle.[3]

This imperative tone may be the impetus of an evolution as the contemporary sense of urgency over the future of a way of life seeks a congruent form. If one compares subject matter, metrics, and tone, this present urgency seems to be replacing most of the past-tense hyperbole about the "good old days" in today's cowboy poetry. Most imitative throwbacks to traditional subject matter ring hollow, obviously inapplicable to life on contemporary ranches and tending more toward oral slapstick entertainment for urban audiences. In most instances, the true, grass-roots voice of livestock culture has been silent since World War II, certainly in poetry, so the explosion of forms deviating from the traditional after nearly fifty years is a dam breaking.

Using McRae's metrics again as an example, the first stanza of his "Outlaw Acres" seems more concerned with stress-counting than with a strict adherence to the metrical foot. McRae's innovative stresses add flow and pause more congruent with a twentieth-century cowboy vernacular, less regimented than most schools yet depicting the imperative and accelerated pace and the sure thought processes and language of today's livestock owner:

"Outlaw Acres" now they call it. There's a rustic routed sign
At the entrance on a yucca planted knoll.
It's gumbo-slick and scabby with some sagebrush, stunted pine;
Not the paradise their smooth brochures extoll.[4]

Perhaps the old poetic laments for a disappearing way of life were premature. Like the buffalo, cowboy poets have apparently risen from the dead to flourish, although it is a more domestic strain of buffalo and cowboy than in the past.

One example of contemporary hyperbole is Rod McQueary's "Chicken Outfit," a poem about a rancher who applies cowboy techniques to a flock of inherited chickens. But even with its outrageous suppositions and exhaustive and humorous extended metaphor, it describes the realities of judges, courts, and inheritance as well as the necessity of pleasing the banker:

But then I missed a payment—
And Gee, it sure seemed sad,
The Dream-Land Bank foreclosed
Upon the place my uncle had.

The sheriff was a Christian soul

But he gave me quite a shock.
He said just the land was mortgaged
And I had to keep the stock.[5]

As Hal Cannon of the Western Folklife Center suggests, the flood of poetic expression from contemporary cowboys is essentially a grass-roots reaction by a culture under siege. As real as are the attacks from wilderness-at-all-costs environmentalists, from continuing governmental intervention with its new programs and regulations, and from vegetarian and animal-rights advocates, I suspect that the writing seed was planted decades earlier. In a good many cases, cowboy poets were writing issue-centered, politically active verse well before cowboy poetry became popular.

Western ranching culture has been an endangered species since World War II, and cowboy poetry has responded to that crisis. Blake Allmendinger argues that true cowboy culture ended around the end of the nineteenth century and therefore so did oral cowboy poetry as an expressive genre unique to that work culture.[6] Although the culture is obviously not in its prime politically or economically, Allmendinger's thesis ignores the men and women of that culture who have begrudgingly adapted and survived and whose offspring continually wrestle with the straightforward values and ethics by which they were raised and that still serve them well yet fly in the face of the values of most folks in town. College educations are common among contemporary cowboy writers, most of whom have been exposed to concentrated doses of urban living and values as well as the questioning chaos of the Vietnam War.

In my case, I began writing in earnest in the late 1960s, wrestling with the contrast, with my sense of non sequitur, between rural and urban worlds and quite aware of the paradoxical misconceptions that urban folks had of their country cousins. At fourteen I was transplanted to a private school in southern California, a planned extension of my education begun when my parents, among others in the rural area where we lived, had founded their own school when I was ten. With two full-time teachers for seventeen students in five grades, I was well-grounded in Latin, French, and literature when I left my ranch home, but I was not prepared for southern California. At the University of Southern California I was a small frog in a huge pond, humbled by the genius and wealth of classmates.

During the Vietnam War, I lived on the outskirts of Watts a year after the riots, blocks from the Shrine Hall and Auditorium, which was a mecca central to a musical rebirth based on country folk music with anti-war and anti-establishment lyrics. These were extreme times, magic and turbulent, yet the contrast with USC, a virtual country club for many upper-class young people in southern

California, was often difficult to comprehend. I began writing poetry in high school, but it was in L.A. that writing became a solace and a vital part of my life.

Although I had been introduced to the work of Gary Snyder when I was packing mules and tourists during summers in the Sierras, I knew very little about contemporary poetry. I would drive to a bookstore in Westwood near the UCLA campus and spend hours in the poetry section, reading, educating myself, and eventually buying the work of a few writers I liked: Robert Creeley, William Butler Yeats, William Carlos Williams, James Dickey, E. E. Cummings, and Donald Finkel. Poetry had purpose and value at a chaotic time in my life.

The importance of the Vietnam War and its effect on all poetic expression must not be taken lightly because at that time (the late 1960s and early 1970s), more than any other in the history of this nation, it became acceptable, almost politically correct, to protest the actions of the U.S. government. Subsequently, writing by veterans of that war has found its way into contemporary literature, and their poetry has also become a vehicle for political outrage, a grass-roots voice in cowboy culture. The historic genre-crossing work of cowboy poets Bill Jones and Rod McQueary not only garnered them a place among the strongest Namvet poets in this country but also spawned some second looks at what was happening in cowboy poetry, both from inside and outside the genre.[7]

Although early cowboy poetry may have helped shape the myth of the cowboy for cowboys, it was Hollywood's artificial polishing of this American icon that was sold to the American public. The image of the cowboy on celluloid encompassed heroic virtues that perhaps were necessary and believable before and after World War II. But the reality is that men and women who raise cattle are cast as second-class citizens, spoilers of the range, hayseeds, oafs, and rednecks—or all that and worse. William Kittredge has responded to the necessity of understanding and changing this myth:

> What's happening in the American West is we're staying with an official mythology that is in the process of being revised, but a lot of people want to hang onto the old version, mostly because they have some economic interest in doing so, and you can't blame them. . . . What we do as human beings more than anything else is invent ourselves in a story over and over again all day long. Recognitions, which are understandings of the world, never hold up, really. They work for awhile. Then we have to do it over and over again. In an individual life or in a society when you lock on some recognition or some version of some mythology and stay with it too long you're bound for disaster.[8]

Kittredge's comments well fit the state of affairs in cowboy poetry as well as the West, for cowboy poets are using new forms and new ideas to portray a West very different from the traditional myth, as, for example, Keith Wilson does in "Portrait of a Father":

My father was a hard man, closed
off from what he could not understand.
One night he tried to pry off the ring
from my mother's hand, she in a coma

he with a new woman waiting for the bright
glimpse of diamond in the darkened room—
it flashed and mother sighed, moved
as he slipped back through the door.[9]

The weightiness of Wilson's beginning stanzas would be difficult to match in metered rhyme, and often I suspect those advocating only the traditional line would rather avoid such introspection and reassessment of the myth of the West. Although I do not believe that to be the crux of the controversy over form, it is a factor, although subliminal in many cases.

If the resurgence of cowboy poetry is a reaction by a culture under siege as Hal Cannon suggests, that siege includes a grappling for identity in a larger world where the majority no longer sees cowboys in white hats. Subsequently, cattle people can no longer ride on the serial heroics of *Rawhide* and *Bonanza;* they must reinspect and sort out those cultural values worth saving from the behavior and attitudes they need to amend. That is a difficult task for a culture of poor communicators that is steeped in chauvinism—but people are learning, and this is cowboy poetry at the millennium:

That woman there
She can be a lead mare
Has watched horses so long
And so well she can tell what goes on
In their minds

In many respects, Sue Wallis's strong poems, like "Coyote Bitch," "Grandpa Lew," "Jenny Jo," and "Lead Mare" (quoted), have opened the door for wide-open female expression within the cowboy genre.[10] That "Lead Mare" may be about more than horses and her mother is but one example of the way many women of the West are honestly speaking their minds. Two anthologies attest to the power of women's poetry: Teresa Jordan's *Graining the Mare: The Poetry of Ranch Women* and *Maverick Western Verse,* which I edited. Both were published simultaneously by Gibbs Smith in January 1994, and in the early editorial stages Teresa and I were both concerned about diluting the "woman's voice," yet we only duplicated a couple of poems in offering forty-one different female poets from the West in the two projects combined.

The woman's voice in cowboy poetry may be more instrumental in the evolution of the genre than anyone has acknowledged to date. With such forthright poets as Linda Hussa, Ruth Daniels, Doris Bircham, Thelma Poirier, Laurie Wagner Buyer, Jo-Ann Mapson, Jennifer Olds, Audrey Hankins, Peggy Godfrey, Penelope Reedy, and a host of others, it is reasonable to conclude that women may keep their male counterparts honest in rewriting the West. These women, among others, write cowboy poetry from deeper in their guts than men, and their learned powers of observation, silent and unexpressed for the most part until recently, constitute another dam breaking, consistent with the explosive nature of the genre. Women's expression contains a tough stoicism and powerful honesty, as exemplified by Audrey Hankins's "Relapse":

AA books and Coors cans—
Fresh starts, forgotten vows.
Everything of yours
Wears the "hard-use" brand
Earmarked by neglect.

Through prisms of tears
Somber shadows and fears
I watch you mount
That same old bronc
And I know he'll kill you yet.[11]

What has happened with the advent of free verse, in addition to the ongoing (but going-nowhere) resistance to the form, is less humor. Once almost synonymous with cowboy poetry, humor has given way to more serious issues that face the ranching community politically, environmentally, socially, and economically. Cleverness is rare among those reassessing their place in the West and facing a constantly changing lifestyle. Baxter Black makes his living with rhymed and metered humorous verse, but the open form humor is wry and dry. Jim Green, Jay Dusard, Elizabeth Bancroft, Doris Bircham, Drum Hadley, Paul Zarzyski, and Charles Potts also demonstrate this ironic tone in *Maverick Western Verse,* yet the form is capable of more. A lack of humor is a function of the times as well as a deliberate and conscious effort by some poets to separate themselves from the slapstick stuff that tends to depict cowboys as buffoons; it is not a stance for a culture that is trying to save itself. Nevertheless, Greg Keeler walks the tightrope between seriousness and humor as well as any in "Llamas in the Landscape":

And sorry ol' Paint,
but your hooves,
your flat iron clodhoppers
are too fat and careless
for what's left
of the trail.
Yes bring on Phoebe
and Fauntleroy
floating over their bird-toes
like mottled balloons,
leaving the path intact
for this new age
of huge moist eyes
and batting eyelashes—[12]

Humor is inherent in the cowboy lifestyle because there is much to laugh about in the less-regimented reaches of cowboy experience. Most were taught to laugh at themselves when young and learning new skills, to laugh at tenderfeet doing the same, and then they learned to find relief in that helpless, humble humor that comes when the best-laid plans go amuck due to the incalculable and unpredictable happenstances that go with raising livestock. Humor is too intrinsic to cowboy poetry not to resurface more boldly in the open forms.

As the editor of *Dry Crik Review,* which has published more free verse than rhymed and metered poetry, I have been in the middle of a controversy over form for several years and subsequently privy to numerous opinions forecasting the demise and ruination of cowboy poetry. Throughout, I have tried to offer a balance between written and oral expression, knowing that the written word is and always has been a personal inspiration, and to provide a forum for communication between rural and urban worlds.

What concerns me most, because the debate has become divisive, is the loss of commonsense experience and orality, whether in the search for original rhyme or the loss of spontaneity in that search. I am saddened by what appears to be a closed-minded, defensive stance from traditional rhymers, yet I'm proud of those individuals for holding fast to their authentic guns, which come from, in most instances, a lifetime of hands-on experience. Perhaps it is just another stage in the father-son generational battle played out within the genre. Nevertheless, it is real and full of that pioneer, never-say-die spirit from which we all have evolved.

Personally, I find the nonconformist route more consistent within a trailblazing cattle culture. More often, my manifest destiny becomes a quest not only for my nature but also for human nature, which the ever-present benefits of progress have temporarily or partially domesticated. Half a dozen cowboy poets are writing of men's and women's issues and delving into their hard-core cowboy psyches to take good, long, honest looks at themselves. In doing so, they are using simple metaphors tied to daily experiences with animal behavior and nature to offer insightful and unique perspectives on the complicated beasts we have all become. That this kind of explorative inquisitiveness comes from a macho cow culture packed with powerful paradoxes undermining age-old paradigms is very interesting. And as these poets inspire others, and are in turn inspired, their poetry matters as part of the evolution of all western verse.

Whether it remains labeled as cowboy poetry is of little importance as more and more appears in small-press publications throughout the United States. That this verse has appeal outside cowboy circles and is circulated ever more widely is a sign of bridge-building between the urban and the rural.

Lingering perhaps in redundancy, the contemporary vision of many cowboy writers may be less cluttered than their urban or academic counterparts. As such, their expression is more lucid and uses old terms and language with common work-related meanings, lending a more visual and intellectual accessibility to the page. If one compares the utility of poetic maps from rural and urban worlds, cowboy expression has the potential to take the reader farther down the trail with fewer diversions or quizzical ambiguities. Rod McQueary and Bill Jones's volume of Vietnam poetry has received exceptional reviews from academic circles. What is more interesting in terms of poetics is how McQueary uses the white spaces of the page as oral pauses, somewhat as the Beat Generation poets did. Even though McQueary has not been directly influenced by them, his work is consistent with theirs in the evolution of a deliberate oral presentation. Even his pause-filled recitation of "For Woody," although based on a rhymed and metered template of Henry Herbert Knibbs, is unique and effective as McQueary manipulates his recitation for emphasis.

In the process of editing his poem "for souls," published in both *Blood Trails* and *Maverick Western Verse,* I opted to place spaces consistent with Rod's pauses to make this lyric, open-form poem more accessible to the reader, as in the first stanza:

Perhaps,
He said, it's not a man's heart or mind
That drives him down to surging sea
To straining mast.
Not mind, he said, that makes him fill
Some quivering stirrup   eagerly
To float across the grunting

Pounding range,
Hat fanning reckless, loose and fast.
Not mind that sends him high
    beyond the tether of the wind   or cloud,[13]

It was Gary Snyder's influence that suggested editing Rod's poem in this manner. The most original and innovative force within the genre is Paul Zarzyski, an ex-rodeo cowboy and a student of Richard Hugo, who effectively explores the margins between academic and cowboy poetry. Exposure to his work inspires more experimentation and illustrates that cowboy poetry is no longer isolated, although it was never a totally free or pure expression that popped mystically out of the heads of cowboys on cattle drives.

Headed in a different, perhaps opposite, evolutionary direction is the melodic, perfectly metered work of J. B. Allen, who would insist that he doesn't know an iamb from a trochee. His closely woven verse continually threads allegorical wisdom consistent with the traditional storytelling nature of the culture and its individualism, which insists that no one be left without pride. Allen uses experimental, nontraditional line breaks as pauses in tight stanzas to allow more time for introspection in his poetry than is evidenced by most of the classic cowboy poets, as in "KINGS AND SLAVES":

FIERCE AS GRIZZLIES IN THE SPRINGTIME
PROUD AS SAGE HENS CAUGHT IN RUT
TOUGH AS RAWHIDE CURED IN SEASON
HARD AS GRANITE SHAVINS—BUT

    INSIDE

THERE LIVED AN ARTIST'S EYE
A POET'S WAY WITH WORDS
RESPECT FOR PROPER WOMEN FOLK
AND SLAVE TO GRAZIN HERDS.

RIDING DRAG OR WRANGLIN HORSES
SERVIN HOODLUM TO THE COOK
SEEMED A DANG SIGHT MORE EXCITIN
THAN A WALKIN PLOW OR BOOK.[14]

When one considers the independent and individualistic nature of cowboy culture, born out of an adaptive instinct to survive based on hands-on experience and celebrating thinking for oneself apart from the herd, there is great potential here. Combined with the honest and powerful new voices of women, the encroaching outside pressures on the land and the lifestyle, and the necessity to reidentify in a changing West, many of the necessary ingredients for an explosion of western expression are already in place. In a larger political arena, the chaotic pressures facing westerners remind me of my days at USC, writing nights in my apartment, a converted stable once a part of a great estate.

Because television is an equal-opportunity polluter equating self-esteem with more consumption, and because the psychological ill-health of the United States is bent on pointing fingers away from home, cowboys have much to reconcile as a minority trying to preserve their distance, lifestyle, and sanity. The best of cowboy expression is yet to come, although I suspect that label will change to encompass a more rural perspective. Nevertheless, the tentative beginnings of cowboy poetry gatherings and the selfless spirit and networking that have evolved may spawn poetry as a hands-on art tool, like a rawhide riata, to become a major influence in western American literature.

Notes

1. Hal Cannon, ed., *Cowboy Poetry: A Gathering* (Salt Lake City: Gibbs Smith, 1985); Hal Cannon, ed., *New Cowboy Poetry: A Contemporary Gathering* (Salt Lake City: Gibbs Smith, 1990).

2. Ian Tyson, "The Coyote and the Cowboy," on *Cowboyography,* a 12-inch L.P. (Eastern Slope Records, ESL-01, 1986).

3. Wallace McRae, "Put That Back . . . Hoedown," in McRae, *Cowboy Curmudgeon* (Salt Lake City: Gibbs Smith, 1992), 86–88.

4. The complete text of Wallace McRae's "Outlaw Acres" was first published in *Dry Crik Review* 2–3 (Fall 1992–Winter 1993): 40.

5. Rod McQueary, "Chicken Outfit," *Dry Crik Review* 4 (Winter-Spring 1994): 40–43.

6. Blake Allmendinger, *The Cowboy: Representations of Labor in an American Work Culture* (New York: Oxford University Press, 1992).

7. Bill Jones and Rod McQueary, *Blood Trails* (Lemon Cove, Calif.: Dry Crik Press, 1993).

8. Kevin Bezner, "A Communal Story of the West: An Interview with William Kittredge," *Writers Northwest Handbook,* 5th ed. (Hillsboro, Ore.: Blue Heron Publishing, 1993), 5–7.

9. Keith Wilson, "Portrait of a Father," in *Maverick Western Verse,* ed. John C. Dofflemyer (Salt Lake City: Gibbs Smith, 1994), 150–51. The poem was first published in *Kayak* and also appears in Keith Wilson, *Bosque Redondo: The Encircled Grove* (Santa Fe: Pennywhistle Press, 1997).

10. Sue Wallis, "Lead Mare," in Wallis, *The Exalted One* (Lemon Cove, Calif.: Dry Crik Press, 1991) and in Wallis, *Another Green Grass Lover* (Lemon Cove, Calif.: Dry Crik Press, 1994). The poem is also in *Graining the Mare: The Poetry of Ranch Women,* ed. Teresa Jordan (Salt Lake City: Gibbs Smith, 1994), 147.

11. Audrey Hankins, "Relapse," in *Graining the Mare,* ed. Jordan, 64. The poem was first published in *Dry Crik Review* 2 (Winter 1992): 17.

12. Greg Keeler, "Llamas in the Landscape," in Keeler, *Epiphany at Goofy's Gas* (Livingston, Mont.: Clark City Press), 1991; see also *Maverick Western Verse,* ed. Dofflemyer, 64–65.

13. Rod McQuery, "for souls," in *Maverick Western Verse,* ed. Dofflemyer, 76.

14. J. B. Allen, "KINGS AND SLAVES," *Dry Crik Review* 2 (Summer 1992): 22.

27

Making Ourselves at Home

William Kittredge

Ross Dollarhide was the great man in the make-believe of my childhood, king of the mountain in our backlands kingdom and buckaroo boss for my grandfather on the MC ranch in Warner Valley, over in southeastern Oregon. Ross took me on my first trip to what we called "the desert" just before the beginning of World War II, when I was nine years old.

It was a long and serious day, in which I began to discover how to feel sheltered however far from the gentleness of my mother and her household. We left before sunup in Dollarhide's black 1939 Ford V-8, and he returned me to home long after midnight, a transformed boy who had traveled maybe three hundred miles of dusty, jolting wagon-track road across the sagebrush and creosote flats and rimrocks with a hard-handed legendary gentleman.

Some sixty miles out as the crow flies we reached our farthest remove from the irrigated enclave of Warner Valley at a place called Ackley Camp, an unpainted two-room lineshack with a long vista over the sagebrush expanses of Hawk's Valley to the south and east. Alongside the shack there was a hillside spring where skunk cabbage grew, a watering trough, and a woven willow horse corral. Dollarhide found black and red ants in the sugar. "Piss ants," he said, and he shook his head.

"Maybe they taste like piss," he said, when I asked him where they got the name. No matter the heat of July, he built a fire in the wood stove, heated a can of stew, and fed me.

An old man I knew only as John the Swede held down the line camp there at Ackley Mountain from May to early November, riding each day to look after MC cows and calves scattered across a territory the size of Rhode Island. It was a good sign that he was nowhere to be found; he had to be out horseback and working.

We stacked a few crates of assorted canned goods on the kitchen floor, and Dollarhide left him a laboriously written note.

John the Swede was famous in our world because of his trips to the Labor Day Rodeo in Lakeview. After four months at Ackley Camp with no way to spend his money, the Swede would gear up with a full rig of new clothes, a barbershop bath and haircut and shave, and settle into a room in one of the half-dozen whorehouses out on the far side of the rodeo grounds, in the little village of whores called Hollywood. After a week or so, the rodeo over, John would be ready to go back to the ringing silences on Ackley Mountain, sexually spent, worn out from the booze and the talking, and broke.

You have to wonder if he was eager to return into a lifetime of dialogue with himself. Those men who went to the line camps seemed to cherish the isolation. "For a week or two," one of them told me, "you worry about what's going on in town, then you get so you can't much remember town, and you sure as hell don't give a shit what they're doing."

While Dollarhide sat at the little kitchen table and composed his note with the thick stub of a carpenter's pencil, I nosed around like a boy and found a few words and even some phrases and verses inscribed into the softwood walls and doorjambs of the cabin. Not just written but inscribed, marked over and over with a heavy hand, cut into the grain of the wood. A few lines of rhyming poetry, some words from "The Strawberry Roan," the names of a woman, a man, and another woman, listed in a row, like a mantra.

That's almost fifty years ago, and I cannot recall any sense of those lost words and none of that verse. I would like to imagine that John the Swede spent some of his time at Ackley making up poems as men will in such isolation. I wish I could believe that the words he chose to inscribe into his walls would have helped me in my battle against my own isolations.

During the years of my young manhood after World War II we developed the habit of listing the names of men traveling with the MC chuck-wagon crew on the off-white oilcloth tacked to the kitchen walls of another camp, a place in Guano Valley, an abandoned homestead called the Dougherty place. Each time the wagon visited, at least once during the early summer branding and again in the late fall, moving the cattle back home to winter on the meadows in Warner, we would print our names on the wall in order of rank, starting at the top with Dollarhide and ending with the cook and wrango boy. I was proud to be on those lists and still am. I stopped to visit them any time I was in the country.

But those lists are gone now. There was a highway built across our deserts in the 1960s, close by the Dougherty place. Hitchhiking travelers camped in those barren rooms and added their names to the lists on the walls. Then, in the last half-dozen years, someone came in and stripped the place of all that oilcloth.

I like to imagine some anthropologist has it now, preserved in a room with precisely controlled humidity, and that our scribblings will someday be cherished as we cherish the cave paintings in France. Which is ridiculous, I know. The paintings in the caves at Altamira and Lascaux are sacred expressions of a dream inhabited by animals, which was life. And they are profoundly beautiful. Our lists of our own names on that oilcloth reflected the same instincts, our yearning to pin down our connection with significances, but they were beautiful only to us.

That yearning for connection inhabits my inclination to keep revisiting that country and writing about the people I knew there, just as it stands a good chance of accounting for much of whatever it was John the Swede wrote on the walls at Ackley. We keep trying to find some name for the dream we inhabit.

John Charles Frémont came through that desert country with a troop of U.S. Army when it was almost entirely uninhabited by whites, during the winter of 1843, mapping as they went, naming everything. They plowed through three-foot drifts of snow to reach a rim from which they looked down on green meadows alongside hot springs at the shore of an alkaline lake, Winter Rim and Summer Lake. A few days later they celebrated Christmas at a place in Warner Valley called the Narrows, on a twisting waterway between swampy lakes where the Shoshone hunted. At their backs loomed the great cliffs of Hart Mountain; those soldiers fired their howitzer into the falling snow and thousands of waterbirds lifted to clamor in the wilderness sky; they drank their brandy and listened to the sighing of wings and must have known they hadn't mapped the significances of anything. Such naming is not so easy.

But it's the way we make ourselves at home in the world, one act of the imagination after another, telling stories, all the time after the meaning of things: saddlehorse, remuda, piss ant, Shoshone. We all know the poetry of such names, if we grew up to the country.

We spend our lives trying to name the dream we inhabit. On an October afternoon in 1982, cruising highway passes through the San Juan Mountains in southwestern Colorado, a friend and I took to making fun of ourselves and the ease of our lives. We were talking about John Colter, who entered the West by going up the Missouri with Lewis and Clark.

A few years later Colter walked hundreds of wintertime miles in the Yellowstone country (Colter's Hell), the first white man in such vast territory. For that he is legendary.

Colter, we said, would have just walked over the San Juan Mountains if they were in his way. We imagined some raggedy man in greasy buckskins, standing on a cliff, looking down on the bright upscale verities of Telluride. We saw him on the streets like a creature left over from another age of man.

We were mostly laughing at ourselves. It was a way of placing ourselves and our lives in history, in relationships to people who had no choice but to walk over mountains if they wanted to see the country beyond.

Storytelling is a prime way of figuring out who we are and should be. Each morning as we wake, we start telling a story to ourselves. It is a story starring ourselves. We listen to it as long as we live. The telling is almost as involuntary as breathing.

Think of the child you were, that distant creature. Remember what you thought you were going to be as an adult and how you learned to imagine such a story.

◇◇◇◇

My father had a genius for friendship, highjinks, and conversations conducted while leaning against a pickup truck with a bottle of beer in his hand, studying the sunset. As those men talked and I listened, I began learning to be whatever kind of man I am.

To my mother's endless consternation, my father also had an affinity for poker, nights on the town, and hunting trips. To quiet her, I think, he would take me along. Without plans having been made, we would stay out overnight.

When I was about eight he took me to the Cedarville Rodeo, where he ran into Butch Powers, a Surprise Valley rancher who later became lieutenant governor of California, a sweet and convivial man. After the rodeo was long over, when it had been planned that we would be well on our way toward home, we ended up in one of the old Basque eating establishments, the Golden Hotel, a two-story frame building under lombardy poplars along the main street of Cedarville. What I recall are the bright faces in that room with its yellow-painted walls, families at table. I recall the way they laughed when my father said, sure, go ahead, drink some wine like the other kids.

Later, I woke up sick in the woodbox beside the black ironwork stove in the kitchen. One of the cooks was washing the last of the dishes, soapsuds to her elbows. The dining room was thick with the talk and laughter of a half-dozen men who were playing cards and happy, my father among them. His face shone in the lamplight as he laid down his cards and rubbed the top of my head, looking around to his friends like someone blessed, and the child I was—even half sick and disoriented—saw how they loved him and even me.

What I did was pile some coats on a bench and go back to sleep. I don't know how we got home, but I do remember that my mother thought it was all right this once, since we'd been at the Golden Hotel, a family place, where she seemed to think nothing could go seriously wrong.

My father is dead, Butch Powers is dead, most of the people in that dining room are dead, and the Golden Hotel has been closed and lost to us for decades.

My mother is a very old woman. Not so long ago when I laughed and asked if she remembered the night my father took me to the Golden Hotel, she studied me a long moment and said, "Your father was the only man I ever wanted to marry."

Any society capable of naming itself lives inside stories; we ride them like rafts, they help us recall and define our lives and the lives of our people. We use them like maps, to locate ourselves and make sense of our purposes.

We invent and reinvent ourselves with stories. Stories are our prime way of naming ourselves, claiming our territories, and defining our emotional boundaries. Without them we aren't much of anybody. Our stories are gifts to ourselves and one another.

My mother and I understand a story about my father, in our separate ways, which allows us to express our profound regard for one another, and our lives are more significant because of it, and, of course, because of my father.

We hear, often quite justifiably, a lot of complaints about environmental damage caused by livestock grazing. Driving north along a willow-lined creek in Idaho, I found myself cursing a rancher whose cows had tromped reaches of the streamside into mud and dust. That, I thought, is a sorry goddamned way to do business.

Ranchland society, we know, those of us who grew up in the life, has often been deeply unfair. The men worked outdoors in the glorious world, sporting around with their horses and guns and pickup trucks and properties, and the women washed dishes and raised kids, sort of second-class citizens. Native Americans for the most part weren't treated like citizens at all.

Laulette Hansen grew up near the Missouri Breaks, where Charlie Russell roamed as a young man in Montana. She writes in a kind of lamentation, "There is a sense that we do not belong on the land, that we bring nothing positive to it; the last people to exist as an integral part of the land were the Native Americans but we are cursed: where we put our feet, we bring knapweed." She goes on, "If we once convince ourselves that our presence on the land was nothing but a long, tragic mistake, that what we knew as love was never anything but rape and abuse, I think we are in for a despair so deep we would be capable of taking out ourselves and the landscape with us. All we care about."[1]

And it's true. Our society in the West is evolving with enormous rapidity, and the changes are tough on people who thought they had a way of life locked down. A lot of working ranch people are angry. They know they aren't to blame. There is great sadness in the West, a pervasive sense of betrayal.

Who's to blame? No one, so far as I can tell, except maybe those who refuse to consider the necessity of change. It's a necessity that has always existed, everywhere. Giving in to anger is a way of giving up on ourselves and our ability to imagine our lives in fresh ways.

A rancher boy, bringing a half-dozen cows out of the rimrocks toward his father's home fields in the vast country north of the Black Rock Desert in Nevada, dreams of girls down by the Humboldt River in Winnemucca. While the snow blows, a woman in a barn out in those sagebrush distances listens to jazz on National Public Radio while braiding a rawhide riata. Both are making their lives inhabitable by acts of faith and imagination. That woman is trying to make her riata as perfect as the music; she is an artist. The boy is a hero of perseverance.

People on the laboring end of the livestock business should mostly be blessed for their endless efforts, which can be thought of as acts of devotion, ways of adding to the beauty of things, gifts to us all.

The world is everywhere symbolic, a wave of metaphor, our own invention, constructed from the flowering energies. We wouldn't be able to make sense of it otherwise.

Our stories, call them metaphors, are like filters or lenses. To a great degree they determine what we are capable of experiencing (or, more exactly, what we are capable of noticing that we have experienced).

It's pointless to mourn, because we can't go back to that time when it was possible to think our societies were changeless and going to last forever.

Our old isolated West doesn't exist any more. It was never just cowboy country; it was always more various than we imagined. Warner Valley, where I grew up, was predominantly Irish Catholic, families from County Cork. Heading south from Missoula I go down the road from culture to culture, enclave to enclave—from friends in the bars in rugged old Butte to ranchers along the Beaverhead and physicists from Arco who live in Idaho Falls among the country Mormons, from Gentile intellectuals among downtown Mormons in Salt Lake City to radical environmentalists in Moab and professional rafters in the Grand Canyon. It's a mix I sort of love to think about. And there's more—Hopi villages, Sun City after Sun City, cowhands, and cotton farmers.

What we know is that we must cherish and care for one another. Mary Oliver has written, "There is only one question: / How to love this world."[2]

All over the American West, cowboys and ranchwomen and farmhands and sheepherders have been gathering to declaim verse to one another. Such gatherings are heartbreaking in their openness, celebrations of things ranchland people respect and care about most deeply—the land they have chosen to live on, their work, and, right at the center, one another, this companionship.

We can all take heart from their willingness to name those things they take to be sacred. Their storytelling is as useful as anything we have.

Notes

Part of this essay is adapted from sections of *Hole in the Sky: A Memoir* (New York: Knopf, 1992). Used by permission of Alfred A. Knopf, Inc. The portion about the Golden Hotel was previously published in somewhat different form in *Sunset* 201 (Sept. 1998): 38.

1. A portion of this quotation first appeared in Laulette Hansen-Malchik, "A Piece of Forever," *Whitefish* (Winter–Spring 1995): 71. Used by permission of Laulette Hansen.
2. Mary Oliver, "Spring," in Oliver, *House of Light* (Boston: Beacon Press, 1992), 6.

Contributors

Jon Bowerman, originally from the Willamette Valley, now starts colts and works with problem horses on his ranch near Fossil, Oregon. Although he occasionally mixes cowboy poetry with an anti-drug and anti-alcohol message for a school assembly or combines poems and scriptures in a country church, he prefers the freedom offered by open range on a good horse.

Hal Cannon is founding director of the Western Folklife Center and the Cowboy Poetry Gathering in Elko, Nevada. He has published a dozen books and recordings on the folk arts of the American West, including *Cowboy Poetry: A Gathering* and *New Cowboy Poetry: A Contemporary Gathering.* Three of his books received Wrangler Awards from the National Cowboy Hall of Fame, and in 1998 he received the Will Rogers Lifetime Achievement Award. Currently producing radio programs for public radio stations throughout the country, he lives in Starr Valley, Nevada.

John Dofflemyer is a fifth-generation cattleman on the western slope of the Sierra Nevadas in California. He has also been the editor-publisher of *Dry Crik Review* and has published collections and chapbooks of several cowboy poets as well as other western rural writers under the Dry Crik Press imprint. He edited a collection of contemporary cowboy poetry, *Maverick Western Verse.* He attributes his first invitation to the 1989 Cowboy Poetry Gathering in Elko, Nevada, as being the catalyst for not only his publishing activities but also his own writing.

CAROL EDISON is the coordinator of the Folk Arts Program of the Utah Arts Council, where since 1978 she has worked to document and publicly present Utah's folk and ethnic arts and artists. In 1985 she wrote and edited *Cowboy Poetry from Utah: An Anthology.*

JIM GRIFFITH recently retired as coordinator of the Southwest Folklore Center, located in the library of the University of Arizona, where he also taught folklore. He has heard cowboy song and poetry since his teen years and likes to recite Kipling and other favorites while driving alone. A presenter of cowboy reciters at festivals and on stage since 1976, he helped with the first few Cowboy Poetry Gatherings in Elko, Nevada. He also works on the folklife of the Arizona-Sonora border region and has written *Southern Arizona Folk Arts, A Shared Space: Folklife in the Arizona-Sonora Borderlands,* and *Beliefs and Holy Places: A Spiritual Geography of the Pimería Alta.*

TERESA JORDAN was born and raised as part of the fourth generation on a Wyoming cattle ranch. She is the author of two works of nonfiction, *Cowgirls: Women of the American West,* an oral history, and *Riding the White Horse Home,* a memoir. She edited *Graining the Mare: The Poetry of Ranch Women* and, with James Hepworth, *The Stories That Shape Us: Contemporary Women Write about the West,* a collection of personal essays. She lives in rural Nevada with her husband, Hal Cannon, with whom she produces *The Open Road,* a public radio series on the American West.

BILL KATRA first strummed the rhythms of Argentine and Uruguayan cowboy songs while in the Peace Corps during the 1960s. Since then, his major teaching and research interest has been the cultural and intellectual history of those two countries during the nineteenth century. Having grown up in Seattle and studied in California and Michigan, he now calls La Crosse, Wisconsin, home, where he teaches at Viterbo College.

WILLIAM KITTREDGE recently retired from teaching creative writing at the University of Montana. His short stories, essays, and anthologies have made him one of the best-known contemporary western writers. In addition to *Hole in the Sky: A Memoir,* he is the author of *The Van Gogh Field and Other Stories, Owning It All, We Are Not in This Together,* and *Who Owns the West?* He also edited *The Last Best Place: A Montana Anthology* and *The Portable Western Reader.* He is in the throes of finishing a book called *Reimagining Desire.*

Ray Lashley was born and raised on a farm in the Missouri Ozarks at a place and time when horses or mules were about the only sources of power and transportation. He has been raising horses since 1970, first in Utah and now in Colorado. He started memorizing poetry, mostly cowboy poetry by the old writers—Curley Fletcher, Charles Badger Clark, and S. Omar Barker—in grade school and writing it in high school. Since appearing at the first Elko Cowboy Poetry Gathering, he has recited at a number of gatherings throughout the western United States.

For more than forty years Guy Logsdon has collected, written books and articles, and compiled and annotated recordings about cowboy songs, poetry, and lore, as well as about Woody Guthrie, Hopalong Cassidy, Bob Wills, western swing music, and the Dust Bowl. He has taught public school, raised cattle, and is now retired from the University of Tulsa, where he was director of libraries and professor of education and American folklife. Logsdon was a Smithsonian Institution Senior Post-Doctoral Fellow in 1990–91 and currently works as an entertainer, writer, and publisher of cowboy music and poetry. He is the author of *"The Whorehouse Bells Were Ringing" and Other Songs Cowboys Sing.*

Bill Lowman was born and raised in the badlands of western North Dakota, where he still ranches. A skilled cartoonist and storyteller as well as a poet, he has appeared at dozens of cowboy poetry gatherings throughout the West.

Jens Lund is an independent folklorist who lives in Olympia, Washington. In recent years, he has specialized in cultural tourism projects. The author of *Flatheads and Spoooneys: Fishing for a Living in the Ohio River Valley* and *Folk Arts of Washington State* and also of articles on fishing, logging, and other occupational traditions, he is an adjunct faculty member at the University of Washington.

Keith McKenry is an Australian poet and folklorist. He was a member of the Committee of Inquiry into Folklife in Australia and coauthor of its report, *Folklife: Our Living Heritage.* He also chaired UNESCO's Special Committee of Technical and Legal Experts on the Safeguarding of Folklore. There being no jobs for folklorists in Australia, Keith is also an alpaca breeder and assistant commissioner of taxation. He is also president of the organizing body of Australia's National Folk Festival. He has presented many workshops in Australian folklore and social history and often appears in concert as a poetry reciter at festivals and folk clubs. Keith has published two books of his own verse and has issued on CD and cassette a solo album of classic Australian ballads, *Bugger the Music, Give Us a Poem!* Earlier, with his friend and bush singer the late Alan Scott, he issued two pioneering albums of Australian bush songs and poems, performed in the traditional style: *Battler's Ballad* (1989) and *Travelling through the Storm* (1996). All these books and albums are available from Fanged Wombat Productions, 5 Bonney St., Ainslie, ACT 2602, Australia.

Jim McNutt is director of the North Carolina Museum of History in Raleigh. He is also a folklorist, scholar, and administrator who has conducted research, published, and created exhibits and other programs on topics as varied as nineteenth-century ranch women, Mexican American instrument makers, adobe housing, and folk music. Formerly director of research and collections for the Institute of Texan Cultures in San Antonio, he has written on the career of cowboy poetry and song collector John Lomax and edited a collection of Melvin Whipple's poetry, *Echoes of the Past.*

Craig Miller is a graduate of Florida State University with an M.S. in geography and of the University of Utah with an M.F.A. As a folklorist, he specializes in studies of cultural diversity in the American West. A former land surveyor and gold miner, he has worked for the Utah Arts Council's Folk Arts Program since 1983, researching and documenting traditional culture in Utah. In that capacity he has assisted at every Elko Cowboy Poetry Gathering. He is now working on projects documenting traditional dance in the state of Utah.

Warren Miller is education director of the Sharlot Hall Museum in Prescott, Arizona, a museum of territorial Arizona history named for poet-historian Sharlot M. Hall (1870–1943), one of the first woman cowboy poets. Warren has served as a staff member at most of the Cowboy Poetry Gatherings in Elko, including the first, and also founded the Arizona Cowboy Poets Gathering in 1988. He has edited an anthology of contemporary cowboy poetry, *Cattle, Horses, Sky, and Grass.*

Glenn Ohrlin was raised in Minnesota, hit the rodeo trail at an early age, and traveled throughout the American West. He soon became interested in cowboy poetry and song and began collecting from those he met. Since the early 1960s he has been a popular performer of cowboy songs at festivals and gatherings around the world. He ranches in the Ozark Mountains of Arkansas and is the author of *The Hell-Bound Train: A Cowboy Songbook.*

Scott Preston dropped out of college in 1979 in Michigan to relocate, after a period of travel, in Idaho. Among other occupations, he has worked as a ranch hand, projectionist, house painter, ski-lift operator, and express courier. A self-taught writer, his poetry and prose have been published by small presses throughout America, including numerous essays and reviews on the cowboy poetry movement, which he has followed since the first Elko Gathering in 1985.

Buck Ramsey (1938–98) as a young man punched cows and snapped out broncs on some of the big ranches along the Canadian River in the Texas Panhandle. Despite being injured in a bucking accident in 1962, he was able to keep his hand in as something of a cowboy by writing poetry and prose about the cow-country West and by singing the traditional cowboy songs that he learned as a youngster. He won two Wrangler Awards from the National Cowboy Hall of Fame for his recordings of cowboy song, *Rolling Uphill from Texas* and *My Home It Was in Texas,* and in 1993 he published a long poem about cowboy life, *And as I rode out on the morning.* In 1995 he was named a National Heritage Fellow by the National Endowment for the Arts.

Charlie Seemann is executive director of the Western Folklife Center in Elko, Nevada, the sponsor of the annual Cowboy Poetry Gathering. He was previously deputy director for Collections and Research at the Country Music Foundation in Nashville, Tenessee. He has written numerous articles on cowboy and western music and has produced and annotated a number of documentary record/CD reissues, including *Back in the Saddle: Songs of the American Cowboy,* which was nominated for a Grammy and received a Wrangler Award from the National Cowboy Hall of Fame.

Ronna Lee Sharpe is state folklorist for western Colorado and represents the Colorado Council on the Arts and Colorado Mountain College. Since marrying Tom at the 1991 Durango Cowboy Poetry Gathering, she has acquired a horse called Buddy and spends her spare time riding the high country and helping work cattle. The Sharpes live in Grand Junction, Colorado.

Tom Sharpe collects, recites, and researches classic and contemporary poetry. His original poetry is based on forty years' cowboying experience. He rides day labor at every opportunity and is trying "to make one more good horse." Working as a farm and ranch realtor, he must daily balance his personal respect for traditional agricultural land use with the professional realities of a rapidly developing region of the West.

Kim Stafford holds a Ph.D. in medieval literature from the University of Oregon and is the author of several books of poetry and of *Having Everything Right: Essays of Place.* He has also written essays and introductions for books of photography and other collections and recorded a compact disk of his own songs, *Wheel Made of Wind.* He lives in Portland, Oregon, with his wife and children, where he directs the Northwest Writing Institute at Lewis and Clark College.

David Stanley teaches folklore and American literature at Westminster College in Salt Lake City. He has served as a staff member at all but one of the Cowboy Poetry Gatherings in Elko and frequently uses cowboy poetry in his classes to demonstrate the roots of poetry in the history and culture of the West.

Elaine Thatcher is president of Heritage Arts Services, a consulting firm that provides research, management, and technical assistance for cultural projects. She has worked with traditional artists and developed folk arts programs throughout the West.

Cynthia L. Vidaurri is a folklorist at the Smithsonian Institution's Center for Folklife and Cultural Heritage. She has taught folklore and U.S.-Mexico Borderlands Studies at Texas A&M University-Kingsville. She has documented ranching traditions of Mexican American and African American cowboys from South Texas and Coastal Plains ranches.

Sue Wallis was raised in a multigenerational ranching family with roots in Montana, Wyoming, and Arizona. She is a poet and writer who runs an Internet publishing and event management business with her husband, Rod McQueary, near Recluse, Wyoming. They write about ranching culture, rural issues, and the complexities of living in the West.

John I. White (1902–92) was a scholar and singer of cowboy songs in the 1920s and 1930s. A native of Washington, D.C., he graduated from the University of Maryland and worked for a map-making company most of his life. His true interest was the music and song of the American West, and he won fame as "The Lonesome Cowboy," singing between acts of the radio show *Death Valley Days.* He wrote many articles about cowboy song and cowboy poetry and was the author of *Git Along, Little Dogies: Songs and Songmakers of the American West.*

Index

(Page references in italics refer to quotations of poetry; persons' names in italics are cowboy or logger poets or reciters.)

Typeset in 10.5/13 Adobe Garamond
with Handel Old Style display
Designed by Dennis Roberts
Composed by Jim Proefrock
at the University of Illinois Press
Manufactured by Braun-Brumfield, Inc.

University of Illinois Press
1325 South Oak Street
Champaign, Illinois 61820-6903
www.press.uillinois.edu